THE WAR AT HOME

THE

MINNESOTA DURING THE

WAR

GREAT WAR, 1914–1920

AT

GREG GAUT

HOME

The publication of this book was supported
though a generous grant from the
Elmer L. and Eleanor Andersen Publications Fund.

Maps on pages viii, ix, and 230 created by Janet Xiong.

mnhspress.org @mnhspress

The Minnesota Historical Society Press is a member
of the Association of University Presses.

Manufactured in the United States of America

10 9 8 7 6 5 4 3 2 1

♾ The paper used in this publication meets the minimum
requirements of the American National Standard
for Information Sciences—Permanence for Printed Library
Materials, ANSI Z39.48-1984.

International Standard Book Number
ISBN: 978-1-68134-307-5 (paper)
ISBN: 978-1-68134-315-0 (e-book)

Library of Congress Control Number: 2024948730

For Branden, Rachel, Remi, and Theia, and as always, for Marsha

In memory of my grandfather Frank Gaut (1889–1976)

CONTENTS

Minnesota Counties

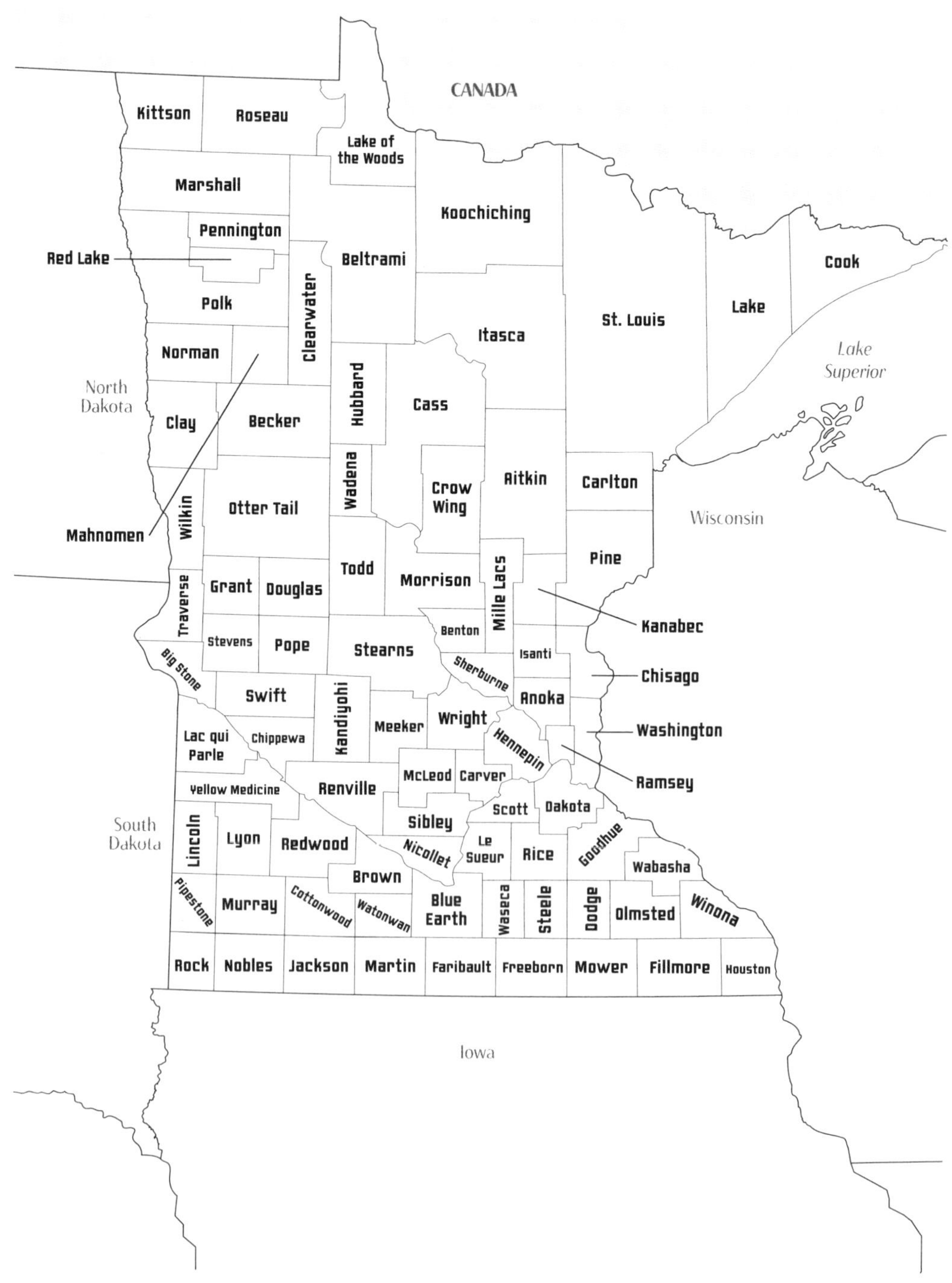

Minnesota County Seats

INTRODUCTION

WHEN I WAS YOUNG my grandfather told me that he emigrated from Austria-Hungary as a teenager in 1907 to avoid being drafted into the army of the Habsburg empire. Like many Europeans, he was trying to avoid the big war that seemed to be coming. As it turned out, migrating to Chicago was not enough. In 1917, the United States declared war on Germany and conscripted men to fight in Europe, requiring all men twenty-one to thirty to register. My grandfather showed up on June 5, 1917, the national registration day.

According to family lore, he would have done anything, even broken his arm, to avoid being drafted. Fortunately, his draft board exempted him because he was married and had a four-year-old son. Unfortunately, his wife died in November 1918, a victim of the influenza pandemic that spread across the country largely through the army's huge training camps. My grandfather's experience was my first glimpse of the wrenching impact of World War I on individual Americans.

People "make their own history," Karl Marx observed, "but they do not make it just as they please." We are born into a specific set of geographic, social, cultural, and economic circumstances that open opportunities, at least for some, but also put limits on individual lives—limits that for many are stark and brutal. The impact of world-changing events on individuals comes into sharp focus during times of massive social upheaval, like periods of invasion or total mobilization for war. Lev Tolstoy famously demonstrated this in *War and Peace.* Once Napoleon decided to invade Russia with a huge army, the lives of every Russian in his path would never be the same. A century later Vasily Grossman, another great Russian writer, published two massive novels showing how Hitler's army, even larger than Napoleon's army, trampled on the personal life of every Soviet citizen, particularly those of Jewish ancestry.[1]

The impact of World War I on Europeans needs no introduction. The armies of the belligerent states suffered more than thirty million casualties, of which about ten million were fatalities from combat or disease. The wounded were often permanently disabled or horribly disfigured. Millions of civilians also perished, often the victims of war crimes. Postwar Europe was a continent of mourners, especially the three million war widows. Personal lives were thrown up for grabs by the collapse of the Russian, German, Habsburg, and Ottoman empires. Even victorious countries like Britain and France limped into the 1920s in debt and clinging precariously to their empires. The stage was set for fascism, which also came to have a profound impact on individual lives.[2]

Americans also experienced serious disruptions in daily life during World War I, even though our country entered the war late and suffered only a small fraction of the casualties sustained by Europeans. Citizens faced a massive propaganda campaign to build support for the war, as well as food rationing, aggressive Liberty Bond drives, government-sanctioned vigilantism, prosecutions under the Espionage Act for dissenting speech, and of course, the drafting of young men, many of whom had recently arrived from Europe to escape conscription. There was no avoiding the war even half a world away from the western front.

When the conflagration broke out in Europe in 1914, Americans were living through a wrenching transition to a new, centralized form of industrial capitalism, dominated by corporations rather than entrepreneurs, where "trusts" held near monopolistic power in banking, mining, steel, and transport. Industrialization stimulated relocation, immigrants continued arriving from Europe, and African Americans began the Great Migration to northern cities. Economic inequality reached astounding levels, with men like Carnegie and Rockefeller rich beyond belief while millions lived at subsistence levels.

As passionately divided as Americans were about the war, it was hardly the only source of tension. The United States entered World

War I during a contentious period when farmer and worker militancy challenged entrenched economic power, the elected mayors in several cities (including Minneapolis) were Socialist Party members, African Americans struggled against Jim Crow and white nationalist terrorism, women were in their final surge toward suffrage, and millions campaigned for "prohibition" in the belief that alcohol was a fundamental source of the country's problems. As David Kennedy wrote in his indispensable book on the American home front, "Americans went to war in 1917 not only against Germans in the fields of France but against each other at home." What happened on the home front, he continued, "was a deadly serious contest to determine the consequences of the crisis for the character of American economic, social, and political life."[3]

Over a century later many find it hard to believe that relatively peaceful and well-mannered Minnesota was an explosive hot spot in this "war at home." Exploring Minnesota's history from the beginning of the European war in August 1914 through the 1920 election provides a unique vantage point from which to assess the impact of World War I on American society. Those years in Minnesota were marked by bitter political polarization, ethnic intolerance, a flagrant disregard for democratic norms and the rule of law by business leaders, and intense conflicts sometimes punctuated by violence.

This was partly the result of timing. The controversial declaration of war on Germany coincided with an intense period of battles between Minnesota's grain milling industry, mining conglomerate, big banks, and railroads on the one hand and the organizations representing farmers and workers on the other. The success of the Nonpartisan League (NPL) in organizing farmers and the influence of the Industrial Workers of the World (IWW) among miners and loggers sent shock waves through the state's business elite. As a result, ongoing economic, social, and political conflicts merged with new ones generated by the war and the draft. Soon editors of German-language newspapers were investigated as possible spies, farmers arguing for market equity were attacked as "disloyal," and workers trying to get union contracts were branded as "Bolsheviks."

Lives in the Balance

This book attempts to understand Minnesota's home front conflicts by focusing on the personal experiences of several noteworthy men and women whose lives were profoundly changed by the war, with John F. McGee and Charles A. Lindbergh Sr. the leading characters in the drama.

As war was declared, the legislature created the Minnesota Commission of Public Safety (MCPS) and gave it nearly unlimited power until the armistice. The commission consisted of Governor Joseph Burnquist, the attorney general, and five men appointed by the governor, mostly conservative businessmen. John McGee became the dominant personality in this powerful body, and until the war ended, the most powerful man in Minnesota. McGee was the oldest son of Irish immigrant farmers, and he became a successful Minneapolis lawyer representing banks and railroads. He set a tone of uncompromising nationalism and maintained that anything less than 100 percent support for the war effort was treasonous. McGee focused on building the Home Guard, an armed force available to enforce "loyalty," curb the growing political power of angry farmers, and block trade unions trying to break through employers' resistance to collective bargaining.

For McGee, the most dangerously disloyal man in the state was Charles A. Lindbergh Sr., the Little Falls lawyer who in 1914 was elected to his fifth consecutive term in the US Congress. Lindbergh, the only son of Swedish immigrant farmers, had emerged as a leader of the Minnesota Republican Party's Progressive wing. While in Congress, he fought a determined battle to limit the power of Wall Street bankers. Lindbergh's radical populism put him in the same camp as Robert La Follette, known as "Fighting Bob," the fiery senator from Wisconsin. Having left Congress, Lindbergh accepted the nomination of the Nonpartisan League to run against Joseph Burnquist in the 1918 Republican primary for governor. Their electoral battle was the climax of the war for the Minnesota home front, and the most violent campaign in Minnesota history. Lindbergh is one of the most important figures in Minnesota political history but largely forgotten, eclipsed by the fame of his aviator son who bears his name.[4]

In addition to McGee and Lindbergh, the impact of the war on several other Minnesotans will be traced. Some were wholehearted loyalists, including the young governor Joseph Burnquist, who veered so sharply to the right that he found his political career stymied after the war; Ambrose Tighe, the St. Paul attorney who wrote the statute creating the MCPS but later had misgivings; and Jens Grondahl, whose newspaper expressed the deep hostility that small-town businessmen felt for the Nonpartisan League. Others were dissidents who questioned the war and were attacked as disloyal, including Thomas Van Lear, who walked a fine line as the Socialist mayor of Minneapolis and the father of two draft-age sons; Albert Pfaender, who learned that commanding a National Guard regiment defending the border was not nearly enough to prove his patriotism; and James Manahan, an attorney who barely escaped an angry mob while trying to defend an NPL leader. Still others were focused on democratic reform at home, like the architect Clarence Wigington, who saw the war as an opportunity to crack open Jim Crow segregation of Minnesota's military forces; and Sarah Colvin, who sought to enfranchise women as a tool to achieve economic justice.

* * *

This book is divided into three sections. Part one introduces the main historical characters and charts their role from the outbreak of the European war in August 1914 until the US declaration of war on Germany in April 1917, the period when our country was officially neutral but increasingly divided. During those years, the Progressive movement peaked nationwide, and workers and farmers in the Midwest were on the move. With every month, the debate about how the United States should react to Europe's war grew more intense.

Part two focuses on the period when the United States went to war in Europe, starting with the April 1917 declaration of war and ending with the November 1918 armistice. During this time Minnesota's National Guard units were absorbed into the federal army; meanwhile, 40,000 Minnesotans volunteered and 75,000 were drafted. The "war at home" raged. The Minnesota Commission of Public Safety did all it could to ensure that the bitter Twin Cities transit workers strike did not end with union recognition. The Nonpartisan League, fresh from a remarkable electoral victory in North Dakota, attempted to replicate its success in Minnesota. This set the stage for a political showdown, climaxing in Lindbergh's campaign against Governor Burnquist in the summer of 1918.

Part three assesses the war's aftermath, and in particular its impact on Minnesota politics and on Lindbergh, McGee, and others. Those influential Minnesotans' postwar lives will be briefly surveyed. The soldiers returned home, except for the 3,480 Minnesotans who died in battle or from disease, many from influenza. The authority of the MCPS ended with the coming of peace, but the war at home continued as business organizations sought to institutionalize some of their wartime gains. The wartime struggles of farmers and workers led to the birth of the Farmer Labor Party, to which Lindbergh devoted his final years. The vigilante violence and nationalism of the period set the stage for the rise of the Ku Klux Klan. John McGee was appointed a federal judge, and he made headlines in his new role and with his shocking demise.

The War about the War

The Minnesota Commission of Public Safety understood, as Viet Thanh Nguyen would later write about the Vietnam War, that "all wars are fought twice, the first time on the battlefield, the second time in memory." Even before the armistice, the commission began constructing and publicizing its version of Minnesota's home front during the war. In 1919, the MCPS published a book-length report on its work, and following its urging, more than thirty counties published books memorializing the efforts of local MCPS units, the Home Guard battalion, draft boards, and other patriotic organizations. These volumes claimed that Minnesota was saved from spies, saboteurs, Bolsheviks, and pro-German elements because the MCPS used the "strong arm of force to suppress disloyalty" and wielded "a mailed fist" against its political opponents.[5]

Eventually, historians began to construct evidence-based chronicles of Minnesota during World War I. Scholars like William Folwell and Theodore Blegen concluded that the MCPS had exceeded its mandate in a "dictatorial" manner. The most comprehensive and significant analysis of the "war at home" was Carl Chrislock's *Watchdog of Loyalty: The Minnesota Commission of Public Safety during World War I.* A disturbing picture emerged, one in which, as Chrislock put it, the

MCPS, "endowed with almost dictatorial powers," spent more time "defending the existing socioeconomic order against a rising tide of radicalism on the prairies and growing labor militancy in the mines, forests and working-class wards" than cooperating with the federal government in supporting the war effort.[6]

These historical analyses of the Minnesota home front have had little impact on popular understanding of the period. In fact, Americans have limited interest in World War I, even though the United States was on the winning side. This may be because exactly what was won is murky. Readers of history have gravitated more to the Civil War and World War II, which present less ambiguous storylines. It is also true that the repressive rule of the MCPS fits poorly into the comfortable and enduring myths of Minnesota as an unusually well-governed place where people are "nice."[7]

In fact, Minnesota repressed civil liberties more aggressively than most other states during the war. Wartime animosity toward citizens of German ancestry played a role, but civil liberties suffered in Minnesota primarily because the business establishment convinced the legislature to turn control of the state government over to a small unelected commission for the duration of the war. This body used its unprecedented power to suppress the rising movements of farmers and workers, and especially the alliance of the Nonpartisan League and the Twin Cities labor unions, which eventually became the Farmer Labor Party. Branding all opponents as "traitors" (whatever their ethnic background), the commission fostered an atmosphere of intolerance, encouraged vigilante action, and condoned violence. This toxic atmosphere continued after the war.

The Minnesota experience differs significantly with that of neighboring Wisconsin despite their commonalities. Each were agricultural states with one large industrialized urban area. The largest city in each state had a Socialist mayor. Both had many immigrants, including Germans, Scandinavians, and Irish who were cool toward war with Germany. In fact, the two states were among the most reluctant to declare war. When the US House voted overwhelmingly in April 1917 for war with Germany, nine (of eleven) Wisconsin and four (of ten) Minnesota congressmen voted "no."

All this might predict that the two states would share a common experience once war was declared. But unlike Joseph Burnquist, the governor of Wisconsin took a relatively moderate course. The legislature created a State Council of Defense to supervise war activities, but it was not a businessmen's club like the MCPS. Wisconsin mandated that the council include at least one member representing "labor" and one representing "the farmers." Whereas the MCPS established its own militia, the Home Guard, to replace the Minnesota National Guard that had been federalized, Wisconsin created no militia. As a result, Wisconsin had to deal with labor disputes by negotiation, while the MCPS could mobilize the Home Guard, as it did during the transit workers strike in St. Paul. Wisconsin also had no "slacker raids" (the sweep arrests of hundreds of young men by the Minnesota Home Guard in a search for draft evaders). Speech was suppressed in Wisconsin, and there was widespread vigilante violence. However, the Wisconsin governor tried to curb the vigilantism, while Burnquist and the MCPS actively encouraged it.[8]

Although Minnesota's home front experience was the product of a particular confluence of events and personalities, the issues it raises have not been left safely in the past. Studying this history can alert us to how extreme economic inequality can warp democracy, how patriotism can be used to suppress fundamental rights, how politicians can harness racism and anti-immigrant nationalism to further their agendas, and how the wealthy sometimes resort to authoritarianism when their power is threatened. Hopefully exploring these years of sharp polarization can help us navigate our own perilous times.

PART I

The War across the Ocean

ONE

LET US BE NEUTRAL

JUNE 1914 TO MAY 1915

'Tis the Madness of the Monarchs 'neath whose lash the nations groan!
And humanity, obedient, rushes on to slay its own—
Marches on, in servile millions, to appease the royal wrath—
Oh, what feast awaits the vultures in that dark and bloody path!

JENS K. GRONDAHL, from an editorial poem on the front page of the *Red Wing Daily Republican*, August 5, 1914

It is true that Europe is ablaze and the destruction of life and property is tremendous; but nothing should be destroyed here as a result of the war, so why should we allow the European war to destroy our reason.

CHARLES A. LINDBERGH, Sixth District congressman, speaking in Congress, September 24, 1914

THE GREAT WAR eventually changed the lives of every Minnesotan, but it would have been hard to convince anyone of that future outcome when the European powers stumbled into war in the summer of 1914. The headline story of the *Minneapolis Morning Tribune* on June 29, 1914, reported that a Serbian student had assassinated the heir to the Austrian monarchy and his wife in Sarajevo. In the following weeks, the newspapers closely monitored the fateful steps that led France, Russia, and Britain to war with Germany and Austria-Hungary. From a safe distance half a continent and a whole ocean away, Minnesotans watched the European conflict unfold. Whether they favored one side or simply believed that Europe as a whole had become unhinged, Minnesotans were sure the conflict would not involve them.

After all, President Woodrow Wilson proclaimed that "the United States must be neutral in fact as well as in name during these days that try men's souls." In September, civic organizations led by the Rotary Club organized a mass meeting at the Minneapolis Auditorium in support of neutrality. One speaker celebrated Minnesota as a haven for immigrants, noting that representatives of the warring European nations lived together peacefully in the state. Another speaker emphasized the need to be rigorously fair to all belligerent countries. "Let us be neutral," proclaimed George Vincent, president of the University of Minnesota, who argued that a neutral United States might "play her part in making war impossible." The meeting was chaired by Frederick B. Snyder, a well-known local leader. Snyder told the crowd that "collectively we may serve as evidence" of Wilson's proclamation of neutrality.[1]

During the period of American neutrality, men of Snyder's social, ethnic, and religious background gradually dropped the language of benevolent internationalism and replaced it with the rhetoric of belligerent nationalism. Snyder's parents, who were Presbyterians of Dutch and Scot ancestry, moved to Minneapolis from Pennsylvania in 1855. They came with money and quickly made more in real estate and banking. Fred Snyder earned a law degree at the University of Minnesota and established a successful law practice. He married a daughter of John S. Pillsbury, the cofounder of the milling firm and Minnesota's eighth governor. After four years as a Minneapolis alderman, he

■ Fred Snyder, a big-city lawyer and politician with Yankee roots, was appointed to the University of Minnesota's Board of Regents in 1912 and served until shortly before his death in 1951. He chaired the board from 1914 to 1950 and was a close confidant of many university presidents. *MNHS collections*

served terms in the Minnesota House and Senate as a Republican. He withdrew from political office in 1902, except that he was a regent of the University of Minnesota from 1912 until his death in 1951. Like most of his peers, Snyder would soon be advocating for an American military expansion in preparation for a war on Germany.[2]

The Madness of Monarchs and Capitalists

Newspapers editors across Minnesota tended to blame the war on Europe's antiquated political system, where autocrats, aristocrats, and generals still held power. At first, they did not single out any country for blame. Jens K. Grondahl, for example, the editor of the *Red Wing Daily Republican*, published an editorial poem on his August 5 front page that explained the war as "the Madness of the Monarchs 'neath whose lash the nations groan!" Six months later, many newspapers were blaming the Kaiser for the war. Grondahl would reinvent himself as an ultranationalist supporter of war and a fiery advocate for suppressing German culture.[3]

Snyder, a big-city lawyer, and Grondahl, a small-town newspaperman, were typical of Minnesota men who moved from promoting neutrality to campaigning for intervention. But whereas Snyder was a quintessential old stock American, Grondahl was an immigrant born in Norway. Grondahl's parents brought him to the southeastern town of Red Wing in Goodhue County when he was eleven years old. Raised a Lutheran, he attended public school and then the Red Wing Seminary, from which he graduated with honors in 1887. He won an oratorial prize and used the money to open a small confectionary shop that sold sundries and newspapers. Soon Grondahl began working at a newspaper, and eventually became the editor of both the *Red Wing Daily Republican* and *Nordstjernen*, a Norwegian-language weekly. He was elected to represent Goodhue County in the Minnesota House in 1894, a position he held for six years. He often used poetry to make his editorials more engaging. In 1898, for example, he wrote "While We Were Fighting for Cuba" to support the war against Spain. He had it set to music and it became a widely sung patriotic song. Grondahl's 1914 poem about "the Madness of the Monarchs" had a different feel, representing an immigrant's disdain for the hierarchical European society he had left behind.[4]

On the eve of World War I, more than 70 percent of Minnesotans were European immigrants or had at least one parent born abroad. Most hoped their adopted country would stay out of the war, although their reasons differed by ethnicity. German Americans were the largest immigrant group, and quite naturally had no interest in fighting Germany. In fact, until the United States declared war on Germany in 1917, German American newspapers across the country unabashedly took the German side. Minnesota was the home of the *Westlicher Herold*, published in Winona, and it was the second-largest German-language weekly in the United States. Under the leadership of Emil Leicht, the paper reported extensively on the war from a pro-German perspective. He attacked the British blockade of German ports and demanded a general arms embargo. At first, the German press attracted little criticism. An arms embargo might favor the German cause, but it was, after all, consistent with a policy of strict neutrality, which was the official stance of the US government.[5]

▪ **Jens Grondahl, a Norwegian immigrant, briefly served in the legislature but made his mark as a small-town newspaper editor, managing the *Red Wing Daily Republican* for nearly forty years. *MNHS collections***

The war had an outsized impact on the southern Minnesota city of New Ulm, where many citizens took pride in their *Deutschtum*, or Germanness. In 1897, the Sons of Herman Lodge built a grand monument on a hill overlooking the city to Herman the Cheruscan, a German national hero who defeated the Romans in 9 CE. In 1907, the German government sent the city an autographed portrait of Kaiser Wilhelm as a gift, and it was put on view inside the monument. The city's split

STATUE 32 FUSS HOCH BIS ZUR SPITZE DES SCHWERTES. HOEHE VON FUSS ZU KOPF 25 FUSS. FUNDAMENT DES MONUMENTES 41 FUSS IN QUADRAT. HOEHE DES UEBERBAUES 17 FUSS. HOEHE DER SAEULEN 25 FUSS 2 ZOLL. HOEHE DER KUPPEL NEBST GESIMS UND FUSGESTELL FUER DIE STATUE 28 FUSS. GESAMMTHOEHE DES MONUMENTES 102 FUSS 2 ZOLL.
JULIUS BERNDT
ARCHITECT

■ **A postcard commemorating the Herman monument in New Ulm.**
MNHS collections

personality was on display at the ceremony accepting the gift. The 2nd Regimental Band of the Minnesota National Guard band played both "America" and "*Die Wacht am Rhein*" ["The Watch on the Rhine"]. The crowd raised cheers to the Kaiser, President Theodore Roosevelt, and Abraham Lincoln.[6]

Dr. Louis Fritsche, the New Ulm mayor, was traveling in Britain and France when war broke out in 1914. He made a quick trip to Germany to visit friends and relatives, many of whom, he discovered, had already left for the front. When he returned home, he gave a speech at Turner Hall, blaming the war on France and Russia. "Germany is fighting for its very existence," he told the audience. Throughout the war, people in New Ulm worried about friends and relatives in the old country.[7]

Minnesotans of Irish ancestry also tended to oppose war against Germany. The *Irish Standard*, a Minneapolis weekly published for Irish Catholics across the upper Midwest and the West, viewed the conflict through the lens of nationalism. The Irish had no quarrel with Germany, and many Irish Americans thought that Britain's time of trouble might be Ireland's moment of opportunity, when the Irish could finally break free of British colonial rule. Minnesota's Scandinavians also favored neutrality, a strong tradition in their homelands. They were similarly put off by the fact that France and Britain were allied with Russia, a traditional adversary of Sweden. They remembered that the Russian empire had historically fought Sweden for control of the Baltic Sea.[8]

Newspapers associated with the trade unions lamented the war, emphasizing the terrible price European workers would pay for the quarrel among monarchs. In Duluth, the editor of *The Labor World* reprinted Jens Grohdahl's poem from August 15. Two weeks later, the editor expressed frustration with those who were "praying for peace." More than prayer, the editor advised that the United States needed to "starve the beast that is ravaging Europe, hinder him in his work by withholding the material necessities for his existence from him," and only "then an answer to your prayers will speedily come." In Minneapolis, the *Labor Review* took a more radical line, reflecting the influence of the Socialist Party in the local Trades and Labor Assembly that published it. The paper reported favorably on an August rally where workers of many ethnicities passed a resolution holding that "this war has been precipitated by the powers that be, Monarchist and Capitalist, for the perpetuation of the damnable system of exploitation, destruction, and waste." In September, the *Labor Review* published local Socialist activist Thomas Van Lear's article "War Against War," in which he prophesized that "if the capitalists are going to be permitted to lend money to help those nations at war" and send goods to them in American ships, then eventually a ship will be sunk, and "the bankers of Wall Street and all those who will profit by the war will be patriotically waving the flag." Wilson's administration, he said, should inform capitalists seeking wartime profits that they act "at their own risk and with the disapproval of the government."[9]

Thomas Van Lear's roots were quite unlike those of Snyder or Grondahl. He was born to working-class parents in Maryland and worked in the Appalachian coal mines as a youth, after which he moved to the Midwest and served four years in the army. He settled in Minneapolis, where he became a machinist and eventually a leader of his union, the International Association of Machinists (IAM), and of the Minneapolis Trades and Labor Assembly. Van Lear was an advocate of industrial unionism, an articulate spokesperson for the Socialist Party, and a powerful stump speaker. He was also a savvy politician capable of upending the two-party politics of Minneapolis.[10]

Minnesota's preference for neutrality also found expression in popular culture. In the early days of sound recording, hit songs were primarily distributed by sheet music, and then sung in public places and at home accompanied by the ubiquitous piano. In the first twelve months of the war, popular songs nationwide overwhelmingly favored neutrality, with titles like "No Matter What Flag He Fought Under (He Was Some Mother's Boy After All)," "I'm Glad My Sweetheart's Not a Soldier," and "If They Want to Fight All Right, but Neutral Is My Middle Name." One of the biggest hits of 1915 was "I Didn't Raise My Boy to Be a Soldier," which sold 700,000 copies in 1915 and continued selling until war was declared. The *Duluth Herald* published an excerpt of the song, complete with music, and noted that "the beauty of the thought is so apparent and the music so skillfully woven that the song is achieving popularity second to no other musical work written within a century."[11]

Twilight of Progressivism

The United States was in the final years of what historians call the Progressive Era when war broke out in Europe. Most Progressives initially favored neutrality, but by 1917 many had become enthusiasts for intervention, having made an ill-advised bet that the war would foster Progressive reform. With the benefit of hindsight, most historians agree that World War I marked the end of the Progressive Era.

In the early 1900s, ministers, authors, and journalists (the "muckrakers") aggressively examined American society in sermons, in books, and especially in popular magazines. They painted a dire picture of the Gilded Age, criticizing economic inequality, rampant materialism, political corruption, and environmental devastation. Progressives argued that a reformed government could tackle these problems and more efficiently serve "the common good," although what that meant was not always clear. Some Progressives were influenced by the Populists and those Protestant preachers associated with the Social Gospel movement, and spoke in moral terms about economic inequality. Others promoted managerial efficiency, arguing that professional expertise could make government a more effective purveyor of social welfare.[12]

Both major national parties embraced Progressive reform, up to a point. Under the presidency of Theodore Roosevelt, a Republican (1901–08), Congress imposed some regulation on the railroads (the Interstate Commerce Commission) and on the food processing industry (the Pure Food and Drug Act, meat inspection laws), and began protecting natural resources (the US Forest Service). Antitrust litigation that had begun under Roosevelt continued under the administration of William Taft (1909–12), his handpicked successor, along with other significant reforms, such as authorizing the US Post Office to act as a savings bank for wage earners. The first term of Woodrow Wilson, a conservative Democrat turned Progressive reformer, saw more legislation, including the first federal income tax (which applied only to the very rich), an eight-hour day for railroad workers, and the Federal Reserve Act that led to a national banking system. Progressives supported women's suffrage and prohibition, although constitutional amendments protecting women's right to vote and banning the manufacture and sale of alcohol were not ratified until after the war.

Long-developing tensions within the Republican Party broke out into a deep schism between the Progressives, often called "insurgents," led by Senator Robert La Follette of Wisconsin, and the conservatives, who called themselves "stalwarts," personified by politicians with close ties to the business community such as Senator Henry Cabot Lodge of Massachusetts. Insurgents were often from the Midwest and West, while stalwarts usually represented the Northeast. Among other things, they disagreed about tariffs. The Republican Party supported high tariffs to protect American industry from foreign competition even though it led to higher consumer prices. In 1909, the stalwarts managed to pass the Payne-Aldrich Tariff Act that generally preserved high tariffs, even though the insurgents joined Democrats in opposition.

In Minnesota, the Progressive Era began in 1898 when John Lind, a Democrat, became governor. Lind served only one two-year term but established a reform agenda that subsequent governors, whether Republicans or Democrats, generally followed. Although Republicans dominated Minnesota politics in the early twentieth century, the high point of Progressive reform was the governorship of John Johnson, another Democrat, who took office in 1905 and served until his death in 1909. During his tenure, the legislature reformed the insurance industry, increased control of the railroads, strengthened the state's power to tax the mining industry, and cleared a path for municipal ownership of public utilities. Minnesota Progressives failed to achieve a statewide prohibition of alcohol sales but did pass a "county option" bill in 1914 that allowed counties to ban alcohol by local referendum. Soon thirty of the eighty-six counties were "dry." In 1915, the Minnesota Senate came one vote short of placing a women's suffrage amendment to the state constitution before the voters. Minnesota women could vote only in library and school board elections until after World War I.[13]

Every member of Minnesota's congressional delegation except one voted against the Payne-Aldrich tariff bill. Only the First District congressman, James A. Tawney of Winona, sided with conservative Republican leadership. In September 1909, President Taft gave a speech in Winona praising the unpopular tariff bill and congratulating Tawney for supporting it. This was no help to Tawney, who lost his seat a year later to a Progressive young lawyer from Lanesboro. Taft's speech also contributed to his failure to carry the state in the

1912 election, as local insurgent Republicans broke ranks to back Roosevelt in his third-party bid.

When the dust settled on the 1912 election, Progressive Republicans held a majority of the Minnesota congressional delegation. The 1910 census had given Minnesota a tenth seat in the House, an at-large seat won by James Manahan, a Republican identified with La Follette. A fiery lawyer, Manahan was known for his defense of farmers and close relationship with George Loftus of the Equity Co-operative League, the farm organization that later spawned the Nonpartisan League in 1915. Manahan returned to his law practice when his at-large seat was replaced by the Tenth Congressional District in 1914. In 1917, he found himself in the center of divisive state politics as an attorney for the Nonpartisan League.[14]

In 1914, Minnesota's Senate seats were held by two very different Republicans: Knute Nelson, a former governor who by this time sat resolutely in the conservative camp, and Moses Clapp, a Progressive who had been a senator since 1900. Like many Progressives, Clapp favored neutrality and opposed expanding the military. In 1907, he had joined La Follette and a few other Republicans in voting against President Roosevelt's bill to expand the navy by building two dreadnaught battleships. Clapp said a larger navy was a "menace to the peace of the Republic."[15]

Progressives tended to be people from the middle and upper class who viewed workers, many of them recent European immigrants, through a lens of paternalistic humanitarianism. Progressive reformers were reluctant to support the growing trade union movement and, in fact, often opposed what business leaders called "the closed shop" (that is, a workplace with a union contract). The idea of workers organized to fight for their own interests made many Progressives nervous. Small-town Progressives felt the same way about organized farmers, especially when they were organized by the Nonpartisan League.

Progressives generally were European Americans who made little effort to break with the racism that was so deeply embedded in their culture. Confronting Jim Crow laws or protesting the scourge of lynchings was not a priority. Although Roosevelt once invited Booker T. Washington to the White House, the administrations of Roosevelt, Taft, and Wilson extended segregation and took no action to protect African Americans from violence.

Progressives held little interest in the overseas empire the United States had established following the Spanish-American War. Foreign policy issues were low on their agendas. As a result, Roosevelt won the support of many Progressives who were unconcerned that he was hell-bent on expanding the military and extending American power by force. Roosevelt, of course, became a national hero by leading the Rough Riders against Spain in Cuba. This cavalier attitude toward US interventions abroad would contribute to the downfall of Progressivism when faced with the European war.

Historians have long debated the significance of the Progressive movement, with some arguing that its main accomplishment was turning the regulation of banking and industry over to agencies controlled by the bankers and industrialists themselves. Whether Progressives capitulated naively or intentionally, it is fair to say that in the years before 1914, the managerial, efficiency-minded faction of Progressivism triumphed over the democratic, anti-privilege side.[16]

The limitations of Progressivism left many people wanting more than the reforms achieved by Republican or Democratic parties. The Socialist Party, organized in 1901, was an attractive alternative for many. In 1910, Socialists elected mayors in several cities, including Milwaukee. In 1912, Eugene V. Debs, a former railroad fireman and union leader, won 900,000 votes (6 percent) when he ran for president on the Socialist Party's ticket. The party had a substantial following in Minnesota, although by 1914 it had elected only one member to the Minnesota legislature: Arthur Devold, an editor of *Gaa Paa* [Press Forward], a Norwegian-language Socialist paper published in Minneapolis. In that year, Thomas Van Lear ran as a Socialist for Fifth District congressman and lost by a small margin. Four of his Socialist colleagues won seats in the twenty-six-member Minneapolis City Council.[17]

Little Falls Insurgent

Among the many Progressive Republicans that Minnesota sent to Congress, the congressman from the Sixth District stands apart. More than any other Minnesota politician, he represented the democratic, Populist-inspired side of Progressivism. During the period of neutrality, he staunchly opposed American intervention in the European war.

Charles August Lindbergh was a Swedish immigrant from the central Minnesota town of Little Falls. He was a successful lawyer who represented the local Weyerhaeuser lumber mill, speculated in real estate, and sat on the boards of several banks. Nevertheless, Lindbergh emerged as one of the nation's most ferocious critics of "the Money Trust," the term Progressives used to describe the East Coast banking establishment. He believed the banking oligarchs were largely responsible for dragging the country into an unnecessary war.

Charles Lindbergh's childhood was typical of many young men whose families migrated from Sweden and scratched out a farm on the prairie. His father and mother, August and Louisa Lindbergh, arrived in 1859 when Charles was eighteen months old. The couple settled in Stearns County and began farming near the town of Melrose on land recently taken from the Dakota. August took an active role in local affairs, serving as a postmaster, justice of the peace, school board member, and township clerk.[18]

The young Charles liked to roam free, contributing to the household by hunting ducks and deer. He was an indifferent student, even though his father had organized the common school he attended. When Charles was about twenty, his father sent him to Grove Lake Academy, a secular school with a rigorous curriculum run by a Catholic priest. Charles made progress, and after two years he passed the University of Michigan law school admission examination. He graduated in 1883, passed the Minnesota bar, and established a practice in the Mississippi River town of Little Falls. He specialized in real estate law and speculated in real estate himself. Working with a local builder, he developed residential and commercial properties. He bought farmland, and he invested in two local banks, the German-American National and the First National, and a printing company that published a newspaper.[19]

Little Falls was a good place for a young lawyer to hang a shingle. Frederick Weyerhaeuser and his partners bought timberland in northern Minnesota and floated logs down the Mississippi to the large, modern lumber mill they built in Little Falls in 1890. Weyerhaeuser sent his son Charles and a partner's son, Drew Musser, to Little Falls to manage the operation. The mill was a success, and the population of Little Falls more than doubled, from 2,354 in 1890 to 5,774 by 1900. The lumber company became Lindbergh's most important client, and

Charles Weyerhaeuser and Drew Musser became the most important members of Lindbergh's social circle.[20]

In 1887, Lindbergh married Mary LaFond, a daughter of one of the town's founding families, and they had three daughters, one of whom died as an infant. This contented period of his life ended abruptly in 1898 when Mary LaFond died after surgery to remove a tumor. Two years later he married Evangeline Lodge Land, a young woman from Michigan who was teaching science in the high school. The couple built an opulent three-story house near Little Falls on the west bank of the Mississippi. In 1902, they had a son and named him Charles Augustus Lindbergh. In 1905, disaster struck again: this time a fire destroyed their home. Soon the couple along with Lindbergh's daughters, Lillian and Eva, and the young Charles, then three years old, moved into a smaller house built on the same site. About this time their marriage deteriorated, and Evangeline handled the tension by taking her young son on extended trips to visit her family in Detroit.[21]

Lindbergh explored ideas of agricultural reform, working with an experimental farmers' cooperative in Little Falls and publishing a short-lived reform-minded farm magazine. Then he decided to channel his reformist ideas into a run for the Sixth District congressional seat. Almost a quarter of the population of this central Minnesota district were foreign born, primarily Germans and Swedes. In 1906, Lindbergh beat the incumbent in the Republican primary, and then cruised to victory over his Democratic opponent in the general election.[22]

Lindbergh moved to Washington to prepare for his new role, and the entire family joined him when the next congressional session began in late 1907. A year later, Evangeline moved out of their Little Falls home, though she continued to spend time in Washington so that Charles could see his father. Between 1906 and 1916, the young Charles lived in Little Falls only during the summer. Lindbergh's eldest daughter, Lillian, left the University of Minnesota after her sophomore year to marry. His younger daughter, Eva, graduated from Carleton College in Northfield, Minnesota, in 1914 and accepted a teaching position in northern Minnesota.[23]

Lindbergh ran unopposed in the 1908 Republican primary, and he won an easy victory in the general election. By the time he began his second term in 1909, he was recognized as one of the most radical members of the insurgent wing of the Republican Party. Lindbergh opposed the Payne-Aldrich tariff bill, arguing that it forced working people to pay more for sugar, coffee, lumber, and many other everyday goods while enriching the "trusts" that controlled these products. He joined other insurgents in amending the Mann-Elkins railroad bill. The unfair rates of the railroads, he argued, were a key reason why "80% of the wealth in America is owned by 3,000 estates, corporations, and individuals." Lindbergh's brand of radical Progressivism played well back home, and in 1910 he won 73 percent of the votes in the Republican primary and was unopposed in the general election.[24]

In his third term, Lindbergh earned a national reputation for taking on the Money Trust, the popular name for the groups who controlled the largest banks and industries, particularly those led by financier J. Pierpont Morgan and John D. Rockefeller. Lindbergh proposed an independent congressional committee to investigate their oligarchic control of the economy. The House leadership opened an investigation, but declined to give Lindbergh a role, even though it was his idea.[25]

In 1912, Lindbergh backed La Follette's bid to take the Republican nomination away from President Taft, but then threw his support to Roosevelt when the former president entered the race. After Roosevelt failed to win the nomination and decided to run as a candidate of the newly created Progressive Party, Lindbergh backed Roosevelt while running for his own reelection as a Republican. This balancing act did him no harm. Roosevelt carried Minnesota, while nationwide Wilson won a landslide victory over both Taft and Roosevelt. Lindbergh sailed to another easy victory and began his fourth term in the House.[26]

Wilson won by repositioning himself as a Progressive, and he began his presidency by attacking the Money Trust. Before long, Lindbergh became a critic of the Wilson administration's signature monetary reform, the 1913 Federal Reserve Act. Conservatives from both parties thought big bankers should run the Federal Reserve, and Progressives

▪ **OPPOSITE**
Charles A. Lindbergh Sr. won the Sixth District seat in 1906 and was reelected four times, establishing himself as the leading congressional critic of the Money Trust. ***MNHS collections***

CHAS. A. LINDBERGH

Republican Candidate for
Re-Election As

CONGRESSMAN

SIXTH - DISTRICT - MINNESOTA

JOURNAL-PRESS PRINT ST. CLOUD

led by Lindbergh argued that the federal government must control the reserve system and the currency supply. Lindbergh contributed to the debate by publishing *Banking and Currency and the Money Trust,* a book-length critique of oligarchic control of the financial system that focuses on how that control leads to economic inequality. He proposed a credit system that was both more stable and more democratic. Ida Tarbell, one of the leading "muckraking" journalists of the Progressive Era, published an article crediting Lindbergh, "a Swede from Minnesota," as being the first in Congress to raise the issue of the Money Trust.[27]

Progressives like Lindbergh and La Follette were disappointed with the Federal Reserve Act because big banks had so much control. Lindbergh called it a "Christmas present to the Money Trust." By this time, he had become what later in the century would be called a social democrat. The unfair distribution of wealth in the United States, he argued, could be ended either by socialism, which he acknowledged did not have popular support, or by government regulation of banking and currency to guarantee that farmers and workers received the same "reasonable return" on their labor as banks expected from their capital.[28]

Lindbergh spoke out on one foreign policy issue during his fourth term. In 1911, a revolution broke out in Mexico, overthrowing the dictatorship of Porfirio Diaz. The United States hoped that Francisco Madero would establish a parliamentary democracy. When Madero was overthrown in 1913 in a military coup led by General Victoriano Huerta, Wilson refused to recognize Huerta and sent aid to opposition forces. Wilson also sent former Minnesota governor John Lind to Mexico as his personal representative, hoping that Lind could bring the warring parties together to form a democratic government without Huerta. This was not likely to happen, and in any case Lind was a novice diplomat who knew little about Mexico and spoke no Spanish. He spent eight months in Mexico, mostly reporting to Wilson on Mexican political developments.[29]

In April 1914, Wilson used a petty dispute about whether Mexican troops would salute US warships in Mexican ports to justify sending the Marines to Veracruz. This gave Huerta the opportunity to act as the defender of Mexican sovereignty. Lindbergh spoke out in Congress against intervention "because we cannot run the domestic affairs of other countries." Not only that, he argued, wars impede social progress and lead to huge debts, ultimately paid for by working people. US troops withdrew after seven months, and the Mexican civil war continued.[30]

In Word but Not in Deed

Neutrality was immensely popular during the first year of the European war, especially in midwestern states like Minnesota. Nevertheless, the United States was soon neutral in name only and certainly not in deed. Those who wanted to keep the United States out of the war found themselves fighting a losing battle.

Mainstream newspapers quickly turned against Germany as reports of its army's brutal treatment of Belgium were published. The German high command faced the problem of fighting on two fronts: on the west with France, and on the east with Russia. Their strategy required a quick defeat of France to concentrate forces on the eastern front against Russia's larger army. Germany planned to invade France by marching quickly through Belgium and heading straight for Paris. Any resistance by the Belgium army or civilians frustrated and enraged them. Hence, the German army took murderous reprisals against civilians suspected of resistance and burned the historic city of Louvain.

The German occupation of Belgium led to a food crisis. As an occupying force, the Germans had the duty to supply adequate food, but they argued that this was impossible because the British navy blocked the shipment of any food supplies into German-occupied Belgium. Herbert Hoover, a wealthy engineer working in England, created the Commission for Relief of Belgium (CRB), a private philanthropic organization that supplied the civilian population for the duration of the war. Minnesota grain millers donated to this effort, and in fact, William C. Edgar, editor of the *Northwestern Miller*, the trade journal of the Minnesota millers, had independently organized a ship loaded with grain for Belgium even before the CRB was founded. The Washburn-Crosby company made the largest donation of flour, and James Ford Bell, its vice president, helped Edgar organize the Minnesota effort.[31]

British propaganda publicized the German army's brutal behavior in Belgium but added stories of horrendous atrocities that had no factual basis. At first, most Minnesota newspapers handled atrocity reports with some skepticism. The British, however, got the upper hand in the battle for American public opinion by cutting the transatlantic cable lines between Germany and the United States. After that, all war news came over heavily censored British cables. The frequent reporting of British, French, and Belgium charges of German atrocities was effective. Many Americans began to think of "the Huns" as barbarians who delighted in bayoneting babies. Despite this, public opinion continued to favor neutrality throughout the first year of the war.[32]

Besides propaganda, the British had economics on their side. The United States entered a recession in the summer of 1914 that was worsened by the war, leading to significant unemployment and the closing of the New York Stock Exchange for four months starting in July. This made trade with the European belligerents especially attractive to American manufacturers and farmers. The British blockade, however, cut off trade with Germany. The British navy mined German ports and stopped neutral vessels at sea, forcing them into "control stations" where they might be held for months. Their goal was to starve Germany into submission. The Wilson administration protested, weakly, noting that the blockade violated international agreements.[33]

Although trade with Germany was impossible, American businesses were compensated with increased orders for war supplies and food from the British and the French, "the Allies." To finance their purchases, the British sought loans from US bankers. Somewhat reluctantly, the Wilson administration gave its approval. By early 1915, the British government had borrowed heavily from J. P. Morgan and appointed him as their exclusive purchasing agent in the United States. Prosperity returned stateside based on a system in which US firms exclusively supplied the Allies and US banks financed the sales. If the United States were to challenge the illegal and immoral British blockade of Germany, it might jeopardize this lucrative trade.[34]

Neutrality had in effect been redefined as open support for the Allies. In response, German Americans mounted a futile campaign for an arms embargo that would ban the sale of weapons to either side. This position was supported by the German-language press and by many mainstream newspapers, especially those in small towns throughout the Midwest. The National German-American Alliance, a loose organization funded behind the scenes by the German Embassy, sponsored rallies in many major cities. A large crowd at the St. Paul Auditorium in January 1915 heard former governor Adolph Eberhart and New Ulm city attorney Albert Pfaender advocate "a nationwide movement against the exportation of arms and munitions to the belligerents." In Washington, anti-interventionist senators proposed an arms embargo amendment to a shipping bill in February. The Wilson administration successfully defeated the amendment, although thirty-five senators voted in favor.[35]

As it became clear that the stalemate on the western front meant a long war of attrition, the German military responded to the British blockade by trying to prevent trade with the British Isles. Their surface fleet was not strong enough to challenge the British navy, so they relied on submarines to destroy ships approaching British ports. Over Wilson's protests in February 1915, the Germans announced a policy of "unrestricted submarine warfare," which meant they might torpedo any ship without warning, even those flying a neutral flag. Submarines were a new technology, and the first German U-boats were small, slow, and few. Initially, however, the British had no effective defense.

American peace advocates realized they could not rely on their government's so-called neutrality policy. Long before the war, organizations called "peace societies" advocated that international conflicts should be resolved by negotiation. Most prominent was the American Peace Society, founded in 1828, and whose officers in 1914 included former president Taft, secretary of state William Jennings Bryan, and Andrew Carnegie. The local affiliate was the Minnesota Peace Society, which had 70,000 members. The society sought to build public opinion in favor of "arbitration or other methods of settling international disputes." It was a blue-ribbon organization, led by Cyrus Northrop, president emeritus of the university, and James Wallace, a Macalester College professor of political science. Other prominent members were Governor Joseph Burnquist and former governor Adolph Eberhart. In defense of diplomacy, the society opposed the Wilson administration's decision to intervene militarily in the Mexican Revolution. When war in Europe broke out, the Minnesota Peace Society hosted Rosika Schwimmer, an internationally known peace activist traveling the United States urging the Wilson administration to organize a coalition of neutral nations to negotiate an end to the war. Schwimmer told a crowd at the Universalist Church in downtown Minneapolis that the "situation in Europe shows that civilization cannot be masculine exclusively and succeed."[36]

Many women from the suffrage, prohibition, and women's club movements believed the European catastrophe required new organizations willing to confront militarism more aggressively than the peace societies. In August 1914, fifteen hundred women from the feminist peace movement marched down Fifth Avenue in New York City in silent protest of the war. At the urging of Rosika Schwimmer and others, three thousand women gathered in Washington in January 1915 to create the Woman's Peace Party. They chose as their leader Jane Addams, a veteran peace advocate. The new organization proposed that neutral nations come together to create a peace plan and mediate among the warring parties. Woman's Peace Party branches quickly sprouted across the nation, including in Minnesota. In April, Addams led a delegation to neutral Holland for an International Conference of Women. She invited Mary Catherine Judd, Minnesota state chair of the Woman's Peace Party, and Ella Patterson, secretary of the Minnesota Peace Society, to attend the conference.[37]

By 1915, Theodore Roosevelt was a fierce critic of Wilson's neutrality policy and anyone who opposed intervention. He was particularly agitated by the Woman's Peace Party, which he called "silly," "base," "hysterical," and "influenced by physical cowardice." Throughout his various political transformations, Roosevelt never abandoned his core belief that American prosperity had made the country soft, unmanly, and prone to avoiding fights. He thought the European war provided an opportunity for the United States to cleanse itself of effeminacy. His call to toughen up the nation resonated with many, especially the rich. East Coast bankers and industrialists formed the National Security League to agitate for universal military training and an expanded military. The organization was bankrolled by wealthy magnates like Cornelius Vanderbilt, Henry C. Frick, and Simon Guggenheim.[38]

In the fall of 1914, Charles Lindbergh ran successfully for his fifth term in Congress. In a speech on the floor of the House, he tried to counter what he saw as an irrational drive toward war. The country was in no danger, he argued, "so why should we allow the European war to destroy our reason." Shortly before the election, Lindbergh charged the Wilson administration with proposing a war tax even though the

United States was not at war. With international trade disrupted, the Wilson administration proposed a special tax to make up for lost tariff revenue. The tax was aimed at beer, wine, and tobacco manufacturers and bonds, mortgages, and other business transactions. Lindbergh argued unsuccessfully that the cost of these new taxes would be passed on to consumers, most of whom were underpaid.[39]

By early 1915, Lindbergh had concluded that Wall Street loans to Britain and influential organizations like the National Security League would eventually drag the United States into war. In a letter to his daughter Eva, he expressed his belief that "we are going in as soon as the country can be sufficiently propagandized into the war mania."[40]

TWO

NEUTRALITY UNDER SIEGE

MAY 1915 TO NOVEMBER 1916

> The war-lords unceasingly call us enthusiasts and mollycoddles. We will not try to find names for them, but simply answer that if the accepted principles of Twentieth Century civilization were lived up to among nations as among men, war would vanish like its comrades—dueling, slavery, and cannibalism.
>
> MARIA SANFORD, retired University of Minnesota professor, speaking at the Orpheum Theatre, Minneapolis, October 11, 1915

> Whether it be moral or immoral, I believe in the maxim, if it may be called such: "My County, right or wrong."
>
> JOHN F. MCGEE, Minneapolis attorney and former judge, in a letter to congressman George R. Smith, March 1, 1916

THE YEAR WHEN NEUTRALITY, in word if not in deed, dominated public discussion in Minnesota ended abruptly on May 8, 1915. On that day, the *Minneapolis Morning Tribune* reported that U-20, a German submarine, had sunk the *Lusitania*, a British ocean liner operated by the Cunard Lines. Most of the passengers were probably unaware that the cargo hold was full of armaments bound for Britain. Of the over 2,000 passengers and crew, 1,201 did not survive, including 121 Americans. It was shocking but not surprising. The German government had made clear that all ships entering the war zone around Britain were subject to attack. The German Embassy even published warnings in New York newspapers, some of which ran next to advertisements selling passage on the *Lusitania*.

President Wilson demanded that Germany repudiate the sinking and pay compensation. He maintained that Americans had a fundamental right to travel anywhere and trade with anyone. William Jennings Bryan, the secretary of state, wanted the president to protest both the U-boats and the British blockade, which not only restrained the rights of Americans in a similar way but also aimed to starve the German people. When Wilson refused, Bryan resigned, and was replaced by Robert Lansing, an outspoken advocate for the Allies. Bryan may have been the only high official of the administration who believed in neutrality.[1]

Many in Congress feared the United States would be drawn into war by the reckless actions of a few citizens. In February 1915, Democrats associated with Bryan introduced resolutions in the House, asking the president to warn American citizens against travel on armed merchant ships, and in the Senate, prohibiting the issuance of passports to Americans traveling on ships of the warring nations (the Gore-McLemore resolutions).

The administration succeeded in killing the Senate version by getting it tabled. Only fourteen senators voted against tabling, one of whom was Moses Clapp of Minnesota. The House also voted to table, but the entire delegations from Iowa, Nebraska, Wisconsin, North Dakota, and Minnesota voted in support and warned Americans against travel in the war zone. Then in March, a German submarine sank a French channel steamer with American passengers. The German government said the submarine captain had acted in error and suspended unrestricted submarine warfare. However, Germany reserved the right to reconsider if Wilson failed to persuade Britain to relax its blockade.[2]

Meanwhile, the British increased their harassment of American shipping. In December 1915, they began seizing US first class mail and parcels from neutral ships traveling to neutral Scandinavian ports. Then in July 1916, the British released a "blacklist" of eighty-five American firms suspected of trading with Germany or Austria-Hungary. British subjects could have no contact with these firms. Wilson privately said that he was "about at the end of my patience with Great Britain and the Allies," but he took no action against them.[3]

Theodore Roosevelt claimed that Wilson was afraid to use military force. The president, however, ordered the invasion of three countries during this period. In July 1915, Wilson sent the Marines to occupy Haiti and install a new pro-American government. They stayed until 1934. In May 1916, the Marines landed in the Dominican Republic. They stayed until 1922. The third and largest operation was Wilson's second invasion of Mexico. Forces led by Venustiano Carranza had forced General Huerta out of power. When civil war broke out between Carranza and Pancho Villa, the leader of a peasant army, Wilson supported Carranza. Feeling betrayed, Villa crossed the border to raid a New Mexico town to provoke a US intervention. Wilson sent a punitive expedition led by General John Pershing, who marched around northern Mexico in a fruitless search for Villa. Pershing eventually clashed with the Mexican army, risking a larger war with Mexico.[4]

Wilson then federalized the National Guard of the various states to defend the Mexican border, including the three infantry regiments and the field artillery regiment of the Minnesota National Guard. Mobilized in June, they spent eight frustrating months defending the border, returning in January 1917. Their mission exposed the fact that the Minnesota units had far fewer men than their official troop strength and were deficient in uniforms, tents, horses, and other necessities.[5]

Readying the Nation for War

Those supporting the Allies organized a national movement around the term "preparedness," which meant the rapid expansion of the army and navy and universal military training and conscription. At the center of this movement was the National Security League, which grew rapidly after the *Lusitania* sinking, organizing chapters in cities across the nation. Powerful East Coast bankers and industrialists bankrolled the league, and it was no secret that they were heavily involved in supplying the British and French with war materiel and credit.[6]

Minnesota businessmen quickly became advocates of preparedness and a firm stand against Germany. Chapters of the National Security League were formed in Minneapolis, St. Paul, and Duluth. The president of Northwestern National Bank, Edward W. Decker, led the Minneapolis chapter. Throughout the state, local chambers of commerce generally backed preparedness, and *Commercial West*, the state's leading business periodical, took a pro-Ally position that echoed leading East Coast newspapers.[7]

When the British and the French sent delegations to New York seeking new credit, J. P. Morgan agreed to underwrite a $500 million unsecured loan, with most bonds purchased by East Coast businesses who were beneficiaries of British orders. Seeking to broaden support, Morgan telegrammed James J. Hill, Minnesota's best-known businessman, who took the Twentieth Century Limited to New York to meet with Morgan and the Allied representatives. Realizing the loan would be unpopular in the Midwest, Hill asked in vain if the credit could be used only for purchases other than munitions. When he returned home, he ordered the First National Bank of St. Paul, which he controlled, to subscribe heavily to the loans. He also wrote a short pamphlet entitled "Preparedness for Peace" that was distributed for free by the bank, presumably to soothe the concerns of its depositors.[8]

Wilson caught the preparedness fever and proposed a major expansion of the navy, with a goal of parity with the British, and an expansion of the army to include a permanent force of 250,000. He continued, however, to reject conscription. In early 1916, he embarked on a Midwest tour to build support for his plan in areas where skepticism about a military expansion was strongest. Meanwhile the National Security League and similar groups organized large "preparedness parades" in New York, Washington, DC, Chicago, San Francisco, and other cities during the summer of 1916. President Wilson declared June 14 to be Flag Day, and led sixty thousand people in a preparedness parade in Washington, wearing a straw hat and carrying the Stars and Stripes over his shoulder. Anti-interventionist forces in Congress tried to put the brakes on military buildup, and in the end Congress passed compromise bills that moderately increased the army and navy while authorizing Wilson to "federalize" the National Guard units of the states in a national emergency.[9]

Theodore Roosevelt and US Army general Leonard Wood were the biggest cheerleaders for preparedness. The two men were fellow veterans of the Rough Rider campaign in Cuba during the Spanish-American War. Roosevelt argued for an expanded army and navy, coastal fortifications, and mandatory military training for all American men starting in high school. He dismissed opponents of preparedness as the "peace at any price men." He was particularly incensed by the popular song "I Didn't Raise My Boy to Be a Soldier," which he called "unspeakably base." Singing that song, he wrote, was as bad as singing "I Didn't Raise My Girl to Be a Mother." In 1916 he published a bestseller entitled *Fear God and Take Your Own Part*, a collection of his interventionist articles, many of which hurled personal insults at President Wilson.[10]

A group of New York City professionals and businessmen asked General Wood to organize a military training camp for them during the summer of 1915. Roosevelt was delighted when three of his sons enrolled in the camp that Wood created at Plattsburg, New York. Bankers, lawyers, brokers, and retailers, almost all with Ivy League degrees, drilled in the summer heat seeking to increase their chances of becoming officers once war was declared. Roosevelt visited the camp at the end of the summer and entertained the young men with a speech in which he called opponents of preparedness "poltroons" and "college sissies."[11]

Preparedness advocates organized the Training Camps Association, which began establishing other "Plattsburg" camps for businessmen around the country. In Minnesota, the National Security League tried to establish a camp at Fort Snelling in the summer of 1916. The project was led by Donald R. Cotton, sales manager of the St. Paul office of the Illinois Steel Company. Cotton had trained at Plattsburg in 1915. He had the backing of the St. Paul Association of Commerce, but the camp never materialized because the regular army officers slated to act as trainers were sent to the Mexican border. However, the idea of providing military training to businessmen was just getting started in Minnesota.[12]

Standing apart from Roosevelt and Wood but still in the interventionist camp was the League to Enforce Peace, organized in 1915 and led by former president William Taft. The group proposed a "league of nations," dominated by the Allies, which would arbitrate conflicts between member nations and respond with collective military forces to any country which unilaterally went to war. Roosevelt thought this was "childish make-believe" that distracted from the task of building American's military might. President Wilson found the league's ideas congenial, and he later became the world's leading proponent of a "league of nations."[13]

Taft appointed former governor John Lind to chair the Minnesota chapter of the League to Enforce Peace. A political maverick who started as a Republican and then became a Democrat, Lind strongly supported Wilson's handling of the war issue. He had just returned to Minneapolis after eight months as President Wilson's personal representative to Mexico. Like Wilson, he likely saw the league as a humane and realistic response to international tensions, one which avoided both isolationism and nationalism.[14]

Two distinct forces leaned toward war against Germany, each with its own rationale. The approach of Wilson and Taft attracted internationalists who sought a world ordered by liberal principles. Roosevelt's rhetoric mobilized nationalists whose priority was enhancing American power.

Yes to Neutrality; No to Militarism

In early 1916, anti-war Progressives organized the American Union against Militarism (AUAM) to counter the preparedness movement and the growing culture of militarism, a combination they feared would undermine Progressive reform. The AUAM held anti-preparedness rallies around the country, including one at the Minneapolis Auditorium presided over by W. F. Webster, a high school principal. He told the crowd that "patriotic business men" do not fear war, but "fear that war may sometime come to an end." Rabbi Stephen Wise, the leader of Reform Judaism, stressed that militarism undermined the Progressive agenda, including women's suffrage and regulation of labor conditions. "Before I would go out to fight for the honor of America," he told the crowd, "I would go out to fight the exploiters of child labor."[15]

In Minnesota, support for neutrality stayed strong in the German, Irish, and Scandinavian communities, in the women's movement, in the trade unions, among most Progressives, and generally in agricultural areas of the state. The most vocal advocates for neutrality tended to see the preparedness movement as a Trojan horse for advocates of aggressive support for Britain and France up to and including a declaration of war on Germany.

As the preparedness movement grew, German American organizations and newspapers fought back with increased intensity. The German-language press, which had a circulation of about 125,000 in Minnesota, generally condemned the Wilson administration for tolerating what was called Britain's "starvation blockade" of Germany. Winona's *Westlicher Herold* claimed that citizens of German ancestry were better citizens than those with ancestral ties to Britain because German Americans could see through the lies of British propaganda. Pro-German lecturers toured the state, speaking to large German crowds. Eugene Kuehnemann, professor of German literature at Breslau University, spoke—in German—to a large New Ulm audience in June 1915. He argued that "Germany was a greatest democratic state in the world" and was fighting for its life against Russia, France, and Britain. Both the local newspapers, the *Brown County Journal* and the *New Ulm Review*, continued to support the German side. Citizens of New Ulm held fundraisers for the German Red Cross during 1916, and they waited anxiously for news of German casualties, fearing that old friends or relatives might be among the fallen.[16]

The *Irish Standard*, the newspaper of the Irish American community in the Twin Cities, took a pro-German line when the war began in 1914, and only shifted to support for strict neutrality after the sinking of the *Lusitania*. When the British decided to execute sixteen leaders of the 1916 "Easter Rebellion" in Dublin, many Irish Americans were even less inclined to aid Britain in the European war. Former St. Paul mayor Daniel W. Lawler, the state's best-known Irish politician, stood squarely for neutrality and against preparedness. Running as the Democratic candidate for US Senate in 1916, he argued that "if we had placed an embargo on munitions the war would have been over a year ago." Referring to the admiral behind Germany's naval buildup, he called Theodore Roosevelt "the Von Tirpitz of the United States, who with Von Tirpitz, the Theodore Roosevelt of Germany, still is breathing fire and slaughter."[17]

However, most established politicians and Catholic bishops of Irish ancestry kept a low profile, not wanting to undermine their influence within the Democratic Party and with the president himself. John Ireland, the archbishop of St. Paul, was no friend of the British, but his main goal was to integrate the Irish into American society. Even before the war he had written that "I would have Catholics be the first patriots of the land."[18]

Just after the sinking of the *Lusitania*, Jane Addams led a delegation of the Woman's Peace Party, which visited leaders of Germany, Austria-Hungary, and Britain to advocate for their plan to end the war. Since late 1915, the party had been encouraging the United States to lead other neutral countries in a united effort to mediate the conflict. The Minneapolis branch of the Woman's Peace Party passed a resolution in favor of this plan in November. Addams was received politely in London, Berlin, Vienna, and Budapest but got nowhere, although in Rome Pope Benedict XV offered himself as a mediator. At home, the Woman's Peace Party tried various tactics, including a two-mile-long peace petition signed by 350,000 children who pledged "to work for schools instead of battleships." They also sponsored a lavish touring production of *The Trojan Women*, the classic anti-war play by Euripides.[19]

The Minneapolis branch of the Woman's Peace Party also used theater to counter the preparedness movement. One of the most successful plays on Broadway in 1915 was *War Brides*, a feminist anti-war play starring the renowned actress Alla Nazimova. The touring company, featuring Nazimova, came to the Orpheum Theatre in Minneapolis on October 11, 1915. The local Woman's Peace Party arranged with Nazimova to have Maria Sanford, professor emeritus of the university, speak from the stage following the performance. After retiring from the university in 1909, Sanford continued to lecture widely, and was well known for her soaring oratory. She delivered a blistering attack on militarism, calling war not only "brutal and barbaric" but also "unnecessary and useless." Taking on the preparedness movement, she argued that "war hides itself under such names as patriotism, courage, loyalty, and devotion," but that these virtues would be better employed in fighting disease and injustice. The newspaper account reported that she received an ovation both before and after her brief talk.[20]

■ **After Maria Sanford retired from the University of Minnesota in 1909 she continued her public speaking career, delivering speeches from coast to coast. *MNHS collections***

The labor movement continued to be strongly in the anti-preparedness camp, especially as labor leaders noticed the unbounded enthusiasm of the wealthiest bankers and industrialists for preparedness. When the Minnesota Federation of Labor held its state convention shortly after the *Lusitania* sinking, it passed a resolution "condemning all forms of militarism as a menace to humanity." In Duluth, *The Labor World* complained that the greatest danger facing the United States was not a foreign foe, but rather that the United States "will be called upon to supply the market for the millions of dollars' worth of wholesale and retail murder tools when Europe gets sick of buying them." *The Labor World* concluded that if the country needed more protection, "then the government itself must manufacture the munitions and build the ships."[21]

In Minneapolis, the Socialist-influenced *Labor Review* took a more militant line, arguing that if the United States went to war, workers should not fight to protect the loans of "Kaiser Morgan," referring to Wall Street banker J. P. Morgan. The Minneapolis Trades and Labor Assembly, publisher of *Labor Review*, threatened to form its own armed militia if the War Department authorized the establishment of a Plattsburg-like camp in Minnesota. These businessmen, the assembly resolved, "are obtaining military training not for so-called national defense, but for the purpose of commanding strikebreakers and thugs in time of labor troubles."[22]

Rural Minnesotans also tended to stick with neutrality, in part because the war seemed to have a negative impact on local economies. The cost of living rose in 1915, and credit got more expensive, which farmers attributed to the enormous loans made to Britain and France to fund their purchase of munitions, most of which were manufactured in the East. Some farmers tried to increase their income by expanding acreage, but this led to greater mortgage indebtedness. Economic conditions tended to bolster the argument that support for the Allies was good for Wall Street but not for Main Street.[23]

There was no professional opinion polling at the time, but the ten members of the Minnesota delegation to the House likely took the temperature of their districts before they unanimously voted against tabling the resolutions aimed at discouraging Americans from sailing on Allied ships (the Gore-McLemore resolutions). Along with Moses

Clapp, their colleague in the Senate, they were confident their constituents leaned strongly toward neutrality.[24]

Of the eleven, Charles Lindbergh emerged as the most radical advocate of neutrality. He blamed the Money Trust, the big bankers organizing the loans to the Allies, for encouraging involvement in the European war. He condemned mainstream newspapers for uncritically reporting the pro-Allied propaganda produced by the chamber of commerce and other organizations. In a speech explaining his vote on the McLemore resolution, he asked why "all America may be juggled in order to protect foolhardy or designing speculators whenever they wish to travel on armed ships controlled by nations at war."[25]

For Lindbergh, "preparedness" was essentially a euphemism for "armaments," most of which were being manufactured for export to the Allies. A better policy would be an embargo on arms shipments to the warring nations. More generally, he thought his country would be better prepared for the future if it would dismantle the "dollar plutocracy" by which "two percent of the people own 60% of the wealth." As he saw it, the enormous profits the munitions industry had made during the war not only increased inequality but encouraged them to seek expanded and prolonged warfare. The only way out of this dilemma, he argued, was to nationalize the armament industry.[26]

During the debate, many argued that congressmen should vote to table the Gore-McLemore resolutions to "stand by the President" and preserve his prerogative to manage the international relations of the United States. Lindbergh responded that a citizen had a duty to stand by their own convictions since "this is not a monarch's country."

But the times were changing. Many newspapers had by now joined the preparedness movement. The *Duluth Herald*, for example, held that "to the everlasting shame of Minnesota," the vote of the Minnesota delegation in the House was "0 for Wilson and America" and "10 for von Tirpitz and the Submarine." Some newspapers predicted Clapp and the ten congressmen would be swept out of office in the coming election.[27]

There were also signs that the war would eventually divide the Progressive movement. When the *Lusitania* was attacked, reporters sought a comment from Dr. Cyrus Northrop, president of the Minnesota Peace Society and president emeritus of the University of

Minnesota. He coolly responded that since Germany and Britain were at war, and since Germany had warned that it would sink British merchant vessels, the sinking was "horrible, as all war is horrible," but not necessarily "contrary to the laws of war." However, when the National Security League was organized in Minneapolis a few months later, Northrop became one of its most visible members. When war finally came, he joined the many Progressives who supported the war because they believed it would lead to democratic reforms.[28]

The Open Shop, a Film about the Klan, and the Hyphen

The European war increasingly intruded into the lives of Minnesotans, but it was far from the only conflict during 1916, a year which saw intense labor struggles, including a bitter strike by miners on the Iron Range of northern Minnesota. The growing intensity of labor organizing and the equally staunch determination of employers to block union recognition played a big role in what happened in Minnesota once war was declared on Germany.

The first two decades of the twentieth century were a period of unprecedented industrial conflict nationwide. Employers fought to maintain the "open shop," the phrase they used to designate a workplace where each employee had to deal individually with the employer about wages, benefits, procedures, and working conditions. Skilled workers, who tended to be of northern European ancestry, formed the American Federation of Labor (AFL) to fight for what employers called a "closed shop," where the workers negotiated collectively, and with much greater success. The unskilled workers, whose numbers were swelled by recent immigration from southern and eastern Europe, gravitated to the Industrial Workers of the World (IWW), which organized workers in industries like mining and lumber.

In Minneapolis, the bankers, grain millers, manufacturers, and other commercial interests formed a highly organized and insulated community, led by a small group that held oligarchic control over the grain industry. They shared common "Yankee" roots; that is, most traced their ancestry back to the British Isles and attended Presbyterian, Episcopal, or Congregational churches. Their finances were handled by Northwestern National Bank and the First National Bank. They belonged to the Minneapolis Commercial Club, which was reorganized in 1911 as the Minneapolis Civic and Commerce Association (MCCA). In 1905 they built the Gothic revival Minneapolis Club downtown to serve as their social hub. They lunched there, and golfed and played tennis at the Minikahda Club on the edge of the city. To prepare their sons for Harvard and Yale, they founded the Blake School, and for their daughters, the Northrop Collegiate School.[29]

Their most important project was the Citizens Alliance, a semi-secret association of businessmen formed in 1903 to keep Minneapolis an "open shop" city, that is, to block the recognition of unions as the collective bargaining agents of workers. It conducted an anti-union propaganda campaign, organized a surveillance apparatus to monitor union organizers, and if a strike broke out, aided individual members by suing the union, recruiting replacement workers (known as "scabs" in the labor movement), and arranging for armed guards if necessary.[30]

Employers in St. Paul were not as organized, militant, or homogeneous. St. Paul society was less dominated by "old stock" Protestants. Germans, Scandinavians, and especially the Irish played significant roles in St. Paul society, the result in part of the influence of Bishop John Ireland and James J. Hill, its leading businessman, who married an Irish Catholic woman. Whereas the Minikahda Club was a "Yankee" enclave, about 20 percent of the members of St. Paul's elite Town and Country Club had recognizably Irish surnames in 1915. In general, they were more interested in social peace than their Minneapolis colleagues, and less committed to enforcing a strict adherence to "open shop."[31]

The Minnesota Federation of Labor, the local affiliate of the AFL, built a growing network of craft unions, but had no interest in organizing unskilled workers in the mining and lumber industry. Moderate trade unionists led the MFL, but they were challenged by a more militant Socialist minority. The Socialists for a time controlled the MFL's newspaper, the *Labor Review*, which led more conservative unions to start a rival paper, the *Union Labor Review*. The IWW was active in northern Minnesota, looking for opportunities to lead strikes of iron miners, loggers, and lumber mill workers. For a time, the IWW operated an office on Hennepin Avenue in Minneapolis, from which it sent organizers to the north. The "Wobblies," as they were called, were especially successful in organizing Finnish miners.[32]

Labor progress was slow and difficult. In May 1916, for example, the Minneapolis teamsters went on strike, seeking better wages and union recognition. When the employers refused to negotiate, the Minneapolis Trades and Labor Assembly held a meeting in a downtown theater, where members passed a call for a general strike. The next day the Citizens Alliance hosted a luncheon at a downtown hotel attended by two hundred businessmen who affirmed the doctrine of "open shop," demanded better police protection for non-striking drivers, and pledged collective support to break the strike. Edward Decker, president of Northwestern Bank, and F. A. Chamberlain, president of First and Security National Bank, spearheaded efforts to raise funds to finance their campaign. The strike failed, and the Citizens Alliance emerged stronger, more unified, and better funded.[33]

Meanwhile, a spontaneous walkout by disgruntled miners sparked a major strike on the Mesabi Iron Range at the beginning of June. Getting no response from the AFL, the miners turned to the IWW, which quickly sent seasoned organizers to lead the strike. Soon mines in and near Hibbing, Eveleth, Virginia, and Chisholm were closed. The rapid spread of the strike, and especially the involvement of the IWW, alarmed the Oliver Mining Company, a subsidiary of United States Steel. However, the miners lacked the resources to survive a long strike, and the company was heavy-handed in its repression. The strike petered out in September, although after it was over the company granted some concessions.[34]

The governor at the time was Joseph Burnquist, a St. Paul lawyer who had earned a reputation as a Progressive Republican while representing the east side in the Minnesota House. He became lieutenant governor in 1912, and unexpectedly became governor when Winfield Hammond died a few days before the end of 1915. Burnquist instructed the St. Louis County sheriff to summon a posse to stop the strike and bring arrested miners to Duluth for trial, presumably because they could be more easily convicted there. The sheriff responded by deputizing four hundred of the mining company's private guards as police officers. This was the first evidence that Burnquist was crossing over from the Progressive to the conservative side of the Republican divide, and it was a move bitterly criticized within the labor movement.[35]

The labor movement got some help from President Wilson in the summer of 1916. The railway worker unions demanded an eight-hour day, which the railroads refused to consider, even after Wilson tried to mediate. To avert a nationwide strike, Wilson pushed Congress to pass the Adamson Act, which mandated an eight-hour day for interstate railroads. The business class was infuriated. *Commercial West*, the business weekly published in Minneapolis, editorialized that unless "the labor unions sober up and use some realism in their demands, this country will be forced into adopting an autocratic form of government that can control by military power the industrial situation." For some business leaders, a piece of pro-labor legislation raised the question of whether democracy should be abandoned in favor of authoritarianism.[36]

Charles Lindbergh supported the Adamson Act, arguing that an eight-hour day was an "absolute right" and that the refusal of the railroads to compromise justified the threat of a strike. He also criticized the railroads for arguing that the railroad workers should not ask for more than workers in other industries. If the railroads wanted to open the question of "comparative pay," Lindbergh argued, compensation in all fields should be analyzed and compared. If this was done, he suggested, all working people would end up getting a raise.[37]

Wilson's labor policies bolstered his claim to be the more progressive candidate in the 1916 election, but he played a reactionary role by fostering white supremacy. In addition to segregating the civil service and turning a blind eye to lynchings, Wilson publicized D. W. Griffith's *The Birth of a Nation*, a film that glorified the Ku Klux Klan during the Reconstruction period, by hosting a screening of the film at the White House in 1915. The film was based in part on Wilson's own *History of the American People* and even included a quote from the book. The National Association for the Advancement of Colored People (NAACP), founded just three years earlier, tried to stop screenings of the film, arguing that it was a blatant call for violence against African Americans.

In Minneapolis, a distributor rented the Shubert Theatre to show the film in October 1915. Mayor Wallace G. Nye banned the film on the grounds that it might "endanger public morals by inciting race prejudice." A judge, however, allowed it to be shown while the distributor appealed. The Minnesota Supreme Court affirmed Mayor Nye's authority to ban the film, but he betrayed the NAACP by delegating his authority to a censorship committee. That committee did not include a single African American. The committee lifted the ban, and the film went on. In St. Paul, the city council allowed the distributor to show the film in the St. Paul Auditorium, a public venue. The St. Paul NAACP, led by Dr. Valdo Turner and Jose Sherwood, mobilized the African American community to lobby the city council to ban the film. The Minnesota Woman Suffrage Association also supported a ban. The council decided to allow the film to be shown if two inflammatory scenes were cut. The film went on, and only when it was too late did the council approve an ordinance banning the film. The NAACP fought an uphill battle, but the fight did help the organization grow nationally and in Minnesota.[38]

About a year later, African American leaders were confronted with nearly a thousand people parading through Minneapolis and St. Paul dressed in the white robes and pointed hats of the Ku Klux Klan. This horrifying spectacle was staged by Walter Wilmot, manager of the 1917 Minneapolis Auto Show, as an attention-grabbing way to kick off the event. Harry Pence, the pioneer car salesman who led the local trade association, endorsed the idea, as did the Minneapolis chief of police. Wilmot offered Klan outfits for sale (ten for $17.50 or one for $1.15). The local newspapers joined in, producing lighthearted stories under headlines like "Nightriders to Ride in Broad Daylight." There was probably no KKK organization in Minnesota at the time, and the Klan did not become a mainstream organization until after the war. Very likely it was Griffith's film that taught many Minnesotans of European ancestry to look favorably upon what was a terrorist organization enforcing white supremacy with unrestrained and unpunished violence.[39]

Wilson also encouraged the nativist backlash against immigrants. In 1915, newspapers and politicians began criticizing the "hyphen," shorthand for "hyphenated Americans," for example, "German-Americans," who were accused of not fully assimilating to American culture. Many "old stock" Americans, especially those associated with the National Security League, thought immigrants' failure to "Americanize" explained the German American opposition to preparedness and the IWW's success in organizing immigrants. Wilson joined them in demanding that immigrants drop the "hyphen" and become true Americans. He attacked foreign-born "creatures of passion, disloyalty, and anarchy." In his June 14, 1916, Flag Day address, Wilson proclaimed that there is "disloyalty active in the United States and it must be absolutely crushed."[40]

In 1915, Minnesota got on the short-lived bandwagon to transform the Fourth of July into "Americanization Day." The Minneapolis Civic and Commerce Association organized a rally at the Minneapolis Armory where four thousand people heard patriotic songs and speeches. Together they recited the Pledge of Allegiance, and then heard speeches by John Lind and Knute Nelson, two former governors who had been born in Europe. Lind said "we have no place for groups which have any other purpose than the welfare of our whole nation and all the people." The *Minneapolis Morning Tribune* followed up with an editorial about "taking out the hyphen" from local politics.[41]

Theodore Roosevelt, the biggest voice for Americanization, traveled the nation giving rabble-rousing speeches to packed auditoriums. He came to Detroit in May 1916, for example, because Henry Ford supported the peace movement. He told a huge crowd that the issues of "Americanism and preparedness were inseparably bound together," and that the country faced a crisis like 1776 or 1861. Attacking German American organizations and their campaign for neutrality, he said "the political-racial hyphen is the breeder of moral treason."[42]

Roosevelt quietly parted ways with the Progressive Party when he saw that conservative Republicans were backing intervention. Conservatives like Henry Cabot Lodge welcomed him back into the Republican Party. They cheered his call to spend more on the military and to introduce universal military service. As for the business-oriented Anglophiles, they applauded Roosevelt's anti-hyphenism.[43]

Judge McGee's Red-Blooded Nationalism

Minnesota had its own nationalist firebrand, John F. McGee, although he was not yet a well-known public figure. McGee echoed Roosevelt's intolerant belligerence, and then pushed it even further. Roosevelt was the Harvard-educated son of an "old money" New York family that traced its roots back to the early Dutch colonists and their Protestant culture, while John F. McGee was the Midwest-born son of Irish Catholic immigrants. He graduated from high school but was self-educated after that. Nevertheless, McGee became the dominant

John McGee, a successful Minneapolis lawyer representing railroads and grain millers, was a confidant of Senator Knute Nelson and well regarded by conservative business leaders. *MNHS collections*

Lieutenant Colonel Hugh McGee, son of John McGee, was a West Point graduate who fought in the Philippines. *MNHS collections*

personality on the Minnesota Commission of Public Safety in 1917, the man Minnesota business leaders trusted to advance their interests during the war.[44]

McGee was indeed an exceptional case. His father immigrated from Ireland around 1850 to a northern Illinois town, where he eventually was able to buy land and become a farmer. He and his wife had twelve children, and John, born in 1861, was the second. By his twenty-first birthday, the precocious young man had graduated from high school, read law with local lawyers, and been admitted to the bar. A year later he moved to Dakota Territory, where his law practice included criminal prosecution. In 1886, John McGee was part of a prosecutorial team that tried Billy Oswald for shooting a man in a Devils Lake tavern. The case was a notorious spectacle tried in a roller rink to accommodate an audience of five hundred. The defendant was represented by W. W. Erwin of St. Paul, famous for defending workers, including American Railway Union leader Eugene Debs and the union members charged during the infamous strike of Andrew Carnegie's steel mill at Homestead. Still only twenty-five, McGee won a jury verdict of manslaughter. Refusing to be intimidated, he confidently traded insults with Erwin during the trial.[45]

McGee married Elizabeth Ryan in 1884, and three years later they moved to Minneapolis, where he built a law practice specializing in complex commercial cases. Ten years later he was appointed judge of the district court in Minneapolis. In 1898, he was elected for a full term of six years. He and his wife bought a home on Pillsbury Avenue in the fashionable neighborhood west of Fair Oaks Park, near the location where in 1912 wealthy businessmen would build the Minneapolis Institute of Arts. He resigned from the bench in 1902 and returned to private practice, forming a partnership with William Lancaster, another former judge. At that time, he noted, he had six children and his annual salary as a judge was $5,000, about a quarter of what he had made in private practice.

Like Roosevelt, he took great pride in his sons' military prowess. In 1915, Roosevelt was delighted that three of his four sons were training at the Plattsburg camp. McGee had something more to brag about. His eldest son, Hugh, graduated from West Point in 1909 and then served in the Philippines as a US Calvary officer. He was wounded in 1912 during General John Pershing's campaign against the Moros, the

Islamic people in the southern part of the archipelago who were rebelling against US rule. In 1916, he was promoted to lieutenant colonel and transferred to the 1st Minnesota Infantry, one of the National Guard units that had been federalized for service at the Mexican border.[46]

John McGee's clients included railroads and grain millers. In the 1890s, he represented a coalition of grain elevator companies who sued to overturn North Dakota's regulatory laws. McGee took the case to the US Supreme Court, where he ultimately lost in a 5 to 4 vote. Another case that reached the Supreme Court involved Minnesota's attempt to regulate railroad rates. Representing railroad stockholders, he obtained an injunction against the state. The Supreme Court eventually held that Minnesota's attempt to regulate the railroads was unconstitutional.[47]

McGee was a member of the MCCA and the prestigious Minneapolis Club, where conservative businessmen strategized in comfort and privacy. Irish Catholics were not typically part of this social milieu. In any case, attorneys, whatever their ethnicity, were generally not part of the leadership strata of the business class. McGee was welcome in these circles because he represented the oligarchs who owned the grain mills, the banks, and the streetcar monopoly and aggressively protected their interests. Consistent with this role, he developed a deep hostility toward trade unions, the Socialist Party, the IWW, and especially the Nonpartisan League. Although a former judge, he was impatient with the rule of law and prone to loose talk, sometimes metaphorical and sometimes not, about suppressing his opponents with violence.[48]

McGee was a frequent correspondent with Senator Knute Nelson, with whom he shared a common political outlook. McGee vented his anger and frustrations freely in letters to the senator, confident of a sympathetic hearing. Nelson was also somewhat of an anomaly, being one of the first politicians of Scandinavian ancestry to become an acknowledged leader of the conservative wing of the Republican Party. The two men shared hostile attitudes toward the labor movement, as evidenced, for example, by McGee's letter thanking Nelson for voting against the Adamson Act, the law which brought the eight-hour day to the railroads and averted a nationwide strike. "That was the most vicious act and most cowardly that ever went through Congress," McGee wrote, "and I might add the most threatening to the future of this country and to the stability of Republican institutions."[49]

McGee's commitment to the Allied cause also made him somewhat exceptional, since most Irish Americans, even if part of the preparedness movement, were less than enthusiastic about aiding Britain so long as Ireland remained a British colony. The fact that elected Republicans in Minnesota tended to support neutrality angered him. In February he wrote a long letter to Moses Clapp, Minnesota's other senator, criticizing his support for an embargo on all arms sales to the warring powers of Europe. McGee was exasperated that Clapp advocated blocking arms sales on moral grounds. "I am probably by instinct a barbarian," he told the senator, in that he could not consider the morality of an embargo apart from its impact on US national interest. He counseled the senator that "it is pleasing to get up in the clouds and listen to the flapping of angels' wings," but a senator must be "hard-headed and practical." Besides mockery, McGee also tried threats embellished with violent images. Politicians who do not prepare Americans for war, he told the senator, will not be able to hide themselves from "the vengeance that will be wreaked upon them," like when the heads of French aristocrats rolled into the baskets below the guillotines.[50]

McGee concluded by urging Clapp to heed the words of two clergymen. The *Minneapolis Morning Tribune* had just reprinted a sermon by Pastor John Bushnell of Westminster Presbyterian in downtown Minneapolis, "the most prominent Protestant church in the city," which argued that peace and prosperity had weakened the manliness of Americans. "A people that has become effeminate through the lack of the need of self-sacrifice for a great cause," he warned, "will put peace first and self-abnegation as secondary." These words echoed Theodore Roosevelt's speeches, which often focused on "manliness" or the lack of it. McGee also recommended Archbishop John Ireland's eulogy for Josiah King, the first Minnesotan to volunteer to fight in the Civil War. Ireland, a Civil War veteran himself, used the occasion to argue that preparedness was "a religious as well as patriotic duty." Condemning "peace at any price," he said that "he who as a citizen of this country is not ready when the nation is threatened to sacrifice his life for its honor is a shame and a disgrace to humanity." McGee told Clapp that Ireland's sermon was "studded with plain red-blooded American thoughts."[51]

On the eve of the vote on the Gore-McLemore resolutions, McGee sent Senator Nelson a copy of the letter he had just written to his own congressman, George R. Smith, another Minnesota Republican who leaned toward neutrality. He warned Smith that the "scuttlers and copperheads" who vote for Gore-McLemore would pay in the 1916 election, or, as he put it, "the axes that have already been bought (and nearly every person with red American blood in his veins has purchased one) can be used without hesitation next November." He expressed his uncompromising nationalism in blunt terms: "Whether it be moral or immoral, I believe in the maxim . . . 'My County, right or wrong.'" Any person who would not stand by his country no matter what the controversy, he added, "would be found, if an autopsy were held, to have serum or rainwater instead of red blood in his veins." In the same letter he suggested a "deportation fund" for people of German extraction opposed to preparation for war.[52]

McGee's letters to Clapp and Smith apparently had little effect, because a month later Senator Clapp joined all nine Minnesota congressmen, including Congressman Smith, in supporting the Gore-McLemore resolution, which responded to German submarine warfare by calling on Americans to avoid booking passage on ships entering the war zone. McGee was left to hope these men would pay in the election coming up in the fall of 1916.[53]

The Mixed Messages of the 1916 Election

The 1916 election was a referendum on Wilson's presidency, especially his foreign policy. In a brilliant public relations coup, his campaign used the slogan "He kept us out of war," a sentence carefully worded in the past tense. Wilson met with AUAM leaders, and many of them publicly supported his candidacy. The republicans nominated Charles Evans Hughes, a lackluster conservative Republican who was not a strong advocate for intervention. However, Theodore Roosevelt went out on the road to give firebrand speeches in support of Hughes, leaving no doubt that a Republican victory would likely mean war. Both the Hughes and the Wilson campaigns pounded the theme of "Americanization."[54]

In Minnesota, all ten congressional seats and the senate seat of Moses Clapp were on the ballot. Eight of the incumbent congressmen won their primary elections, one lost in the primary, and Charles Lindbergh decided not to run for reelection for the Sixth District seat.

George R. Smith was the one losing incumbent, but he was defeated by Ernest Lundeen, who was at least as committed to neutrality as Smith. In April 1917, Lundeen would be part of the minority of congressmen who voted against declaring war on Germany.[55]

After five terms in Congress, Charles Lindbergh was frustrated, restless, and unsettled. He felt that his efforts to create a money and banking system that served the needs of farmers and workers had achieved little, and that, in fact, the Money Trust was pushing the country toward war. In October 1915, he announced that he would seek the Republican Party nomination to run against incumbent governor Winfield Hammond, a Democrat. Then fate intervened. Hammond died unexpectedly during the Christmas holidays of 1915. Lieutenant Governor Joseph Burnquist, who was only thirty-four, became governor on December 30, 1915.[56]

Lindbergh was faced with a dilemma. Instead of a Democrat, the incumbent was now a Republican with a record as a Progressive. After meeting with Burnquist in early 1916, Lindbergh announced he was ending his candidacy because he thought Burnquist's principles and goals "are in accord with my own." In February, he wrote a letter to Burnquist stating that "he had no personal favors to ask except that which I stated to you when I saw you and that was that you administer affairs in your office in such a way as to not cause me to regret that I will take myself out of the field." This was before the Iron Range strike during which Burnquist began to shed his Progressive image. Even after the miners' strike, Lindbergh could not have guessed how much reason he would have to regret his assessment of Burnquist.[57]

Shortly thereafter Lindbergh made another decision that he might have regretted, and one that is hard to understand. Even though he had withdrawn from the governor's race to avoid running against a fellow Progressive, he decided to challenge incumbent senator Moses Clapp, a longtime Progressive, in the June 1916 Republican primary. This would be Lindbergh's first attempt at running statewide. Frank B. Kellogg, an attorney who had earned a national reputation prosecuting antitrust lawsuits in the Roosevelt administration, and Adolph Eberhart, a former governor, were also candidates. Kellogg campaigned as a strong advocate of preparedness. Eberhart had a long record of antagonizing Progressives. Senator La Follette feared Clapp and Lindbergh would split the anti-interventionist vote, leading to a win for Kellogg or Eberhart. He urged Progressive Republican James

Manahan to encourage Minnesotans to stick with Clapp to avoid losing the seat to a conservative.[58]

The campaign gave Lindbergh an opportunity to spend time with his son. He pulled him out of school in Washington so that the boy, who was fourteen, could act as his driver. Charles Jr. drove his father's new Saxon automobile over three thousand miles around Minnesota, passing out campaign literature wherever they stopped, all to no avail. As La Follette feared, Kellogg won easily. Meanwhile, Clapp and Lindbergh dueled to a virtual tie, together attracting fewer votes than Kellogg.[59]

In November, Wilson was reelected to a second term by sweeping the south and the west. Hughes barely won Minnesota, defeating Wilson by only four hundred votes. Kellogg won the senate seat in a three-way race, defeating Democrat Daniel Lawler and Prohibitionist W. G. Calderwood. Both men campaigned against militarism. Kellogg's victory indicated support for preparedness, although he received less than 50 percent of the vote. All eight congressmen on the ballot who had voted against tabling the Gore-McLemore resolutions were reelected. Their survival indicated strong and enduring public support for neutrality.[60]

In Minneapolis, Thomas Van Lear, a well-known labor leader and Socialist Party member, was elected mayor. Van Lear had few allies on the city council and limited power under the law. He did, however, control the police department. The teamster strike, for example, might have had a different outcome if Van Lear had been mayor. The men who lunched at the Minneapolis Club were dismayed that a Socialist had become mayor on their home turf.

John McGee may have been buoyed by the defeat of Moses Clapp, but overall the results alarmed him, not only because Wilson was reelected, but also because the "axes" of those with "American red blood" in their veins had not fallen on the necks of the congressmen who supported Gore-McLemore as he had predicted. In a letter to Knute Nelson, McGee wrote that the congressional election results "made him sick," and still worse was the election of a Socialist as mayor of Minneapolis: "That was the last straw."[61]

But it was not the last straw, and a minor irritant compared to what had just happened in North Dakota, where the Nonpartisan League had achieved a remarkable victory. It was no secret that the NPL hoped to repeat this achievement in Minnesota.

THREE

THE WAR COMES HOME

NOVEMBER 1916 TO APRIL 1917

There isn't any such thing as a war for democracy. All real democrats will suffer just as deeply and mortally as the soldiers in the trenches. . . . Instead of more democracy, either politically or industrially, there will be less. Dictators will spring up, perhaps even here.

CHARLES A. LINDBERGH SR., Sixth District congressman, in conversation with his friends Lynn and Dora Haines on February 2, 1917

If the Governor appoints men who have backbone, treason will not be talked on the streets of this city and the street corner orators, who denounce the government, advocate revolution, denounce the army and advise against enlistment, will be looking through the barbed fences of an interment [*sic*] camp out on the prairie somewhere.

JOHN MCGEE, Minneapolis attorney and former judge, in a letter to Senator Knute Nelson, April 11, 1917

THE CARNAGE IN EUROPE CONTINUED, no more than at the Battle of Verdun, where France and Germany had together suffered a million casualties. On the eastern front, the Russian Army inflicted 600,000 deaths on the German and Austro-Hungarian armies, but lost a million men in the process. Meanwhile, the Italians, now allied with Britain and France, sustained horrendous losses fighting Austria-Hungary. All the belligerent nations neared the breaking point, but the scale of the bloodbath led leaders on all sides to press for a military breakthrough and a tangible victory. How else could they justify the millions of lives lost and the millions of survivors permanently scarred in body and mind?

President Wilson's ability to influence events peaked in the months after his reelection. John Maynard Keynes, at that time a young official overseeing British purchases from the United States, warned that British credit would soon be exhausted. Wilson might have used the credit squeeze to pressure Britain to end its blacklist of US firms, stop its censoring of US mail, and ease the blockade of food to Germany. This path was not taken. A ban on further loans might eventually force Britain to the negotiation table, but it would also disrupt the massive American exports to Britain and France that were generating huge profits and a general prosperity.[1]

On December 18, Wilson asked both sides to state their war aims and called for a league of nations to keep the peace after the war. A few days later he delivered a dramatic speech in the US Senate calling for a new international order based on "a peace without victory," by which he meant that the war should not end with a "peace forced upon the loser, a victor's terms imposed upon the vanquished." Peace advocates like Robert La Follette and Jane Addams were pleased, while advocates of intervention like Theodore Roosevelt argued that Wilson got his inspiration from the Tories of 1776 and the Copperheads of 1864. In any case, the British and the Germans rejected Wilson's initiative.[2]

Socialists, Wobblies, and the Nonpartisan League

At the Christmas holidays, Minnesotans who wanted a neutral United States to mediate an end to the war felt that Wilson was on their side. Business leaders were frustrated by Wilson's moderation, but for now they were focused on developments closer to home. Their reaction to three events set the stage for Minnesota's unique experience once war was declared.

The first was Thomas Van Lear's victory in the Minneapolis mayoral election. The Socialist first ran for mayor in 1910, blindsiding the business community by coming in third, just a few votes behind the Republican and Democratic candidates. In response, the legislature created a nonpartisan primary so that the two candidates with the most votes could proceed to the general election. In 1912, however, Van Lear got on the ballot after the primary by petition. When it looked like he might win a three-way race, a "citizen's non-partisan committee" led by retailer George D. Dayton and banker E. W. Decker convinced the Democratic candidate to withdraw two days before the election, paving the way for a narrow Republican victory.[3]

Van Lear ran a strong but unsuccessful race for the Fifth District congressional seat in 1914, and two years later he was poised for another run for mayor. This time the Democrats sat out the election, and Van Lear went head-to-head with the Republican Otto Langum, the Hennepin County sheriff, who was closely allied with the Citizens Alliance. Van Lear won with 54 percent of the vote, and eight Socialists were also elected to the twenty-six-member city council.

▪ **Thomas Van Lear was a pragmatic Socialist who became mayor of Minneapolis by focusing on bread-and-butter issues like the contract with the private company that provided streetcar service in the Twin Cities.** ***Courtesy of Hennepin County Public Library Special Collections***

How did he do it? Van Lear was a pragmatic Socialist who campaigned as an anti-corruption reformer. His issue was the renewal of the contract with the Twin Cities Rapid Transit Company, the private firm that held the franchise for the streetcar system. The company maneuvered to get its value assessed much higher than Van Lear and other observers thought fair. The contract was based on a fixed rate of return on investment, so the higher the valuation, the greater the allowed profit, meaning higher fares for the public. Van Lear favored public ownership, but in the short run he campaigned against what he called the "streetcar franchise grab." The other key to Van Lear's victory was his broad support among workers, including conservative trade unionists opposed to socialism. This was partially the result of the Citizens Alliance's heavy-handed response to strikes during 1916. Trade unionists could see the deck was stacked against them until they had more control over city hall.[4]

The new mayor was intent on negotiating a better deal with the transit company and cleaning up the city, especially the brothels. About a month after his January 1917 inauguration, the war took center stage and swamped his reform agenda. He played a major role in last-ditch efforts to keep the country out of the war. Once war was declared, he walked a fine line, trying to be both a responsible mayor and a determined critic of the war policy.

The second development was the ongoing labor strife in northern Minnesota. The IWW-led Iron Range miners' strike ended in September 1916, but in December a new strike broke out among sawmill workers at the Virginia and Rainy Lake Lumber Company in the city of Virginia. The strike spread to International Falls, and the IWW had some success encouraging the lumberjacks to walk out of the logging camps. The lumber companies, backed by the local police and hired guards deputized by the local sheriff, broke the strike by arresting anyone who could be identified as an IWW member. The mills were running again by February, and the IWW was banished from the Iron Range. Business leaders concluded that the IWW must be driven out of Minnesota by whatever means necessary, and most newspapers agreed.[5]

The third event was the victory of the Nonpartisan League in North Dakota. The league grew out of the efforts of wheat farmers in the Dakotas and western Minnesota to gain leverage in their dealing with the Minneapolis grain millers, who were represented by the Chamber of Commerce, the original name for the Minneapolis Grain Exchange. In 1908, farmers organized the Equity Cooperatives Exchange as a terminal grain marketing agency to market the grain collected by local cooperative elevators. The Minneapolis grain millers fought back and derailed this effort. Then Albert E. Bowen and Arthur Townley, two men who had some experience organizing farmers for the Socialist Party, envisioned a new approach. They sought to create a party of farmers that would seek state ownership of grain elevators and mills, state regulation of grain trading, and state crop insurance. They borrowed some ideas from the Socialist Party, but the goal was not socialism. Farmers joined the NPL because they thought that state institutions could even the playing field and allow them to bargain fairly with the corporations. They joined to become more successful entrepreneurs.[6]

Townley and Bowen called their experiment the Nonpartisan League because the strategy was to run candidates in the open primaries of the two established parties. At its Fargo convention in March 1916, the NPL selected candidates, most of whom ran as Republicans, and in June they won big in the North Dakota primary. They then took control of the Republican Party's central committee, bought one of the state's major daily newspapers, and swept to victory in November. The NPL candidate for governor, Lynn Frazier, won 80 percent of the vote. When the dust settled, they controlled most state offices and the state house of representatives. At the next election, the NPL gained control of the state senate.[7]

The NPL hoped for a similar result in Minnesota, where victory would require more than the votes of wheat farmers. Agriculture was more diverse than just wheat, and the NPL would need to win votes on the Iron Range and in the cities. Nevertheless, Townley decided to move into Minnesota even before the North Dakota election. By late summer 1916, he had already sent ninety organizers across the Red River to sign up farmers in western Minnesota. In early 1917, the NPL moved its national headquarters from Fargo to St. Paul.[8]

Business leaders believed their struggle with workers and farmers had reached a critical stage. How could they preserve the "open shop"? How could they maintain the power of the grain millers? How could they thwart the Socialist Party and the NPL at the polls?

▪ With a few experienced organizers, Arthur Townley created the Nonpartisan League and led it to power in North Dakota, a victory he hoped to repeat in Minnesota. *MNHS collections*

How could they drive the IWW out of Minnesota? In the next few months, a plan emerged.

The Crisis Begins

Shortly after New Year's Day 1917, Germany made the fateful decision to return to unrestricted submarine warfare, figuring the navy now had enough submarines to choke off supplies to Britain. This action would likely provoke the United States, but the German command calculated that they could defeat the Allies before the United States could train an army and deploy it in France. On January 31, the German ambassador informed the Wilson administration that German U-boats would sink without warning all ships in the waters around Britain, France, Italy, and the eastern Mediterranean. Full-scale submarine warfare began the next day.

Wilson told Congress on February 3 that he had broken diplomatic relations with Germany. Most newspapers, including even some German-language papers, responded favorably to Wilson's response, arguing that Americans should "stand by the President." On February 7, the Senate passed a resolution supporting the president, with only five dissenting votes, one of which was La Follette's. Anti-war groups like the American Union against Militarism and the Woman's Peace Party realized the moment of truth had come. They put together a new umbrella group, the Emergency Peace Federation, whose very name signaled desperation. In a last-ditch effort, they adopted the slogan "No War without a Referendum."[9]

Several anti-war congressmen, including Charles A. Lindbergh, introduced bills requiring a national referendum before the United States could declare war on Germany. Lindbergh's bill stated that if the president severed diplomatic relations with any country, the Bureau of Census would conduct a referendum in which all citizens over the age of eighteen, regardless of sex, could vote for or against a declaration of war. The balloting would be conducted through the post office. Lindbergh's bill never made it out of committee.[10]

In Minneapolis, Mayor Van Lear spoke out against war. The present crisis, he said, was the result of the "unneutral" position of the United States since the beginning of the war, and as a result, the country had "always been in a position to being forced into the conflict."

Van Lear argued that the US involvement would suit the Allies but not be in the interest of the American people. The *Minneapolis Morning Tribune* responded with an editorial claiming that the mayor did not "speak for Minneapolis," because "Minneapolis stands by the President. Minneapolis is loyal."[11]

In response, Van Lear called for a mass meeting on February 10 to demonstrate the broad support for neutrality. About three thousand attended, with others participating in an overflow meeting in the street. Van Lear attacked the *Tribune*, the MCCA, and generally business leaders whom he called "patriots for revenue only." He suggested that the preparedness movement was organized to support the loans that J. P. Morgan had made to Britain, and he noted that St. Paul businessman J. J. Hill had an interest in those loans. He argued that criticizing the policies of the government was a right and a duty. Among the other speakers were Scott Nearing, the well-known economist who had been fired from Wharton School of Business at the University of Pennsylvania in 1915 for his radical views; Lynn Thompson, a member of the Minneapolis Board of Education; and Sylvanus A. Stockwell, a Progressive who had represented Minneapolis in both chambers of the Minnesota legislature. Rebutting the campaign against "hyphenism," Stockwell noted that his ancestors came to this country in the seventeenth century, but that his views should be given no more weight than "the last man who settled on our shores." Thompson invoked the image of the famous "Christmas truce" of 1914, when British, French, and German soldiers briefly took control and celebrated the holiday together. The crowd endorsed a resolution reminding President Wilson that he had been reelected for keeping the country out of the war. The resolution also criticized the press for trying "to stampede our great nation into war" and rejected the notion that only those who sought war were "loyal" Americans.[12]

On that very day, the Socialist Party held its own rallies in Minneapolis and St. Paul featuring Jacob Bentall, the Socialist Party's candidate for governor. After war was declared, Bentall would be arrested by federal officers for speaking out against the war. *New Times*, the Socialist newspaper, continued to demand an arms embargo on the warring countries, and argued that capitalists were dictating the march toward war to protect their profitable trade with the Allies. The trades and labor assemblies of Minneapolis, St. Paul, and Duluth called on the president to keep the United States out of the war. The St. Paul assembly asked the Minnesota congressional delegation to support a referendum on the war because, they argued, workers would bear the entire burden of a war.[13]

The day after Van Lear's rally, the Minneapolis Loyalty League, created just a few days earlier by the MCCA, held a "patriotic rally," also in the Minneapolis Auditorium, to demonstrate the "true sentiment" of the great majority toward the war issue. The league filled the hall and the overflow crowds filed into Westminster Presbyterian and Wesley Methodist churches. The rally was called "to stand by the President." Cyrus Northrop, former president of the university, and now president of the Loyalty League, asked citizens to endorse a message to President Wilson pledging the support of the people of Minneapolis, and making clear that they "earnestly hope and devoutly pray" for peace, but not "peace at any price." Senator Knute Nelson delivered this message, signed by 36,000, to the president. Northrop, who was still president of the Minneapolis Peace Society, echoed Theodore Roosevelt when he stated that "nothing, I am sure, will indulge our government to resort to war except a condition that would stamp us as a nation of degenerates and cowards if we refused to fight for our rights." He apparently had in mind the right to book passage on a ship sailing for the war zone.[14]

Other speakers included Maria Sanford, the retired university professor who a year earlier had bitterly attacked militarism and proclaimed the uselessness of war from the stage of the Orpheum Theatre. Now she focused on the German attempt to keep ships from reaching Britain, asserting that she supported the president "in whatever steps he may have to take to preserve our liberties." George E. Vincent, current university president, who in 1914 eloquently defended the benefits of neutrality, now spoke as if he assumed that war was not only unavoidable but positive. He called on the audience "to accept the inevitable obligation which will open up new vistas of national opportunity, national duty, national achievement."[15]

Vincent's comment typified how some Progressives who had earlier advocated for neutrality now found a way to embrace the war. The philosopher and educator John Dewey, for example, wrote in *The New Republic*, the flagship of Progressive thought, that the war would lead to social reform. Walter Lippman, the rising young Progressive journalist, confidently predicted that a war to overthrow Prussian autocracy would lead to "the overthrow of our own tyrannies—in the Colorado mines, our autocratic steel industries, our sweatshops, and our slums." Progressives like Dewey and Lippman were confident that Wilson saw things the same way, especially when he talked about a war for democracy and a war to end war.[16]

In addition to the Progressive argument articulated by Northrop, Sanford, and Vincent, the audience heard the nationalist case laid out by Judge Eli Torrance, former president of the Grand Army of the Republic, the organization of Civil War veterans. He told the crowd that they were the "real Minneapolis," as opposed to those who attended the event called by Mayor Van Lear the previous evening. Like all speakers, he declared his love of peace, but he also warned that "the exigencies of this hour call for a manifestation of manly patriotism, rather than for the cooing of doves." He praised the country's wars in Cuba and the Philippines, asserting that America "will lead the stricken nations of Europe onto the highway of justice, righteousness, and an enduring peace." He articulated a view that would soon evolve into the pervasive call for "100% Americanism," a slogan that implied dissent was inexcusable during wartime. "A faltering, apologetic, criticizing patriotism in this time is worthless," he said, "and those who indulge in it will be held in aversion by the American people."[17]

The St. Paul Association, the counterpart of the MCCA, quickly organized the St. Paul Patriotic League, led by Charles W. Farnham, an acolyte of Theodore Roosevelt. Other core members included attorney (and future US Supreme Court justice) Pierce Butler, who represented railroads, and Ambrose Tighe, a corporate attorney and politician. The leaders of the St. Paul Patriotic League favored war with Germany, but they were also concerned with the home front. In fact, they conceived the initial idea to create the body that became the Minnesota Commission of Public Safety. Ambrose Tighe wrote the legislative act that created it.[18]

Tighe was raised in New York and educated at Yale College, where he was a member of Phi Beta Kappa and the Skull and Bones secret society. He started a law career after graduating in 1879, but he then returned to Yale, where he studied, and eventually taught, Roman history and law. He even published a book on the Roman constitution for which Yale awarded him a graduate degree. In 1886, he moved

■ Ambrose Tighe, an attorney who operated within elite circles in St. Paul, wrote the legislation that created the Minnesota Commission of Public Safety and became its chief counsel. *MNHS collections*

to St. Paul, where his law practice prospered. He represented national firms like Mutual Life Insurance Company and Eastman Kodak. He also invested in railroads and lumber. He started a suburban railway company, for example, which was eventually bought by the Twin Cities Rapid Transit Company, and he then became that firm's attorney. In 1900, while president of the Ramsey County Bar Association, he helped found the St. Paul College of Law. Running as a Progressive Republican, he represented St. Paul in the Minnesota House between 1903 and 1907. He pursued his intellectual bent in the Informal Club, a group dedicated to "rational good-fellowship and tolerant discussion." Only successful St. Paul men were admitted to this invitation-only club, whose members included both Pierce Butler and Charles Farnham.[19]

War at Last

In Washington, preparedness advocates used the war crisis to secure passage in the House of a $368 million naval bill during the final days of the sixty-fourth Congress. The appropriation was intended to fund three battleships, three cruisers, fifteen destroyers, and eighteen submarines. The bill passed 353 to 23, and one of those "no" votes was cast by Charles Lindbergh, now a "lame duck" congressman serving his last weeks in Congress.[20]

Because American ships were reluctant to sail for Europe, Wilson asked Congress to authorize the arming of merchant ships for defense against submarines. During an intense debate in the House, opponents argued that if armed American merchant ships entered the war zone, the United States would soon be at war. Nevertheless, the House passed the "armed ship" bill by a vote of 403 to 13 on March 1. Charles Lindbergh was again in opposition, joined by Third District congressman Charles R. Davis of St. Peter. Lindbergh noted that Congress took this step toward war only because munition makers had trouble delivering their goods.[21]

Lindbergh disagreed with those Progressives who argued that the war would lead to democratic reform. In early February, shortly after Wilson ended diplomatic relations with Germany, a dejected Lindbergh visited the Washington office of his friends Lynn and Dora Haines and told them that the war would be a great setback for the cause of good government. "There isn't any such thing," he told them, "as a war for democracy." When someone in the office argued that the war would promote Progressivism, he responded that this "sounds logical," but "it won't work" because "war-born things never do." He expected that the war would lead to less democracy, and that "dictators will spring up, perhaps even here."[22]

In the Senate, Robert La Follette and four other senators filibustered the bill until the sixty-fourth Congress adjourned. Although Moses Clapp of Minnesota, also a "lame duck" in his last days in Congress, did not join the filibuster, he opposed the bill. A few days later Wilson armed merchant ships by executive order and called Congress back for a special session starting April 16.

Congress was influenced by the dramatic disclosure on February 28 of a telegram sent by Arthur Zimmerman, the German foreign minister, to Mexico, proposing that if Mexico allied with Germany, it could recover the territory lost in 1848. The British had intercepted this message and passed it on to Wilson, who chose this day to release it to the press. Predictably it led to a patriotic backlash against Germany.

The St. Paul Patriotic League passed a resolution condemning the votes of Lindbergh and Davis as "un-American, unjustifiable, and cowardly." To bolster patriotism, the league then began a flag crusade, which resulted in Governor Burnquist issuing an official proclamation on March 11 mandating flags over all public buildings and requesting that private citizens display the flag. The legislature passed a bill requiring the Department of Education to provide a flag to every school, and then a second bill requiring the schools teach "subjects including patriotism" at least one day per week. George H. Sullivan, a conservative senator from Stillwater, moved to amend the second bill to include a requirement that all schools "teach the necessity for military preparedness." This amendment was defeated.[23]

On March 15, the news broke that Nicholas II, the Russian tsar, had been swept away by a spontaneous mass uprising, and that a Provisional Government committed to a Western-styled constitutional republic had taken over. Wilson could now avoid the blatant hypocrisy of fighting a "war for democracy" as an ally of Russian autocracy. Most Western observers were wildly optimistic about the new government's ability to continue fighting the war.

On March 18, the newspapers carried the news that German U-boats had sunk three merchant vessels clearly marked as American in the war zone. Two of the ships were empty, but the German captains made no effort to verify their cargo before sinking them. None were armed. Wilson's cabinet was unanimous for war, although several members envisioned a limited intervention that did not include sending troops to France. On March 23, Wilson moved up the opening of the new Congress to April 2. Few doubted he would ask for a declaration of war.

Minnesotans favoring neutrality frantically campaigned for peace. Some traveled to Washington in response to a call from the Emergency Peace Federation to lobby their representatives to resist a declaration of war. Sylvanus Stockwell, one of the speakers at Van Lear's rally, told the press that at least twenty-five Minnesotans were going to the capitol. On March 28, the American Neutrality Society, one of the organizations formed primarily among German Americans to campaign for an embargo on all belligerents, held a rally in downtown Minneapolis. Speakers criticized Wilson for his tilt toward Britain, and the audience passed a resolution opposing war against Germany.[24]

On March 31, the newly organized St. Paul Peace League held a rally attended by three thousand at the St. Paul Auditorium, chaired by Anna Maley, an assistant to Mayor Van Lear. A major figure in the Socialist Party, she had returned to her native Minnesota in 1915 because of failing health after an extensive career as an organizer, journalist, and orator. Robert La Follette was scheduled to speak, but at the last minute decided he could not leave Washington. He was replaced by James Peterson, a former Hennepin County attorney who had run an unsuccessful primary campaign against Senator Knute Nelson in 1912. He criticized the massive publicity campaign encouraging a declaration of war. "Who put up the money for spreading of this propaganda?" he asked the crowd, which shouted back "Wall Street!" Yes, he said, and "why don't they go and fight the war themselves?" He would soon find himself under federal indictment. John W. Willis, a former district court judge, also spoke against the war. He felt the need to devote the first part of his speech to defending his freedom to speak. He argued that there was nothing disloyal about opposing a war that had not yet been declared. He then noted that the United States had as much cause to fight Great Britain as Germany, since both countries violated American maritime rights. Wilson was willing to negotiate its differences with Britain, and should do the same with Germany. In Willis's view, this policy would be consistent with the Gospels, whereas to go to war would be to revert to paganism.[25]

About a thousand people packed the New Ulm armory on March 30 to hear anti-war speeches from mayor Louis Fritsche, city attorney Albert Pfaender, professor Adolph Ackermann, newspaper editor Albert Steinhauser, businessman Frank Retzlaff, and Rev. Robert Schlinkert, a Catholic priest. The crowd approved a resolution demanding a referendum on the war and sending Fritsche, Steinhauser, and Retzlaff to Washington, DC. When they arrived, they found the atmosphere hostile to the movement for peace. Peace delegates were handed yellow ribbons and the peace federation's building was smeared with yellow paint.[26]

Meanwhile St. Paul Loyalty League and other groups favoring war held frequent rallies, culminating in a major event on April 5 chaired by Pierce Butler. This event featured Henry L. Stimson, the secretary of war under President Taft, and Frederick R. Coulter, a New York lawyer who was on a speaking tour to promote universal military training. The next day, Stimson and Coulter spoke to eight hundred in Minneapolis at a West Hotel luncheon, joined by F. C. Walcott, a Wall Street banker, "who had a big role in the floating of Allied loans in America," according to the *Minneapolis Morning Tribune*. The newspaper reported that the attendees became "smoldering volcanoes of patriotism" when a military band opened the meeting with the national anthem.[27]

One group of European immigrants came out in favor of war. On March 29, about a thousand Polish Americans met at Kozlak's Hall in Minneapolis to pledge their loyalty to the United States and their readiness to fight. Poles had a much different relationship to the warring European nations than their German, Irish, and Scandinavian neighbors. Because Prussia, Austria-Hungary, and Russia had conspired to destroy the Polish state through conquest and partition, Poles supported war against the first two, and tolerated an alliance with Russia after the tsar was overthrown. The defeat of the German and Austro-Hungarian empires would clear the way for the rebirth of a Polish state, the goal of every Polish nationalist.[28]

Modern readers may be surprised to learn that college faculty were generally pro-war and often passionately intolerant of those who disagreed. When David Starr Jordan, the former president of Stanford University, toured the East on behalf of the Emergency Peace Federation in March, he was heckled at Harvard and Princeton and driven off the stage at Yale by a hail of rotten eggs. When he tried to speak at the Baltimore Academy of Music, a crowd of businessmen and Johns Hopkins University professors stormed the hall and disrupted the meeting.[29]

At the University of Minnesota, 135 faculty members signed a telegram to President Wilson demanding war with Germany. The organizers claimed that only one faculty member in ten declined to sign. Macalester College professor James Wallace publicly resigned as vice president of the Minnesota Peace Society, arguing that "an American who preaches peace and submission [to Germany] invites his country to play the role of arrant coward." Like his fellow academic Cyrus Northrop, who had been president of the Peace Society, he advocated intervention by invoking a sense of national manhood. He also argued that the existence of the German and the Turkish empires constituted "a moral crisis confronting the world" and that anyone who could not see this "ought to be disenfranchised on the ground of stupidity."[30]

One exception to the academic hunger for war was quickly overwhelmed. In March, the Neutrality and Peace Association, a student organization at Macalester College, sent a statement signed by eighty-seven male students to Congress that defended neutrality, criticized both Britain and Germany for their blockades, advocated the nationalization of the munitions industry, censured the press as "jingoistic," and praised the courage displayed by a small minority in Congress. This set off a brouhaha in the press. Clarence B. Miller, the Eighth District congressman from Duluth, published an open letter in the Twin Cities newspapers attacking the petition as "pro-enemy and anti-American" and "the cry of a yellow-streaked and cowardly soul." To rescue the college's reputation, the neutrality statement was refuted by fourteen of the seventeen Macalester faculty members, by an alumni petition, and finally by a student "loyalty" petition, to which some of the signers of the neutrality statement added their signatures. Once war was declared, most of the original signers entered the military. Led by Professor Wallace, faculty members telegrammed President Wilson urging an American declaration of war. Their proposed war aims were expansive. Permanent world peace was impossible, they wrote, until the German and Turkish empires were destroyed.[31]

Wilson told Congress on April 2 that Germany's submarine warfare had created a state of war they must formally acknowledge. He did not suggest that the security of the United States was jeopardized. Instead, he argued that the United States must go to war both for the specific need to protect American maritime rights and for the general goal of overcoming Prussian autocracy and making the world "safe for democracy." He called for new taxes, financial support for the Allies, a fully equipped navy, and 500,000 new troops. For the first time, he spoke favorably about conscription. Wilson understood the country was deeply divided about entering the European war. "If there should be disloyalty," he told Congress, "it will be dealt with with a firm hand of repression." Few then understood how firm a hand he had in mind.[32]

The legislators, or most of them, interrupted Wilson repeatedly with prolonged applause. A minority, mostly insurgent Republicans and William Jennings Bryan–inspired Democrats, were quiet. When the Senate debated the declaration of war two days later, Wisconsin senator Robert La Follette and Nebraska senator Charles Norris spoke in opposition. La Follette ridiculed the idea that fighting alongside the British and the French empires meant fighting for democracy. Norris observed that the British blockade, enforced by submerged mines, was no better than the German blockade, enforced by submarines. He argued that the United States was going to war only to protect the profits of Wall Street and the armaments industry. On April 4, the Senate voted 82–6 for war. Minnesota senators Kellogg and Nelson both voted yes.

The House debate started on April 5 and continued till 3:00 AM the next morning, which happened to be Good Friday. The representatives voted 373 to 50 for war, with most of the "no" votes coming from the Midwest. Four of Minnesota's ten congressmen voted against the war resolution, an indication of the continuing strength of neutralist sentiment. Three represented districts with large German American populations: Charles R. Davis of St. Peter, Carl C. Van Dyke of St. Paul, and Harold Knutson of St. Cloud, who held Lindbergh's Sixth District seat. Had Lindbergh still been in Congress, he most certainly would have voted "no." The fourth, Ernest Lundeen of Minneapolis, cited a poll of people in his district resulting in a ten to one vote against going to war. Neutralist sentiment in neighboring Wisconsin was even stronger, where nine of eleven congressmen voted against the war resolution.[33]

John McGee was infuriated that four Minnesota congressmen, including his own representative, Ernest Lundeen, had voted against the war. He was already disgusted with Lundeen for arguing that war with Germany should be put before the voters in a referendum. In a letter to Nelson, McGee expressed his contempt for Lundeen by writing that "if you . . . backed him up against a wall and bumped his head, he probably would pay some attention to you." Despite their anti-war votes, only Lundeen lost his seat in 1918, while Davis, Van Dyke, and Knutson easily won reelection.[34]

Many legislators who voted for war did not believe Wilson would send soldiers to France. Since the tangible reason for war was maritime rights, some assumed the war would be fought at sea. Others felt the declaration of war was simply a way to facilitate financial aid to the Allies. They would soon find out that Wilson intended to draft millions of young men and send them across the ocean to fight Germany in the trenches.

Seizing the Moment

The declaration of war triggered irrational fears. Newspapers in the Twin Cities printed stories about "an assassin" arrested with a suitcase full of dynamite, guardsmen wounded in a gun battle with saboteurs, and a foiled conspiracy to blow up a Washburn-Crosby mill. All these stories were baseless. Nevertheless, the National Guard was assigned to provide round the clock protection to mills and grain terminals in Minneapolis and St. Paul; to mines and ore docks in Duluth, Two

Harbors, and the Iron Range; and to railroad bridges throughout the state. No sabotage was reported, either at this time or any time during the war. The atmosphere of fear and anxiety, however, was real.[35]

While many Minnesotans were caught up in the emotional drama of the war crisis, cooler heads in business circles were making plans for the home front. Leaders of the MCCA and the St. Paul Association understood that while war would be very good economically, it could also lead to instability. They worried about how immigrants would react to the war. The campaign that German Americans had waged for neutrality raised concerns about their loyalty during wartime. These business leaders were more concerned, however, about organizations that directly threatened their economic interests. They feared the war might provide fertile ground for trade unions, the IWW, the Socialists, and the NPL to make advances. They realized the Minnesota National Guard, their last line of defense in case of strikes, would soon be federalized and sent to France. However, the war might provide an opportunity to get the upper hand over their adversaries. They were keenly aware that the legislature was about to adjourn and would not reconvene until 1919, barring a special session.

The leaders of the St. Paul Patriotic League, especially Charles Farnham and Ambrose Tighe, grabbed the initiative. On March 17, Tighe wrote a letter to Governor Burnquist suggesting that the legislature pass an alien registration law. Meanwhile, Tighe began drafting a bill to create the Minnesota Commission of Public Safety, an emergency body to govern the state during the war. On March 24, two weeks before the declaration of war, state senator George Sullivan of Stillwater introduced an early version of the bill. Tighe continued to refine it, adding many of the powers the final bill contained, including the power to subpoena witnesses and remove elected officials. At one point, Tighe's bill empowered the commission to suspend "the privilege of the writ of habeas corpus." This provision, which would give the unelected commission the ability to declare martial law, was not included in the final version.[36]

On March 31, Sullivan introduced an expanded version of the bill. It called for a commission of seven members, including the governor, the attorney general, and five others appointed by the governor. The proposed legislation contained an alien registration requirement. A companion bill was introduced in the house the next day. It was an unprecedented piece of legislation, but nevertheless became law in just a few short days, with little public notice. Looking back on the final days of the 1917 legislative session, the secretary of state noted that Senator Sullivan "put the measure through in probably the shortest period of time ever experienced in the passage of important legislation in Minnesota probably through patriotic fervor which was high at that time."[37]

The bill had one public hearing. On the evening of April 3, the Senate Finance Committee took testimony from business leaders. The *Minneapolis Morning Tribune* reported that "representative business men of Minneapolis and St. Paul crowded the Senate chamber" to urge passage of Sullivan's bill. They were something of a who's who of the rich and powerful. The Minneapolis delegation included A. M. Sheldon, president of the MCCA; Albert C. Loring, president of Pillsbury Flour; A. C. Magnuson, vice president of the Minneapolis Chamber of Commerce; and F. M. Prince, board chair of First National and Security Bank and a founding member of the MCCA. The *Minneapolis Journal*, whose executives were also members of the MCCA, editorialized that the bill would "gather the sovereign powers of the State in a few responsible hands for quick and effective use in case of need." Among the speakers from St. Paul were Charles Ames, president of West Publishing, who was closely associated with the leadership of both the MCCA and the St. Paul Association; Alex Janes, an attorney for the Great Northern Railway, who represented the Patriotic League; and Robert M. Olds, a partner in the law firm of Davis, Kellogg, and Severance, St. Paul's well-connected power firm.[38]

Meanwhile, a separate alien registration bill was introduced in the house, provoking a bitter debate. Supporters of the bill suggested that only "copperheads" could oppose it, while an opponent called it "jingo legislation." Legislators who were born in Europe, or whose parents were immigrants, testified on both sides of the issue. Magnus Johnson, a Litchfield farmer born in Sweden, stated that he was "willing to shoulder a gun to defend the United States, but that he was not going to vote for this bill and I am not a copperhead." After the war, Johnson would represent Minnesota in the US Senate. On the other hand, Oscar Seebach, an American-born son of German immigrants, proclaimed that he was "German to the backbone but I am for this bill." Seebach had been wounded in the Philippines during the

Spanish-American War, and within a few weeks he would be recalled to military service. After two hours of acrimony, the bill was tabled to let tempers cool. Eventually, the bill was dropped, as was an alien registration requirement in the MCPS bill, with the understanding that the commission, once established, would have the power to register aliens if it saw fit.[39]

On April 7, Burnquist issued a public statement urging the legislature to suspend the rules and quickly pass Sullivan's safety commission bill. He noted that the legislature was about to adjourn and a special session would be required if they failed to create the commission. On April 10, the senate voted 63 to 0 to pass the bill with several amendments, including one authorizing the commission to create its own military force, the Home Guard. Two days later, the house passed the bill by a vote of 161 to 1. Only Ernest Strand, a Socialist from Two Harbors, voted against it. Andrew Devold, the other Socialist in the house, did not vote.[40]

There was one final hurdle. The senate and house bills were out of sync because the house had amended the bill to give the governor veto power over the actions of the commission. Sullivan and his senate colleagues worried that Burnquist, who had earlier been a Progressive, might hesitate to wield the commission's ample powers. In conference committee, they made sure the final bill stated that "all official acts of the commission shall require a majority vote of the entire Commission." As a result, unelected commissioners were given the power to override the will of the governor. On April 16, Governor Burnquist signed the bill.[41]

The legislature passed three other "war measures." The most important was the Minnesota version of the federal Sedition Act that Congress would pass in June 1917. It outlawed interference with or discouragement of enlistment in the armed forces. Because any criticism of the government could be construed as discouraging enlistments, this law would prove a potent weapon against the Nonpartisan League, even though the league officially supported the war effort. There was also a far-reaching "criminal syndicalist" bill aimed at the IWW, which included severe penalties not just for those who advocated violence but for those who sold "syndicalist literature" or were members of a syndicalist organization or attended a syndicalist meeting or even rented a hall for a meeting deemed "criminal syndicalist."

A third bill prohibited the possession of firearms or explosives by enemy aliens.[42]

Although McGee was not a member of the legislature, he played an active role in the development of the MCPS bill. He told Knute Nelson that he had seen a copy of the bill while "in the Governor's office," and that he was pleased because it had "teeth in it eighteen inches long." The bill gave the seven commissioners, five of whom were unelected, such extensive powers to govern that he was worried it might not survive a court challenge. He told Nelson that since sections of the bill were "unconstitutional and palpably so," he had instructed a legislative ally "to inject an amendment into it" so that if one or more provisions were held unconstitutional, the entire law would not be invalid.[43]

McGee told Nelson that "if the Governor appoints men who have backbone, treason will not be talked on the streets of this city" and those who oppose the government and the war effort "will be looking through the barbed fences of an interment [*sic*] camp out on the prairie somewhere." He confided to Nelson that many people "in banking, grain and milling circles" hoped he would be appointed to the commission. His big moment was about to arrive.

PART II

The War at Home

FOUR

FORGING THE WEAPONS

SPRING & EARLY SUMMER 1917

America, my country, I come at thy call; I plight thee my troth and I give thee my all;
In peace and in war I am wed to thy weal—I'll carry thy flag through the fire and steel.
Unsullied it floats o'er our peace-loving race, on sea, nor land shall it suffer disgrace;
In rev'rence I kneel at sweet liberty's shrine: America, my country, command, I am thine!

JENS GRONDAHL, from "America, My County," *Red Wing Daily Republican,* April 6, 1917

Of what avail is it to a freedom-loving and peace-loving citizen of a foreign country to leave his fatherland to escape military conscription and universal military servitude imposed by a military bureaucracy and make this his adopted country, only to find that the country of his adoption is setting up another military bureaucracy to conscript him and impose upon his sons the system of universal service patterned after that of the fatherland from which he has flown?

CARL C. VAN DYKE, congressman for Minnesota's Fourth District, speaking against the Selective Service Act in the House of Representatives on April 26, 1917

THE DECLARATION OF WAR on Germany was a great victory for the British and the French. Advocates of intervention in the United States also celebrated. Theodore Roosevelt, who had publicly insulted Wilson as a coward for two years, paid a surprise visit to the White House to congratulate the president. It was a bright day for industrialists and bankers. As the historian Niall Ferguson wrote, one may well imagine "the state of elation" in the offices of J. P. Morgan because "it was Morgan as much as Britain which was bailed out in 1917." The fact that Britain had exhausted its credit was now irrelevant, and orders for war materiel would continue.[1]

The Allies welcomed the money but also needed American troops. Nearly three years of war had taken a terrible toll on Russian, British, and French armies. In May, for example, significant parts of the French army on the western front refused orders to begin new offensives, a strike against the strategy of attrition. A new commander was appointed who made some concessions to the troops and executed fifty-five soldiers for insubordination.

Conscripting Men but Not Wealth

When the United States entered the war the so-called "regular army" numbered only about 128,000 men. In addition, the law allowed the president to call the national guards of the various states into federal service in a national emergency, a force of about 164,000. The day after war was declared Secretary of War Nelson Baker brought to Congress a bill to expand the regular army to 298,000, to "federalize" the national guard and expand it to 440,000, and, most controversially, to authorize the president to conscript 500,000 men with the possibility of another 500,000 later, through a selective, rather than universal, national draft.[2]

A majority in both the Senate and the House of Representatives opposed conscription, with members from the South and Midwest the most ardent adversaries. After more than a month of debate, however, Wilson succeeded in passing the Selective Service Act. The law subjected men age twenty-one to thirty to the draft, set pay for privates at thirty dollars per month, and outlawed liquor sales and brothels near army camps.[3]

Three of the four Minnesota congressmen who had voted against the declaration of war also voted against conscription. Ernest Lundeen of the Fifth District (Minneapolis) argued that forcing conscription on the American people "is to enslave millions in the interest of foreign nations." Carl Van Dyke of the Fourth District (St. Paul) observed that it was a bitter irony for someone to emigrate to the United States to escape "universal military servitude" only to find himself once again ensnared by a military bureaucracy. Charles R. Davis of the Third District opposed conscription "as militaristic and savoring too much of the methods of autocratic governments in Europe." Davis was a captain in the Minnesota National Guard. Lundeen and Van Dyke were veterans of the Spanish-American War.[4]

Their votes reflected the widespread opposition to the draft, expressed in the labor press, the foreign language newspapers, and some small-town newspapers such as the *Hibbing News* and the *Park Region Echo* of Alexandria. The Socialist-influenced *Labor Review* came out against conscription, but the more moderate *Labor World* in Duluth echoed the Minnesota Federation of Labor view that if men must be conscripted then wealth should be conscripted too. The Swedish and German newspapers tended to be anti-conscription, although the latter took a low profile on the issue. Small-town newspapers that opposed conscription tended to characterize it as un-American, unconstitutional, incompatible with free institutions, and even a step down the path toward a Prussian-style militarism.[5]

Once Congress decided to build an army through conscription, there were difficult logistical problems to be solved. For starters, the government had no list of men between age twenty-one and thirty from which to "select" its army. The only way to create such a list was to ask men to register themselves with the Selective Service System. The government announced that every man between those ages must present himself on June 5, 1917. Many government officials were surprised how smoothly this day went. About 9.6 million men registered, although it was clear that many had not reported, especially in the southern and western states. The government then set July 20 for the first lottery drawing, at which the order of call would be established. Shortly after that, men around the country would receive draft notices.

Critics argued that conscription not only negated individual liberty but also dangerously centralized power in the hands of the federal government. Long-term opponents of war also felt that it would further militarize society. The Wilson administration calmed fears by designing a decentralized institution based on local committees of civilians—the draft boards—which could exempt individuals based on several legal categories. The government cleverly christened the bureaucracy as the "Selective Service System," highlighting the fact that conscription would not be universal and encouraging men to think of a draft notice as an invitation to fulfill an already existing duty to serve one's country.[6]

The law allowed for some accommodation for members of "any well-recognized religious sect" whose creed forbade its members "to participate in war in any form." Men who received status as conscientious objectors were inducted into the army and assigned to noncombatant service. In practice, draft boards were willing to grant this status to members of historic peace churches with which they were familiar, like the Mennonites and Quakers, but were reluctant to exempt other religious objectors. Conscientious objectors often faced harassment and even court-martial once in the military.[7]

Meanwhile, Congress debated how to pay for the war. Wilson and his treasury secretary William G. McAdoo had hoped to pay at least half the cost through taxation. Progressives like Robert La Follette and Claude Kitchens argued for a "pay as you go" approach, in which taxes on the wealthy would pay the bulk of the costs. They had some success, but in the end about two-thirds of war expenditures were financed by borrowing. The loans were a combination of Treasury Bonds sold mainly to Wall Street and small denomination Liberty Bonds sold to the public during five nationwide campaigns, the last of which, called the Victory Loan, came after the armistice. Encouraged by an enormous publicity campaign, and in the later bond drives by considerable coercion, sixty million Americans subscribed to at least one bond.[8]

The first Liberty Bond campaign was in May 1917. The federal reserve bank in each of the twelve districts organized the sale and issuance of bonds. Bonds were sold in denominations from $50 to $10,000 at 3½ percent interest with a thirty-year maturity. Although the market rate for similar bonds was 4 percent, bond sales nationally surpassed the goal of $2 billion. However, the Ninth Federal Reserve District, which included Minnesota and the Dakotas, fell $10 million short of its $80 million quota, and Minnesota in particular fell $2 million short of its $37 million goal. Bond sales were strong in cities across the upper Midwest but disappointing in rural counties. Officials recognized that they needed to mount an intensive campaign before the second drive in October to convince farmers and workers to invest in the war.[9]

Concerned about the supply of food for the military, the Allies, and the home front, Woodrow Wilson asked Herbert Hoover to take on the role of food administrator. When Hoover, who was in Europe managing the Committee for Relief of Belgium, returned in May, he called a meeting of grain millers, who agreed to voluntarily comply with government efforts to stabilize food prices. Hoover appointed James Ford Bell, a thirty-eight-year-old vice president at the Washburn-Crosby Company in Minneapolis (and later its president), to head the milling division of the Food Administration. Bell moved to New York for the duration of the war, managing the nation's production and distribution of grain.[10]

Businessmen Take Charge

Several days after the declaration of war, Secretary of War Newton Baker asked the states to create councils of defense to implement on a local level the policies of the Council of National Defense (CND), an institution created by Congress to coordinate nationwide support for the war effort on the home front. Burnquist informed Washington that the Minnesota legislature was just about to create the Minnesota Commission of Public Safety (MCPS), a body with powers far beyond what Washington had in mind. It remained to be seen to what extent the MCPS would cooperate with the Wilson administration.[11]

The bill creating the MCPS gave it the "power to do all acts" necessary and proper for the public safety and the protection of life and public property or private property, so long as these acts did not violate Minnesota law or its constitution. The commission was also tasked with doing everything necessary to make sure military, civil, and industrial resources were efficiently employed in the successful prosecution of the war. The commission had the power to seize property, to require people to appear before it and testify under oath, and to investigate and remove elected public officials. A separate section granted the commission the power to create and arm a Home Guard of as many units as it saw fit. The Minnesota legislature had created what may have been the most powerful of all the state defense councils.[12]

The legislature appropriated $1 million to support the work of the commission, equivalent to about $20 million in today's dollars. The bill set aside some of this money for a bonus to be paid to all Minnesota National Guard members who served on the Mexican border, calculated at fifty cents per day of service. The statute also authorized the commission to spend funds to provide for the "comfort" of Minnesotans in military service and of dependents of soldiers. In the end, the MCPS spent about half of its appropriation for these purposes.[13]

Burnquist signed the bill on April 16. The next day, the senate quietly approved the five men he nominated to join him and the attorney general Lyndon A. Smith as commissioners: Charles W. Ames, president of West Publishing Company in St. Paul; John Lind, an attorney, a former Democratic governor, and most recently President Wilson's personal envoy to Mexico; Colonel Charles H. March, Spanish-American war veteran, mayor of Litchfield, and an attorney whose clients included the Great Northern Railroad; John F. McGee, attorney and former judge, Minneapolis; and Anton Weiss, publisher of the *Duluth Herald*.[14]

The press took little notice of the governor's appointments, although the *Minneapolis Morning Tribune* published a short editorial praising him for choosing men who have "the courage to meet the emergency, no matter how serious it may become, and safeguard the peace and quiet of the commonwealth so long as the war should last." Soon critics of the commission, especially in the labor movement, complained that all commissioners except Weiss and Lind were associated with the conservative wing of the Republican Party, and that Weiss, a conservative Democrat, published a pro-business newspaper. No commissioner represented the trade unions or farmers, and only Lind was even vaguely sympathetic to those constituencies.[15]

As the elected governor, Burnquist was chair, but the legislature had decreed that the commission could act only by majority vote. John F. McGee, who was eighteen years older than the governor, quickly became the de facto leader, by virtue of his experience, self-assurance, and clear agenda. The commission retained Ambrose Tighe as its legal counsel and appointed John Pardee, an experienced journalist, as secretary. The secretary was key, since he was a full-time employee and the commission members were unpaid volunteers. In daily correspondence, Pardee interpreted the meaning of the commission's orders. Pardee, Tighe, and Lind stood somewhat apart from the other figures of the MCPS in that they were moderate Progressives who hoped the war would drive positive reform. Pardee, for example, told the Progressive journalist Lincoln Steffens he thought his work for the MCPS, although routine, would influence "the shaping of the new world in which we are to live." In the early days of the MCPS, Pardee, Tighe, and Lind had not grasped the extent to which John McGee intended to use the commission to defend the status quo. Something, or somebody, would have to give.[16]

For the moment, the newspapers were more interested in the governor's call for a patriotic festival on April 19 to mobilize support for the war, although the stated reason was to honor Paul Revere and the battle of Lexington in 1775. In the Twin Cities, the festival involved a large convocation at the University of Minnesota, a daytime parade in St. Paul, and an evening parade through downtown Minneapolis to Parade Stadium. At the university, President George E. Vincent made a passionate speech about "Americanism." The Minneapolis parade featured National Guard companies, newly formed volunteer militias, veterans' organizations, fraternal lodges, and delegations from various companies, including the Northwestern National Bank and Donaldson's department store. The *Tribune* reported that retired university professor Maria Sanford, "in spite of her four score years, jumped from an automobile to climb into an army wagon," from which she told the crowd that those who could not enlist "must give our last dollar and our last ounce of strength" to support the troops who will do the fighting.[17]

Similar events were held in Duluth and elsewhere around the state. Those who had advocated intervention were thrilled, and many who had resisted the drive toward war surrendered to the patriotic fervor. Jens Grondahl, editor of the *Red Wing Daily Republican*, who had poetically dismissed the war as the "madness of monarchs" in 1914, reinvented himself as Goodhue County's most visible cheerleader for the war effort.

Grondahl published "America, My Country," a nationalist verse written in the overheated poetic diction of the time, on his front page. The poem made national news when Representative Isaac Seigel, a congressman from New York City, read it during the debate on the war resolution. According to the *Minneapolis Tribune,* the poem was greeted with applause on the floor of the House of Representatives. Thrilled by this moment of fame, Grondahl had the poem set to music and published the song with the subtitle "The New National Anthem." Combining the roles of entrepreneur and patriot, Grondahl printed huge quantities of the sheet music and launched a campaign to get the song recognized as the official national anthem. This was not completely quixotic, since Congress did not designate "The Star-Spangled Banner" as the official anthem until 1931, although it was already widely accepted as such.[18]

Grondahl played a big role in Red Wing's Loyalty Day parade on April 19. His newspaper reported that over six thousand marched in a procession through town, including about twenty members of his staff, who carried a "monster American flag." Besides the usual marching bands, veterans' groups, Boy Scouts, and the like, the newspaper noted the participation of ten Mdewakanton Dakota men from the nearby Prairie Island reservation. University president Dr. George E. Vincent told the crowd that the war was "a fight between the form of government represented by France, England, and the great democracy of America and the despotic and autocratic rule of Germany." The colonial holdings of Germany were meager compared to those of Britain or France, but he used the word "empire" only when referring to the former.[19]

Creating a Wartime Government

At the MCPS's first meeting on April 23, the commission effectively enhanced its power by deciding that its meetings would not be public. The press would learn about its activity only from press releases and other publications. The commission's minutes were remarkably terse, recording decisions but giving no sense of the reasons behind them.[20]

During its first three months, the MCPS created a statewide network of institutions and operatives to execute the commission's agenda. The first step was to appoint a director for each of Minnesota's eighty-six counties. The commission chose Donald R. Cotton, a steel company executive and National Security League leader, to be the Ramsey County director, with the understanding that he would be "mutually the agent" of the commission and of the St. Paul Association, the business group which had initiated the idea of the MCPS.

Across the river, the commission appointed Minneapolis lawyer Fred Snyder as the Hennepin County director, with the understanding that he would be both the agent of the commission and of the Minneapolis Civic and Commerce Association, of which he was a leader. Directors in the other eighty-four county-level commissions came from more diverse backgrounds, but since they were recruited through the Minnesota Bankers' Association, many were bankers. William Putnam, for example, a well-known Red Wing banker and former president of the local Commercial Club, was appointed the director of the Goodhue County Public Safety Commission. Even in predominantly rural counties, directors tended to be businessmen rather than farmers.[21]

The commission organized agencies to facilitate a smooth transition to a wartime economy. Even before the MCPS was created, Burnquist appointed the Committee on Food Production and Conservation, chaired by A. D. Wilson from the university's Department of Agriculture. This group, which was semiautonomous but reported to the MCPS, was charged with maximizing Minnesota's food exports by overseeing agricultural production, farm labor, food marketing, and consumer conservation. The MCPS conducted a farm labor census to gauge the need for farm labor during the harvest, and then set up a State Employment Office in Minneapolis to meet this demand. This office also acted as a clearinghouse where men, and increasingly women, could be matched with openings in factories and shops. These efforts were among the most successful, and least controversial, of the commission's work.[22]

However, the MCPS put most of its energies into achieving the unwavering allegiance of every Minnesotan, by persuasion if possible and coercion if necessary. The commission understood that despite the patriotic rallies and parades, most Minnesotans, especially in urban working-class wards and in rural counties, had wanted the United States to stay out of the European war. In the belief that "unity in thought is the basis of unity in action," commissioner Anton Weiss chaired the publicity committee, which produced and distributed 150,000 copies of a pamphlet called "Why We Are at War" and 100,000 copies of Wilson's war address in the first months of the war. The commission instructed the county directors to organize local speakers' bureaus. In this work the commission followed the lead of President Wilson, who issued an executive order creating the

Committee of Public Information (CPI). He appointed George Creel, a well-known muckraking journalist and a longtime Wilson supporter, to head the massive propaganda agency. Creel hoped to mold public opinion by supplying newspapers, schools, libraries, citizens' groups, and the like with mountains of advertising intended to build support for the war and hate for the Germans. The CPI famously created the "Four Minute Men" program, which trained local speakers on how to make short speeches supporting the war, sometimes by invitation but often to otherwise captive audiences, for example, to people waiting for a motion picture to begin.[23]

When the newly appointed county directors gathered in St. Paul for a training session on June 13, John McGee informed them that they were to mount a campaign of "100% loyalty" throughout the state:

> Every citizen of the United States owes fealty and loyalty to his government. A citizen of the United States who declares since April 6 that he has been and is neutral, in effect declares that he is a traitor. There can be no such thing as a neutral citizen in a warring nation. The claim is simply a thinly veiled cover for treason and cowardice. . . . A man can no more be half loyal than he can be half honest, no more than a woman can be half chaste. It is all one thing or the other. He is either a patriot or a traitor.[24]

His speech had what later in the twentieth century might have been labeled a "totalitarian" tone, since he implied that citizens must not only support the government (for example, by enlisting in the army or buying war bonds) but also align their thoughts and attitudes with the official views of the government, in this case to the seven men of the MCPS. He justified this program of thought control by depicting the European war as an existential crisis for humanity.[25]

> This is no time for hostile criticism of our own government in its conduct of the war. . . . This is a struggle between autocracy and democracy. The underlying principle of autocratic government is that everything that is necessary to its success is right and proper and is made so because it is necessary to its success. The fact that it is necessary to success makes it right without reference to the laws of God or man. . . . I believe that the future of the race requires the destruction of the autocratic form of civilization. . . . In my judgment the struggle will go on until the world is made safe for democracy, and by that I mean, will go on until Prussian autocracy is pulverized.

McGee's criticism of autocracy as lacking a moral basis seems somewhat hypocritical coming from a man whose creed was "my country right or wrong." He also appeared oblivious to the contradiction inherent in his claim that citizens must conform their attitudes to the current government's worldview to "make the world safe for democracy." In any case, his fellow commissioner Charles Ames reinforced McGee's threats by telling the county directors that although thousands of Minnesotans were still uncertain about the war, "the time will come when we shall regard every fellow citizen who is not supporting the Government with his whole heart, as unpatriotic, disloyal, treasonable."[26]

While McGee and Ames were lecturing the county directors, President Wilson was signing the Espionage Act. Although part of the law was aimed at espionage—that is, spies working for enemy governments—Congress broke new ground by criminalizing speech. The act made it a felony, punishable by up to twenty years and a $10,000 fine, to "willfully cause or attempt to cause insubordination, disloyalty, mutiny, or refusal of duty, in the military or naval forces of the United States." The act also gave the US Post Office the power to ban publications criticizing the government from using the mails. The slippery term "disloyalty" was critical, and public officials and their civilian supporters were quick to brand any criticism of the government as "disloyalty."[27]

The next day, June 14, was Flag Day, an annual event established by President Wilson in 1916. In his address, Wilson warned that only those who were "friends or partisans of the German government" denied that the United States was fighting "a war for freedom and justice and self-government." He concluded his speech with a threat: "Woe be to the man or group of men," he threatened, "that seeks to stand in our way."[28]

The Commission's Armed Forces

To put muscle behind the rhetoric, McGee became the chair of the commission's military affairs committee. Although he had never been a soldier, McGee was known as an avid student of the Civil War. In addition, he knew something of military life by following the career of his eldest son, Hugh McGee, the West Point graduate, who had fought in the Philippines and was currently a lieutenant colonel in the federalized Minnesota National Guard.

Under McGee's leadership, the MCPS quickly took three steps to build its coercive power. McGee won approval for the creation of the Home Guard, a volunteer force, to take the place of the Minnesota National Guard, which was expected to be "federalized" and transferred out of state. Business leaders looked to the MCPS to create a replacement for the MNG because the national guard was their last line of defense during labor unrest and, in fact, intervening in strikes was the most common use of the national guard in the years before the world war. Secondly, the commission augmented these forces by authorizing six hundred of its own "peace officers." The third action was the creation of a surveillance operation to supply information on dissenting groups and individuals.[29]

On April 28, the MCPS approved Order No. 3, which created the Home Guard, composed of units like the MNG and made up of men over the age of twenty-six, that is, men not subject to conscription under the Selective Service Act. When the federal law was changed to make men eligible for the draft through age thirty, the commission ordered that Home Guard applicants had to be at least thirty-one or show that they were exempt from federal service. Members of the Home Guard served without pay unless ordered to duty away from their homes or for more than five days of continuous duty. Soldiers furnished their own uniforms or they were supplied by their home communities. The state was supposed to supply arms. The term of enlistment was until peace was declared. Order No. 3 authorized seven battalions, and a month later McGee asked the MCPS to increase this to ten. By the armistice there would be twenty-one battalions, at least on paper, composed of over 8,300 men. The Home Guard reported to the governor, which in practice meant they were under command of the adjutant general of the MNG.[30]

At McGee's request, the MCPS hired Oscar Seebach, a state legislator representing Red Wing, to organize the Home Guard battalions. Seebach was a well-known war hero, having been shot through the lungs while leading a company into battle during the Spanish-American War. McGee was surely aware that Seebach, a first-generation German American, had passionately supported the Alien Registration bill during the legislative debate. When a Home Guard company was organized in Red Wing, Burnquist commissioned Oscar Seebach's brother Fred to lead it. No one doubted the loyalty of the Seebach brothers.[31]

McGee was confident that businessmen and professionals would enthusiastically join the Home Guard. In fact, even before the declaration of war, businessmen in several cities had already organized militias, which laid the groundwork for the Home Guard. They were inspired by the Plattsburg movement, a national mobilization of young professionals and businessmen named after the summer camp in upstate New York where Ivy League college students and businessmen had come together for military training as part of the movement for military preparedness in 1915.

The St. Paul Association and the National Security League had hoped to establish a Plattsburg-like camp at Fort Snelling in 1916. The project fell through when the regular army officers scheduled to act as trainers were mobilized for the Mexican incursion. Their plans to organize the camp in the summer of 1917 were derailed by the declaration of war. Instead, the St. Paul Association established a militia called the Civilian Auxiliary and began training at St. Thomas College. In a few months it had grown to over six hundred "mostly business and professional men, including local leaders in business, banking, industry, education, politics, and the law." Meanwhile, the Minneapolis Civil and Commerce Association assembled its own Civilian Auxiliary, which also trained at St. Thomas. The two auxiliaries trained separately one weekday evening a week, and had a joint drill on Saturdays, involving over a thousand men. A similar process unfolded in Duluth, where the Commercial Club organized a Citizens' Training Corps, which assembled about a hundred "younger professional and business men" for weekly drills at the armory. By late April, their numbers had doubled and they were split into two platoons. In Moorhead, a judge and a lawyer organized a local militia that attracted thirty-five men to its drills in April.[32]

Seebach traveled around the state recruiting officers who began to fill the new Home Guard companies with volunteers. By July, several Home Guard battalions were beginning to take shape. Four companies from St. Paul formed the 1st Battalion, and in Minneapolis four companies were recruited to the 2nd Battalion. Through the end of 1917, the Civilian Auxiliaries in both cities continued to function

Home Guard units parading past the federal building in downtown St. Paul, 1917. *MNHS collections*

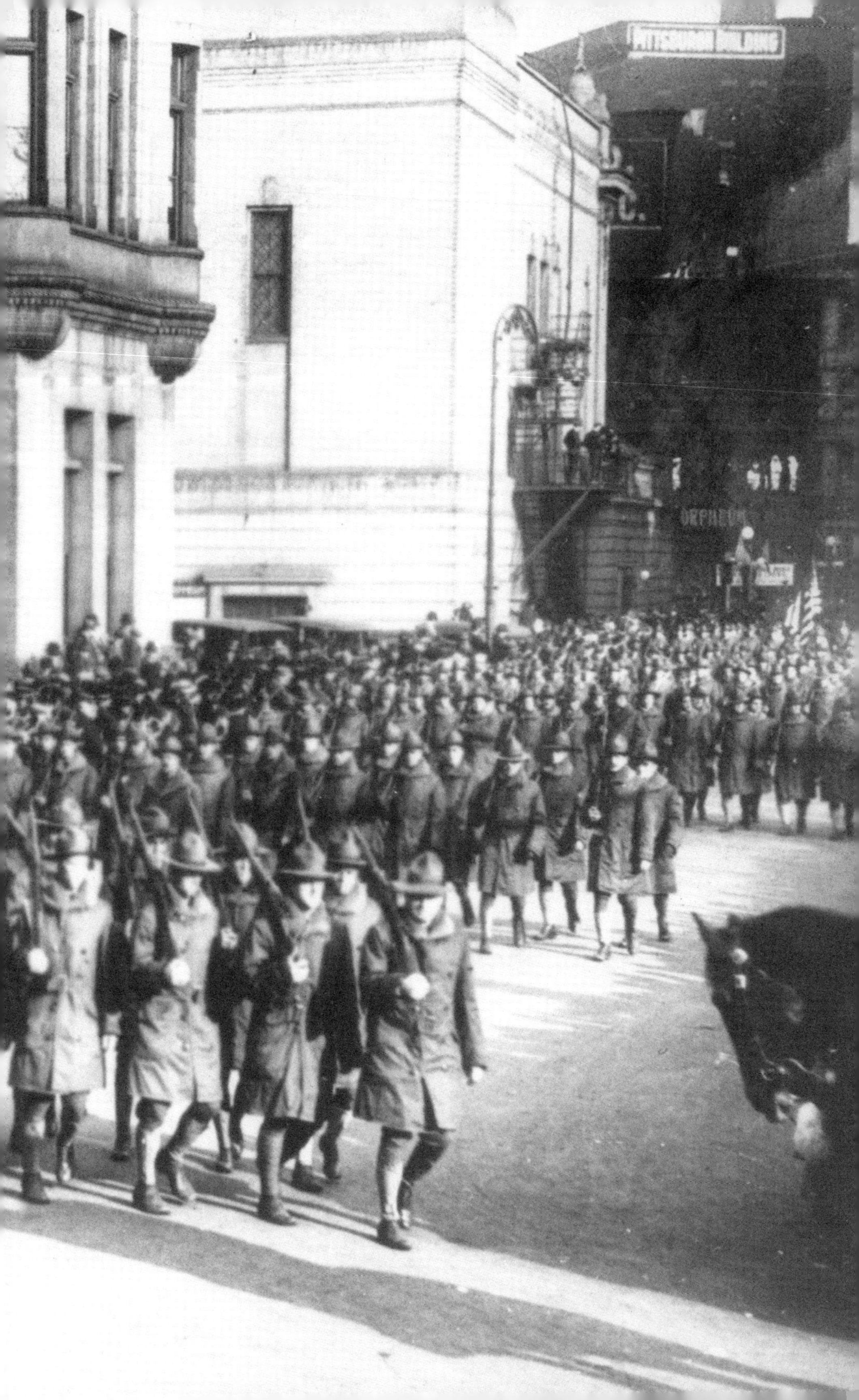
PITTSBURGH BUILDING

as independent forces, although some of their members joined the Home Guard companies. In Duluth, the 3rd Battalion was organized with four companies (a fifth from Two Harbors was added later), taking over the work of the Citizens' Training Corps. Several Iron Range cities organized companies, which formed the 4th Battalion headquartered in Virginia. Companies in southeast Minnesota formed the 5th Battalion, whose command was stationed in the Winona armory. Companies from five southern Minnesota cities formed the 6th Battalion, headquartered in Mankato, and Faribault was the headquarters of the 7th Battalion, composed of four companies from nearby towns. More would follow, and in the far corners of the state some were still in development when the war ended. Having established the first seven battalions, Seebach resigned and entered the US Army. He eventually served in Germany as part of the occupation force after the war.[33]

The MCPS augmented the Home Guard by issuing Order No. 4, by which it empowered itself to commission up to six hundred "peace officers" with full police powers. They were supplied with a metal badge that said "Minnesota Public Safety Commission, Peace Officer." The only qualification for peace officers was that they be "voters" in the state of Minnesota. No oath of office or bond was required, and no remuneration was provided. The order invited "any person, corporation, or co-partnership who desires to have property guarded by any such Peace Officer" to submit names of applicants to the MCPS. McGee took charge of commissioning peace officers; and as we shall see, this allowed him to grant police powers to allies around the state, including county directors, draft board members, Home Guard officers, and even private citizens. Applicants were not vetted in any way, except that they had to be "loyal" in his eyes.[34]

The commission's third action was the development of an intelligence service, essentially a group of undercover agents sent around the state to collect information about individuals and organizations perceived to be opposed to the MCPS agenda. On May 21, the commission passed McGee's motion to establish a "secret service system" and assign Commissioner Ames to work out the details. On May 29, Ames hired the Pinkerton Detective Agency, the nationwide firm that employers often used when they wanted to break a strike with violence. Oliver R. Hatfield, who led the Pinkerton local office, sent about six agents throughout the state during the summer looking for opposition to the war, and especially to conscription. Generally, the agents found acquiescence wherever they went, even in areas populated primarily by immigrants. For example, the agent reporting from New Ulm found some pro-German sentiment but no visible dissent. Similarly, the agent who visited saloons in the Scandinavian neighborhood of Arlington Hills on St. Paul's east side heard grumbling about the war but no indication that anyone was going to do anything. Northern Minnesota was an exception, where some immigrants, especially Finns, were actively resisting the draft.[35]

In June, the commission appointed Thomas G. Winter, a Minneapolis grain dealer, as the superintendent of intelligence, and he became the clearinghouse of the agents' reports. It is not clear why he was chosen, but he had been sending intelligence reports to the commission from the beginning, and probably not coincidentally he was the brother-in-law of commissioner Charles Ames. The Pinkerton contract ended late in the summer, and Winter then relied on his own agents. Hatfield advised Winter that the commission's agents should focus on the IWW, the Socialist Party, and the Nonpartisan League. He thought their newspapers should be shut down and a regime of censorship created for the foreign-language press.[36]

An Autonomous Auxiliary

In the early twentieth century, social and fraternal organizations, which mostly excluded women, often had a "ladies auxiliary." The MCPS followed this model and approved a Women's Auxiliary Committee, headed by Alice Ames Winter. Under her leadership, it operated autonomously from the commission, in part because she wore two hats. The Council of National Defense (CND) in Washington organized state-level committees of women to support the war effort, and Winter had been appointed the Minnesota state chair. The CND chose her most likely because of her national reputation both as a women's movement leader and as a writer. The MCPS chose her to lead its women's auxiliary because she was well connected in elite society and a recognized leader of women's organizations in Minnesota. She was also the half sister of Commissioner Ames, and the wife of Thomas G. Winter, the superintendent of the commission's intelligence bureau. The commission paid for a secretary and for office supplies, but Winter opted to work out of her expansive Minneapolis home on Lake of the Isles.[37]

Alice Ames Winter was the daughter of Charles Gordon Ames, a clergyman and politician. She earned a bachelor's and master's degree at Wellesley College, and taught high school for a time. She married Winter in 1892, and while she was raising their two children she found time to publish two novels. She was one of the founders of the Minneapolis Women's Club in 1907, and served as its first president until 1915. On a national level, she chaired the literature department of the General Federation of Women's Clubs. After the war, she would be elected chair of the federation.[38]

Under Winter's leadership, the women's auxiliary set a more moderate tone than the MCPS. She gave unquestioning support to the

■ **Alice Ames Winter led the Women's Committee of the Minnesota Commission of Public Safety from her home in Minneapolis.** ***MNHS collections***

war but stood somewhat apart from the belligerent nationalism of the commission's male leaders. This was partially because her organization mobilized club women who were committed to the social programs of Progressivism, at least as understood by well-to-do urban women of European ancestry. Her stance was also the result of her association with the Committee of National Defense, which generally took a more moderate approach than the MCPS.

She quickly appointed women from around the state to lead county-level committees of the women's auxiliary, and they in turn created township-level committees. Winter had an ambitious agenda that included food conservation, support for the Red Cross and Liberty Loan drives, recruitment and protection of women in war industries, child welfare activities, programs to counter the sexual degradation of women associated with war, the "Americanization" of immigrant populations, and patriotic education for all Minnesotans.[39]

Food conservation was a priority from the very beginning. In May 1917, President Wilson by executive order created the Food Administration office, tasked with swiftly increasing food output while at the same time controlling rapidly rising prices, and appointed Herbert Hoover to lead it. Instead of food rationing, Hoover opted for a massive campaign to persuade households and restaurants to willingly schedule "meatless" and "wheatless" days, to use less sugar and fat, and to eat more locally produced fruits and vegetables. The campaign included pledge cards that allowed housewives to publicly announce their patriotic commitment to the conservation program. The MCPS printed 275,000 "Hoover Pledge" cards, and the women's auxiliary distributed the cards through its network around the state. The organization also worked with the state's Committee on Food Production and Conservation and the university's Agricultural Extension Service. Women were urged to fill out the cards, affix a one-cent stamp, and mail it to Washington. In return, they would get information on the food conservation program, with practical tips.[40]

The women's auxiliary also made the "Americanization" of immigrant communities an early priority. At least at the beginning, Winter articulated a pluralistic approach that focused on incentives and avoided the threatening rhetoric of the anti-hyphen campaign. With the outbreak of war, Alice Winter believed, the time had come for the many peoples living together in the United States to become a nation. The country needed the "fine character and genius of all these races," and combined they will "make the greatest race on earth." She urged her members to include immigrant women on committees and Mother's Clubs, to hold celebrations for newly made citizens, and to help immigrants learn English. She also recommended respect for the culture of immigrants, suggesting that programs for children include both patriotic songs of America and songs of other lands. Finally, she supported the teaching of foreign languages in schools, so long as the language of instruction was English. She found it difficult to sustain this moderate approach as the atmosphere became increasingly anti-immigrant, a situation that was fostered by the MCPS.[41]

How Minnesotans Went to War

By the end of the war, the United States had mobilized four million men, and of these over 118,000 were from Minnesota. They served mostly in the army, and they joined in one of three ways. Some volunteered for one of the existing Minnesota National Guard units before they were federalized and left the state, some enlisted in the army, navy, or marines of the United States while that was still allowed, and the rest were drafted into the new national army.[42]

In 1917, the Minnesota National Guard was composed of three infantry regiments and one field artillery regiment. There was also a naval militia composed of men who lived around Lake Superior. The Minnesota National Guard did not admit African Americans, even to segregated units. Almost immediately, the state's naval militia was federalized and its members entered the US Navy. Starting in late August, companies of the three infantry units began moving to Camp Cody, New Mexico, where they would begin training as part of the new 34th Division. Hugh McGee, the son of John McGee, became the chief training officer of the 34th Division, and eventually was promoted to chief of staff. The 1st Field Artillery was sent to Camp Mills, New York, where it joined the 42nd Division, known as the "Rainbow Division" because it was made up of guard regiments from around the country.[43]

Meanwhile, military recruiters worked hard to encourage voluntary enlistments in the army, navy, and marines up until December 15, 1917, and to the navy and marines after that date. Local political leaders encouraged enlistments in their towns and staged celebrations for young men as they boarded trains bound for training camps. The Military Training Camps Association, led by Donald Cotton, took on the task of recruiting candidates for the officer training campus set up at Fort Snelling. Cotton, who was also the Ramsey County director of the Minnesota Commission of Public Safety, ran the local branch of the Intercollegiate Intelligence Bureau, which surveyed college campuses seeking men with special skills. This led to the creation of the Hamline Ambulance Unit, composed of volunteers associated with Hamline University. Meanwhile the Mayo Clinic and the University of Minnesota collaborated to create the University of Minnesota Base Hospital #26, a self-contained unit of 25 physicians, 65 nurses, and 125 support staff. Both units were in France by the early summer of 1918 and served through the end of the war.[44]

The overwhelming majority of the Minnesotans who entered the military were draftees. A statewide bureaucracy registered them, medically examined them, and processed their claims for exemption. Outside the cities, the draft boards were often composed of the sheriff, the county auditor, and a physician. Local county and city officials generally made the appointments. Although the MCPS had no legal basis for doing so, it reviewed the appointments in Minneapolis, probably because the commissioners could not abide the fact that Thomas Van Lear, the Socialist mayor, controlled who would serve on the city's thirteen draft boards.[45]

This provoked the first open conflict between John McGee and John Lind. McGee felt that Van Lear, "being a Socialist," was trying to pack the Minneapolis boards with Socialists and pro-Germans. He had Oliver R. Hatfield of the Pinkertons supply him with reports on the people Van Lear had nominated. Lind apparently saw no reason to veto Van Lear's nominations. After a contentious meeting in late May, McGee wrote to Knute Nelson that he had managed to eliminate eighteen of Van Lear's thirty-nine nominations, but that he had to fight with Lind for two hours to do it. "I really think that Lind is a Socialist in his view," he concluded. At that same meeting, the commission passed a resolution that nobody should serve on draft boards "who is opposed to the execution of the law for registration and conscription."[46]

McGee was sure there would be armed resistance to the draft. In Hennepin County, Sheriff Otto Langum, the conservative whom Van

Lear had beaten in the mayoral race the previous year, announced that he had assembled five hundred special deputies to maintain order on June 5, the national registration day. As a precaution, the MCPS banned "all traffic in intoxicants" on registration day and ordered every city to enforce the order. In fact, Socialists were urging men to boycott the registration, not disrupt it. As it happened, registration went smoothly, and about 227,600 Minnesotans showed up and registered. Langum never mobilized his deputies.[47]

Immigrants from Finland and Austria-Hungary apparently failed to register in significant numbers on the Iron Range, and large numbers were indicted in July by Alfred Jaques, the US attorney for Minnesota. The Finns tended to be obstinate, and many were convicted in federal district court in Duluth. Judge Page Morris lectured them and gave out sentences of up to a year. Although the newspapers referred to the citizens of Austria-Hungary as "Austrians," they were likely Czechs, Serbs, Croatians, Italians, and other groups from the multiethnic Habsburg empire. Many convinced authorities they failed to register because they misunderstood the law, and they received light sentences or had their charges dropped.[48]

In the Twin Cities, a sizable group of Socialist Party members refused to register, some very publicly, which resulted in speedy arrests. The US attorney prosecuted twenty-nine young men in the St. Paul federal court for refusal to register in 1917, many of them associated with the Socialist Party. In early July, four of them—Joseph Arver, Alfred Grahl, and Otto and Walter Wangerin—were convicted and sentenced to one-year prison terms and induction into the military after release from prison. Their attorneys appealed, arguing that the constitution did not grant Congress the power to conscript men, and that in any case, the Selective Service System violated the Thirteenth Amendment's prohibition of "involuntary servitude." The Supreme Court combined the Minnesota cases with several others, heard arguments in the fall, and issued its opinion affirming the constitutionality of the draft in January 1918.[49]

On July 20, 1917, the federal government held a drawing to set the order to be followed by each draft board in summoning registrants. Shortly thereafter, states received their quotas based on their population, which were then translated into the quotas for each draft board. With credit for the voluntary enlistments into the army and National

Guard, Minnesota needed to draft 17,778 men. Local boards had to call three times this number to meet their quotas, due to the high percentage of men who were not physically fit, the large number of exemption claims, the temporary hold on African American inductions, and the significant numbers who did not show up.

The Segregated Army of Democracy

The army with which Wilson proposed to protect democracy was strictly segregated, a fundamental contradiction that Wilson never acknowledged. There were two African American infantry regiments and two African American cavalry regiments, the so-called "Buffalo Soldiers" who fought in the wars against the Indians. These four regiments, totaling about ten thousand soldiers at full strength, had seen service in Cuba and the Philippines during the Spanish-American War, and in the subsequent suppression of Filipino independence. In addition, about five thousand African Americans served in eight segregated National Guard Units, and another five thousand as cooks, waiters, and coal handlers in the navy.

Generally, African American units were not led by African American officers, and in fact the army excluded African Americans from its officer training schools. Senator Newton Baker understood that many southern politicians opposed the very concept of armed African American soldiers, and did not want African American soldiers to receive combat training at southern camps. While he weighed his options, he assigned the four African American regular army units to guard military installations in the United States rather than serve overseas, and he ordered that no draft notices be sent to African Americans.[50]

Many African Americans reacted with indifference to what they saw as a "white man's war." It was difficult to swallow Wilson's "war to make the world safe for democracy" when they were disenfranchised, subject to terroristic violence, and living in a Jim Crow world with a segregated military. However, many African American leaders, fully aware that Wilson and many of his cabinet were white supremacists, calculated that support for the war might bolster their demands for racial equality. As a result, the NAACP, the National Urban League, and important newspapers like the *Chicago Defender* affirmed their loyalty, but also pressed their claims for racial justice. Many felt, as

James Weldon Johnson, the NAACP field organizer, put it, that African Americans could not afford to be perceived as disloyal, given the toxic atmosphere of violence that already existed.[51]

In the Twin Cities, the African American middle class vigorously supported the war effort. William T. Francis, an attorney who was a leader of the St. Paul community, accepted the governor's appointment to represent the Minnesota Commission of Public Safety in his area, charged with overseeing the work of his local draft board. The African American press gave full support of the war, but made clear that the best way to fight a war for democracy was for Congress to pass an anti-lynching law and desegregate the armed forces. In April 1917, John Quincy Adams, the editor of *The Appeal*, published an open letter to W. E. B. Du Bois in his role as head of the NAACP in which he donated five dollars toward a fund to fight "any Jim Crow army legislation which may bob up in Congress." In the *Twin Cities Star*, editor Charles Sumner Smith wrote that "this is our fight," but noted that the Negro "is a slave of Race-hatred, Discrimination, and that prejudiced Americanism—the Southern propaganda of the present administration." Nevertheless, "he must fight to save his Country—that he might enjoy Liberty in the fullest sense."[52]

Throughout the state, most African American men registered as required. To preserve the strict segregation of the armed forces, the Selective Service System separated African Americans as they registered. When young men reported on June 5, they were given a card that required them to fill in their name, address, age, and possible exemption claims. They also had to fill in the blank after the words "Race (specify which)?" The card instructed draft officials to tear off the bottom left corner of the card "if the person is of African descent." Under this system, 1,765 of the Minnesotans who registered were classified as African Americans.[53]

In *The Appeal*, Adams raged that this process was "an infamous insult" to which no other group, not even German aliens, was subjected. He reprinted an editorial from another newspaper that characterized the process as "Jim Crow registration." Charles Sumner Smith, editor of the *Twin Cities Star*, was more philosophical, arguing that if the intent was to keep African Americans out of the military, the discrimination would boomerang against the southern politicians. In fact, politicians in southern states would soon realize that if no African Americans were drafted then the entire burden of meeting state quotas would fall on the rest of the population.[54]

Most African American men who were drafted were destined to be assigned to service battalions and never see combat. In St. Paul, Samuel L. Ranson, a popular bachelor known for his singing voice, found a way to fight in France as a real soldier. In July, he traveled to Chicago to enlist in the 8th Regiment, a segregated unit of the Illinois National Guard, but one led by African American officers. The 8th eventually became the 370th Infantry Regiment of the 93rd Division, one of the two African American divisions created in late 1917. General John Pershing loaned the 93rd to the French army, and it fought to great acclaim. Ransom's bold act thrilled the African American community in St. Paul, which feted him at a gala banquet when he briefly returned home before entering the service. William Francis and other leaders made speeches attesting to his character and patriotism. Members of the Minnesota Club, where he had worked for several years, presented him with a gift of $550.[55]

The NAACP wanted to desegregate the military, but also shared the general belief that the struggle for civil rights would be advanced if African American units, led by African American officers, had the opportunity to fight in France. As W. E. B. Du Bois put it, African Americans were faced with a "damnable dilemma" of bad choices. He and NAACP president Joel Spingarn argued that a segregated officer training camp was the lesser of two evils, since without it no officers would be trained. More militant voices bitterly criticized the NAACP, especially William Monroe Trotter, the fiery editor of the *Boston Guardian*, who charged that Du Bois had "betrayed the race." However, many African American college students and young professionals voiced their approval. On May 19, Secretary of War Newton Baker announced the creation of an officer training camp for African Americans at Fort Des Moines, Iowa, a site chosen to appease congressmen from the South. On June 15, the camp opened with a thousand civilian recruits and 250 noncommissioned officers from the army's four African American units. A month later, a second camp opened at Fort Des Moines to train African American medical officers and others for the Army Medical Corps.[56]

The federal government's obsession with segregating African Americans meant that, in Minnesota for example, Ojibwe and Dakota men were grouped with registrants of European background, in other words, classified as "white," at least for purposes of military service. This was the case even though many Indians were not legally citizens and under the law could not enlist or be drafted. Before 1924, when all Indians born in the United States were recognized as citizens, only those Indians who had left their tribes and settled on land received under the Dawes Allotment Act of 1887 or otherwise lived independently from their tribes were considered citizens.[57]

Many Indians, whatever their legal status, were anxious to join the military both as an act of patriotism and as an expression of the warrior traditions of their tribes. William Little Wolf, for example, an Ojibwe from the White Earth Reservation in northern Minnesota, ran away from the Carlisle Indian Industrial School in Pennsylvania to join the navy in 1917. Serving with distinction on the battleship USS *Utah*, he was promoted to third class petty officer and led a crew servicing one of the ship's twelve-inch guns. He was discharged in 1919 and given a hero's welcome when he returned to the reservation.[58]

Washington left it to draft boards to determine who was a citizen, and the boards often applied the criteria loosely to fill their draft quotas. When they did, the Indian draftee helped meet the "white" quota. When bluntly asked by a southern governor whether Indian registrants could be classified as "white," Major General Enoch Crowder, who ran the Selective Service System, stated that "Indians must be classed as white men" during the registration and induction process. "What we desire," he went on to say, "was to prevent numbers of the African race from moving with the white contingent."[59]

Keeping Soldiers and Workers Dry

Of the first ten official orders issued by the commission, five regulated the sale of alcohol. Secretary of War Baker asked local committees of national defense to shield from temptation young recruits "who have not yet become accustomed to contact with either the saloon or the prostitute." The commissioners were eager to comply, and they were also convinced that drinking sapped the morale of those who stayed at home to work the farms and factories. Their zeal to suppress liquor was fueled by the fact that one ethnic group whose cultural traditions prioritized social drinking—German Americans—was also suspected of harboring disloyal elements.[60]

The commission came to power just as the nationwide prohibition movement led by the Woman's Christian Temperance Union and the Anti-Saloon League was reaching the height of its influence. In 1915 the Minnesota legislature approved a county option law that allowed 25 percent of the voters of a county to force a referendum to create a ban on liquor licenses. By the time national prohibition began in January 1920, more than half of Minnesota's eighty-six counties had voted to become "dry." The law also provided a local option that allowed cities and towns to ban alcohol, and in 1917 prohibitionists succeeded in making Duluth a "dry" city.[61]

The public safety commissioners did not want to get mired in the alcohol controversy, but they were respectable middle-class men who frowned on drinking, at least when the drinkers were working-class men. McGee claimed he had "never used intoxicating liquor," and he took the lead in advancing the commission's anti-liquor policies. Following the commission's first meeting, McGee, Lind, and March toured the Bridge Square area of downtown Minneapolis along with Mayor Van Lear and police chief Lewis Harthill. The next day, the commission issued Order 1, closing all saloons, pool halls, and moving picture theaters in the Bridge Square and milling districts of Minneapolis. More than alcohol was involved. The IWW had opened an office in the area, hoping to organize the seasonal farm and timber workers who gathered in Bridge Square, sleeping in the boardinghouses and socializing in the saloons. The commission also had the IWW in mind when it issued Order 8, which outlawed the sale of intoxicating beverages in St. Louis County outside of Duluth except in licensed saloons and drugstores. Unlicensed establishments, called "blind pigs," were places where iron miners and lumberjacks might gather to air their grievances, and perhaps be swayed by a Wobbly organizer after a beer or two.[62]

The *Minneapolis Labor Review* complained that with Order 1 the MCPS had closed forty saloons and put several hundred people out of work without even granting these businesses a hearing. The commission, the labor paper wryly noted, "unfairly and unjustly blackened" the reputation of Minneapolis by making it appear that its saloons were worse than "the toughest saloons in Frisco and the New York waterfront," all of which were still open.[63]

To protect soldiers, the commission issued Order 2, which banned the sale of alcohol within two and a half miles of Fort Snelling Military Reservation. In this case, the neighboring cities of Minneapolis, St. Paul, and Mendota were required to revoke any liquor licenses for establishments within the prohibited area. In support of conscription, the commission issued Order 6, which mandated the closure of all saloons statewide on June 5, 1917, the day set for the draft registration.[64]

The commission encountered little opposition until it issued Order 7 to mandate statewide rules, including the diktat that women and girls were not allowed to enter any saloon. This raised questions. What if a saloon owner had a wife who regularly tended bar in a family establishment? What about Salvation Army women who visited saloons seeking donations? The commission's secretary responded that there were no exceptions. The order also required all saloons to be closed by 10:00 PM and not open again until 8:00 AM at the earliest. These hours of operation were also imposed on all cafes and restaurants serving intoxicating liquor. Women could enter these places, but could not be served intoxicating liquor. Finally, the order prohibited "dancing and cabaret performance" in any Minneapolis, St. Paul, or Duluth establishment where intoxicating liquor was sold. These cities were expected to pass ordinances consistent with the order.[65]

The president of the Minneapolis Trades and Labor Assembly telegrammed Secretary of War Newton Baker asking the Council of National Defense to intervene. Order 7, he argued, was "a drastic order" that put several hundred cooks, waiters, bartenders, and musicians out of work. He suggested that the core of the problem was the absence of labor representation on the MCPS. He was told that regulating liquor establishments was a local matter outside of federal jurisdiction. The *Minneapolis Labor Review* took a more militant view, arguing that the MCPS, which it called a "grotesque little party of autocrats," had "cast a shadow over all women in the state" by implying that their mere presence in a saloon was morally suspect. A week later the paper claimed that McGee was calling for the indictment of the editor for treason, on the theory, according to the paper, that "the King can do no wrong." The editor had concluded that the MCPS was an institution of the business elite because the "bankers, brokers, corporation managers, and food gamblers are listened to most attentively" but had little use for farmers and workers.[66]

Mayor Van Lear signaled that the city would enforce the commission's order, but he refused to make the commission's regulations part of a city ordinance until forced to do so by the city council. He noted that Phil Cook, who owned a saloon at the corner of Washington and Hennepin Avenues in downtown Minneapolis, was challenging the order in federal court. Cook told district judge Wilbur F. Booth that his saloon normally stayed open until 11:00 PM, and that the 10:00 closing significantly hurt his business. His attorneys argued that Order 7 went beyond the powers delegated to the commission by the legislature. The unelected commission, they argued, should not be allowed to make statewide laws imposing restrictions on a particular category of business.[67]

Representing the commission, Ambrose Tighe convinced the court that Order 7 was well within the commission's powers. The court agreed that the legislature gave the commission the power to do all acts "necessary or proper for public safety." In his view, liquor regulation was clearly part of protecting public safety, and in any case, Order 7 was not legislation, but merely an "administrative detail" necessary to fulfill the commission's mandate. Tighe had shepherded his creation through its first court challenge unscathed.[68]

The commission's early orders regulating alcohol encouraged prohibitionists to ask for more. On June 19, the commission proclaimed that it was "overwhelmed with complaints" and that given its many important duties it "cannot fritter away its time prosecuting violations of the license laws of the State." It warned, however, that if the liquor industry continued to flout the law, the commission would ban liquor sales statewide. The commission never took this step, but it did continue to issue orders in response to local violations, and even to mobilize the Home Guard to enforce them. By the end of the war, the MCPS had issued fifty-nine orders, twenty of which regulated alcohol. In this way, it played a major role in suppressing the state's liquor business.

FIVE

OPENING SALVOS

LATE SUMMER 1917

> Avowing our loyalty to this country and pledging in its defense the highest sacrifice to the extent of life itself if need be, and with full realization of the difficulties that beset a government in times of war, we respectfully petition the president and Congress of this nation not to transport or force across the ocean to the battlefields of Europe any men outside of the regular army, contrary to their desires but that such matter be left to voluntary enlistments.
>
> Petition signed by several thousand attendees of a New Ulm rally on July 25, 1917

> Any man now talking treasonable doctrines ought to be shot on the spot.
>
> ALBERT R. ALLEN, Martin County Attorney, speaking at the Minnesota State Bar Association Convention, August 9, 1917

THE WAR OF ATTRITION on the western front continued. On July 31, the British began the ill-fated offensive near the Belgium village of Passchendaele. On the Eastern Front, Alexander Kerensky, the Russian minister of war, ordered an offensive against the Austro-Hungarian army. When the Germans counterattacked, the collapse of the Russian army began.

General John Pershing, commander of the American Expeditionary Force (AEF), arrived in France in June 1917 with his staff but little more. The Allies wanted to integrate the American troops into the British and French armies, but Pershing refused, insisting that his army must retain its autonomy on the western front. It was not until October that enough AEF troops had arrived in France that they could take positions on a quiet sector.

On the home front, the Minnesota Commission of Public Safety continued to expand its armed forces. Seven Home Guard battalions were training weekly. Some units participated in loyalty parades or escorted draftees to railroad stations for transport to training camps. New battalions were being organized in western and northern Minnesota.

Because the Home Guard battalions were composed of lightly trained volunteers who had daytime jobs in banks, offices, or stores, John McGee convinced Governor Burnquist to rebuild the Minnesota National Guard by creating the 4th Infantry, a new battalion composed of two companies in Minneapolis and two in Duluth. This unit made its first public appearance on August 14 when its two Minneapolis companies marched with the Home Guard's 2nd Battalion at a military review at the Parade, a Minneapolis park. John McGee, his son Lieutenant Colonel Hugh McGee, Captain Walter Rhinow, at that time the governor's military secretary, and Captain Perry Harrison of the Minneapolis Civilian Auxiliary reviewed the troops. The Home Guard's battalion band, which was in fact the ensemble from the Shriners' Zuhrah Temple, provided the music. Two weeks later the same units marched again at the Parade, this time before a reported crowd of ten thousand.[1]

In July, the MCPS advised its county directors to encourage local sheriffs to organize motorized "rural guards" to supplement the Home Guards. The commission envisioned squads of automobile owners ready to transport deputized armed men to the scene of any trouble, such as an attempt to disrupt the harvest. Nothing came of it, perhaps because there were in fact no attempts to disrupt the harvest. The concept would be resurrected in 1918 with the creation of the Motor Corps, a new addition to the Home Guard.[2]

In August, seventy-six of the state's eighty-six sheriffs attended a meeting called by the commission. They heard rousing loyalty speeches and discussed the enforcement of federal and state sedition laws. Attorney General Lyndon Smith told the sheriffs that they could not arrest someone merely for possessing seditious material. They needed evidence of intent to circulate the material, but after all, a person with a sack full of subversive literature "is not lugging it around for ballast." Several sheriffs reported how they had banned anti-draft meetings. The sheriffs unanimously pledged their full obedience and promised to do everything "that is asked of us by the Government of the United States." Many of the sheriffs proved themselves to be extremely aggressive agents of the commission's agenda.[3]

Fractured Movements

The declaration of war put advocates of neutrality in a difficult position. Some Socialists continued to oppose the war, and especially the draft, even to the point of facing imprisonment. Many supporters of neutrality bowed to a reality they could not change and gave full support to Wilson's program. These supporters convinced themselves either that the country's national honor was at stake or that the war would lead to democratic reform. There were also those who walked a fine line, declaring allegiance to the country but reserving the right to advocate for an early "peace without victory," as Wilson had once suggested, or, more provocatively, to criticize how the war was being financed. Most likely, many of those who had favored neutrality quietly acquiesced to the powerful forces that demanded their loyalty.

Like their colleagues in the cities, small-town business and political leaders organized "loyalty" parades and festivals to counter the deeply felt support for neutrality among farmers. A common event was a parade to celebrate local men who had enlisted or been drafted into the army. Most small-town newspapers took up the demand for loyalty with gusto. The German-language press, however, had difficulty expressing enthusiasm for the war. Emil Leicht, editor of the *Westlicher Herold* in Winona, wrote that German Americans would be loyal, but that they could not be expected to greet the war with smiling faces. As war approached, he abruptly ended a serialized novel about the adventures of the Imperial German Navy. Political cartoons also disappeared from his paper. National advertisers stopped placing advertisements, the first sign that German-language newspapers were entering a difficult period.[4]

Nationally, many leading members of the American Union against Militarism (AUAM) jumped ship, leaving stalwarts like Jane Addams and Max Eastman to carry on a campaign for diplomacy and peace.

The AUAM organized a Civil Liberties Bureau to defend draft resisters and other anti-war dissenters. Directed by Roger Baldwin, it became a lightning rod of controversy. Soon the bureau split off to become an independent organization, and later evolved into the American Civil Liberties Union. The Woman's Peace Party shrunk to half its size, and on its behalf, Jane Addams continued to speak in favor of a negotiated settlement. At the request of Herbert Hoover, she also devoted much time to working for food conservation. "The war years," her biographer wrote, "were the loneliest of Addams' life." Looking back on the war, she wrote how hard it was to "hold one's own" when "the force of the majority was so overwhelming."[5]

Most Progressive intellectuals supported the war policy wholeheartedly. Wilson's argument that the war would lead to reform and democracy won the hearts of Walter Lippman and Herbert Croly, the editors of *The New Republic*, the flagship of the Progressive movement. They were also motivated by a fear of being left out of the action and losing the influence they believed they had with Wilson. Minnesota Progressives shared their passions. Maria Sanford, for example, told an audience of five hundred at Glencoe in McLeod County in western Minnesota that the war was a fight between democracy and autocracy, and that if she were a man, she would consider it an honor and privilege to be drafted.[6]

The brilliant young journalist Randolph Bourne broke with *The New Republic* and bitterly attacked the Progressives who supported the war, especially John Dewey, his former mentor. Like Jane Addams, and as noted by Charles Lindbergh, Bourne scoffed at the idea that the war could enhance democracy, either at home or abroad. Given that they were not strong enough to prevent the war, he pointedly asked his former Progressive allies, "how is it going to be weak enough for you to control and mold to your liberal purposes?" Progressives hoped the call to arms would inspire people to a new sense of social commitment and idealism. Bourne thought most young people reported for the draft because they had no choice. Men like Dewey, Bourne wrote, who had defended reason as the agent of reform, now looked to violence as the answer. Time would tell whether Dewey or Bourne had the better argument.[7]

The Socialist Party, unlike similar parties throughout Europe, refused to accept the legitimacy of the war and actively opposed national mobilization. At an emergency convention in St. Louis shortly after the declaration of war, the party passed a majority report that stated the US entrance into the European war "was instituted by the predatory capitalists" seeking profits from the export of munitions and food and the repayment of the huge loans they had made to the Allies. The party pledged "continuous, active, and public opposition to the war" and "unyielding opposition to all proposed legislation for military or industrial conscription." A minority report conceded that the capitalist class was responsible for the war, but nevertheless held that the defeat of Germany was a goal worth supporting. Both reports agreed that "the conscription of wealth [should] accompany any conscription of man for military service."[8]

The Socialist Party organized the People's Council of America for Democracy and Peace, the PCA for short, as a place where peace activists nationwide could work together. The PCA demanded "peace without annexations and indemnities and the right of people to settle their own destinies," the slogan of anti-war Socialists in Europe. The People's Council debuted with a massive rally in Madison Square Garden in May, followed by rallies in other big cities. PCA leaders planned a national convention for early September. They thought Minneapolis would be an ideal venue, especially since it had a Socialist mayor.

Most of the labor movement supported the government's decision to go to war. Samuel Gompers, leader of the American Federation of Labor, enthusiastically pledged its loyalty. A pacifist in his youth, Gompers endorsed the preparedness movement in 1916. He figured that if the trade union movement supported the war effort, it could bargain more effectively for government guarantees of the right to organize and assurances to preserve union standards of pay and working conditions during the war.[9]

Following Gompers's lead, the Minnesota Federation of Labor also took a pro-war stance. The Duluth newspaper *The Labor World* editorialized that advocating neutrality had been entirely justified, but now that war was declared, the debate was over and the Kaiser had to be defeated to preserve democracy. Not everyone agreed, especially since support for the war meant supporting the draft. At the MFL's July convention in Faribault, Socialist delegates, who formed a large share of the Minneapolis contingent, opposed efforts to endorse the war. The battle began when the leadership introduced a resolution pledging loyalty in florid language: "Hail Columbia, happy land! Grand and glorious nation! The last great charity of a beneficient [*sic*] Creator to the human race. We hear your call and with alacrity and joyful hearts we respond to it." And then went on to genuflect before the president: "Hail, Woodrow Wilson, peerless leader of Columbia's hosts. Matchless expounder of her high principles and pure purposes!"[10]

The Socialists failed to block this resolution and lacked the votes to pass another condemning conscription. They did win passage of a resolution that the "federation declares in favor of the conscription of wealth as being fully as necessary as the conscription of men for the successful conduct of the present war." Significantly, this was a key plank of the Nonpartisan League platform. The dissidents also passed a resolution calling on Burnquist to remove all members of the Minnesota Commission of Public Safety for their hostility to trade unionism.[11]

When the convention voted down a resolution calling on the United States to "clearly state just what are the aims of the Government in this war, and to state the conditions upon which peace will be made," the Socialist delegates walked out. A resolution asking for a statement of war aims might seem utterly reasonable, but everyone understood that it was a criticism of the Wilson administration. In fact, the resolution exposed a crucial flaw in Wilson's policy. His stated goals were so vague—to make the world safe for democracy—as to be meaningless. He had committed the United States to the war aims of the British and French, but the Allies were very cagey about what they intended to do with the territories of the German, Habsburg, and Ottoman empires after victory. Wilson would have to wait until the Paris Peace Conference in 1919 to discover the war aims to which he had committed the United States.

The women's suffrage movement was also divided by the war, with its two major organizations taking divergent paths. The National American Woman Suffrage Association (NAWSA), which had been leading the suffrage struggle for five decades, believed that patriotically supporting the war would lead to the vote. In Minnesota, Clara Ueland, leader of the Minnesota Woman Suffrage Association, agreed, holding that "American suffragists can stand by their country and at the same time give allegiance to the cause of suffrage." Women associated with MWSA dedicated themselves to war work for the duration.

Ueland represented the MWSA on the "war council," the statewide committee of presidents of women's organizations created by Alice Ames Winter, director of the Women's Committee of the MCPS.[12]

The more militant National Woman's Party (NWP) was determined to use Wilson's rhetoric about spreading democracy abroad to embarrass him into supporting democracy at home. The NWP had grown out of the Congressional Union, organized in 1914 by the charismatic activist Alice Paul. She had spent time in Britain working with the Women's Social and Political Union, the militant suffrage group led by Emmeline Pankhurst and Christabel Pankhurst. When Paul failed to get the NAWSA to adopt a more confrontational style, she found many women around the country ready to join a more militant group.

Sarah Tarleton Colvin was already a member of NWP when Alice Paul came to the Twin Cities in 1915 to organize a chapter. Colvin was a southerner whose family moved to Baltimore after the Civil War. She graduated from the nursing school at Johns Hopkins in 1892 and worked as a nurse until her marriage to a doctor in 1897. When the couple settled in St. Paul, she immersed herself in public service, working to improve educational standards in nursing. While on a trip to Washington, DC, she met Alice Paul, whose thoughtful demeanor and militant tactics impressed her. In 1916, Colvin traveled with Paul on the "Suffrage Special," a whistle-stop train tour through the western states to build membership in the NWP.[13]

In January 1917, Alice Paul put militant tactics to the test when the NWP began daily picketing at the White House to pressure President Wilson to support a constitutional amendment to enfranchise women. Paul designated February 28 as "Minnesota Day" on the picket line, and Colvin came to Washington to picket the White House along with other Minnesota feminists. When war was declared, the NWP continued its protests, provoking an angry backlash. In June police began jailing NWP women for obstructing traffic, and in August two Minnesota NWP members were arrested, including Clare Kinsley Fuller, the editor-publisher of the *Little Falls Transcript*. The picketing continued throughout the war, and many more Minnesota women, including Sarah Colvin, would eventually find themselves in Washington jails.[14]

When the police began arresting women at the White House, Clara Ueland published a statement distancing her organization, and the NAWSA of which it was a part, from the militant picketers. Her group, she wrote, was "pledged to a policy of aid and cooperation in this time of the nation's stress, and regrets that a body of suffragists should employ a policy tending to embarrass and discredit our government."[15]

On several days during August, the NWP picketers carried a sign equating Wilson with the Kaiser. An angry mob that included many men in US Army, Navy, and Marine Corps uniforms assaulted the women. Charles Lindbergh thought it "disgraceful" that soldiers attacked women exercising their right to speech and that it was "almost unthinkable" that the police would stand by and not intervene. In a letter to Wilson, he wrote that the president could have, and should have, taken action to stop the mob violence. If the women were in the wrong, he argued, let the courts and not a mob adjudicate it.[16]

Lindbergh and Van Lear Walk a Fine Line

Lindbergh was one of those Minnesotans facing the dilemma of advocating for peace in a nation at war. He surely would have voted against the declaration of war if he had still been in Congress in April 1917. Once war was declared, he felt he must support the government. He told his daughter Eva that once the "thing has been done, and however foolish it has been, we must all be foolish and unwise together, and fight for our country." Maybe some good would come from it, "because it will open the people's eyes to what fools they are for following the rich wherever they lead with their money." A few weeks later he wrote to Governor Burnquist that "if our Nation needs me in any capacity in war, I will be ready to serve." He went on to say he was anxious to complete a "special work" but that would not be an excuse if he was needed.[17]

That special work was *Why Is Your Country at War, and What Happens to You after a War, and Related Subjects*, a book he produced completely on his own. An editor might have refined the text, or at least reworked the unwieldy title, but Lindbergh nevertheless penned an engaging work linking his long-standing critique of Wall Street (the Money Trust) to his opposition to the US entry into the European war. He restated his argument that the big bankers had maneuvered the country into war for their own selfish purposes. He acknowledged that Germany's violation of American maritime rights "made our cause just," but nevertheless questioned the wisdom of entering the European war.[18]

His resistance was grounded in his belief that militarism was the enemy of reform. Warfare, he wrote, even when legally justified, "has the least prospect of doing justice in any way." He was convinced that war feeds upon a false sense of patriotism "that would destroy millions to avenge wrong to an individual when to avenge that wrong by war begets thousands of other wrongs, and secures no reform than could not in most cases be more honorably secured and permanently established by natural means." He lamented that "war hysteria" had become so powerful that Wilson seemed to have forgotten his earlier goal of "peace without victory."[19]

Lindbergh took the long view. The country's biggest problem was not the war, but the conditions that had led to the war, which for him included economic inequality and the lack of true democracy that resulted from the concentration of wealth. Real victory, he thought, would mean overcoming the conditions that led to war. There must be equal opportunity for all and special privileges for none. To create a more level playing field, he proposed to take the profit motive out of the information (telephone, telegraph, mail), transportation, and banking industries, essentially by nationalizing them.[20]

Lindbergh thought the war was a terrible mistake, but nevertheless argued that Americans must support the president and Congress "with all our power." He exposed himself to attack, however, by rejecting as "contemptible to the idea of democracy" the often-heard slogan of "Stand by the President" because it suggested that during wartime citizens forfeited their right to influence policy. The book attracted little notice in 1917. Lindbergh, after all, had only himself to publicize and distribute it. When he next ran for office, however, the book would play an outsized role.[21]

But for the moment, Lindbergh was neither an elected official nor a candidate. He was therefore spared the difficulties faced by Thomas Van Lear, the Socialist mayor of Minneapolis, an impassioned opponent of US involvement in the European war. Hardly a pacifist, Van Lear was proud of his military service in the Spanish-American War. Once war was declared, he felt he had a duty to support it, while reserving the right to criticize government policy. He did not support the

Socialist Party's decision in St. Louis, and in fact his aide Anna Maley, who was a member of the party's national executive committee, voted against the majority report at the convention. He tried to balance criticism of the war with his statutory duties as mayor.[22]

Van Lear was in an awkward position because the Socialist Party in Minnesota, which endorsed the St. Louis platform, was actively campaigning against the draft, even to the point of urging men not to register. Nevertheless, he pledged police support to ensure that the June 5 draft registration day went smoothly. His cooperation did not protect him from the humiliation of having his appointments to the Minneapolis draft boards attacked by John McGee. In July, Van Lear spoke at the MFL convention, warning that Wilson's zeal to carry democracy to the rest of the world might leave so little here that only autocracy would be left at home. From news reports, he apparently said nothing specifically about conscription or the MCPS.[23]

The draft was a political headache for Van Lear, but it was also the cause of personal anguish. He and his wife had two draft-age sons, Howard and Ralph. When they registered as required on June 5, both wrote on their registration cards that they claimed an exemption for "conscientious scruples against war." Later Ralph Van Lear told his south Minneapolis draft board that his exemption claim was based on his membership in the Socialist Party, an organization opposed to war. There was, of course, no such exemption.[24]

Fighting for Democracy

Many African American leaders criticized Joel Springarn and W. E. B. Du Bois when they lobbied the federal government to create an officer training camp even though it would be segregated. The NAACP leaders were pleased when the army opened the training camp for African American officers at Fort Des Moines in June. Now, they thought, African American officers would command the African American troops sent to France.[25]

Their optimism was derailed by three events in the late summer. Across the country, African Americans hoped that Lieutenant Colonel Charles Young, the highest-ranking African American in the US Army, would eventually lead a combat division. He was the third African American to graduate from West Point and had a distinguished service record, commanding an African American unit in the Philippines, serving as a military attaché to Haiti and Liberia, and serving in the Mexican expedition of 1916 under General John Pershing, who promoted him to lieutenant colonel. In 1917, he commanded the 10th Calvary division, "Buffalo Soldiers," at Fort Huachuca, the division's home base in Arizona. "It would be a grand thing," wrote Charles Sumner Smith in the *Twin City Star*, "to have Col. Young as a Brigadier General." Instead, army doctors determined in May that he was unfit for service due to high blood pressure. Du Bois, who was a close friend, helped organize a campaign to save his career. The *Twin City Star*, for example, asked its readers to write their congressman, senator, and Secretary of War Baker, demanding that Young not be forced out of the army. Nevertheless, the War Department promoted him to full colonel and retired him from active duty on July 30.[26]

Even more distressing was the ghastly race riot in East St. Louis, Illinois. Directly across the Mississippi River from St. Louis, the city was a growing industrial center, and one of the places where African Americans from the South were settling, attracted by jobs in factories and steel mills. They were sometimes hired when unions, which did not accept African American workers, were on strike. The rioting went on for several days in early July and left at least thirty-nine African Americans dead, hundreds wounded, and thousands fleeing the city. A *St. Louis Post-Dispatch* reporter witnessed scenes of exceptional brutality, as African Americans were stoned, lynched, and beaten to death by mobs.[27]

In St. Paul, *The Appeal* called the riot a "crime against civilization," and reprinted Du Bois's "A Litany of Atlanta," the impassioned prayer to a "Silent God" he wrote after the brutal 1906 massacre of African Americans in Atlanta. The NAACP organized the first march in US history to protest racial discrimination and terror, a silent demonstration in New York on July 28. Between eight and ten thousand African Americans marched down Fifth Avenue. This "army with banners," as James Weldon Johnson called it, carried signs that read "Make America Safe for Democracy" and "Mother, Do Lynchers Go to Heaven?" Pleas for federal intervention, or even for a public comment from President Wilson, were met with silence.[28]

In August, things got worse. There was another dramatic outbreak of racial violence, this time in Houston, involving a battalion of the

24th Infantry, one of the army's four African American units, which had been assigned to guard a new army camp under construction. Reacting to Jim Crow treatment, and particularly the beating of two of their comrades by Houston police, one hundred members of the 24th marched into the city. In the gunfire that erupted, twenty-one died, including five policemen and four African American soldiers. The army hastily court-martialed 118 soldiers, sentencing twenty-eight to death and forty to life imprisonment. Thirteen soldiers were executed in secret before their cases were reviewed by the secretary of war. In the end, eighteen African American soldiers were hanged.[29]

The day after the "Houston Mutiny," as the army called it, Secretary Baker announced that there would be only one African American combat unit, and that most African American draftees would be shipped overseas for service in labor units as soon as possible. For the time being, he placed a hold on the induction of African American draftees. He lifted the ban in September when southern politicians complained that if no African Americans were inducted then more European Americans would have to be drafted to meet state quotas. To appease racist politicians, he announced that there would be strict segregation within each cantonment, and that African American draftees would not exceed 30 percent of the total population of any camp.[30]

Meanwhile, Baker appointed Emmett Scott, who had been Booker T. Washington's secretary, as special assistant on issues facing African Americans. Scott helped the Committee of Public Information (CPI) organize the Committee of 100 Citizens, made up of African American journalists, clergymen, and educators to build support for the war in African American communities. In October, 639 African American cadets successfully completed their training at Fort Des Moines and were commissioned as officers. Shortly thereafter, Baker announced that there would be two African American combat divisions. The 92nd would be composed of African American draftees and the 93rd would consist largely of the African American National Guard units that had been federalized.

African Americans had succeeded in winning some concessions from the War Department, but in the end, only about 42,000 of the nearly 370,000 African Americans in the military were assigned to these two combat divisions. The rest were assigned to service units deployed in trench digging, stevedoring, latrine cleaning, and the like. African American draftees from Minnesota would only see combat if they were among the few selected to join the 92nd. In any case, the two combat divisions provided unprecedented opportunities for African Americans and heightened their expectations for racial justice after the war.

From a Discussion to a Protest Rally

A peaceful gathering in New Ulm, a prosperous town about ninety miles southwest of Minneapolis, marked a major turning point on the home front. Several prominent citizens of New Ulm, which had a largely German American population, had actively campaigned for neutrality, including Louis Fritsche, the mayor, Albert Pfaender, the city attorney, Albert Steinhauser, the editor of the *New Ulm Review*, and Rev. Adolph Ackermann, president of Martin Luther College. Fritsche and Steinhauser had even gone to Washington to lobby for peace in the days before war was declared. Neutrality had near unanimous support in New Ulm, but once war was declared, the consensus broke down. Steinhauser's newspaper, for example, continued to be critical of the war, while its competitor, the *Brown County Journal*, embraced the war without reservation.

New Ulm had a long tradition of military service, beginning with Joseph Bobleter, an immigrant from Austria who settled in New Ulm after serving in the Union Army during the Civil War. In addition to founding the *New Ulm Review* and several banks, Bobleter served as state treasurer, a state senator, and at the time of his death in 1909, mayor of New Ulm. In 1871 he organized a local militia that became one of the first units of the Minnesota National Guard. He served as a colonel in the Spanish-American War, and in 1903 was made a brigadier general of the MNG. When the guard was mobilized for their assignment on the Mexican border in June 1916, their training camp at Fort Snelling was named Camp Bobleter in his honor.[31]

The three MNG units stationed in New Ulm—Company A of the 2nd Infantry Regiment, the 2nd Regiment's band, and a machine gun company—all used the Turner Hall as their base of operations. The city and guard units lobbied for an armory, and in 1914 the state authorized its construction. In May 1916, Mayor Fritsche presided over a dedication of the new armory, which was followed by a concert by the

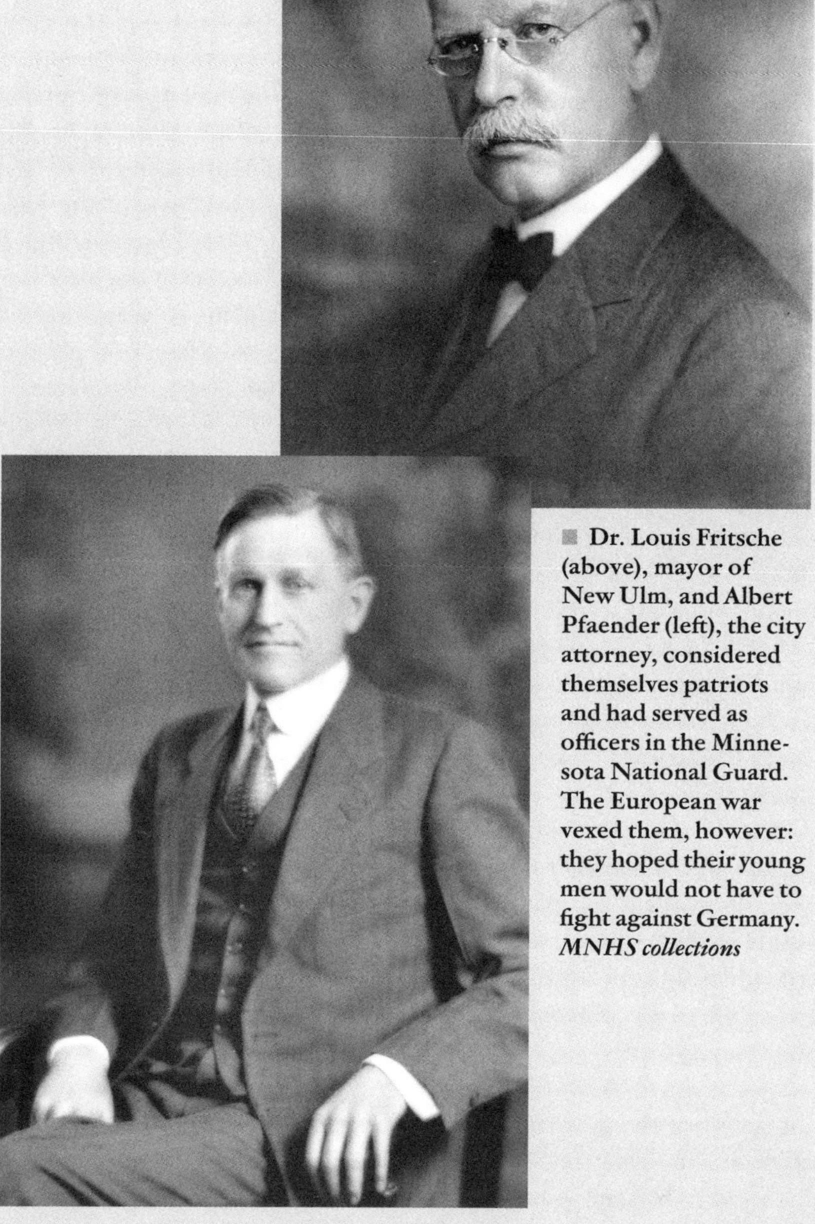

Dr. Louis Fritsche (above), mayor of New Ulm, and Albert Pfaender (left), the city attorney, considered themselves patriots and had served as officers in the Minnesota National Guard. The European war vexed them, however: they hoped their young men would not have to fight against Germany. *MNHS collections*

regiment's band and a "grand military ball." Joseph Burnquist gave the featured address, his first visit to New Ulm as governor.[32]

Steinhauser, Fritsch, and Pfaender were military men. Albert Steinhauser, the newspaper editor, earned a Purple Heart and a Silver Star while serving with a Minnesota unit during the Spanish-American War in the Philippines. Mayor Fritsche, a physician, held the rank of major in the MNG and was second in command of the medical corps. City Attorney Pfaender, who also held the rank of major in the MNG, served on the general staff of the 2nd Infantry Regiment. He had entered the MNG as a lieutenant in Company A, and was later promoted to captain of the company, and then to major of the regiment. He was mobilized in June 1916 along with the 2nd Regiment for service at Camp Llano Grande in southern Texas near the Mexican border. The regiment returned to a hero's welcome in New Ulm in January 1917, just a few months before the United States entered the war against Germany. Citizens of New Ulm had elected Pfaender to the Minnesota House in 1908, 1910, and 1912.[33]

After war was declared on Germany, New Ulm's military tradition ran aground. In preparation for the federalization of the MNG regiments, companies that could not quickly fill their rosters were sometimes moved to other locations. New Ulm's Company A apparently had trouble attracting new recruits, perhaps because of the possibility of fighting Germany. The MNG transferred the three New Ulm units to other cities, with Company A going to Luverne. The armory in New Ulm stood empty. Many in New Ulm protested, especially since Company A had just returned from many difficult months at the Mexican border.[34]

About that same time, Albert Pfaender resigned from the MNG. It may have been that he was exhausted after the seven challenging months in Texas. He may have needed to revitalize his law practice and bring in some revenue. He had also been involved in a dispute among the officers of the 2nd Regiment. Very likely, the fact that the MNG was about to become part of the US Army and be sent to the European war played a role.

Citizens of New Ulm had supported the wars against Spain and Mexico but thought the war with Germany was different. The passage of the Selective Service Act meant that young men from New Ulm could be sent to France to fight a German army which included some of their relatives. Many people in town were distraught, but the June 5 draft registration day passed without incident. In July, Brown County learned it would need to supply 156 men in the first call, less the number of men who had enlisted. When some young men sought advice, Fritsche, Pfaender, and others organized a meeting to discuss the draft and weigh options. News of the event spread, and soon even some Twin Cities newspapers took interest. On July 25, the day of the meeting, the *Minneapolis Morning Tribune* ran an article under the headline "War Protest Meeting in New Ulm Tonight" and connected the planned event with anti-draft meetings organized by the Socialist Party. The *New Ulm Review*, Steinhauser's paper, announced on its front page that a "monster mass meeting" would be held in Turner Park, "under the auspices of the People's Council of America." What connection the PCA had with the event is unclear, but its Socialist links were well known to the MCPS. The meeting had grown into a larger and more oppositional event that Fritsche and Pfaender had envisioned.[35]

County auditor Louis Vogel kicked off the event by leading a parade of young men subject to the draft and several bands from the armory to Turner Park, where at least five thousand had gathered. Mayor Fritsche presided, and by way of introduction stated that the purpose of the gathering was to request that the federal government "not force those drafted to fight in Europe against their will." A petition to that effect was circulated in the crowd and was signed by several thousand. The mayor was at pains to make clear that beyond that one reform there was "no desire on the part of anyone to cause any disaffection with the existing draft law." He then introduced Pfaender, his brother-in-law, who spoke from a prepared text.[36]

Pfaender, who a year earlier was commanding a National Guard battalion at the Mexican border, affirmed the loyalty of German Americans who he was sure would do their duty to their country. He probably sealed his fate when he noted that "we find ourselves in a war which would never have been declared if the common people had had a voice in it." For the future, the remedy was to pass a constitutional amendment requiring a referendum before a declaration of war. For now, people could support the PCA, which was working to keep drafted men from being sent across the ocean. Aware that he was on dangerous ground, he chose his words carefully. "Nothing can be gained by resisting the draft law," he cautioned, ". . . every legal American citizen should honor it until it is declared illegal." He went on to argue that the Constitution does not provide, not even permit, men to be taken across the border unless they are willing to go of their own free will.[37]

Pfaender's notion that draftees should not be sent abroad had been debated in Congress. Representative Hubert Dent Jr., an Alabama Democrat, proposed a two-tier military force in which volunteers would serve overseas and draftees serve at home. This bill had significant support among legislators from rural districts, but was voted down in the House Military Affairs Committee by thirteen to eight. Be that as it may, men like McGee thought Pfaender's comments proved his disloyalty, even though the constitutionality of the Selective Service Act was still being litigated. It was not until six months later that the Supreme Court ruled that the constitution allowed the executive branch to conscript men against their will and send them to fight a war on another continent. In retrospect, the court's ruling may seem inevitable, but at the time many held out hope that the ruling might go the other way.[38]

The next speakers were less guarded in their remarks. Steinhauser focused on the repression of free speech, specifically criticizing postmaster Albert Burleson for suppressing *The Masses*. For some reason, he cited the words from the Declaration of Independence that sanctioned overthrowing the government. Very likely his endorsement of the Nonpartisan League as a defender of common people caught the eye of the MCPS.[39]

Rev. Ackermann gave the most remarkable speech of the day. He maintained that 80 percent of voters did not want the war, and he called on the crowd to make sure congressmen who voted for the war were not reelected. He specifically mentioned the congressman for the 2nd District, which included New Ulm. He then condemned the war in starkly moral terms: "We do not want to fight for Wall Street, England, or France. If they tell us it is a war for humanity, they better create humanity in our own country first. Look at the recent killings of Negroes in East St. Louis and the conditions under which thousands of workmen and women have to work." Critics of the war routinely cited Wall Street and the plight of workers, but Ackermann's mention of the East St. Louis race riot was unusual. Minnesotans of European heritage generally ignored the racist violence across the country.[40]

Seemingly unaware of the backlash that was building against them, Pfaender, Ackermann, and Steinhauser spoke at several other rallies in neighboring counties in the following weeks. At Gibbon in Sibley County, a MCPS representative persuaded the city council to ban a scheduled talk by Pfaender and Ackermann. They spoke instead from a hay wagon just outside the city limits. In several cases, the New Ulm speakers shared the stage with Socialists, as at a well-attended rally at Glencoe, where Ackermann spoke alongside Thomas Van Lear. The local Nonpartisan League organizer helped set up this rally, early evidence of an important alliance just beginning to form.[41]

Many newspapers criticized the New Ulm leaders as disloyal, or even traitorous, and called for them to be disciplined in some way. In an editorial entitled "Treason Must Be Stopped," Jens Grondahl of the *Red Wing Daily Republican* demanded that men like Pfaender be jailed for the duration of the war and then "sent or returned to the countries with which they sympathize." The *Princeton Union* suggested it was no surprise that "there are those who regret that the Sioux did not do a better job in New Ulm fifty-five years ago." In late August, the *Minneapolis Morning Tribune* probably spoke for many newspapers when it called New Ulm a "hot bed of disloyalty," a self-contained community with "an alien language and alien customs and an alien press."[42]

Embarrassed by statewide criticism of their town, the New Ulm Commercial Club organized a loyalty festival on September 4 to fete the Brown County men who had been drafted and to give citizens a way to express patriotic feelings. People came from the surrounding area, and the crowd was estimated at eight thousand. They witnessed a large parade with ten bands and a rally addressed by dignitaries including Governor Burnquist. He told the crowd he was convinced New Ulm was "100% loyal to the United States." At a banquet held at the armory, the drafted men were asked to adopt a resolution pledging their loyalty and asserting that any criticism of conscription "is a menace to us who are about to assist in fighting our nation's battles." According to the *New Ulm Review*, only about a third of the draftees accepted invitations to the banquet, and of those, two refused to endorse the resolution.[43]

The Storm Breaks

The war at home began in earnest in the days following the July 25 rally, ending the relative calm that had prevailed in the months after the declaration of war. The MCPS came down on the New Ulm speakers, the federal government began indicting Socialist Party leaders, and the People's Council of America found that the US Constitution gave it no protection in Minnesota. The IWW came in for special treatment, driven out of the state by government-sanctioned vigilante violence.

Business leaders responded to the New Ulm event by organizing a series of loyalty meetings. The largest was in Minneapolis, arranged by the Stars and Stripes League, a new group that emerged from a meeting at the offices of the Minneapolis Civic and Commerce Association chaired by Fred Snyder, the MCPS's Hennepin County director. The Stars and Stripes League wanted to put "every man on record" as being 100 percent loyal, and the league called for a massive loyalty rally for August 16. The group produced pledge cards that read:

> **He Who Is Not with Us Is Against Us**
>
> **AMERICA FOR ME**
>
> I hereby enroll as a member of the Stars and Stripes League
> and pledge myself—
> That I will speak no word and do no act which will tend
> to lessen the chances of my government for success in this war.

The Stars and Stripes event featured a massive parade down Nicollet Avenue that ended at the Parade park west of downtown, where as many as fifty thousand gathered. For two hours, the crowd heard speeches from three separate stages. Fred Snyder, for example, branded the New Ulm meeting as treasonous and asked the crowd what should be done with such "copperheads." Some in the crowd shouted back: "Shoot 'em, hang 'em." Governor Burnquist stole the headlines by bluntly warning that if local officials could not stop "anti-American meetings," he would use every resource at his command to prevent such gatherings, referring to the forces the MCPS had assembled. He warned that if people were injured or killed in the process, it would be the fault of those who support "un-American demonstrations" with their presence.[44]

About a week later Labor's Loyal Legion, another new organization, hosted a large event to bolster loyalty in Minneapolis. This group claimed to be an "organization of workingmen," although it was organized by William C. Robertson, the managing editor of the *Minneapolis Daily News.* Robertson stated that the purpose of the organization was to give working men a vehicle for combatting the "the traitorous acts of men working against the welfare of the United States." Membership was open to anyone who worked "either with their hands or their brain." Although not initiated by the labor movement, the group attracted workers, including more conservative trade unionists.[45]

Labor's Loyal Legion hosted two nationally known speakers who addressed large crowds on August 24. James M. Gerhard, who had been Wilson's ambassador to Germany, gave a spirited indictment of the German government. Clarence Darrow, the lawyer well known for his defense of unions and criminal defendants, said he had been a pacifist before the war, and would be one after the war, but now it was necessary to fight against "German despotism."[46]

Smaller loyalty events were held around the state. The Cottonwood County affiliate of the MCPS, for example, sponsored a loyalty rally at Windom, where speakers denounced the New Ulm leaders. The fifteen hundred in attendance passed a resolution condemning them as traitors and demanding that they be interned until the close of the war if they could not furnish "proof of their loyalty." The municipal auditorium in Anoka was the venue for an event entitled "Anoka's reply to New Ulm" and featured Marion Burton, president of the University of Minnesota. Similar events were held at Morris in Stevens County and other towns.[47]

In this atmosphere, the MCPS began an investigation of mayor Louis Fritsche, Brown County auditor Louis Vogel, and city attorney Albert Pfaender for alleged disloyalty. Pfaender came to a MCPS meeting on August 14 hoping to convince the commissioners that the July 25 event was not seditious. He failed. The commission concluded that Pfaender's speech was "incendiary" because he cast young men as "martyrs, dragged to an unjust fate by a tyrannical and unjust government." At one point, John McGee told Pfaender that he was "a traitor and ought to be stood against a wall and shot." However, the commission gave Pfaender and his colleagues the chance to sign a public statement affirming their loyalty, admitting their mistake, and promising that no more "seditious gatherings" would be held. They refused, most likely because they would not concede that the July 25 event was "seditious."

On August 22 the governor removed Fritsche, Pfaender, and Vogel from office pending a hearing to be held in late September. Prior to acting, the commissioners asked Ambrose Tighe to confirm the governor's legal power to do so. Tighe noted that the Minnesota Constitution allowed for the removal of officials after a hearing for "malfeasance or nonfeasance in the performance of their duties" (Article 13, Section 2). Tighe decided it was malfeasance for an elected official "to publicly throw discredit on existing laws."[48]

Fritsche and Pfaender submitted their resignations, but the MCPS refused to accept them because the commissioners preferred to make an example of the men at a public hearing. The commission also sought to punish Rev. Ackermann, the president of Martin Luther College, but since he was not a government official, they resorted to demanding that the college fire him. They also recommended that the federal government prosecute Albert Steinhauser for statements made at the rally and in the *New Ulm Review*.[49]

Pfaender found himself also under attack from his fellow lawyers. At the Minnesota State Bar Association convention in early August, a resolution was introduced charging him with "giving aid and comfort to the enemy" and demanding that he be disbarred. In response Pfaender sent a telegram welcoming an investigation and affirming that he had "consistently and publicly urged cooperation of draft-age men with officials charged with execution of the draft laws." He noted that he had been a National Guard officer for fifteen years and had recently served at the Mexican border "at considerable sacrifice." He did admit, however, that he did not favor sending troops to foreign lands, but insisted that these issues could only be contested in a lawful manner. The resolution passed. Pfaender's troubles were just beginning.[50]

At the same convention, a resolution was introduced demanding that the MCPS remove Mayor Van Lear from office based on his speech at Glencoe. The resolution failed only because there was no written transcript of his speech available. At the banquet that closed the convention, Albert R. Allen, the Martin County attorney, told his fellow lawyers that "any man now talking treasonable doctrines ought to be shot on the spot." The reporter covering the meeting observed that "everyone in the room gave unqualified sanction to his utterance and rose cheering to their feet." In a few months, Allen would be attracting notice for his vigorous prosecutions of Nonpartisan League leaders in Martin County.[51]

Meanwhile, federal prosecutors were using the Espionage Act against the Socialist Party. At President Wilson's request, Congress had passed this groundbreaking legislation not long after war was declared. On August 9, Department of Justice agents arrested Abraham L. Sugarman, the secretary of the Socialist Party of Minnesota, for urging young men in Sibley County not to report for induction. The next day, the federal government arrested Jacob O. Bentall, who had been the party's candidate for governor, for a speech he had made in Hutchinson a week earlier. He was taken into custody while harvesting grain at his farm near Litchfield and brought to jail in Minneapolis, where he sat worrying about his crops for several days and trying to make bail. Mayor Van Lear visited his Socialist colleague in jail and expressed indignation that Bentall had been arrested.[52]

Undeterred by this crackdown, Mayor Van Lear invited the People's Council of America to have their national convention in Minneapolis and pledged police protection. The PCA responded by opening a Minneapolis office to plan the September 1 event. Among the local organizers were James Peterson, a Progressive Republican, Sylvanus A. Stockwell, a longtime state legislator from the south side, and Arthur Le Sueur, an attorney who had recently moved to St. Paul with his wife Marian Le Sueur to manage the Minnesota branch of the Nonpartisan League (although the NPL had not endorsed the council). Some newspapers called on the governor to ban the PCA convention. When the organizers could not find a venue that would rent to them, they planned an outdoor event on land near Minnehaha Park owned by Senator Stockwell.[53]

On August 21, Sheriff Otto Langum told the MCPS that the convention would result "in grave disorder." On August 28, a delegation from the Minneapolis Civil and Commerce Association appeared before the MCPS to ask that the convention be outlawed. McGee then moved that the governor ban the meeting, and the resolution passed with only John Lind dissenting. Burnquist issued a proclamation banning the convention on the grounds that it would be a threat to public order and would render aid and comfort to the enemy. Most of the press approved the ban with little acknowledgment that First Amendment rights might be involved. The proclamation came three days before the scheduled event, leaving the PCA to hastily divert the convention to Chicago. When the beleaguered convention was finally convened, the Illinois National Guard dispersed it.[54]

An Ominous Example

The New Ulm leaders, the Socialist Party, and the People's Council of America got off easy compared to the Industrial Workers of the World (IWW). By the summer of 1917 there was a broad national consensus in the business community, in government, and in the press that the IWW was a special case not deserving of even token protection of legal process. The national press mostly applauded when a local sheriff and a local businessmen's militia arrested twelve hundred copper miners taking part in an IWW-led strike of a Bisbee, Arizona, mine. They were put in railroad cars and left without food and water in the desert for two days, with a warning never to return. In Butte, Montana, the IWW led a copper mine strike after a mine explosion in June killed 164 workers. Among the IWW organizers was Frank Little, a member of the executive board of the IWW. He had taken part in IWW organizing around the country, including the Mesabi Iron Range strike in 1916. In the early hours of August 1, masked vigilantes burst into his hotel room and dragged him through the streets tied to the bumper of their car before lynching him from a railroad trestle.

Mainstream newspapers generally took the view that lynching was deplorable but that somehow the IWW had it coming. Citing no evidence, newspapers like the *New York Times* suggested that "IWW agitators are in effect, and perhaps in fact, agents of Germany." The *Minneapolis Morning Tribune* editorialized that the lynching, although not to be condoned, indicated that the federal government must repress the IWW nationally, especially because there is every reason to believe that its activities "are inspired in many cases by our enemies in war."[55]

The repression of the IWW in Minnesota began during the iron mine and timber strikes in 1916. Sheriffs of several northern counties collaborated to drive all IWW members out of Virginia, Eveleth, and International Falls during the strike against the Virginia and Rainy Lake Timber Company in December. In January, the legislature debated a bill to pay special deputy sheriffs to intervene in strikes. In response, labor representatives in the legislature proposed an investigation of labor conditions, suggesting that strikes might have more to do with poor pay and dangerous working conditions than with the IWW. The bill to fund special deputy sheriffs died in committee when the legislature ended its session in April. However, the business community achieved the same goal with the creation of the Minnesota Commission of Public Safety. In its final days, the legislature also passed the criminal syndicalism bill, which was clearly aimed at the IWW.

On June 20, the MCPS convened a meeting of Iron Range officials to discuss the labor situation. Following that meeting, the commission proposed a model vagrancy ordinance as a weapon against the IWW. The ordinance defined "vagrancy" as any speech or writing that advocated the disregarding of any legal obligation imposed or that advocated a failure to assist the government in carrying out the war. Just three days later, on a Saturday morning, the Duluth city council passed a vagrancy ordinance, and later that day arrested seventeen IWW members at their downtown office. They also arrested Elizabeth Gurley Flynn, a nationally known IWW organizer, at a hotel. She told the police she had split from the IWW and was only in Duluth because she was traveling to the Iron Range to speak at a Socialist Party picnic. A few days later she was released on condition that she leave without delay for the East. Charges against the others were dropped in exchange for a promise to be law-abiding citizens.[56]

John Lind spearheaded the commission's plan to drive the IWW from Minnesota. He wrote Attorney General Thomas Gregory that the commission had sufficient evidence to justify a nationwide federal prosecution of the IWW. Ambrose Tighe was sent to Washington to personally make the case to Gregory, and he enlisted the support of Knute Nelson and Frank Kellogg, the two Minnesota senators. Gregory was convinced, and although the MCPS took credit for the Department of Justice's nationwide raids on IWW offices that began on September 5 and the mass trial of IWW leaders that followed, it was very likely Gregory was lobbied by other states as well.[57]

Before the federal onslaught began, the IWW faced a kind of undeclared martial law in northern Minnesota. In at least three places, groups of vigilantes, sometimes consisting of elected officials and uniformed soldiers, attacked the IWW with the intent of driving all

"Wobblies" permanently out of town. In July, the MCPS sent a Pinkerton agent to Bemidji, a lumber boomtown in north-central Minnesota, to investigate the IWW. Two days after he arrived, the city's largest lumber mill burned down, throwing 450 people out of jobs. The police briefly held five IWW members "on general suspicion" but then released four of them the next day for lack of evidence linking them to the fire or, for that matter, any evidence of arson. They did not release Jesse Dunning, leader of the local branch, because he had a copy of Elizabeth Gurley Flynn's *Sabotage* in the IWW office. He had the distinction of being the first in the state to be charged with criminal syndicalism.[58]

The story might have ended there except that the managers of the mill told the city's Commercial Club that they would not rebuild the mill unless the IWW was run out of town. In response, the mayor led a posse of police, businessmen, and members of the local Home Guard in a roundup of twenty-four men thought to be IWW members. They were held in the baggage room of the Great Northern Depot and then put on a train to the jeers of an angry crowd of a thousand townspeople. In an editorial the next day, the local newspaper celebrated this act of vigilante violence: "Bemidji has been the roosting place of this lawless horde, many of whom are aliens who seem to be allowed the privilege of coming to this country. . . . Into it has come hordes of the scum of south Europe. . . . Bemidji's best citizenship . . . resolved to cleanse their homes of this festering sore. . . . It was not a mob of rowdies, it was a gathering of businessmen, professional men, men who work for a weekly wage and are proud of their labor, their homes and their families, the men who made Bemidji."[59]

In the days that followed, the police and Home Guard members harassed and threatened citizens judged insufficiently loyal, including Morris Kaplan, a Socialist who owned a wholesale grocery business and a hotel, and W. N. Weber, a Socialist lawyer. Weber was beaten, and then he left town; Kaplan stayed and continued to operate his store until his death in 1959. In September, Dunning was convicted of criminal syndicalism for possession of Flynn's book, and in December sentenced to two years in the state prison.[60]

The IWW in Duluth also experienced extrajudicial violence, in this case by a highly organized unit of the US Army. The 3rd Infantry Regiment of the Minnesota National Guard had been federalized during the summer and was waiting to be shipped to Camp Cody. At about 6:30 PM on August 18, about a hundred members of the regiment attacked the IWW office at 530 West First Street. According to news reports, the guardsmen marched in perfect formation down First Street until a leader gave the order "Left Wheel," at which point the guardsmen broke ranks and charged the storefront, smashing the windows and tearing the doors off their frames. Inside they destroyed the furniture and upended everything. They dragged the IWW papers and literature out and started a bonfire with them on First Street. Then they marched off, once again in formation. The newspaper concluded that the IWW office "had all the semblance of a bombarded village on the western European front."[61]

Commanding officers of the MNG insisted that the attack took them by surprise. The newspaper surmised that the attack was the result of an altercation between an alleged IWW member and a guardsman the previous evening. Labor organizations circulated a petition demanding that the guardsmen be prosecuted. They complained that the police had stood by while the soldiers acted as a "mob." The *Duluth News Tribune* took issue with the term "mob." The guardsmen were not a mob because they "formed an orderly body." The soldiers are willing to fight the Germans, "open enemies in battle," the editorial concluded, but they "are not willing to have enemies in the rear, skulking cowards, who would stab them in the back." The city did not prosecute the soldiers, and it is unlikely anything came of the internal investigation. By the end of August, the 3rd Infantry was training at Camp Cody.[62]

Then in September, the Moorhead unit of the Home Guard, Company C of the 9th Battalion, helped deport about thirty-five IWW members from Clay County. Captain A. M. Hopeman, the commander, received a call that Wobblies in nearby Sabin were "threatening disruption of the marketing operations of potato producers." The Home Guard and the local sheriff rushed to Sabin, where they found a camp of IWW workers eating breakfast. They rounded them up and ordered them to start walking down the railroad tracks until they were out of the county. When most of the workers returned the next day, a new posse arrested the group for vagrancy. A few days later, the workers were released when they agreed to leave Clay County.[63]

By this time, the nationwide juggernaut against the IWW rendered local suppression superfluous. On September 5, 1917, federal agents raided the IWW headquarters in thirty-three cities. They arrested hundreds and seized records that would be used in the mass trial of IWW leaders in Chicago in 1918. As the MCPS had hoped, federal agents included IWW offices in Minneapolis, in Duluth, and on the Iron Range on their list of targets. In Minneapolis, federal agents raided three IWW locations, carting off three carloads of records and literature.[64]

The IWW was an easy target because it was politically isolated. The Wobblies had few friends in the labor movement. Most newspapers demonized them and either acquiesced to the abandonment of legal process or, worse, applauded what had become a kind of undeclared martial law. Although the IWW was able to hire competent lawyers, including Clarence Darrow, the legal profession looked the other way when the government abandoned the rule of law in suppressing the IWW.

The neutralization of the IWW accustomed Minnesotans to extrajudicial violence and set the stage for the next phase of the war at home. On August 18, the same day the National Guard attacked the Duluth IWW office, Fred Snyder, the Hennepin County public safety commission director, wrote to Senator Knute Nelson about the "threatening progress" that the Nonpartisan League was making around the state. He had in mind events like the June gathering in Glencoe, where Arthur Townley told three thousand farmers that with their help the NPL could transform Minnesota government through the ballot box, just as it had done in North Dakota. Unless something was done to stop the NPL, Snyder told Nelson, it would take control of state offices and the legislature, a prospect that terrified business leaders.[65]

Soon John McGee was arguing that the Nonpartisan League was even more dangerous than the IWW. He had a point.

SIX

BRANDISHING THE WEAPON OF LOYALTY

AUTUMN 1917

I don't mean to say we hadn't suffered grievances; we had—at the hands of Germany. Serious grievances! . . . They had interfered with the right of American citizens to travel upon the high seas—on ships loaded with munitions for Great Britain. . . . We had a right, a technical right . . . to ride on those vessels. I was not in favor of riding on them, because it seemed to me that the consequences resulting from any destruction of life that might occur would be so awful.

SENATOR ROBERT LA FOLLETTE, speaking on September 20, 1917, at the St. Paul Auditorium to the Producers and Consumers Convention, called by the Nonpartisan League, from the transcript of his speech used in his expulsion hearing in the US Senate

Mr. La Follette is the most sinister enemy of democracy in the United States today. I include, of course, according to their capacities, the shadow Huns, who dance with him—like Gronna, wasn't it, and Lundeen?

THEODORE ROOSEVELT, speaking a week later at the St. Paul Auditorium, referring to Senators Robert La Follette (Wisconsin) and Asle J. Gronna (North Dakota) and Representative Ernest Lundeen (Fifth District, Minnesota), as quoted in the *St. Paul Daily News*

THE BRITISH OFFENSIVE near Passchendaele ground to a halt in early November, gaining a bit of territory at the cost of a quarter million casualties. The German losses were similar. The British had better success against the Turkish army, advancing into Palestine and taking Jerusalem. This set the stage for the Balfour Declaration, committing the British government to establishing a "national home for the Jewish people" in Palestine.

In Russia, Kerensky took charge of the Provisional Government. He ordered an offensive the Germans repelled with such force that the Russian army essentially disintegrated. By autumn, peasants began to seize the land, workers began a series of strikes, and the Bolsheviks became the largest party in Moscow and Petrograd. The pressure was on the United States to train, equip, and ship an army to France.

Training the Segregated Army

The Wilson administration scrambled to build a network of camps where thousands of newly drafted men could be forged into an effective army. The War Department planned sixteen of these cantonments, each designed to house up to forty thousand men, along with administrative offices, a hospital, a rifle range, railroad sidings, bakeries, storehouses, laundries, repair shops, and schools. Fort Snelling was shortlisted as a possible site, but Secretary of War Baker instead chose Camp Dodge near Des Moines, Iowa, very likely because it was in a "dry" county. The MCPS had anticipated this objection by ordering a dry zone around Fort Snelling, but the saloons of downtown Minneapolis and St. Paul would still be accessible to soldiers. The army did conduct officer training camps at Fort Snelling during the war.[1]

Minnesota draftees trained at many camps, but most went to Camp Dodge, where there were three hundred buildings for enlisted men and one hundred buildings for officers' quarters, as well as a civic center where organizations like the Young Men's Christian Association, the Knights of Columbus, and the Lutheran Brotherhood erected buildings to provide services to enlistees. The Young Women's Christian Association had two "hostess houses," one of which served African American soldiers who were segregated from the rest of the camp. The Carnegie Corporation funded a library administered by the American Library Association.[2]

The war department assigned the three infantry regiments of the Minnesota National Guard to Camp Cody, in the desert of southern New Mexico, named for the recently deceased William "Buffalo Bill" Cody, whose nickname called attention to the thousands of bison he

▪ **The army was still building Fort Dodge in Iowa when the first Minnesota draftees arrived for training.** ***MNHS collections***

claimed to have killed. He fought in the Civil War and the wars against the Plains Indians, and then created Buffalo Bill's Wild West, a circus-like pageant that toured the United States and Europe, playing a large role in mythologizing the American West.[3]

The departure of drafted men from cities and towns throughout Minnesota was celebrated on "Dedication Days," which featured parades, speeches, and banquets. On September 5, an advance contingent of about nine hundred men left for Des Moines to prepare Camp Dodge for the thousands to follow. For six days starting on September 19, trains carried another seven thousand Minnesotans to Camp Dodge. Washington then abruptly halted further mobilization of Minnesota draftees, announcing that construction at Camp Dodge had not progressed enough to receive any more men. It was not until February 1918 that trains filled with large numbers of Minnesota draftees again rolled toward Iowa.[4]

Since the Wilson administration had decided to keep the military strictly segregated, African Americans were sent to separate sections of the new cantonments. The induction of African Americans began in September, and eventually over 367,656 joined the military, 92 percent of whom were drafted. African Americans were drafted at higher rates than Americans of European ancestry because they were more often denied occupational and dependency exemptions, and despite

their abysmal access to health care, they were declared physically fit for service at a higher rate.[5]

On November 3, over a hundred African American draftees from Minneapolis, St. Paul, Duluth, and elsewhere left by train for Camp Dodge. Large crowds came to the station to bid them farewell. On the eve of their departure, Louis W. Hill, the son of James J. Hill and president of the Great Northern Railroad, hosted "a chicken dinner" for the draftees in St. Paul at which former mayor Daniel Lawler spoke. Governor Burnquist was expected but did not appear, provoking a bitter editorial in the *Twin City Star*, which called the governor "a slacker when needed by the Negro." The editorial also called on Burnquist and Hill to appoint African Americans to positions of responsibility.[6]

The Commission Extends its Reach

While Minnesotans were training in Iowa, New Mexico, and elsewhere, the MCPS continued to strengthen its forces at home. The county public safety commissions, each led by a director appointed by the MCPS, were gaining experience in enforcing loyalty on a local level. The commission's intelligence service was busy shadowing the allegedly disloyal. The Home Guard grew as new battalions were organized in western and northern Minnesota. The commission could count on most of the sheriffs around the state, some of whom had organized their own "rural guards." The commission also had the enthusiastic support of a growing list of volunteer organizations, including the Loyalty Leagues, Labor's Loyal Legion, and the Stars and Stripes League. In November, the American Protective League, an organization of amateur detectives dedicated to enforcing loyalty, joined this coalition.

Albert M. Briggs, a Chicago advertising executive, formed the American Protective League in 1916. When the war began, he offered

OPPOSITE
African American men depart Duluth's Union Station for St. Paul to join Twin Cities draftees for the journey to the segregated Camp Dodge. *Courtesy of University of Minnesota Duluth, Kathryn A. Martin Library, Northeast Minnesota Historical Collections (from S3005 Minnesota War Records Commission, St. Louis County Branch Records, MNHS collections)*

his services to A. Bruce Bielaski, chief of the Bureau of Investigation (the precursor of the FBI). He proposed that the APL be officially recognized as a civilian auxiliary. Bielaski and his boss, US attorney general Thomas W. Gregory, endorsed the scheme and funded it. Soon Briggs had chapters around the country and more than 250,000 amateur sleuths opening mail, spying on their neighbors, and generally monitoring the loyalty of citizens. The Department of Justice even gave APL operatives badges that said "American Protective League—Secret Service."[7]

The Minneapolis Civic and Commerce Association sponsored creation of a Minneapolis branch of the APL in November 1917 under the direction of Charles G. Davis, a local contractor. The APL worked closely with the local Bureau of Investigation agents, draft boards, and the MCPS. Remarkably, officials gave Davis, who was the civilian leader of a vigilante organization, an office in the federal courthouse in downtown Minneapolis. One of the operatives claimed that by the end of the war, the Minneapolis branch had 491 agents operating in Hennepin County. He also claimed the branch had a card file with 15,446 items, each representing a "case" investigated by the branch's sleuths.[8]

Although the attorney general sanctioned the APL, individual APL members lacked police powers. John McGee solved this problem by conferring police power on APL agents using Order 4, which the MCPS issued to give itself the power to create its own police officers. Charles Davis forwarded names to McGee and asked him to send peace officer badges assigned to each name on the list. On his own authority, McGee conveyed police powers on at least forty of the APL's amateur detectives based only on a statement by Davis that the men were "loyal."[9]

The commission's extensive powers were on display when it punished the elected New Ulm officials charged with playing key roles in the July 26 gathering. Governor Burnquist had removed city attorney Albert Pfaender, mayor Louis Fritsche, and county auditor Louis Vogel from office, but they had a right to a hearing before his order became final. Ambrose Tighe acted as chief prosecutor at a proceeding that began in New Ulm and concluded in St. Paul. Pfaender and Fritsche testified that they supported the war but maintained that citizens could petition the government not to send draftees overseas to fight. The attorney for Vogel asked that his client be reinstated since he had made no speeches at the rally and, in fact, "was training a searchlight on the American flag at the courthouse" when the draft meeting was in progress.[10]

The hearing ended abruptly when Pfaender recalled that during his earlier appearance before the MCPS he had said that some older New Ulm residents did not want to see their former homeland destroyed. Tighe then asked Pfaender if this was the moment when John McGee told him he was a traitor "and ought to be stood up against a wall and shot." Pfaender responded that McGee was in fact responding to his assertion that citizens had the right to petition Congress against sending draftees to France.[11]

In December the governor affirmed the removal of Pfaender and Fritsche and reinstated Vogel to the job of county auditor. The governor found Pfaender and Fritsche guilty of "malfeasance" because the July 25 meeting was "anti-draft" and "in effect pro-German and disloyal to America." The governor held that the "intended effect" of the meeting was to "interfere with the plan of the United States government in the raising of its army and the prosecution of the war."[12]

The MCPS had power over Pfaender and Fritsche because they were public officials. The commissioners also wanted to punish two other speakers at the July 25 rally: Albert Steinhauser, editor of the *New Ulm Review* and *New Ulm Post*, and Adolph Ackermann, president of Martin Luther College. Eventually, they prevailed on the US attorney to indict Steinhauser under the Espionage Act. In the meantime, the commission sent undercover agents to attend Ackermann's public appearances, and even follow him around St. Paul as he attended a baseball game, stopped in a library, and went to the theater. The agents, however, found no evidence of disloyalty.[13]

Undeterred, Ambrose Tighe warned the trustees of Martin Luther College on November 20 that the commission would "not tolerate the continued operation" of an educational institution within which the "teachings and instructors . . . are not unquestionably loyal." The trustees, many of whom were ministers, sought to delay the matter, citing their duties over the Christmas holidays. Tighe waited until January 9, 1918, and then demanded an answer. The board said they would respond by February 20. Tighe told them they had to remove Ackermann by February 5 or face the consequences. On January 30, the board announced that Ackermann had resigned.[14]

Ackermann was not the only academic in trouble. The commission also provoked the firing of William Schaper, head of the political science department at the University of Minnesota. In July, McGee asked Fred Snyder, chair of the Board of Regents, to investigate several university professors infected with the "germ" of disloyalty. McGee wrote that the commission thought the matter could be "safely entrusted" to the regents. This decision was not surprising, given that Snyder was the Hennepin County director of the MCPS and Governor Burnquist sat on the board ex officio. McGee attached an unsigned statement that claimed all but one member of the German department was disloyal, and in addition, "there are two other rabid pro-Germans in official positions," namely Schaper and Alfred Owre, dean of dentistry. Snyder consulted with Marion L. Burton, who had just become university president, and the stage was set for an inquisition.[15]

When summoned before the regents in late summer, most of the professors, including all the German-language faculty, established their loyalty. On September 13, the board interrogated the last two, Dean Akre and Schaper. The regents concluded that Akre, a mild-mannered pacifist, was a harmless eccentric and sent him back to work. Burton then summoned Schaper and informed him that the regents wanted to question him about his loyalty. With no idea why this was happening and no time to prepare, Schaper was ushered into the boardroom. What happened next marks a low point in the university's history.[16]

William Schaper was born in La Crosse, Wisconsin, the son of German immigrants. The University of Minnesota hired him in 1901, shortly after he had completed his doctorate at Columbia University. By 1917, he was the chair of the political science department and a respected scholar, well known for his expertise in state and municipal governance and taxation. He had played a major role, for example, in efforts to create a new charter for the city of Minneapolis.[17]

Schaper bristled at what he felt were ridiculous insinuations and a humiliating process. He told the regents that, although he did not oppose the war effort, he could not "boost for the war" because he had relatives fighting for both sides. When asked what he meant by boosting, he replied "that it was revolting to my conscience to go out to harangue public meetings for the purpose of arousing the war spirit." This response angered regent Pierce Butler, a well-known trial lawyer, who grilled Schaper as Burton sat silently. "You want the Kaiser . . . to dominate the world, don't you?" he demanded. Schaper, just as angry, responded that he thought Butler's question was "utterly absurd." To men like Burton, Snyder, and Butler, however, the question was anything but absurd. They had internalized McGee's "100% loyalty" ideology that branded a person who was not completely loyal as a traitor. Acquiescence was not enough; boosting was exactly what they expected of university faculty.[18]

After almost two hours of tense interchange, the board deliberated and then fired Schaper by unanimous vote. The resolution terminating him said that "the University, the state, and the nation require unqualified loyalty on the part of all teachers at the University, coupled with willingness and ability by precept and example to further the national purpose in the present crisis." The regents made clear they had dismissed Schaper solely for statements he had just made in the boardroom. He probably could have kept his job if he had projected a more obsequious attitude. He was, however, in no mood to cooperate. Schaper left the university that afternoon unemployed, and he would not find another academic job for eight years.[19]

The commission's quest for loyalty may have reached its limit in the case of another teacher. In the fall of 1917, the Minneapolis School Board interrogated O. J. Arness, a high school teacher, about his IWW membership. He was unrepentant, and the board terminated him, with only two members voting to retain him—Mae Snow, one of two women on the board, and Lynn Thompson, a Socialist. This was not enough to satisfy John McGee. He asked his fellow commissioners if something could be done about the two school board members who voted to retain the disloyal teacher. On the motion of Charles Ames, the commission asked Ambrose Tighe to investigate the possibility of removing Snow and Thompson from the school board. There is no evidence that Tighe followed through on this request.[20]

Propaganda and the Press

Led by publicity director William C. Handy, the MCPS mounted a propaganda campaign to build support for the war effort using all available tools, including the press, the schools, organizations, public meetings, and the distribution of printed materials created either by

MCPS staff or the Committee on Public Information (CPI) in Washington. The commission urged county directors to establish local speakers' bureaus and formally incorporated the Loyalty Lyceum, a volunteer organization of patriotic speakers based in St. Paul.[21]

The University of Minnesota played a big role in the CPI. Guy Stanton Ford, a historian who in 1917 was dean of the graduate school, moved to Washington to direct the division of civil and educational programs. He recruited a group of University of Minnesota faculty who produced thirty-five pamphlets, millions of which were distributed nationwide. The division's first pamphlet was an annotated edition of Wilson's war message to Congress prepared by William Stearns Davis of the history department and William Anderson and Cephas D. Allin of the political science department. Wallace Notestein, professor of history, and Elmer E. Stoll, professor of English, wrote *Conquest and Kultur: Aims of the Germans in Their Own Words*, of which more than a million copies were distributed.[22]

In late summer the journalist Charles W. Henke took over as MCPS publicity director. He focused on disseminating the commission's own perspective, especially in its publication, *Minnesota in the War*, which debuted on September 8, 1917, and ran weekly for the duration of the war. Initially a four-page newsletter with a print run of four thousand, it grew to eight pages and a circulation of ten thousand in January 1918. County directors, Home Guard officers, sheriffs, patriotic organization leaders, and journalists followed the newsletter to learn the commission's views, which practically speaking meant the views of John McGee.[23]

The commission supplemented the CPI pamphlets with its own materials. Henke turned to Alice Ames Winter, director of the Women's Committee and a published novelist, to write "Why We Are at War," a handbill issued in many languages. On the Iron Range, for example, the commission distributed the handbill in Finnish (10,000 copies), Croatian (10,000), Italian (5,000), and Bulgarian (2,500). The publicity department also published *Facts About the War*, a fifty-nine-page anthology of short pieces on German aggression, the US cause of war, and other topics, compiled by University of Minnesota faculty.[24]

Henke also produced reprints of work originally published elsewhere, including Edward F. Hale's *The Man Without a Country*, about a Revolutionary War traitor who is sentenced to a life imprisonment on navy ships. No one ever speaks to him about the United States until he comes to understand the true worth of his country and dies a passionate patriot. The department also printed Isobel Field's "Are You Talking Treason Talk or American Talk," a series of paired statements, which started with this one:

> TREASON TALK: Why are we in this war?
> AMERICAN TALK: We are in this war because Germany gave us too many knocks. We were not quick to fight. We said "please don't" many times, but Germany would not stop. We are in this war because we are not cowards.

MCPS publications sought to convince Minnesotans that German actions made the war unavoidable, which required balancing Wilson's liberal internationalist rationale of altruistically spreading democracy and John McGee's conservative nationalist claim that US sovereignty, and the manhood of individual American men, required the destruction of the German state. The commission distributed 100,000 copies of Wilson's war address, but also continued to press the nationalistic argument. Accordingly, *Minnesota in the War* editorialized that "we would have lost our entire self-respect had we chosen to swallow every insult and remain inactive." This justification of the war naturally led to vengeful, unWilsonian conclusions that the war would end "when the Prussian government is made to feel the iron heel of an indignant and resentful civilization upon its neck and a world peace is guaranteed forever."[25]

The commission's publication also sought to rebut the common criticisms of the war, in particular the view stated by Robert La Follette, Charles Lindbergh, and many activists associated with the Socialist Party and the Nonpartisan League. In "Wall Street and the War," the commission sought with "sledge hammer arguments" to refute the notion that the war was "a rich man's war and a poor man's fight." This piece insisted that the burdens of the war and the fruits of victory would be distributed equally, thanks to progressive taxation, Liberty Bonds, and the Selective Service System. It rejected the notion that Wall Street profited by the war, although no specifics were mentioned, including, for example, the enormous loans made by J. P. Morgan to the Allies. Finally, the pamphlet argued, without evidence, that munitions manufacturers would experience a decline in profits during the war.[26]

A third theme in the commission's publications was "100% loyalty," the idea that every citizen must wholeheartedly support the war effort in word and deed. Neutrality was unacceptable. "Anyone who talks and acts against the government in time of war," the commission proclaimed, "is a traitor and deserves the most drastic punishment." A loyal citizen was duty bound to act "as a secret service man" and report the "disloyalty" of their neighbors to the government. The commission's proclivity to demand not just outward compliance with the law but also internalized agreement with government policy anticipated the totalitarian tendencies of the postwar period.[27]

Truth, it has been said, is the "first casualty" of war, and abundant experience demonstrates that one should skeptically evaluate what governments say about the behavior of the enemy. Nevertheless, propaganda about atrocities is common and often effective. During the period of neutrality, for example, the British did a remarkable job of publicizing tales of German atrocities in Belgium. As noted earlier, the German army took murderous reprisals against civilians suspected of resistance and burned the historic city of Louvain. The British reports, however, went further, inventing tales of "the Huns" tossing babies on their bayonets and slicing off the hands of elderly men and women and worse. The reports often had a sexual subtext. These titillating stories were widely reprinted in the American press and played a major role in turning public opinion against Germany. After the declaration of war, the CPI produced posters depicting Germans as bloodthirsty monsters carrying off women. Speakers continued to use stories of German atrocities to promote the sale of Liberty Bonds.[28]

Occasionally, however, someone asked for evidence. Local patriots, for example, might want to prove to skeptical neighbors the barbarism of the Germans. One Minnesotan wrote to the MCPS asking to be put in touch with Belgians who could provide direct testimony of German atrocities. Charles W. Henke responded that while there were such people in the United States, he did not know how to contact them. In lieu of evidence, he suggested going on the offensive. Anyone who does not believe in German atrocities, he wrote, "was either a fool or so intensely pro-German that the best thing to be done with him is to tell him to go back to his beloved Germany as soon as possible." After all, he said, "the records of German atrocities and the mutilation of Belgian children, men, and old women are so thoroughly established in the records of Allied government, that it does not permit the least bit of doubt on the part of any sensible man."[29]

The publicity department also produced materials aimed at the German American community. The author of "What German Americans Owe to Themselves: A Message to Americans of German Stock" bluntly told the German reader that "it is an act of gross and flagrant dishonesty to accept America's protection and withhold from America his undivided fidelity and support." The department also issued reprints, including "The Poison of Prussianism," an address by Otto H. Kahn, a wealthy New York investment banker born in Germany, and the poignant "A Family Letter: From a German American to His Brother," originally published in the *Atlantic Monthly,* in which Rudolph Heinrichs, a patriotic son of German immigrants, complained about his sibling. His brother was "absolutely loyal to the United States," but his loyalty was "passive," in that he would not openly campaign for the defeat of Germany, primarily because their father, their three sisters, and a brother had returned to Germany before the war. Heinrichs criticized his sibling for putting family loyalty before patriotism, concluding that "passive loyalty today is disloyalty."[30]

The publicity department worked hard on its publications, but recognized that the press was the most important molder of public opinion. In 1917, there were about seven hundred newspapers in Minnesota, ranging from the big dailies of the larger cities to the weeklies and dailies published in smaller cities and towns. Minneapolis, St. Paul, and Duluth each had several daily newspapers, and most towns of any size had at least a weekly if not a daily; some towns had two or even three newspapers. The commission sent *Minnesota in the War* as well as weekly press releases and clippings to editors. Most newspapers gave full-throated support to the commission's point of view.

In southeastern Minnesota, for example, Jens Grondahl steered his *Red Wing Daily Republican* down a path that increasingly echoed MCPS talking points. At first a committed neutralist disdainful of the European war, he became an impassioned militarist after the United States entered the war, and had his patriotic poem "America, My Country" set to music and attempted to have it recognized as the national anthem. He adopted the 100 percent American idea promulgated by the MCPS. "You are either for your country, or you are against your country," he editorialized, echoing McGee, "there is no middle ground."

Therefore, "boost for it, stick up for it," or if there is another country you like better, go there. Like McGee, he became an advocate of extreme measures. He wrote that Albert Pfaender and Robert La Follette were "traitors." In the Kaiser's Germany, he believed, "they would be silenced once and for all by the firing squad." Although his constant theme was criticizing German autocracy, he suggested that "a little of that German method . . . would go a long way toward permanently silencing these voices that are prolonging the war and postponing the day of victory."[31]

He continued his campaign to make "America, My Country" the national anthem. In September he produced a "patriotic post card" version of the song, trumpeted in advertisements as "the song-poem that is sweeping the country and helping to 'make the world safe for democracy.'" The postcards were one cent each or six for a nickel. And he produced new patriotic poetry, including "We Go to 'Get' the Kaiser" on the front page of the August 27, 1917, edition. Each stanza ended with the poem's title, as for example this one, focusing on possible future German atrocities:

> Beneath the flag of freedom, we shall do our duty well,
> And save America's womanhood from death or living hell,
> Nor shall you see your children burnt and mangled from the blue—
> We go to "get" the kaiser—or the kaiser will get you.

The MCPS worried about what was being written in the foreign-language press, especially in the fourteen German-language dailies and weeklies published in Minnesota. They had a combined circulation of 120,000, led by the *Westlicher Herold* in Winona, which sold about 60,000 copies. Congress passed the Trading with the Enemy Act in October. This act required foreign-language newspapers to submit translations of any articles touching on the war to the Post Office Department for approval prior to publication. Compliance was critical because the Espionage Act gave postmaster general Albert Burleson the power to revoke the mailing rights of a publication if he deemed it to be treasonous. German-language newspapers either had to actively support the war or adopt a policy of silence. In addition, many businesses that had regularly advertised in German-language papers placed their ads elsewhere. As a result, some newspapers were suppressed by government action, some closed on their own, and some became English-language papers. By the end of the war, the total number of German-language publications in the United States had been significantly reduced.[32]

The *Westlicher Herold* survived by walking a fine line. Publisher-editor Emil Leicht supported the war but refrained from casting Germany as aggressor and, most importantly, defended the rights of its readership to be both American and German. The state's second-largest German newspaper, the *Volkszeitung* in St. Paul, also survived. The MCPS opened an investigation but apparently decided that the newspaper was loyal. However, its editor Frederick Bergmeier was interred by the federal government as an enemy alien. The newspaper continued under Clara Bergmeier, his sister-in-law. *Der Wanderer*, an independent Catholic newspaper, was also closely monitored but allowed to continue.[33]

The commission was also concerned about the Scandinavian press, especially after Senator Knute Nelson demanded they do something about what he considered the pro-German attitude of some Norwegian- and Swedish-language newspapers. The commission appointed Nicolay A. Grevstad, a multilingual journalist and friend of the senator, as "assistant publicity director in charge of the foreign press." Grevstad supplied Scandinavian newspapers with translations of MCPS press releases, speeches by Governor Burnquist and other politicians, and original articles he authored, and generally campaigned to win over the Scandinavian press fraternity.[34]

Senator Nelson was pleased with the results, except for one glaring exception: the *Park Region Echo*, a pro-Nonpartisan League paper in Alexandria, his hometown in Douglas County. Carl Wold, the *Echo*'s editor and a fellow Norwegian, had published an anti-war article by James Peterson, a Minneapolis politician who had challenged Nelson in the 1912 primary. In June, Nelson asked John McGee "if there was any way you can jack up the paper and Mr. Peterson." To be clear, Nelson added, "I wish you would try and squelch both the paper and Peterson." Then in July, Wold criticized a pro-war speech by Constant Larson, leader of the local America First Association and Nelson's former law partner. Nelson then asked A. S. Burleson, the postmaster general, to revoke the *Echo*'s mailing privileges. Eventually Peterson would be indicted under the Espionage Act, but the MCPS lacked authority to ban newspapers and the Post Office declined to act.[35]

Nelson's campaign against the *Park Region Echo* climaxed when Arthur Townley, leader of the NPL and perhaps the most famous graduate of Alexandria High School, came to town to address a large patriotic rally. Farmers came from neighboring counties to hear Townley, who was quoted in the *Echo* as saying that "the only difference between Senator Nelson and me is that the senator is about thru and I have just commenced." The next day, vandals broke into the *Echo* offices and damaged the press and linotype. Six days later Nelson spoke in Alexandria at a banquet honoring the town's draftees. He compared critics of the war to the copperheads of the Civil War, and assured the draftees that "we will do our best to protect you against them." The next night, vandals again broke into the *Echo*'s offices and did more damage.[36]

▪ Senator Knute Nelson was irritated by the pro-NPL newspaper in his hometown of Alexandria and asked John McGee to do something about it. ***MNHS collections***

The *Park Region Echo* weathered these attacks thanks to the financial contributions of pro-NPL farmers in the area. In December, however, Wold was assaulted in downtown Alexandria by a man angered by an editorial criticizing the America First Association. The final blow came in 1918 when he was convicted under the state version of the Espionage Act. He died of stomach cancer in October shortly before his sentencing.

Food, Fuel, Liquor, and Liberty Bonds

Although local business leaders created the MCPS primarily to advance their economic and political interests, the commission also was responsible for Minnesota's overall war mobilization. Accordingly, the commission monitored food production and conservation, fuel supply, the cost of living, energy conservation, liquor sales, and Liberty Bonds.

The Committee on Food Production and Conservation, which reported to the commission, encouraged increased agricultural production in the state. Supported by the MCPS, the committee and the Women's Committee participated vigorously in the federal government's food conservation programs. The MCPS also set up a State Employment Office to ensure that farmers had the labor they needed. The food conservation program asked Minnesota households, hotels, and restaurants to observe "meatless" and "wheatless" days. Conservation programs were also created to reduce demand for coal and gasoline. Most people accepted these small sacrifices without complaint. Despite these efforts, food and fuel prices tended to rise, and the MCPS felt pressure to do something about the cost of living. Although they were vociferous opponents of socialism, the commissioners nevertheless pursued policies that restricted market relations.

The most ambitious effort was the commission's foray into the fishing business. The basic idea was to promote the consumption of so-called "rough fish," such as carp, dogfish, garfish, and other species, to increase the availability of a cheap protein source and lower the cost of living. In October, the MCPS authorized Carlos Avery, the state's game and fish commissioner, to license fishers to catch rough fish with seines as agents of the state. They staked him $1,000 to help cover initial costs. State institutions used the fish, and the surplus was sold through dealers "at a reasonable price taking into consideration . . . the cost of securing such fish." The project was limited to Red Lake and a few other lakes to minimize the interference with commercial fishing.[37]

Commercial fishers protested, but Avery was an adept practitioner of what Carl Chrislock playfully called "piscatorial socialism." He invited the commissioners to the capitol's restaurant for a luncheon, the centerpiece for which was a fourteen-pound carp. A St. Paul woman known for her rough fish recipes prepared the meals and published her recipes in the commission's bulletin. At the luncheon, Avery announced that seven thousand pounds of carp were about to be distributed to retail dealers in the Twin Cities at eight cents per pound with the understanding that they would sell to consumers at ten cents. By the end of the war, the MCPS had sold 1,630,366 pounds of fish through 182 markets at a total cost to consumers of $132,279. The commission estimated that consumers paid about 50 percent of the market rate for commonly sold fish. With the profits, Avery paid back the initial investment, bought new equipment, and returned a net profit to the state in the amount of about $35,000.[38]

The commission's successful fish enterprise was not enough to keep the cost of living in check. On November 2, the commission issued Order 13. This order fixed the maximum price that milk producers could charge Twin Cities wholesale distributers at six cents per quart and the price that distributors could charge consumers at ten cents per quart. A month later, the committee amended the order to raise the maximum prices by 10 percent in view of a rise in the price of cattle feed. This order stayed in place for the duration of the war.[39]

Controlling the price of bread was more difficult. The MCPS temporarily went into the bread distribution business, contracting with a large bakery to furnish pound loaves of bread at five and one-half cents, which the commission sold at thirteen cents for two loaves on a cash and carry system. This seemed to work, but after a month the commission retreated to price-fixing, issuing Order 18. This order required bakers in Minneapolis to deliver bread to grocers for not more than thirteen cents for a two-pound loaf and grocers to sell it at not more that fourteen cents. By March, the commission abandoned price-fixing for bread, in part because the federal government in late 1917 required bread to have at least 20 percent barley or corn flour. This added cost shrank the profit margins of bakers. The commission concluded that it lacked the staff or expertise to calculate a fair price for bread in all the regions of the state.[40]

The MCPS also worked to guarantee that Minnesota would have adequate and affordable coal supplies during the coming winter. A fuel famine would cause great hardship and undercut the production of war materiel. The state relied mostly on coal from the Appalachian coalfields, transported to Minnesota via the Great Lakes. Boats left Duluth-Superior with iron ore for steel plants in the eastern Great Lakes and returned filled with coal. Some boats came back empty, due in part to a shortage of railcars in the coalfields. Governor Burnquist sent urgent telegrams to Minnesota's two senators and to President Wilson, stating that "our people are looking forward to the coming winter with much apprehension," and asked the federal government to curb "the greed of [coal] producers and the inefficiency of carriers."[41]

In July, Burnquist appointed John McGee as the state's "special agent . . . to expedite coal shipments," and in August he traveled to Washington, DC, and Cleveland to investigate the coal situation. In October, he was appointed federal fuel administrator for Minnesota after the Wilson administration created the United States Fuel Administration. McGee set up fuel boards in each county to monitor needs, supply, prices, and the difference between the wholesale and retail price of coal. The federal government made sure that Minnesota and neighboring states received enough coal for the winter of 1917–18 to avoid hardship. It was up to McGee to keep the price under control and guarantee equitable distribution of a limited supply.

McGee issued an order in January 1918 establishing a schedule of retail gross margins, the amount a local dealer could charge for coal based on the wholesale cost, a complicated task because the margins had to be adjusted for different grades of coal and different localities. To ensure equitable supply, the federal fuel administration required every purchaser of hard coal (anthracite) to report to their dealer the details of their heating system, how much coal they had used in previous years, and how much they had on hand. Households were then issued fuel cards to regulate how much they could buy. Inevitably, the commission received complaints of discrimination, including letters charging that a household or business lacked an adequate supply while neighbors were "stocking up on coal."[42]

Energy conservation helped reduce demand for coal. There were federal campaigns urging people to inspect and repair furnaces, to keep room temperatures no higher than 65 or 68 degrees, to shorten office hours, and to use wood instead of coal whenever possible. The severity of the winter of 1917–18 led to more drastic measures. On January 18, 1918, a federal order closed all industrial plants for five days, and then all plants and businesses for the next ten Mondays, with certain exceptions. There were many complaints, but the closings were effective, and the federal administrator suspended the order after the third heatless Monday.[43]

The federal government and the MCPS waged similar campaigns to conserve gasoline and electricity. The federal administrator urged automobile owners to curtail driving for pleasure, and the commission suggested that they limit their Sunday drive to twenty-five miles. The federal government eventually asked people east of the Mississippi, but including all of the Twin Cities, to observe "gasless" Sundays. To conserve electricity, the federal government ordered in December that Thursday and Sunday be "lightless nights," meaning no advertising or ornamental lights, including, for example, retail store windows. Judge McGee followed this with an order that every night be lightless in communities where electricity was generated by burning coal. In the three large cities, electric railways adopted a "skip-stop" system, whereby cars stopped on alternate streets. Later in the war, Congress instituted "daylight saving time," the system of moving clocks ahead one hour in March to gain an extra hour of daylight in the evening and reduce electricity demand, and thereby began an endless debate.[44]

The regulation of liquor continued to find its way onto the commission's agenda. Although many of its orders restricted liquor sales, dry activists were disappointed that the commission would not order a statewide ban of alcohol sales. In lieu of that, they wanted the commission to ban liquor sales in wet counties that harbored saloons catering to crowds from surrounding dry areas. In response, the commission passed Order 10, banning alcohol sales between 5 PM and 9 AM in Martin County (on the Iowa border) and Pipestone County (on the South Dakota border). Prohibitionists then demanded that the commissioners apply the same rationale to the thriving saloons of Blooming Prairie, located in Steele County, a wet county surrounded by dry counties. In December, the commission issued an order closing the town's bars from 5 PM to 9 AM. In most counties, the saloonkeepers acquiesced to the commission's orders, but fourteen residents of Blooming Prairie traveled to St. Paul to petition the commission to modify the order. The commission refused, but resistance in Blooming Prairie was just beginning.[45]

Much of northern Minnesota was saloon free, thanks to the county option and treaties with the Ojibwe. However, shipments of liquor directly to consumers was legal, and dry activists complained that the railroads were shipping enormous amounts of liquor into dry counties. In September, the commission responded with Orders 11 and 12 forbidding the importation of alcohol into Koochiching, Beltrami, and Clearwater Counties, all of which were legally dry. In Koochiching County, which borders Canada, the commission also removed from office the sheriff and the mayors of International Falls and Ranier for their failure to quell the liquor traffic. Later they issued Orders 19 and 20 banning shipment of liquor into Polk County and Clay County. Then in January 1918, they issued Order 24 prohibiting the shipment of liquor into any county in which the sale of liquor was prohibited by either the county option or treaty.[46]

The commissioners operated with some restraint when imposing price controls or regulating liquor, aware that these policies would aggravate many people, regardless of their views on the war. They had no qualms about aggressively promoting Liberty Bonds, however, since they assumed that anyone who did not buy their fair share was a pro-German slacker. As noted earlier, Minnesota failed to meet its quota in the First Liberty Bond campaign in May 1917. In preparation for the Second Liberty Bond campaign in October, the commission announced it would promote bond sales "with every means within its power."[47]

The Federal Reserve Bank, which coordinated the bond sales, mounted an extensive publicity campaign, far exceeding what had been done for the first campaign. Newspapers, including those associated with the labor movement and the Nonpartisan League, carried free advertising for the campaign. Speakers, usually organized by the Four Minute Men, stumped for bond sales. Patriotic rallies kicked off the loan drive in local communities, often with well-known speakers including Theodore Roosevelt. The MCPS mobilized its county organizations to promote bond sales throughout the state. To generate enthusiasm, the commission organized competitions, awarding a banner to the county with the largest percentage of sale in proportion to its quota and to the county with the largest number of individual subscribers in proportion to its population. The banks who sold bonds throughout the state also greased the wheels by offering installment payment plans. The banks were happy to do so, since the bonds would revert to the bank for resale if a buyer failed to make all the payments.

During the second bond campaign a voluntary system of financing the war began to evolve into a system of compulsion. In September, Arthur Rogers, chairman of the Ninth District's bond campaign, told local campaign organizers that his office would maintain a record of bond purchasers. Those who failed to buy bonds when asked would be recorded separately on blue cards. Meanwhile, Commissioner

A rally for the Second Liberty Bond campaign featuring a fire truck in front of the Donaldson's department store in downtown Minneapolis. *Courtesy of Hennepin County Public Library Special Collections*

Ames told the county MCPS directors that the bond campaign was a weapon against disloyalty. "If the Germans know what is good for them," he told them, "they will come across strongly on these government bonds." He also used the bond campaign to threaten Brown County, the county seat of which was New Ulm. He told its MCPS director that "certainly there is no county in the State that is more in need of redemption in the eyes of the world." Brown County exceeded its quotas, but the director did not like to be threatened. "We subscribed," he wrote to Ames, "not because we had any good name that needed redeeming, but because it seemed a patriotic duty."[48]

The more aggressive approach paid off. Minnesotans purchased $141 million in bonds, 35 percent above the goal. About one-third of counties oversubscribed their quotas. Lake County won the prize for oversubscribing by 371 percent, and Nobles County won the prize for the largest percentage of subscribers (about 33 percent). However, two-thirds of counties did not meet their quotas, some not even close, a shortage that was made up by the strong sales in Minneapolis, St. Paul, and Duluth. In its weekly newsletter, the commission suggested that a lack of patriotism was behind the slow bond sales in many rural communities. The next bond campaigns would be even less voluntary.[49]

The Titans of Progressivism Clash in St. Paul

Food, fuel, liquor, and bonds were important, but the MCPS was increasingly fixated on the Nonpartisan League and organized labor, and especially the threat posed by the possible alliance of the two. Senator Robert La Follette's September 20 speech at a large NPL meeting confirmed their fears while at the same time providing an opportunity to paint La Follette and the NPL as treasonous. Theodore Roosevelt, who stormed into town a week later, played the starring role in the anti-NPL reaction. La Follette and Roosevelt were, or had been, the dominant politicians of the Progressive movement. If Roosevelt had not bolted the Republican Party in 1912, the Progressive Party likely would have nominated La Follette rather than Roosevelt as its presidential candidate. La Follette never wavered in his Progressive beliefs. Roosevelt had returned to the Republicans and, in particular, the party's conservative and militaristic wing.

■ **The St. Paul appearances in September 1917 of Senator Robert La Follette and former president Theodore Roosevelt, both Republicans, dramatized the deep divisions within midwestern states like Minnesota.** *MNHS collections*

La Follette was the featured speaker at the Producers and Consumers Convention, which the Nonpartisan League organized to give farmers and workers a voice in the ongoing debate about how the government should regulate the economy during wartime. The four-day event began in Fargo on September 17, and then moved to the St. Paul Auditorium for the final three days. NPL farmers thought the price the federal government set for wheat was too low. Workers felt the cost of living was outpacing the wage growth. The NPL leaders favored price controls that would adequately compensate wheat farmers while at the same time keep the price of bread at a reasonable level. The NPL hoped the convention would help build an alliance between farmers and organized labor, a prerequisite for electoral success in Minnesota.[50]

The NPL leaders were so focused on their economic agenda that they were unprepared when the MCPS and most newspapers mounted a ferocious attack on their loyalty. They were vulnerable because some key NPL figures had come from the Socialist Party, had campaigned against the US entry into the European war, and in some cases continued their opposition after Congress had declared war. The leadership may have thought they were protected because the NPL had officially supported the war effort. In June 1917, Joseph Gilbert drafted a war program that was endorsed by NPL meetings throughout the state and published in a pamphlet. "We stand for our country, right or wrong, as against foreign government with which we are actually engaged in war," the program asserted, but it went on to say that "when we believe our country wrong, we should endeavor to make it right." The NPL war program opposed wars for annexation, "either on our part or that of our allies," and demanded the "abolition of secret diplomacy."[51]

The NPL backed up their statement by vigorously participating in Liberty Bond campaigns. North Dakota, where they controlled state government, far exceeded its bond sale quota in the first campaign. NPL support for the war, however, was complicated by two demands. First, the NPL called on the Wilson administration and the Allies to state their war aims. Conservative politicians and newspapers considered this to be almost treasonous, arguing that there would be time enough to discuss war aims after Germany was smashed. Secondly, the NPL argued that if men were conscripted to fight in Europe, then wealth should be conscripted to support the military. The NPL argued that corporations like U.S. Steel and Dupont were reaping great profits from the war while "a species of coercion" was being used to urge poorly paid workers to buy Liberty Bonds. For business leaders and many newspapers, this sounded like Socialist rhetoric.[52]

The Producers and Consumers Convention got off to a strong start, attracting big crowds drawn by a list of well-known speakers, including Idaho senator William Borah, North Dakota senator Asle J. Gronna, Montana congresswoman Jeanette Rankin, former Minnesota congressman Charles Lindbergh, Minneapolis mayor Thomas Van Lear, and St. Paul mayor Vivian Irvin. Speakers from several federal agencies appeared, including representative of the Federal Trade Commission and the Department of Agriculture. Judge Eli Torrance, former head of the Minnesota Grand Army of the Republic, was invited to make a speech pitching Liberty Bonds. Governor Lynn Frazier and congressman John Baer, two NPL politicians who had won elections in 1916, addressed the Fargo session of the convention.[53]

The convention marked the debut of Charles Lindbergh as a major figure within the NPL. Lindbergh had written a few articles for the *Nonpartisan Leader* in 1915, and in early 1917 he wrote to the NPL suggesting that his new book might be of use to the organization. In the summer, Henry Teigan, the NPL national secretary, invited him to a meeting with Townley, who, Teigan said, "feels that you are in thorough sympathy with this organization." From that point, Lindbergh was part of the inner circles of the NPL. Townley asked him to give a major address on the third evening of the convention. Speaking to a crowd of about eight thousand, he reiterated his populist themes about economic inequality and the great influence Wall Street bankers had on the cost of living. He argued for a pay-as-you-go approach to funding the war, and ultimately for a restructured economy in which money lending would not be a profit-making business. He also mentioned the importance of free speech, and declared that it was not disloyal to speak out about the country's problems during wartime.[54]

Lindbergh's speech was met with a warm response, but was largely forgotten after Senator La Follette's appearance closing the convention the next day. The NPL was playing with fire when they invited La Follette as its marquee speaker. He was perhaps the most famous opponent of the war, and the newspapers warned that La Follette would give a "disloyal" speech. Townley apparently worried that La Follette's planned topic—the right to free speech during wartime—was too provocative. Fearing a public relations disaster, he sent two lawyers, William Lemke and James Manahan, to La Follette's hotel room. After talking to Manahan and Lemke, La Follette agreed to set aside his prepared speech and speak extemporaneously, focusing on wartime finance. Sticking to a prepared text might have been a better idea.

Lemke was one of the founding members of the NPL. He grew up on a North Dakota farm, went east to law school at Yale, and then returned to practice law in Fargo. Well known as an advocate for farmers, he joined forces with Townley in 1915. James Manahan was raised on a southern Minnesota farm and earned a law degree at the University of Minnesota. He had been an ardent supporter of William

Jennings Bryan's presidential campaigns, and in 1908 crossed over to the Republican side as an ally of La Follette. In 1912, he was elected to Minnesota's at-large seat in Congress, and when redistricting ended that seat in 1914, he decided not to run again. He was an active supporter of farmers' organizations like the Equity League, a precursor to the NPL. He was one of the NPL's lawyers, and one of its most effective stump speakers. He was also valuable because of his impeccable credentials as a supporter of the war effort. Manahan, for example, was the featured speaker at the Memorial Day celebrations in Red Wing the previous May, earning the praise of Jens Grondahl, who by that time was refashioning himself as a superpatriot. Grondahl must have been surprised to find Manahan at the center of the organization he detested.[55]

La Follette was greeted by a spontaneous demonstration when he entered the packed auditorium, and his speech was interrupted repeatedly with applause and cheering. At one point, he digressed to mention why he had voted against the war. When a heckler yelled, "Yellow," La Follette and Townley had to intervene to make sure the crowd did not attack the man. "I don't mean to say that we hadn't suffered grievances," La Follette continued, "we had, at the hands of Germany, serious grievances." Referring to the *Lusitania*, he noted that Germany had violated the right of Americans to travel on the high seas, "on ships loaded with munitions for Great Britain." He added that Secretary of State William Jennings Bryan had warned President Wilson four days before the *Lusitania* sailed that it had a large cargo of ammunition and explosives. He told the crowd that "this comparatively small privilege" of sailing on a munition-laden ship flying a foreign flag was in his opinion not enough to justify the involvement of the United States "in the loss of millions and millions of lives."[56]

Twin Cities newspapers blasted his speech as proof of disloyalty. For many, the sinking of the *Lusitania* was the ultimate proof of German barbarity. The fact that few people in 1915 considered it a cause of war had been forgotten. Generally, local newspapers attacked La Follette for what he said, but an Associated Press reporter compounded the damage nationwide by misquoting La Follette this way: "We had no grievances against Germany." Eight months later the AP acknowledged that the word "no" was an "unfortunate error."[57]

The convention passed a resolution pledging full support to the government in the war effort, advancing the league's proposals for war finance and price controls, and advocating close cooperation between farmers and organized labor. The resolution concluded with stirring patriotic language. "We pledge our lives, our fortunes, and our sacred honor to our country and our flag in this, our war." The newspapers showed little interest in the resolution, except to say, with some justification, that the tone of many speeches, including those by Townley, Van Lear, and La Follette, were out of sync with the sentiment of the resolution.[58]

Theodore Roosevelt arrived a week later. Labor's Loyal Legion invited him to boost the Second Liberty Bond campaign, but the timing of his visit was a bonus for conservatives. In a single day he spoke at four venues, including both the St. Paul Auditorium and the Minneapolis Auditorium. He devoted as much time to attacking La Follette and other war critics as selling Liberty Bonds.[59]

It was a big day for St. Paul. Roosevelt was feted in a parade that he led and then watched from a reviewing stand in Rice Park. Newspapers estimated seventy-five thousand lined the parade route. Then Roosevelt spoke to eleven thousand in the St. Paul Auditorium, starting his speech by announcing that "they held disloyalty day last week," referring to the NPL convention, "and we'll hold loyalty day this week." His attack on La Follette hinged on the term "shadow Hun." Referring to German submarine warfare, Roosevelt said he hated "the Hun without our gates, I abhor still more the Hun within our gates who apologizes for, condones, excuses such infamy." He included Senator Gronna and Minnesota congressman Ernest Lundeen among the "shadow Huns," and concluded that Senator La Follette was "the most sinister enemy of democracy in the United States." He said that at one time he had felt "great sympathy" for the Nonpartisan League, but that La Follette's speech had "excited his . . . scornful repudiation" of the organization. At the end of the meeting, the crowd adopted a resolution calling for La Follette's ouster from the Senate.

Taking Aim at the Nonpartisan League

Roosevelt's rhetoric invigorated conservative forces. The *St. Paul Pioneer Press* wrote that the patriotic fervor displayed by thousands "removed the blot cast by the notorious La Follette incident" and put

St. Paul "back on the map as . . . a loyalty center." The former president's blunt rhetoric also set the tone for a multifront escalation of the anti-NPL offensive.[60]

Business leaders had been worrying about the NPL since the 1916 election, and especially after the NPL moved its national office to St. Paul in early 1917. They searched for a way to undermine the NPL's growing popularity among farmers. One early tactic was the creation of a phony league to confuse farmers. In March 1917, a group of St. Paul businessmen incorporated a "Minnesota Nonpartisan League," which published several issues of a newspaper, the *Non-Partisan*, in an attempt to win over farmers attracted to the real Nonpartisan League. This ploy was clumsily executed and abandoned by mid-summer.[61]

A few days after La Follette's speech, the MCPS opened an investigation of the NPL by summoning Arthur Townley to appear for questioning. Townley responded immediately, appearing that same day, accompanied by James Manahan. Townley testified that he had negotiated with La Follette not to address the wisdom of America's entry into the war. Townley replied that "there is no doubt in my mind" that La Follette's speech was "seditious and disloyal." Commissioner Ames questioned Townley about NPL organizing in Brown County, trying to link the NPL to the New Ulm rally. Townley responded that the NPL was successfully recruiting Brown County farmers, but that he instructed organizers not to discuss the war.[62]

When Townley departed, Ames introduced a resolution, prepared in advance, which called on the US Senate to expel La Follette because his speech had encouraged treasonable sentiments. The resolution also called on the federal government to investigate La Follette and NPL speakers for sedition. However, the Wilson administration was at that same time courting the NPL to strengthen the allegiance of midwestern farmers. To the dismay of the MCPS and local business leaders, George Creel, director of the CPI, arranged for Townley to come to Washington in early December to meet with President Wilson and food administrator Herbert Hoover. The meetings apparently went well. The MCPS and the federal government were completely at odds over the NPL, and the breach would continue to grow.[63]

In early October, the MCPS appointed Commissioner Ames to oversee the NPL investigation, citing "numerous complaints . . . alleging that said organization is disloyal and guilty of disseminating sedition and disloyal propaganda." Early reports that reached Ames, however, indicated that Townley's speeches were explicitly loyal, even to the point of appealing for support of the Red Cross and Liberty Bonds. Nevertheless, the MCPS actively encouraged the harassment of NPL around the state.[64]

When Henry Libby, the MCPS secretary, obtained a copy of the speakers' itinerary for the NPL's planned organizing drive, he sent letters to the MCPS directors in fifteen counties where the league was scheduled to speak. He instructed them to have stenographers at the meetings to record any seditious utterances. Some local safety commissions responded by prohibiting all NPL meetings. The director in Otter Tail County, for example, informed Townley that his planned meeting in Fergus Falls was banned, and if he did appear, the mayor had ordered the police not to interfere if local citizens threw "ancient eggs and other missiles" at him. In a letter to Henry Libby, the director reported that the mayor had instructed the police officers "to molest no one who goes after Mr. Townley in a rough way."[65]

Some county directors sought advice. The Becker County director asked if Townley's scheduled speech in Detroit should be banned. Libby sent back the standard reply, which was that the MCPS had taken no position and that banning a meeting was entirely within the discretion of the local sheriff. He sent local officials the October 10 memorandum of Attorney General Lyndon Smith, a member of the MCPS, about the duties of sheriffs. Although "that which disturbs the peace must be prevented," he wrote, "the exercise of legitimate freedom of speech is not a disturbance of the peace." It was up to the sheriff to decide "between these two things." This apparent defense of free speech was undercut by the last line of his memorandum, which stated that "any meeting, the tendency of which is to create or promote disloyalty to the United States in time of war should not be tolerated." Since the MCPS was routinely characterizing the NPL as disloyal, Smith opened the door to suppression.[66]

The NPL sometimes managed to move a banned meeting to another town. Wabasha County sheriff Julius E. Boehlke banned a Townley speech scheduled for early October in Lake City on the grounds that public opposition to the league was so strong that there might be a riot. The sheriff's rationale essentially allowed Townley's opponents to negate his First Amendment rights, but the sheriff's prediction that anti-league forces were capable of violence was undoubtedly true. The NPL moved the meeting to Dumfries, and claimed that the attempt to suppress the meeting had led to a larger turnout. In Blue Earth County, the NPL rented a hall in Mankato for a speech by Townley. When business leaders pressured the venue to return the rental fee, the NPL transferred the event to Nicollet, fifteen miles northwest of Mankato. Townley's scheduled speech in Slayton in Murray County was blocked when the local Commercial Club prevailed on the village council to ban any NPL meeting. The meeting was successfully moved six miles west to the little town of Hadley.[67]

A Pine County incident nearly ended in tragedy. An angry mob led by the postmaster attacked two NPL organizers trying to recruit farmers in November. Fearing for his life, N. S. Randall, one of the NPL organizers, was relieved when the sheriff, the county MCPS director, and a local Home Guard unit arrived at the chaotic scene. The sheriff, however, was a passive observer, and the Home Guard was divided between those who wanted to prevent mob violence and those who wanted to let the mob have its way, which meant the use of hot tar or worse. Fortunately, Randall fell into the hands of the first faction. They drove him to a neighboring town while his fellow organizer escaped there in his car. The county director advised them to leave the county by back roads to avoid the mob. He told them not to come back because the next NPL man might be lynched. In 1918, scenes like these would be commonplace.[68]

County sheriffs, as Carl Chrislock put it, were the "shock troops" of the MCPS. Not all sheriffs were swept up in the anti-NPL movement, however. James Mitchell, Nobles County sheriff, reported to Attorney General Smith that Townley's speech in Worthington "was the most patriotic one heard in this city since the war began." He praised Townley for increasing Liberty Bonds sales. The NPL newspaper reported that the Kandiyohi sheriff attended Townley's speech in Litchfield because Townley was scheduled to speak in Willmar, his county seat. The sheriff told Townley that if he gave the same speech in Willmar, he would have no objection, since "what you said today is what we all believe in."[69]

In the Twin Cities, business leaders met at the St. Paul Hotel in early October to plan a huge convention to "stand as a final, crushing, cleansing answer to the polluting Nonpartisan League gathering in this city." The attendees agreed that the league was a pro-German organization, and more to the point, was endangering "the commercial life of Minnesota." One participant suggested shooting Townley and La Follette, but the group settled on a two-day loyalty rally, with the first day in St. Paul and the second in Minneapolis.[70]

The organizers put out a statewide call for county-level loyalty conventions to choose delegates for the Twin Cities meetings. The call was signed by Marion Burton, the university president, George Lawson, secretary of the Minnesota Federation of Labor, George W. Buffington, president of the Minnesota Bar Association, and a lengthy list of business and media leaders. In Winona, for example, the Association of Commerce organized a meeting attended by five hundred participants who chose delegates. In the keynote address, attorney Edward Lees sounded very much like John McGee when he said that "in a time of war, a citizen who is not for his country is against it—there is no middle ground."[71]

The organizers told the press that delegates from all eighty-six counties were represented at the Twin Cities meetings. Former St. Paul mayor Daniel Lawler presided, and he told the crowd that the purpose of the meeting was to "obliterate completely any stain that might be left from the Nonpartisan League conference where La Follette was the headliner." More ominously, Lawler also said that the "air of the North Star State was too pure for traitors to breathe." Senators Knute Nelson and Frank Kellogg spoke, as did Governor Burnquist. The crowd also heard a brief statement from President Wilson, who praised the loyalty of the "great Northwest." The president, however, did not mention the NPL.[72]

A new organization, the America First Association, emerged from the loyalty rallies, and in the following weeks meetings were held around the state to create county-level affiliates. The organization sought to foster a spirit of "Americanism," grounded in the belief, as one speaker put it, that "the spirit of Prussianism and the spirit of Americanism cannot live in the same world." The goal was to win every Minnesotan over to the belief that the conflict was "not a rich man's war, or a poor man's war, or a politician's war, but a war of every man, woman, and child in America."[73]

SEVEN

URBAN AND RURAL SKIRMISHES

WINTER 1917–1918

You see my friends, the welfare of all who work in the city or out on the land is of one piece; and the welfare of all classes is measured out by the machinery of government. The streetcar company and its franchise to use our streets for profit, is all a matter of law. . . . So too is the Public Safety Commission a creature of law, but that does not give it the right to say you shall not, while at work, wear your union button. . . . That commission was created for war purposes—not to play the childish game of button, button, who has the button?

JAMES MANAHAN, attorney for the Nonpartisan League, recounting his December 2, 1917, speech in St. Paul during the transit workers strike for which he was indicted, in his memoir *Trials of a Lawyer*

Last fall men who ought to be in jail and about whose disloyalty there is no doubt, taking advantage of the distressing war conditions in this state, attempted to organize the employees of the Traction company into a union. . . . Minnesota quickly placed thirty-five hundred troops in the Twin Cities and the rioters were as scarce as hen's teeth. . . . Here the matter ended and never would have been heard from again had Washington not interfered in a matter purely local. . . . A commission was sent here that started the pot to boiling again.

JOHN MCGEE explaining the transit workers strike to the US fuel administrator in a March 11, 1918, telegram

FOR THE ALLIES, the final months of 1917 were bleak. In November, the German and Austro-Hungarian armies ended the stalemate on the Italian front by breaking through at Caporetto, inflicting on Italy a devastating defeat in which 600,000 of its soldiers were captured or deserted. Simultaneously, the Bolsheviks seized power in Petrograd and began to negotiate a peace treaty with Germany, crushing the Allies' ill-founded hope that the Provisional Government that replaced Tsar Nicholas II would rally the Russian people to continue the war against Germany. In fact, the Bolsheviks' popularity was fueled by the fact that they were the only party promising to take Russia out of the war.

The Allies were encouraged by the fact that the United States was preparing a massive army that would eventually fight in France. By the end of 1917, however, only about 175,000 soldiers had arrived, most of whom were not yet on the front lines. Many more were training in hastily constructed cantonments across the United States. Eventually over two million Americans would reach France, although some arrived only a few weeks before the armistice.

Soldiers and Objectors

Most Minnesota draftees were sent to Camp Dodge in Iowa, but some were assigned to Camp Pike in Arkansas, Camp Lewis in Washington, Camp Grant in Illinois, and Camp Wadsworth in South Carolina. The Minnesota draftees arriving at Camp Dodge hoped they would be kept together in companies assigned to the 88th Division that was being organized there. Before long, however, Minnesota draftees were being transferred to other camps and assigned to other units. The regular arrival of new recruits and the frequent transfer of partially trained men slowed the development of the division, leading some to wonder if the 88th would ever sail for France.[1]

In December, the Supreme Court decided the case of the four Minnesota Socialists convicted for refusal to register for the draft. The court rejected the argument that the Selective Service Act violated the Thirteenth Amendment, which outlawed slavery and involuntary servitude. In February, three of those Socialists, Joseph Arver, Alfred Grahl, and Walter Wangerin, began serving their one-year prison sentence. The fourth Minnesotan, Otto Wangerin, had already been drafted because his number had been reached. In September, he joined the other recruits at Camp Dodge, but once there, refused to wear a uniform. In November, he was court-martialed and sentenced to fifteen years at the prison at Leavenworth, Kansas. In January, eleven more Socialists were convicted. This time, however, they were sentenced to time already served and immediately conscripted, even though some of them might have been entitled to exemptions. The army felt it could intimidate dissenters into compliance once it had control of them at the training camps. This often worked, but some of the Minnesota Socialists refused to cooperate at Camp Dodge and were court-martialed, receiving sentences of twenty to twenty-five years.[2]

Two well-known Socialists who chose a different path were mayor Tom Van Lear's sons, Ralph and Howard. When they registered for the draft, they wrote "conscientious scruples against war" as a basis for exemption. Ralph was the first to be called, and his draft board denied his claim, which after all had no basis in law. He was drafted and sent to Camp Dodge, where he was assigned to a field artillery unit. In October 1917, he was sentenced to thirty days in the guardhouse for an alleged breach of sanitary regulations. Fort Dodge officials claimed to be planning further charges against him, expressing frustration with the publicity he was generating, which in their view unfairly painted him as a victim of military injustice. Perhaps to spare his father more difficulties back home, Van Lear came to some accommodation with his superiors while in the guardhouse. When he was released on November 1, he was assigned to the 163rd Depot Brigade, the unit responsible for running the camp. Howard was inducted in 1918, and he apparently did not press his exemption claim.[3]

Most cases of non-registration originated in northern Minnesota, especially among recent immigrants from Finland or the Austro-Hungarian empire (which might include Czechs, Slovaks, Poles, Italians, and others). During the war, US attorney Alfred Jaques charged 416 Minnesota men with evading the Selective Service Act. Of these, 288 were convicted and just a few were acquitted. Most of the remaining cases pending at the armistice were dropped by the federal prosecutors.[4]

At Camp Cody in New Mexico the three Minnesota National Guard infantry regiments were assigned to the new 34th Division, along with guard units from Iowa, the Dakotas, and Nebraska. The

Minnesotans were relieved to find their units were kept intact in the newly formed division, at least at first. However, since most units were short of men, the army began transferring draftees from various cantonments, including Camp Dodge, to fill out the units of the 34th Division. As a result, the division came together slowly, although the pace of its development apparently improved in December when Lieutenant Colonel Hugh McGee, the son of John McGee, was promoted to assistant chief of staff and placed in charge of training. McGee had to deal with a shortage of officers, a lack of equipment, an epidemic of German measles, and, worst of all, sandstorms that brought all outdoor activity to a halt.

Each division of the army had a nickname, and the 34th decided to call itself "the Sandstorm Division," which was more likely a lament about what they were suffering in the desert than a boast about what they would inflict on the enemy. Bjorn Winger, a graduate of St. Olaf College and a member of the Field Hospital unit of the 2nd Minnesota infantry, wrote the poem "The Sands of Cody" for the regimental newspaper, expressing the soldiers' feeling about the camp's environment:

It isn't the cold we fear,
It isn't the snow that flies,
It isn't this hades dear
That troubles us hard-boiled guys—
It isn't the drill or the hike
That curses this starved-out land,
It's the drifting, shifting, every-lifting
SAND, SAND, SAND.

Complaints about conditions at Camp Cody reached Minnesota by the end of the year. After visiting the camp, Harold Knutson, the Sixth District congressman, made a blistering speech in Congress criticizing the camp, which he called an "annex of hades." His fellow members of Congress chuckled when he said that if he were in "fear of the hereafter, I would first go to Camp Cody for a preparatory course." His hyperbolic rhetoric provoked the Minnesota Commission of Public Safety to send a committee led by Governor Burnquist to investigate the camp. The committee recommended that the troops be moved to another camp because the dust and extreme ranges in temperature had caused serious health issues. The War Department responded that the camp was no more harmful to health than any other. The Minnesotans would endure many more months in the desert before sailing for France.[5]

Which Side Are You On?

Back in Minnesota, an attempt by workers at the Twin Cities Rapid Transit Company to organize a union led to an angry confrontation in October and, after a brief truce, a second, more tumultuous battle starting in December. The strike pitted the labor unions against not only the transit company but the Minnesota Commission of Public Safety. This was the most violent labor conflict in Minnesota during the war, and one with lasting implications.

The Minneapolis Civic and Commerce Association had a long tradition of successfully thwarting union organizing, or as they put it, maintaining an "open shop" system. The MCCA sponsored the Citizens Alliance, a coalition of businesses dedicated to actively stopping union organizing. The alliance could rely on the active support of the Civilian Auxiliary, a private militia of businessmen which was organized immediately after the declaration of war. When Secretary of Labor William B. Wilson urged business and labor to avoid conflicts that would disrupt the war economy, the Citizens Alliance took this to mean that the status quo could not be altered during the war: in other words, no union organizing. Trade unions countered that the war should not preclude peaceful organizing of trade unions and collective bargaining.[6]

In August 1917, a group of workers asked Horace Lowry, head of the Twin City Rapid Transit Company, for a raise. When he declined, they contacted the International Amalgamated Association of Street and Electrical Employees, a national union representing transit workers. The union sent representatives to the Twin Cities who quickly organized locals in both cities that were recognized by the Minnesota Federation of Labor. Aware of these developments, business leaders prepared to execute their well-practiced strategy, which involved refusing to negotiate, firing union leaders, hiring replacement workers, and then overwhelming the strikers with superior force. In preparation for the last element, the Civilian Auxiliary met at the Minneapolis Athletic

Club on September 6 to reorganize into four companies of 150 men each. A week later, Hennepin County sheriff Otto Langum, a member of the MCCA, deputized the entire group of six hundred, conferring official status on the employers' militia. Waiting in the wings were the recently formed units of the Home Guard, ready to fill in for Minnesota National Guard units training at Camp Cody.[7]

On September 22, Lowry fired thirty-two union men, and shortly thereafter twenty-five others. The union demanded their reinstatement. He refused, but offered a 10 percent wage increase. The union rejected the offer and began a strike on October 6. The Civilian Auxiliary quickly mobilized in Minneapolis to protect the streetcars and the carmen who reported for work. There was some minor violence, but service was not interrupted. There were four days of violence in St. Paul, however, as mobs attacked streetcars, breaking windows, pulling crews out of cars, and slowing or stopping service. Unlike Minneapolis, no private militia patrolled the streets. Apparently, city, county, and state officials bickered behind the scenes about how to respond. On October 7, a "provost guard" composed of soldiers from the officer training companies at Fort Snelling arrived in St. Paul because the mob of the previous evening had included several soldiers in uniform. The provost guard discouraged rioters at least for that evening. On October 9, the MCPS ordered the end of the strike and the reinstatement of the fired men pending an investigation of each case. The union declared a victory and, quite prematurely, organized a victory parade that evening that degenerated into more rioting. The St. Paul battalion of Home Guard was assembled in the armory, but the governor did not order its members onto the streets.[8]

Striking carmen, and their wives and even children, were involved in the disturbances, but they were joined by others who used the labor conflict to vent their anger about grievances unrelated to the streetcar company. Police arrested only thirty men during the riots, not one of whom was a striking carman or a member of organized labor. Working people felt squeezed by rising prices and wartime shortages. Many in the German, Scandinavian, and Irish communities of St. Paul had reason to be feel unjustly criticized as insufficiently loyal. Soldiers may have had their own reasons for rebelling. Beyond specific expressions of grievance, chaotic scenes attract individuals who revel in destruction when the chance of consequence is small.[9]

■ **The streetcar strike in late 1917 pitted the labor movement against both the Twin Cities Rapid Transit Company and the Minnesota Commission of Public Safety.** ***MNHS collections***

The MCPS stopped the strike but did not settle the dispute. The union continued to recruit members, and Lowry responded by organizing a "company union" called the Trainmen's Co-operative and Protective Association. He named himself president. Thus started the button war. Members of the union and the protective association wore buttons on their caps to clearly identify which side they were on. The union complained that managers harassed union members, and the MCPS responded by appointing a three-man committee to investigate. On November 19, the committee recommended that all buttons be banned and that all union solicitation cease. The next day, the MCPS adopted these recommendations and passed McGee's resolution outlawing union organizing for the duration of the war. Before the union members could vote on whether to remove their buttons, Lowry posted an order prohibiting the wearing of any button. About eight hundred union members interpreted this as a lockout. The MCPS then issued Order 16, giving the committee's recommendations the force of law. The second strike had begun, and the union was now in conflict with both Lowry and the MCPS.[10]

With tensions escalating, the Department of Labor in Washington decided to intervene by appointing a mediator. The union welcomed this development, but Lowry indignantly rejected it. Both the MCCA and the St. Paul Association sent telegrams to Washington opposing this move, and indicating their complete confidence in the MCPS to resolve the dispute. Very likely they feared their chance for a complete victory would be undermined by federal arbitration. The MCCA's telegram to President Wilson stated that "any intervention in the way of arbitration . . . would result in the undermining of the state public safety commission and . . . would impair their influence [and] lessen their hold upon our people and thereby encourage disloyalty and sedition which are now fairly under control." The St. Paul Association expressed its "absolute confidence in the wisdom, ability, integrity, and disinterestedness" of the commission. On the same day, Burnquist telegraphed the secretary of labor, warning the federal government to back off, stating that "interference at this time will simply result in an attempt to defy a duly constitutional authority of Minnesota." His message was clear: "I shall use every power at my constitutional command to uphold the dignity of the State and to protect the rights of all concerned."[11]

The trade union leaders fired back a blistering reply authored by E. H. Hall, the Minnesota Federation of Labor president; James Clancy, president of the St. Paul Trades and Labor Assembly; and L. J. Frank, representing the railroad metal trades. They told the governor and the commission that they opposed the button order as a violation of their fundamental rights and called for federal intervention. Although well known for their moderate views, they went so far as to say that the governor "by attempting to usurp the right of the people in upholding the Safety commission in the issuing of its strike-breaking and slave-making order, cannot escape the appearance of aiming to aid the streetcar company." The leaders concluded that the transit workers were willing to comply with the decision of the federal government but the company was not.[12]

On December 2, a labor rally in a downtown park led to another round of rioting, as frustrated workers once again took out their anger on streetcars and nonunion trainmen. Among the speakers at the rally were Oscar Keller, a member of the city council; T. J. McGrath, who represented St. Paul in the Minnesota legislature; and James Manahan, the former congressman, who spoke as a representative of the Nonpartisan League. Consistent with the NPL's strategy of building solidarity with trade unions, Manahan stressed the common interests of farmers and workers, while criticizing the MCPS for "playing

▪ James Manahan, attorney for the Nonpartisan League, was charged with sedition for a speech he made in Rice Park during the streetcar strike. *MNHS collections*

a childish game of button, button who has the button." All three were subsequently indicted for inciting the riot, although they had spoken against violence and urged the trainmen to express their feeling through the ballot box.[13]

Once again, authorities in St. Paul did not move aggressively against the rioters, while in Minneapolis, Sheriff Langum called upon the Civilian Auxiliary to protect streetcars. Later in the day, Burnquist called out the four companies of the 1st Battalion of the Home Guard, the local unit composed of St. Paul men, under the command of Major W. D. Mitchell, an attorney who would later serve as attorney general under President Hoover. On December 3, the governor dismissed Ramsey County sheriff John Wagener, and his replacement quickly deputized all members of the 1st Battalion. The governor had received a petition from the St. Paul Association, the business group, criticizing Wagener's failure to act, and a statement from Major Mitchell complaining of Wagener's lack of cooperation.[14]

On December 4, Burnquist ordered Adjutant General Rhinow to mobilize Home Guard battalions from around the state. Many Home Guard units were still being organized, but Rhinow was able to call on several battalions that had been training since the summer. About 3,500 merchants, professionals, and businessmen, armed and in uniform, were soon patrolling the streets of St. Paul. Among the first to arrive was the 7th Battalion's Company C, which took a special overnight train from Austin, and the 9th Battalion's Company A from Morris. They were soon joined by companies of the 3rd Battalion from Duluth; the 5th Battalion companies from Red Wing, South St. Paul, and Winona; the 6th Battalion company from Mankato; and companies of the 7th Battalion headquartered in Faribault. Also in St. Paul were companies from the 11th Battalion headquartered in Crookston and the 14th Battalion's Company A from Park Rapids, a group of men who were all members of the National Rifle Association.[15]

The trade union movement called a labor convention to open on December 5 at the St. Paul Auditorium and stay in session until the strike was settled. Fearing this would lead to a general strike, Secretary of War Newton Baker telegraphed Burnquist on December 4 asking him to rescind Order 16 and accept federal mediation. The governor angrily responded that "reopening of the decision now . . . would be a surrender of government by reason of riots and agitation and would

Home Guard units, armed with clubs and pistols, came from around the state to patrol downtown St. Paul during the streetcar strike. *MNHS collections*

be an incentive to further riots and agitation." The federal officials hesitated, worried about the impact of a general strike but unwilling to break with the governor and the MCPS.[16]

The crowd of fifteen thousand who attended the convention heard a variety of speakers. Mayor Van Lear denounced the MCCA and the MCPS, noting that the unions were in accord with the federal government. Mayor Irwin of St. Paul also spoke. Several speakers represented the Nonpartisan League, including James Manahan, reprising the gist of the speech that had recently gotten him arrested. He called on federal officials to intervene in the hopes that "they will not allow the pinheads in control of affairs here to bring disaster on the country." The convention decided to call a sympathy strike if there was no federal intervention by December 11.[17]

When that day was reached, the Minnesota Federation of Labor leaders called a strike to begin on December 13 at 10:00 AM. All liquor stores were closed, the new acting sheriff and the Home Guard stood ready in St. Paul, and Sheriff Otto Langum and the Civilian Auxiliary were on alert in Minneapolis. An estimated ten thousand workers had left their jobs by noon, and at that point Secretary of War Nelson Baker telegraphed William B. Wilson, chairman of the president's Mediation Commission, requesting that the commission come to the Twin Cities to investigate the controversy. When E. H. Hall, president of the Minnesota Federation of Labor, heard this news, he called off the strike, three and a half hours after it had begun.[18]

The moderate union leaders who found themselves leading a militant sympathy strike must have been relieved by Baker's intervention, so much so that when the federal mediators arrived on December 19, they signed an agreement pledging no further strikes pending the resolution of the controversy by the federal mediators. With that, in the words of William Millikan, the leading historian of these events, "the union had signed away their last chance." Lowry and the MCPS had no intention of honoring the recommendations of the president's mediators and, further, understood that the federal government could not force them. The president's commission could only resolve labor disputes when both sides were willing to negotiate in good faith to sustain the war effort. For Lowry, Burnquist, and McGee nothing was more important than maintaining the "open shop," no matter the cost.[19]

After the holidays, while the unions waited for the president's

Mediation Commission to complete its report, Lowry began advertising in small towns across the state to recruit new workers. He had no intention of rehiring anyone connected with the union. On February 14, 1918, the Mediation Commission sent its report to Nelson Baker, who the next day forwarded it to the MCPS. The mediators recommended that the company rehire union men who were available at their prestrike wages and not discriminate against members of the union. The report found that the company had hired twenty-seven men from outside the Cities even though "several hundred of the former employees of the company, many of them with years of service, remain unemployed in the Twin Cities." The mediators noted that hiring rural workers violated the federal government's policy that men employed in agriculture not be hired in non-war industries. Lowry refused to comply, and Ambrose Tighe issued an opinion that the MCPS was powerless to act.[20]

On April 8, 1918, trade unions nationwide were encouraged by President Wilson's proclamation adopting a statement of principles that emerged from the National War Labor Conference, chaired by former president William Taft and labor lawyer Frank Walsh. The conference sought to create a legal framework that would lessen the impact of labor disputes on war production. The guidelines called on unions to forego strikes, but in return they were guaranteed the right to organize unions and bargain collectively. In addition, employers were not supposed to fire workers for union membership or for "legitimate trade union activities." The process would be overseen by a National War Labor Board.[21]

This posed a dilemma for the MCPS and the Citizens Alliance (CA). The federal guidelines could potentially undermine the CA's "open shop" strategy. Privately, some business leaders echoed John McGee's belief that the Wilson administration was a nest of Socialists. Publicly, the MCPS responded by issuing Order 30 on April 16, an attempt to preempt the federal guidelines by creating its own comprehensive labor program based on the Board of Arbitration, a moribund agency that Burnquist reactivated. Order 30 mandated the *status quo ante* principle, that "employers and employees agree in good faith to maintain the existing status, in every phase of employment, of a union, non-union, or open shop." Employers could not try to break a union recognized before the war, nor could workers try to organize a new union. All wage and hour disputes were to be referred to the state Board of Arbitration.[22]

The order was based on an agreement between the Minnesota Employers Association and the Minnesota Federation of Labor. George Lawson signed the agreement, but later claimed that he had been duped. He maintained that he had accepted the agreement only on the condition that the streetcar dispute be settled by the state arbitration board before publication of Order 30. He also claimed that the agreement originally had explicitly barred discrimination against workers for union activities. Finally, he said his signature was conditioned upon acceptance by the MFL council. However, as soon as he had signed the agreement, the governor delivered it to the MCPS, which then issued Order 30.[23]

When the transit workers appealed to the Board of Arbitration, calling for reinstatement of the fired workers, Lowry first refused to accept the jurisdiction of the board, and when the board ordered that a path be open for the fired workers to be reinstated, Lowry refused to accept the decision. The union then appealed to the National War Labor Board, a process that continued until after the armistice and ultimately resulted in no relief.[24]

A Failed Strike with Major Repercussions

The transit workers failed to win recognition of their union, but their strike transformed the political landscape. To begin with, it brought out into the open the growing conflict between the MCPS and the Wilson administration. The Wilson administration sought to mediate rather than suppress labor demands to avoid disruption of war-related production. The MCPS, which was to a significant extent a creation of the Minneapolis Commerce and Civic Association, considered union recognition nonnegotiable. In addition, the Wilson administration sought a working relationship with the Nonpartisan League. For the MCPS, the NPL was a nest of Socialists and traitors.

John McGee's attitude toward the federal government comes across clearly in a long, angry telegram he wrote to Harry A. Garfield, the US fuel administrator, in March 1918. Garfield had apparently commented on the strike in an earlier telegram, and McGee told him he was "misinformed on the facts." The strike in McGee's view was organized by "men who ought to be in jail and about whose loyalty there is no doubt in the minds of all red-blooded Americans in this state." He blamed the strike on "Socialist agitators" and claimed it was financed by the "treasonable Nonpartisan League." When the MCPS mobilized the Home Guard troops, he contended the dispute was resolved and only resurrected by the meddling of the federal government. The arrival of the president's Mediation Commission, he contended, "started the pot boiling again." He asserted that Minnesota had stood "staunchly" behind the president, but did not propose to turn over its local affairs to commissions from Washington. In fact, he argued, the president's commission was "made up in the main of union labor and Socialists" and its only effect had been to undermine the powers of the MCPS. In his signature style, McGee concluded that he had "no doubt whatever that I am right and knowing that I am right there is no power on earth that can budge me one inch from following the path of duty as I see it."[25]

The tensions unleashed by the strike also led to the departure of two active and influential commissioners: Charles Ames was fired and John Lind resigned. On December 4, newspapers reported that Ames was in Washington to discuss the strike with Secretary of War Nelson Baker, Congressman Van Dyke, and representatives of the Department of Labor. The newspapers also reprinted Governor Burnquist's telegram to Ames, warning him not to represent the commission and, ironically as it turned out, informing him that John Lind had been appointed to represent the commission if needed.[26]

Ames either did not understand the message or thought he could finesse the situation. He participated in the meeting, which led to Baker's telegram to Burnquist asking him to revoke Order 16. This would encourage the company to rehire fired employees and to reopen the entire matter with federal mediation. Burnquist fired back a telegram that the dispute was essentially over and federal intervention would only inflame it, while also "impeaching the integrity, intelligence, and competency of the Public Safety Commission." On December 6, Burnquist sent a terse telegram to Ames, also made available to the press, replacing him with Henry Libby, the commission's secretary. Ames was blindsided, telegramming the governor that he was "unable to understand your discourteous action and the reason you assign for it."[27]

Burnquist made a half-hearted attempt to portray the firing of Ames as a concession to labor, noting in the first telegram that Ames should not represent the commission because of "his attitudes to labor." The labor movement did indeed consider Ames an enemy, and the labor convention meeting at the same time in St. Paul passed a resolution calling for his resignation (and the removal of McGee). Burnquist tried to spin the appointment of Libby as a goodwill gesture to the unions. However, Libby's union, the International Association of Machinists, made very clear that he was not, in their view, a genuine union man. In St. Paul, Machinist Lodge No. 459 passed a resolution proclaiming that Libby "does not represent the sentiments, feelings, or convictions of organized labor in his home city or anywhere else in this state." His attitude toward the streetcar strike was "treasonable to organized labor." The machinists were also angry that Libby accused workers of not thanking the governor for "what he has done for them." A few weeks later Libby's own local in Winona expelled him from membership after a formal trial for the same reasons.[28]

Burnquist fired Ames not to appease the unions but to punish him for his "concession in Washington to interference by the United States government in affairs that were solely in the hands of the State." The company, the MCPS, the MCCA, and the St. Paul Association all viewed federal intervention as jeopardizing a victory they had essentially won. For his part, Ames, who was president of St. Paul's West Publishing, might have been anxious to settle the strike, by federal mediation if necessary, not only because he was distressed by the chaos in his hometown but also because he understood that the strike was bringing the unions closer to the NPL.[29]

At almost the same time, John Lind left the commission after a bitter clash with John McGee at the December 5 meeting. McGee chose this moment to again push for the removal of Mayor Van Lear and his police chief Lewis Harthill Jr. from office. Van Lear, in fact, had on that same day addressed the labor convention at the St. Paul Auditorium, criticizing the commission for its "button" decision and calling for federal arbitration. Earlier, McGee had charged that Harthill had not done enough to keep prostitutes away from the military training camp at Fort Snelling. Harthill responded in writing that his officers had cooperated in this effort, even though the fort was outside of the city limits. Lind continued to defend Van Lear. He argued that removing him would be illegal and could lead to disorder, given Van Lear's popularity. Lind's opposition enraged McGee. Several years later, William Watts Folwell, then writing his classic history of Minnesota, asked Lind about the meeting. Lind wrote back as follows: "He called me everything vile you can think of before the committee—with the governor in the chair. The latter sat silent and I walked out. I did not return to any meeting. The governor begged me to come back. I told him that I could not and would not with McGee on board."[30]

On January 7, 1918, Lind resigned from the commission in a letter to the governor, which made clear that he could not "sit through another session with Judge McGee." Burnquist tried to get him to return, writing that "if there is any way in which you can continue your work on the Commission, I would consider it a great favor." He praised Lind for his "valuable work" and "wise advice." Ambrose Tighe also wrote to Lind, telling him that "I miss you very much at the meetings and a great deal of the joy of life is gone because of your absence." Tighe went on to criticize the workings of the commission, stating that "the ruthlessness of the Commission's procedure shows if further evidence was required, how dangerous it is to vest even good men with arbitrary power." This letter is surprising, even somewhat of a mystery, coming from the man who wrote the law creating the commission and often acted as its chief henchman.[31]

Burnquist finally gave up and appointed Thomas Cashman, a conservative businessman from Owatonna, as Lind's replacement. Cashman maintained a low profile on the commission, known primarily as a promoter of Liberty Bonds. The MCPS was now a different body. Lind had been the only commissioner who challenged McGee, and the only commissioner whom trade unions and farm organizations might look to not as an advocate but at least as an honest broker. McGee had been the dominant personality from the beginning, but with Lind gone, it was McGee's commission.[32]

The strike also tended to change the outlook of moderate union leaders. When E. G. Hill and George Lawson, the president and secretary of the Minnesota Federation of Labor, assumed leadership of the labor struggle with the transit company, they probably did not anticipate that they would soon find themselves in bitter conflict with the governor and the MCPS. Until that moment, Hill and Lawson had worked with the commission and kept their distance from the Nonpartisan League. Lawson served on the advisory committee of the Ramsey County Public Safety Commission, and the governor appointed him to the three-person committee investigating bread prices. Their record of loyal cooperation, however, did not stop the commission from doing all it could to block the transit workers union. By the end of the winter, Lawson was alienated from the commission and increasingly open to alliance with the left wing of the labor movement.[33]

The strike also had an important consequence for Minnesota politics over the next several decades. The crucial element in the NPL's Minnesota strategy was building a coalition of workers and farmers. Arthur Townley appointed Joseph Gilbert to lead this effort, and found in James Manahan an inspired orator who had the confidence of both farmers and workers. The coalition became a reality during the strike, as the tactics of the transit company, backed by the MCPS, the MCCA, and the St. Paul Association, encouraged trade unionists and Nonpartisan League farmers to see each other as allies.

This emerging alliance was celebrated at a banquet at the Ryan Hotel in downtown St. Paul in early February. The occasion was the dramatic dismissal of the charges against Manahan, Oscar Keller, and T. J. McGrath for allegedly inciting a riot with their Rice Park speeches on December 2. The judge held that the state had only proved that Manahan was in sympathy with labor and disdainful of the commissioners (for example, he called them "pinheads"). The court noted that Manahan had said the button order was illegal, and the judge agreed that it was most likely unenforceable in any court. The judge also noted that Manahan was correct when he told the crowd that the streets belonged to the people and not the transit company.[34]

An array of labor and NPL leaders addressed the banquet, including Charles Lindbergh, identified in the labor press as a "farmer." Joseph Gilbert stole the show by telling the five hundred diners that they all had the same enemy, "Big Business," which in the past had protected its power by keeping workers and farmers divided. Now, he promised, "we are going to scourge you from the high places which you now occupy, the positions which you have prostituted to individual gain instead of using your powers for the common good." During the banquet several resolutions were passed, including a sweeping indictment of the MCPS, which it charged had "actually interfered with the conduct of the war" by protecting special interests like the transit company. The resolutions called on Burnquist to remove McGee and Libby and replace them with commissioners recommended by the labor movement and organized farmers.[35]

There was no chance, however, that Burnquist would remove McGee, even though he was becoming a political liability. On December 6, 1917, the *St. Paul Daily News* published a front-page article about a speech that McGee allegedly made to a local club in which he expressed the commission's determination to defy Washington's attempt to intervene in the strike, characterized the federal government as "weak and wobbly," and belittled Wilson as a "college man." These charges came from a telegram sent to Senator Nelson, Congressman Van Dyke, and others, that had also been leaked to the press. McGee denied attacking Wilson in his speech at the club. The newspaper recalled, however, that three days prior to the 1916 election, he had fiercely criticized the president, characterizing his signing of the bill authorizing an eight-hour day on the railroads as "a tragedy" and his refusal to recognize the Huerta government in Mexico "as almost criminal conduct."[36]

On the same day, Oscar Seebach, the soldier and legislator from Red Wing, wrote a letter to Governor Burnquist about McGee. Although a German American, Seebach's reputation for loyalty was unassailable. He had advocated an alien registration bill in the Minnesota House on the eve of the declaration of war. Shortly thereafter, McGee hired him to organize the Home Guard battalions. He worked for the MCPS for six months and then returned to active duty service in the army. Now, he urgently recommended that the governor remove McGee and Ames because he thought their lack of good judgement and diplomacy had caused the labor strife. He noted that while working for the commission he had become "well acquainted with them and their methods." Seebach's main concern was that Burnquist retain the governorship, and he feared that McGee and Ames were "losing votes for us every day." He was not aware that Burnquist had already fired Ames; his concerns about McGee were ignored.[37]

Burnquist may have hoped to retain Lind to provide a kind of counterweight to McGee. Now he was completely reliant on McGee, and completely committed to him. Following the strike, for example, the NPL executive committee called on Burnquist to remove McGee and

Libby and appoint in their place "a member recommended by organized labor and another recommended by organized farmers." Burnquist replied that he thought that "union labor has no better friend" than Libby, although he acknowledged his own union had expelled him. As to McGee, he told the NPL that "there is no more patriotic citizen or anyone more anxious to see the United States win this war" and that "you will find that when the rights of union labor or any other organization are involved no one will be more sincere in the securing of justice than he."[38]

Sheriffs, Prosecutors, and the Home Guard Curb the NPL

No longer facing a transit strike in the Twin Cities, the MCPS and its allies refocused their attention on the Nonpartisan League's organizing drive across the state. Local officials continued to ban meetings in some counties. After the holidays, sheriffs and MCPS county directors continued to stop the NPL from organizing in certain locales, sometimes aided by vigilantes and increasingly by local Home Guard units. In the northwestern county of Hubbard, for example, the 10th Battalion's Company D was mobilized when two NPL organizers tried to speak at Akeley. The Home Guard arrested them and put them on a train. When one of the organizers returned in early March, this time to Park Rapids, the county seat, the Home Guard ran him out again.[39]

A similar event happened in the southern county of Freeborn, where the local director of the MCPS got wind of an NPL meeting at the little hamlet of Mansfield. He called the county attorney, who "ordered the meeting stopped." The local Home Guard commander mobilized a detachment to rush from Alden, about five miles north, to enforce the order. The county attorney told the local newspaper that he "advised all Germans to let the league alone, as it was alleged to be pro-German and was fomenting trouble in many communities." The local newspaper reported that the county attorney was "not attempting to stop free speech, but he will stop any attempt at disloyalty that is started in his jurisdictions."[40]

Vigilantes sometimes acted on their own without the approval of local officials. In early March, several hundred citizens of the Goodhue County town of Kenyon met to nominate candidates for town offices. Andrew Finstuen, owner of the *Kenyon News* and a future state legislator, chaired the meeting. When someone burst into the room to report that NPL organizer George Breidal was in town, they adjourned and stormed out. When they grabbed him, he was ordered to kneel and kiss the American flag. Carrying the flag, he was escorted by the crowd to the hotel, where he paid his bill, and then the crowd took him to the train station. He wanted to go north, but the next train was going south, and that is where he went. The *Kenyon News* concluded its news story on this event by commenting that the incident "ought to be a warning to others of his kind to give Kenyon a wide berth."[41]

By the end of February, the NPL counted nineteen counties that had formally banned their speakers and recorded about forty meetings that had been stopped or disrupted. In response, the NPL leadership petitioned the governor for protection. In February 1918, Magnus Johnson and A. C. Welch, both legislators, led a delegation of NPL farmers who met with Governor Burnquist to detail the violence they were experiencing and to demand protection of their right to recruit members. They specifically charged officials in Jackson and Rice Counties with illegal acts. Burnquist was polite, but within a week the attorney general ruled that the charges did not warrant disciplining the officials.[42]

The NPL could not have expected much help from the governor. He was, after all, just one vote on the John McGee–dominated MCPS. In any case, the MCPS maintained that it had no official position on whether the NPL should be banned. Henry Libby, the secretary, consistently told local officials that they should use their own discretion when dealing with the NPL. He usually referred them to Attorney General Hilton's October 1917 memorandum that said sheriffs must protect free speech, but added "any meeting, the tendency of which is to promote disloyalty to the United States in time of war should not be tolerated." The MCPS at the same time made it very clear that the NPL was a disloyal, even traitorous organization, and further, that traitors might appropriately be suppressed with violence.

The MCPS message was reinforced in January, when its publicity department sent newspaper editors a brief article entitled "One Cure for Disloyalty" with a suggestion that they run it in their papers. Without specifying the locality, the author noted that "a member of a certain 'gang' pulled a Red Cross button off a young man's chest and threw it into a spittoon with a curse." The offender was then "beaten to a pulp" by a crowd of loyalists and later jailed, fined, and forced to sign a pledge of loyalty. The crowd's actions "had a very salutary effect on . . . the disloyal element." The article warned that there was no "half-way" citizenship, and that soon "a disloyal utterance or lukewarm attitude will be resented by the American people in every section."[43]

The NPL then turned to the federal government for help. In April, they published a 120-page booklet entitled *Memorial to the Congress of the United States Concerning Conditions in Minnesota, 1918*, with an identical companion version addressed to President Wilson. The booklet was composed of sworn affidavits by NPL organizers detailing various incidents in which they were forcibly denied the right to hold a meeting. The Wilson administration, however, had neither the inclination nor the resources to intervene on the NPL's behalf.[44]

While sheriffs, local MCPS directors, and Home Guard units continued to ban and disrupt NPL meetings, the county attorneys from three southern Minnesota counties charged NPL organizers with crimes under state law. McGee and his allies wanted Alfred Jaques, the US attorney for Minnesota, to prosecute the NPL in Minnesota's federal courts under the Espionage Act. Jaques was willing to charge Socialist Party leaders under the act but declined to charge NPL leaders, who, after all, enjoyed friendly relations with the Wilson administration. However, ultrapatriotic county attorneys could charge NPL organizers with violations of state law, including the version of the Espionage Act passed by the Minnesota legislature in April 1917 as part of a package of bills that included the MCPS.

The first attempt by a county attorney to prosecute an NPL speaker was a clumsy one, more of a farce than a crime drama, although it could have easily degenerated into a lynching. When Jackson County officials got wind of an NPL meeting scheduled for January 23 in Lakefield, E. H. Nicholas, the county attorney, wrote a letter to the NPL promising to "use every measure at our disposal to prevent you from speaking here, and to prevent your organization from holding any future meetings in this County." Joseph Gilbert, the most important NPL leader after Townley, decided to personally challenge the ban. Standing on a wagon, he began speaking to a group of farmers. When he said, among other things, that some county officials spelled patriotism with "P-A-Y," the sheriff arrested him for "riot." Several farmers made his bail, and he agreed to return for trial on February 11.[45]

Attorneys James Manahan and H. A. Paddock came south to Lakefield to defend Gilbert at trial. The original charge of "riot" had been changed to unlawful assembly. Looking back years later, Manahan felt he underestimated how deeply small-town business owners and professionals hated the NPL. He thought he had made the prosecution's case look ridiculous. The pro-NPL farmers in the courtroom were gleeful. However, after most of the farmers went home to milk their cows, the judge called an evening session. During an extended dinner break the prosecution found new witnesses. Near midnight, Manahan moved for adjournment till the morning. The judge refused but did allow a man in the audience to auction a parrot, named Kaiser Bill, for the benefit of the Red Cross. Manahan saw a trap: if he bought the bird, he would be pro-German, but if he did not, he was anti–Red Cross. He outbid everyone and bought the parrot for fifteen dollars, and then jumped on a table to start a new auction, challenging Nicholas to prove his patriotism by bidding.

In the ensuing uproar, the sheriff rearrested Gilbert. In a fit of anger, Manahan told the hostile townspeople that he would ask the farmers to boycott the town if Gilbert was not released. Farmers bailed Gilbert out a second time, and as the crowd grew more threatening, Manahan, Paddock, and Gilbert attempted a retreat. In his memoir, Manahan wrote that the mob caught him before he could reach the hotel. Someone yelled, "get a rope." He sheepishly recounted how he saved himself by telling the crowd that he was "only a lawyer, trying a case for a living," and that he had "no use for those damn Socialists." The crowd agreed to let him go if he would drop Gilbert's case and leave town. The next day Gilbert was convicted and was freed pending appeal.[46]

Nicholas, however, let the misdemeanor drop, preferring instead to charge Townley and Gilbert with violation of the Minnesota sedition statute, which provided for a prison term of up to one year for discouraging enlistments either in writing or in a public speech. It was also a crime to advocate that citizens should not aid the country in prosecuting the war. Nicholas based the charge on the NPL pamphlets that reprinted the "war resolutions" approved by the NPL executive board in June 1917 and on the resolutions passed at the Producers and Consumers Conference in September. In addition, Nicholas alleged that Gilbert and Irving Freitag, an NPL organizer, had made speeches that violated the statutes. This case would not come to trial in the summer of 1918.[47]

In a coordinated effort, Albert Allen, the country attorney of neighboring Martin County, charged Townley and Gilbert a few weeks later under the Minnesota statute with discouraging enlistments. Since Townley and Gilbert had never spoken in Martin County, the charges were based exclusively on the NPL pamphlets. In a speech at the Minnesota State Bar Association Convention in August 1917, Allen had said that "any man talking treasonable doctrines ought to be shot on the spot." Fortunately, he did not follow his own advice, instead sending his sheriff to St. Paul to arrest Townley and Gilbert and bring them back to Fairmont, the county seat, for trial. The sheriff arrested them, but they succeeded in getting a judge in St. Paul to release them after posting bonds. When the sheriff returned home empty-handed, Allen sent him back to St. Paul. He grabbed Gilbert, but Townley had left town. The sheriff put Gilbert on a train to Fairmont in the custody of his deputy, while NPL attorneys obtained a writ of habeas corpus, which required the sheriff to return Gilbert to Ramsey County court, where the original bonds were honored.[48]

Townley and Gilbert appeared in Fairmont for trial on March 11. Before the trial could begin, their attorneys entered demurrers, meaning they admitted the facts charged (that the NPL had published the two pamphlets) but argued that the facts did not constitute a crime. The judge denied their motion but agreed to send the case to the Minnesota Supreme Court to settle the matter prior to the trial. The court would not rule until the summer.

Meanwhile, Thomas Mohn, the Goodhue County attorney, persuaded the local grand jury to indict nine defendants. Three were NPL organizers Joe Gilbert, Louis Martin, and N. S. Randall, all charged with discouraging enlistments at a speech made in Kenyon in August 1917. The other six were county residents, including John Seebach, who managed a flour mill, and his son Carl, both charged with speaking against the draft. Ironically, John Seebach was the uncle of Oscar Seebach, the soldier-legislator whom McGee had hired to organize the Home Guard, and Fred Seebach, the commander of the local Home Guard unit, Company A of the 5th Battalion. The other defendants were farmers charged with speaking out against the war or the draft. The three NPL organizers were tried separately in Goodhue

County court. John Seebach was later indicted for violating the Espionage Act and tried in federal court. The other defendants were never brought to trial.

After indicting the nine men, the twenty-three members of the grand jury passed a loyalty resolution directed at those county residents who they thought were either "pro-Germans" or "fifty-fifty Americans." From now on, they warned, "these people are going to be very carefully watched and we . . . feel that it is their duty to come out in the open and commit themselves to the successful prosecution of the war. . . . From now on we must all be boosters for the war and 100% Americans."[49]

Jens Grondahl, editor of the *Red Wing Daily Republican*, celebrated the indictments and the resolution, which he heralded as the "first vigorous step" to make Goodhue County "100% American." The county would no longer tolerate "pro-Germanism, fifty-fifty, or lukewarmness toward the government in prosecuting the war." He also warned that anyone who had knowledge of "seditious or treasonable acts or utterances" and failed to report it to the proper authorities would be an accomplice and should be punished. The indictment also inspired Grondahl to write the most remarkable of his many editorials, where he argued that the local pro-Germans "are branding their children and their children's children with the mark of Cain." He went on to say that they "are murderers pure and simple, committing at the same time the crime of treason and murder to which they will be called to account, as sure as there is a God in heaven. . . . Their descendants shall curse the memory of these fathers and mothers for disgracing their country and their progeny, for standing in the way of human liberty and in defense of Hun savagery and bestialism. The mark of Cain is upon them because they have helped in the murder of American citizens."[50]

During the spring and summer, the NPL attorneys would be busy defending Townley, Gilbert, Randall, and Martin in the courts of three counties. They would have some success, but the prosecutions complicated the NPL's attempt to defeat Governor Burnquist in the Republican primary in June. In addition to being prohibited from campaigning in many counties and encountering the threat of violence everywhere, the NPL was burdened by the fact that its leaders were facing sedition charges.

Monitoring Aliens and Curbing German Culture

A common feature of modern warfare is the demonization of the enemy. Most American newspapers depicted Germany as a barbarian, evil power during the period of neutrality, especially after the sinking of the *Lusitania*. Leaders of the preparedness movement preached hatred and fear of Germany as a strategy for achieving its goals of an expanded army and navy, universal military service, and, ultimately, a declaration of war. Once war was declared, the federal government's Committee of Public Information mounted a massive propaganda campaign to depict Germans in bestial terms. This campaign built public support for the Wilson administration's stated goal of fighting until Prussian autocracy was defeated and the world was once again "safe for democracy."

This was the age of nationalism, and each belligerent government sought to rally its people by presenting the war as a clash of nations, of our nation against the enemy nation, of "us" against "them." The United States, however, had just experienced a massive immigration. A sizable portion of the population was born in Europe, and in Minnesota, the largest group of immigrants had come from Germany. They had left behind relations and friends, some of whom were fighting in the German army. The MCPS, the business organizations like the MCCA and the St. Paul Association, and organizations like the America First Association and the American Protective League, were convinced that German communities harbored people who hoped that Germany would win the war. The leadership of these organizations were prosperous, native-born Americans, usually of English or Scot ancestry. For many of them, the only immigrants they knew were the employees of their companies and the servants in their homes.

The MCPS was primed to assume the worst about the New Ulm draft rally in July 1917, and came down hard on the leaders, seeking to send a message to German Americans statewide. The governor removed Mayor Fritsche and City Attorney Pfaender from office despite their record of military service. Newspaper editor Albert Steinhauser would be charged under the Espionage Act despite the Purple Heart he earned fighting for the United States in the Philippines. The commission leaned on the board of Martin Luther College until they fired Rev. Adolph Ackermann, the college's president. At about the same time, the MCPS sought and won the dismissal of William Schaper at the University of Minnesota, not for opposing the war but for failing to "boost" it. Most likely, the regents would not have fired Professor Schaper, or even taken notice of him, had he not been of German ancestry.

Across the United States, there were countless incidents of harassment and violence against German immigrants, even when they were naturalized citizens. The most infamous case involved Robert Praeger, a German immigrant who lived in southern Illinois across the river from St. Louis. He had taken out his first citizenship papers and tried to enlist in the navy. Rejected because he was blind in one eye, he eventually found work in a mine. He ran afoul of some fellow workers, who denounced him as a spy, and after being forced to parade draped in a flag, he was lynched from a tree. Rather than prosecute the lynchers, Attorney General Gregory argued that the Praeger lynching demonstrated the need to pass the Sedition Act. More repressive legal enforcement, he hoped, would preempt the need for vigilante action.[51]

Minnesotans of German ancestry suffered in Minnesota too, but overall, popular backlash against Germans was not as vicious as it was in some states. There were few reported incidents of violence against German Americans solely for their ethnicity. However, there was considerable violence against members of the Nonpartisan League, many of whom were of German ancestry. Very likely, this violence was motivated by a blend of ethnic and political animosity. An NPL farmer with a German name was probably more likely to be a victim of discrimination or violence.

On the eve of war, the Minnesota legislature debated but ultimately failed to pass an alien registration bill. Some argued that the federal government should handle alien registration, and in fact the Wilson administration ordered the registration of German male aliens in February 1918. Washington decided, however, that it was not necessary to register aliens from the Habsburg empire, for example Austrians and Hungarians. The MCPS went further, issuing Order 25, which required the registration of all aliens except for German male aliens (who were subject to federal registration). Aliens were ordered to report between February 25 and 27 and complete under oath a form with thirty-five questions, including whether they had registered for the draft, whether they had begun the naturalization process, and whether they had relatives fighting in the war on either side. They also had to provide a complete inventory of their real property, bank accounts, and personal property such as farm animals and machinery. It was even necessary to reveal the location of any safe deposit vaults. In a related move, the commission issued Order 32, barring aliens from teaching children in any public, private, or parochial school, or teaching future teachers in any normal school. Higher education was excepted, and the superintendent of public instruction could grant permits to aliens in special cases.[52]

The MCPS registered 225,000 aliens, many thousands of whom were property holders. The state estimated that several thousand aliens left for Canada or Wisconsin, either because they were actively working against the war and feared exposure or because they had falsely claimed to be aliens to evade the draft. Order 25 may have successfully limited the activities of immigrants who opposed the war, since it sent a message that they were being watched. But the order also sent shock waves through the entire German community, scaring even the most loyal, since it seemed to lay the groundwork for a wholesale confiscation of alien property. Fortunately, these fears were not realized.

The MCPS was also worried about the influence of German language and culture, especially in schools. In the fall of 1917, the MCPS asked superintendent of public instruction Carl G. Schulz to investigate the extent to which students were taught in German and other languages in private and public schools, and to evaluate the acceptability of textbooks used in German-language classes. Based on a partial survey, Schulz estimated that about two hundred schools used a foreign language as the medium of instruction for at least some classes. Alarmed, the MCPS approved a resolution urging all schools, "as a patriotic duty," to require that English be the only language of instruction, except for "the study of those foreign languages themselves, or as a medium of religious instruction." The commission never issued a formal order to this effect. Schulz also made a preliminary report about textbooks, and in response, the commission asked him to create a "white list" of acceptable German-language books from which schools could safely make their selections.[53]

After Charles Ames was dismissed as a commissioner, he agreed to continue his investigations of the NPL and the German-language "problem." He looked deeper into the state's parochial schools, and found that of 307 schools surveyed, only ninety-four used English exclusively. German was the language of instruction in some classes in 195 schools. He also found that some schools were following the commission's recommendations for German textbooks, but that many objectionable books were still being used. Very likely, the commission failed to completely remove German as a language of instruction during the war.

Overall, the MCPS proved to be relatively restrained in its language policy, aware of the large numbers of Minnesotans for whom English was a second language. It never ordered, or even discussed, a ban on the public use of the German language, as happened in Iowa. Nevertheless, Ames found that the number of schools offering German-language instruction declined. Very likely, the general hostility to Germany made the study of the German language less attractive to many. For schools, the need to have textbooks approved by a government agency was just one more reason to cancel a class. In the years before the war, the board of education graded about five thousand state board examinations in the German language, but only 340 in 1919.[54]

Even without MCPS encouragement, however, many people became hostile toward any manifestation of German culture. This posed a difficult problem for symphony orchestras, some of which had German-born conductors, and all of which performed a repertoire that relied heavily on German composers, especially Beethoven, Bach, Mozart, Brahms, and Wagner. Dr. Karl Muck, for example, conductor of the Boston Symphony Orchestra, got into trouble when he chose not to start a concert with the "Star Spangled Banner," apparently on aesthetic grounds. Soon, he was the target of a frenzied backlash, culminating in his arrest, just as he was about to conduct Bach's *St. Matthew Passion* in March 1918. He had been born in Germany but was in fact a Swiss citizen. Nevertheless, he was interred as an enemy alien.[55]

The Minneapolis Symphony Orchestra also had a German-born conductor, Emil Oberhoffer. He came to Minnesota in 1897 and worked as a teacher, performer, and conductor. With the help of the wealthy elite, he organized the Minneapolis Symphony Orchestra in 1903. Two years later, the Northwestern National Life Insurance Company offered to build an auditorium if the orchestra and its supporters could sell insurance policies worth $2 million. The quota was reached, and in 1905, the orchestra held its inaugural concert at the new building at Eleventh Street and Nicollet Avenue. In 1907, the Orchestral Association was incorporated to ensure the financial stability of the orchestra, and its board included many of the founding members of the Citizens Alliance, which had been organized a few years earlier to keep unions out of Minneapolis.[56]

The orchestra attracted top-ranked soloists and pursued a vigorous touring schedule. At first, the war had little impact on the orchestra. Oberhoffer continued to perform a repertoire heavily weighted toward German composers, and through most of the winter season of 1917–18 he faced no backlash. He was careful to announce that he considered himself an "intensely patriotic" American, and he roused audiences with a stirring rendition of the "Star Spangled Banner" in each concert. The orchestra's program for March 14–15, 1918, for example, included Beethoven, Brahms, and Wagner. Then he took a step too far. The season finale on March 31 featured an all-Wagner program. The orchestra apparently received so many complaints that the Orchestral Association made a last-minute decision to cancel the Wagner selections and substitute a program of non-German music.[57]

When the orchestra opened its next season in October 1918, German composers were absent, and the repertoire now featured, among others, Bizet, Berlioz, Dvorak, Grieg, Saint-Saens, Sibelius, Tchaikovsky, and Verdi. Oberhoffer's caution was understandable. The orchestra, for example, was forced to suspend Emil Schulze, a bass horn player, because someone had reported seeing pictures of Emperor Franz Joseph and Empress Elizabeth of Austria in his home. Schulze, an American citizen, also displayed Liberty Loan signs in the window of his northside house. After an investigation the orchestra found no evidence of disloyalty and reinstated him, but only after conferring with the Department of Justice. Schulze held onto his job, but had to weather an investigation, reported in his hometown newspaper, about whether he harbored criminal thoughts.[58]

In Red Wing, newspaper editor Jens Grondahl took up the fight against German culture with his customary vigor. In 1904, the city built the lavishly decorated Sheldon Memorial Auditorium in Renaissance Revival style with a large gift from a local businessman. The lobby walls were embellished with the names of ten cultural figures. In an editorial, Grondahl suggested that the auditorium board should remove the three German names, Beethoven, Wagner, and Goethe. When someone from the board protested, Grondahl lashed out against German culture:

> Our schools are barred against her language, her music is being discarded by our musical organizations everywhere, everything "made in Germany" bears the mark of Cain. If Goethe is barred officially from being read in our public schools is there any reason why he should be flaunted from the decorations of the Auditorium. If Wagner and Beethoven are discarded from our classical music activities because we don't want to know or hear or meet anything that is German, is there not ample reason why these should be removed from places of honor in an auditorium maintained by Americans for Americans and supported by the taxes of the community.

Grondahl overstated the case. The MCPS had not "barred officially" the study of the German language and Goethe in the schools. Still, his editorial expressed a view which was gaining currency during 1918.[59]

This growing anti-Germanism eventually found a culprit inside the Minnesota State Capitol, in the very restaurant where legislators ate their lunch. In 1905, the state finished its impressive new capitol building, designed by Cass Gilbert in the Beaux Arts version of the classical revival style. In the basement, Gilbert designed a rathskeller, a restaurant that echoed the German tradition of eating and drinking establishments in town halls. The rathskeller acknowledged the state's largest immigrant group, and true to the German tradition, the room was decorated with twenty-nine mottoes in German. Mostly the sayings are benign comments such as "A cheerful guest is always welcome" and "May God bless your entrance and exit." Several of the mottos refer to drinking ("Better be tipsy than feverish" and "After hearty eating you can do some hearty drinking"). In the winter 1918, patriotic visitors to the capitol began sending protests to Governor Burnquist demanding that the German decorations be removed. Pursuant to his orders, German mottoes were "obliterated" and a crew of decorators were assigned "to blot out all other signs of German kultur" from the rathskeller.[60]

In this atmosphere, companies decided to delete the word "German" where it appeared in the names of their banks, insurance companies, or other commercial ventures. In Charles Lindbergh's Little Falls, for example, the German American State Bank had proudly announced its name with large letters on the stone frieze below the

cornice of its classical revival bank building. In 1917, however, the bank was renamed the American State Bank. The bank simply removed the word "German" from the building's exterior, but in such a way that over a century later the outlines of the word are still visible. A more spectacular change happened in St. Paul, where the Germania Life Insurance Company bowed to public pressure and removed a two-story-tall bronze statue of Germania, the female figure representing the German nation, from its perch high above the entrance to its massive Richardsonian Romanesque building in downtown St. Paul. After removing the statue in March 1918, the company changed its name to the Guardian Life Insurance Company.[61]

Many in the German community reacted to the anti-German backlash by trying to match the patriotism of the most ardent ultrapatriots. In New Ulm, for example, the leaders responded to the deposing of Fritsche and Pfaender by holding a massive patriotic rally to which Burnquist was invited. In St. Paul, a group of German Americans announced the creation of a new organization, called the League of Patriotic Americans of German Origin, which pledged its complete support of all activities geared toward winning the war. According to their bylaws, the league would "search the hearts of people of German origin . . . converting those whose course is wrong." They also pledged to help in the detection and punishment of the disloyal.[62]

The need for German Americans to prove their loyalty led one St. Paul man to rename himself. Captain Robert Auerbach led Company H of the Home Guard's 15th Battalion, the unit headquartered in St. Paul. As anti-German attitudes grew more intense, he apparently felt that his German ancestry compromised his position. He petitioned the Ramsey County District Court to change his name, and that of his wife and family, to Rice, his mother's maiden name. Identifying himself as Robert A. Rice, he issued a public letter explaining that he hoped to save his children "from the odium attached to a German name, and the fact that they will have to live it down in every new community to which they may go."[63]

▪ **OPPOSITE**
Workers prepare to lower the statue symbolizing the German nation from its perch above the main entrance of the Germania Life Insurance Company building in St. Paul, April 1918. ***MNHS collections***

EIGHT

THE DECISIVE BATTLE

SPRING & EARLY SUMMER 1918

The Non-Partisan League lecturer is a traitor every time. . . . Where we made a mistake was in not establishing a firing squad in the first days of the war. We should now get busy and have that firing squad working overtime. . . . These men who are fighting against our soldiers this side of the water and stabbing them in the back are going to die. All Socialists should be in internment camps.

JOHN F. MCGEE, testifying in Washington before the Senate Committee on Military Affairs as reported by the *Minneapolis Morning Tribune* on April 20, 1918

You people in town should not be fooled into believing that the League is fighting little business. We need the banks and the stores and we are not going to fight them if they let us alone. It is the profiteers, grafters, speculators, the unnecessary middle men . . . the league is fighting. . . . Now one more thing. Do you suppose the farmers appreciate such treatment as tearing the banners off their cars and the refusal of business men to display a single picture of their candidate for Governor in their places of business.

GEORGE W. MATHIESEN, a Nonpartisan League farmer, in a letter published in the *Windom Reporter*, June 14, 1918

IN EUROPE, everyone knew what was next. With Russia out of the war, Germany would move troops from the eastern to the western front for a massive attack on the British and French lines, trying to win the war before significant numbers of American troops arrived. In March, the German army launched the first of a series of successful offensives, finally ending the trench war stalemate. The final struggle had begun, and the Germans would gain considerable territory before the Allies, now including General Pershing's troops, mounted a counteroffensive in the summer.

Increasing numbers of American soldiers had crossed the Atlantic, but not many Minnesotans. In September, the induction of Minnesota men was suspended until the construction of barracks and other buildings at Camp Dodge could be completed. At that point, only about half of Minnesota's draft quota had been met. In February, inductions resumed, and over eight thousand men boarded trains for Iowa. Minnesotans arriving at Camp Dodge expected to join the new 88th Division. However, the army continued to transfer soldiers to other camps to fill out units in formation. The development of the 88th continued to lag.[1]

The Minnesota National Guard soldiers at Camp Cody in New Mexico were frustrated by the constant transfer of men in and out of the still-forming 34th Division. In May 1917, the army announced that several thousand men would leave the camp to fill out units that were about to embark for France. Minnesota officials complained that the war department had turned the 34th into nothing more than a replacement unit. Governor Burnquist traveled to Washington to protest, but the war department informed him that the German offensive required the transfer of as many infantry and machine gunners to France as possible. As the transferred troops were replaced by new draftees, the local character of the original national guard units was gradually extinguished.[2]

The generals were focused on training troops and sending them to Europe to fight against Germany. But another enemy, invisible but ultimately more deadly, was sweeping through the cantonments. It began in Kansas, when on March 4, the hospital at Camp Funston admitted its first soldiers with influenza. Within three weeks, eleven hundred soldiers at Funston were sick enough to be hospitalized. As soldiers were moved around the country, influenza spread to other camps, and then to nearby towns and cities. When troops boarded ships for France, the virus went with them. There were serious outbreaks on troopships, and soon the disease spread to the armies of all belligerents. This first wave of the influenza epidemic did not produce massive fatalities, but something unusual was happening. Doctors were accustomed to influenza killing the very young and the very old. This time, a surprising number of young men died.[3]

The League Challenges the Governor

In Minnesota, the stage was set for the decisive battle of the home front. Following the North Dakota playbook, the NPL planned to run a slate of candidates in the June 17, 1918, Republican primary. Minnesota NPL members, about fifty thousand in number, gathered for precinct caucuses on February 22. This began a process that resulted in farmers representing forty-six of the state's sixty-seven senatorial districts gathering in St. Paul on March 19 to choose a slate. The nineteen districts not represented were located either in large cities or on the Iron Range where there were few farmers. In those districts, the NPL generally backed labor-endorsed candidates.

The delegates put Charles A. Lindbergh at the top of the ticket as candidate for governor. The rest of the slate for state offices was a combination of farmers and labor leaders. Lindbergh had developed close ties with the NPL since leaving Congress a year earlier. In letters in early 1918, his daughter Eva urged him to run for the Sixth District seat that he had held for ten years. He replied that he had no interest in returning to Congress unless there were forty or fifty Progressives to work with. On the other hand, he thought that he could accomplish something as governor, and that Burnquist was vulnerable because he had alienated both unionized workers and NPL farmers. Reflecting on the governor's political evolution, he told Eva that Burnquist "fell in with a gang of profiteers, perhaps not intentionally, but can't cut loose now."[4]

In many ways, Lindbergh was the ideal NPL candidate, popular among both farmers and trade unionists, and comfortable with the organization's platform, which pledged unqualified support to the federal government's battle to defeat German autocracy and also reaffirmed the NPL's economic program of state-owned agricultural enterprises (stockyards, creameries, etc.). There were also labor demands, such as an eight-hour day, state old-age pensions, and a state insurance system. The platform also called for several wartime measures, including increased taxes on large incomes and excess profits and government operation of munitions plants and those industries in which labor disputes could not be settled by federal mediation. It was a platform written to hold together the developing alliance of farmers and workers.[5]

The MCPS and the conservative press would probably have branded any NPL candidate as a Bolshevik and a pro-German traitor. Lindbergh, however, was particularly vulnerable. He had passionately opposed the preparedness movement, and he had cast controversial votes for the Gore-McLemore resolutions and against the arming of merchant ships. No one doubted that he would have voted against the war resolution in April 1917 if he had still been the Sixth District congressman. Then there was his self-published 1917 book, *Why Is Your Country at War*, which echoed the Socialist Party argument that a certain "inner circle," by which he meant the Money Trust, had maneuvered the country into the war "for selfish purposes." He made clear in the book, however, that once Congress and the president decided on war, "we must support them with all our power," no matter how Americans felt about the decision. This was not just a political ploy. In a private letter to his daughter in early 1918, he wrote that he was "very sorry we got in the war, but once in we must all support it with all our power till, we get peace and end it that way."[6]

Although few people had seen the book, or ever would, Lindbergh's critics made it the focal point of their attack. The *New York Times*, for example, editorialized that Lindbergh's argument that the Money Trust brought the country into war "for selfish reasons" proved that he was a kind of "Gopher Bolshevik." The *Times* also took notice when the Eighth District congressman, Clarence B. Miller of Duluth, devoted an entire speech on the floor of the House to attacking the NPL and Lindbergh's "poison book," a speech that was published as a pamphlet. Miller argued that the leaders of the NPL were "Socialists and nothing but Socialists," and that the book was so traitorous that "it seems incredible that any person allowed to be at large . . . could entertain or express such a view as this."[7]

After the delegates had chosen Lindbergh as their candidate, there was a two-day rally at the St. Paul Auditorium attended by thousands of farmers and workers. They were addressed by NPL luminaries like Arthur Townley and Lynn Frazier, the North Dakota governor, and by Mayor Van Lear. William Kent, a former congressman who was a member of the Federal Tariff Commission, and Gilbert Hyatt of the

Department of Labor, also spoke, evidence that the NPL continued to enjoy friendly relations with the federal government.

One invited speaker did not attend. For reasons difficult to fathom, the NPL extended a "cordial invitation" to Governor Burnquist to speak "for such time and on such subjects you may desire." Burnquist declined the invitation, but not cordially. On March 11 he sent the NPL a blistering letter, which was widely reprinted in the press. During the war, he wrote, "there were but two parties, one composed of loyalists and the other of the disloyalists." He declined the invitation because the NPL leadership had proven itself disloyal, and had in fact "drawn to it the pro-German element of our state," including the IWW, the Socialist Party, pacifists, peace advocates, and the radical wing of the labor movement. The governor recalled Senator La Follette's "unpatriotic utterances" at the NPL gathering in September 1917, which "put a stamp of disloyalty" on the league that "can never be erased."[8]

Arthur Le Sueur wrote the invitation to Burnquist in his role as the NPL national secretary. Burnquist attacked him for acting as defense counsel for Wobblies and for supporting the People's Council of America for Democracy and Peace. He also criticized NPL director Joseph Gilbert, noting that a jury had found him guilty of making "disloyal utterances," and James Manahan, NPL attorney, for slandering members of the MCPS in his attempt to unite farmers and workers to advance the agenda of the NPL. The NPL leaders, he said, were "neither real farmers nor workers, but self-seeking demagogues." He did not mention Charles Lindbergh, who had not yet been nominated, but he left no doubt that a vote for any NPL candidate was treasonous.

Inviting Burnquist was, as Carl Chrislock noted, "a serious blunder." It provided the governor the opportunity to make loyalty the defining issue of the election. The NPL leaders could not have expected the governor to speak at their convention, the whole purpose of which was to rally support for the campaign to defeat him. Perhaps they thought the governor's inevitable rejection would cast the league in a favorable light. In any case, Le Sueur responded to Burnquist's denunciation with a second letter in which he claimed that "our invitation was wholly sincere." He said they had hoped Burnquist would attend and deliver a "high-minded message that might result in conciliation and a better understanding."[9]

Governor Joseph Burnquist claimed that loyalty was the only issue in the Republican gubernatorial primary, an attempt to put Charles Lindbergh, shown here on the front page of the NPL newspaper, on the defensive. *MNHS collections*

Lindbergh formally accepted the NPL nomination on March 21 and immediately confronted the charge of disloyalty. The main problem, he argued, was to win the war but manage the war effort "so as to lose the least number of lives, and save the people from as much burden as possible." It was true, Lindbergh said, that the state was divided into two classes, but the difference between the two is "that a few would destroy democracy to win the war, and the rest of us would win the war to establish democracy." The governor, Lindbergh continued, failed to understand that we were at war to win the world for democracy. In fact, "for many months democracy has not existed in our state." With just a few isolated exceptions, Lindbergh maintained, Minnesotans were loyal. There were, however, "profiteers who subvert their loyalty to selfish action," and the politicians who follow them. The NPL opposed these monopolists and sought industrial democracy, because "we must put into practice at home those principles for which we have sent our boys to fight abroad."[10]

A bitterly fought campaign was about to begin, characterized not only by extreme rhetoric but also by suppression of the NPL's ability to campaign widely. Many counties had already banned the NPL, and three counties had ongoing sedition prosecutions of NPL leaders. The repression of the NPL would increase during the campaign, including the mobilization of the Home Guard to stop NPL campaign rallies and, finally, even the arrest of Lindbergh. Arthur Townley hoped to replicate the North Dakota victory with a campaign that focused on the economic needs of farmers and workers. Instead, the campaign would be about "loyalty" as defined by John McGee.

Something Like Martial Law

As generally understood, martial law is the temporary suspension of civil rights up to and including arrest without cause and summary executions. It has seldom been formally invoked in the United States because it is an extreme measure justified only when the survival of the government is in question. The fighting in Europe did not threaten the existence of the United States. Germany could not possibly invade. No insurgency threatened to storm the capitol in St. Paul. Nevertheless, McGee made a provocative call for martial law, which created a small scandal for the governor while he was running for reelection.[11]

In April 1918, Senator George Chamberlain held hearings before the Senate Military Affairs Committee in Washington on his bill that gave military tribunals jurisdiction over citizens charged with sedition. John McGee was invited to testify, and he took full advantage of his appearance on the national stage. McGee told the committee that the US attorney in Minnesota "lacks a fighting stomach," a blunt criticism of Alfred Jaques. He said he favored military courts because they would not be as "chicken-hearted" as regular judges nor as undependable as juries. "Where we made a mistake," he told the senators, "was in not establishing a firing squad in the first days of the war. We should now get busy, and have that firing squad working overtime." He startled the committee by asserting that the Nonpartisan League was twice as dangerous as the IWW. "A Non-Partisan League lecturer is a traitor every time," he said. "In other words, no matter what he says or does, a League worker is a traitor." Twin Cities newspapers characterized his testimony as "sensational."[12]

Following the hearing, reporters interviewed McGee at his hotel. He told them that convicting traitors was difficult in counties dominated by Germans and Swedes. For example, it was hard to get a jury to convict someone of treason in Brown County (where New Ulm, a largely German American town, was the county seat) or in Chisago County, home of many Swedes. Military tribunals should try sedition cases because juries in such places were unreliable.[13]

McGee did not get his military tribunals and firing squads, but when he returned from Washington, he pushed through a number of changes that strengthened the power of the MCPS and brought Minnesota closer to a kind of undeclared martial law. In May, the commission issued Order 33, which made the violation of its orders a misdemeanor punishable by up to three months in a county jail or a $100 fine. Prior to this, the commission had relied on counties and cities to create ordinances enforcing the commission's orders. Now the commission backed up its orders with a criminal sanction enforceable by its own peace officers or Home Guard units. In June the commission issued Order 37, the "work or fight" law, which obligated every Minnesota man to be "regularly engaged in some useful occupation." Sheriffs and other law enforcement officials were instructed to diligently seek out able-bodied men who were not employed and report them for prosecution to the local county attorney. The order stated that it was a defense to the charge if you were under sixteen, a bona fide student, physically unable to work, or temporarily unemployed "owing to differences" with an employer.[14]

The sweeping nature of the order, coupled with its vagueness, confused many people, including county attorneys. What exactly was a "useful occupation"? What if you were physically able to do some work but not others? What if you were leasing your farmland and living off the rent money? Many employers found the open-ended language congenial, however, and posted the order in their workplaces as a warning to employees. A worker had better think twice before quitting his job, and although the order seemed to exempt workers on strike, the MCPS might decide that any strike was illegal. The order also contributed to military recruitment, since unemployed men could be coerced into enlisting to avoid a criminal charge.

The military power of the MCPS was greatly increased in May by the formation of the Motor Corps, which gave the commission the capacity to quickly transport peace officers and Home Guard troops to trouble spots around the state. When the MCPS invited county sheriffs to St. Paul in August 1917, there was talk of a Motor Reserve, which could provide a local sheriff with a volunteer motorized posse in emergencies. This idea stagnated until May 1918, when Winfield R. Stephens, a motorcar salesman, proposed to Adjutant General Rhinow the creation of motorized units as part of the Home Guard. Stephens managed retail sales for the Pence Automobile Company, owned by pioneering auto dealer Harry Pence. As a leading industry official, Pence had supported the public relations stunt of advertising the 1917 automobile show using hundreds of marchers dressed in Ku Klux Klan costumes.

Rhinow gave Stephens "his hearty approval" and made him commander of the Motor Corps section of the Home Guard with the rank of major. Stephens recruited volunteers who could supply their own five-passenger motorcar. Rhinow bragged that Minnesota was the only state that had a "uniformed, armed, and thoroughly military body of business and professional men who have offered their own motor cars for any duty the state may see fit to call them on." Eventually, the Motor Corps grew to ten battalions composed of about 2,450 men.[15]

The Motor Corps went right to work. Discovering that three saloons in the southern Minnesota town of Blooming Prairie were

■ Over a thousand business and professional men driving more than six hundred cars attended the Motor Corps encampment at Camp Lakeview near Lake City in September 1918. They trained to respond to strikes and other disturbances. ***MNHS Sound and Visual Collection***

violating an earlier order, the commission had permanently closed them for the duration of the war. When Burnquist learned on July 1 that they were still in business, he ordered Rhinow to send troops to the town. Within hours, Rhinow and his troops, conveyed by eight Motor Corps vehicles, were on the road to Blooming Prairie, "at a high rate of speed." The adjutant general closed the saloons, posted guards who stayed in town for three weeks, and then rode back victorious to St. Paul with the Motor Corps. One of the saloonkeepers went to court in St. Paul and won an order stopping enforcement of Order 34. Tighe quickly got the state supreme court to quash the order and rule that the governor was acting within his legal powers.[16]

The most spectacular example of the move toward martial law

was the slacker raid, the popular term for the organized dragnets of draft-age men. The American Protective League took credit for inventing this new form of repression, which involved unjustified mass arrests. All men age twenty-one to thirty were required to register for the draft on June 5, 1917, and over nine million young men did so. There were additional registration dates during 1918. When it became clear that not everyone was complying with the Selective Service System, Albert Briggs of the American Protective League proposed that his agents concentrate on finding young men who were not registering or who were evading induction.

At first, the APL conducted investigations of individual men suspected of being in violation of the Selective Service Act. Briggs, however, took note of the federal government's nationwide raids of IWW offices and the sweep arrests of hundreds of Wobblies. He proposed a similar approach to draft evaders, taking advantage of the fact that the law required men to carry proof of their draft status. The APL enlisted the cooperation of local draft boards (to verify the draft status of detainees), the Bureau of Investigation (to legitimize their arrests of civilians), and Home Guard and National Guard companies (to supply the armed manpower).[17]

The Minneapolis APL claimed the distinction of staging the very first slacker raid in the nation on March 26, 1918. About 130 APL agents, a Minneapolis Home Guard company, and local Bureau of Investigation agents raided lodging houses in the downtown Gateway district after midnight and took twenty-one men into custody. Pleased with the result, the APL decided to conduct a larger operation on April 6, in which about 250 APL agents joined twelve Home Guard companies in raids throughout the city. Over a thousand men were arrested and held in a "bull pen" at the county courthouse. The newspaper recounted various stories, such as how the Home Guard invaded a dance hall downtown and lined up all the women on one side and all the men on the other. Over fifty of the men were arrested, leaving many women without their escorts. Another story concerned a traveler whose papers were in the baggage he had checked at the train station. He sat in custody while his train left without him. Hennepin County sheriff Otto Langum said the raid was "very successful." However, only twenty-four of those arrested were still being held the next day, and they were all awaiting the delivery of their credentials from home. The "mammoth raid," the *Minneapolis Morning Tribune* reported, would likely not result in the capture of a single real slacker. Very few of the men detained in these sweep arrests were draft evaders, although they were technically in violation of the law for leaving their homes without their draft papers.[18]

Inspired by the Minneapolis example, a larger, more efficient slacker raid was organized on May 11 in Duluth. The Duluth raid was a collaboration between George Warren, who supervised the draft boards in Duluth, and Adjutant General Walter Rhinow, who authorized the participation of the 3rd Battalion of the Home Guard and the newly formed 4th Regiment of the Minnesota National Guard. The four companies of the Home Guard were supplied with long pine clubs, which they dubbed "persuaders." A fleet of trucks, mobilized by a committee of businessmen, was on hand to transport soldiers and prisoners.

The Home Guard and the 4th Regiment blockaded the main streets in downtown Duluth and demanded identification and draft papers from every young man. Guardsmen went into pool halls, dance halls, and stores. Crowds emerging from theaters were confronted with squads of soldiers demanding draft papers from all draft-age men. Couples were separated; in some cases, the women rushed home to find their husband's or boyfriend's draft papers. When all the men trapped in the downtown cordon were arrested or released, the troops moved to other parts of the city. Over a thousand men were arrested that evening in what the *Duluth News Tribune* approvingly called a "city wide loyalty coup." By the next day, about 175 had not yet proven their draft status, and it is not clear how many evaders were found. Neither the Home Guard nor the Minnesota National Guard had the legal standing to arrest civilians, at least without being deputized by the sheriff or after a formal declaration of martial law. Nevertheless, General Rhinow characterized the conduct of his troops as "perfect." In fact, as the *Duluth Herald* put it, "the city was practically under martial law, that is, as far as young men were concerned." But of course, no government body had declared martial law. The slacker raids would continue through the summer months.[19]

Minnesotans also experienced a tightening of the screws during the Third Liberty Bond campaign, which began in April. Minnesota had exceeded its goal in bond sales in the second campaign, but many rural counties fell short of their quotas. Campaign organizers recognized that bond sales were weakest where anti-war sentiment had been strongest. In response local bond committees were instructed to compute an "allotment" for everyone based on ability to pay, determined by property holdings, debt obligations, and income, with allowances made for bonds purchased earlier. The new system was augmented by a massive educational campaign.[20]

The organizers hyped the allotment system as a democratic reform of the Liberty Bond campaign. In practice, however, threatening individuals for not meeting a government-imposed quota was one more step in transforming a voluntary system into a coercive one. In any case, the new system resulted in increased bond sales. In Minnesota, the Third Liberty Bond campaign brought in $99 million, exceeding the state's goal by $27 million. Many rural counties reported big numbers, and overall, rural counties now accounted for more than half the bond sales.[21]

The final step in making the purchase of Liberty Bonds mandatory came with the Fourth Bond campaign in the fall, when the MCPS authorized its county directors to subpoena citizens who had not bought enough bonds. In Martin County, home of the aggressive County Attorney Allen, however, this was already the norm during the Third Bond campaign. In April, the sheriff delivered subpoenas to farmers requiring their appearance before the local public safety commission. Once there, they either bought the required bonds or were publicly questioned about their property holdings, expenses, and patriotism. One farmer, Martin Theide, said he could not afford to buy the required $500 in bonds because he had ten children at home to clothe and feed. The board told Theide to borrow money to buy the bonds, which the board estimated would cost him $18.75 a year in interest. When Theide said he could not spare even that much, a board member pledged to "take the bonds off your hands at the end of the year" if Theide would buy them now. The farmer agreed, but only after getting the pledge in writing.[22]

The Damnable Dilemma in Minnesota

In the spring, the MCPS commissioned a new Home Guard battalion that was quite unlike all the others. Generally, men joined Home

Guard and Motor Corps battalions to protect the status quo. This new unit, the 16th Battalion of the Home Guard, was organized to challenge a deeply entrenched social norm.

Nationally, most African Americans leaders declared their patriotism while at the same time demanding urgent reforms like an anti-lynching law. They hoped that loyalty during wartime would lead to improved civil rights in peacetime. In this spirit, the NAACP had faced the "damnable dilemma," as W. E. B. Du Bois put it, and campaigned for the training camp for African American officers even though it reinforced the army's segregation. The camp's graduates helped fill out the officer ranks in the two African American divisions of the US Army and eventually went to France.

African Americans in Minnesota faced the same dilemma. The St. Paul and Minneapolis communities honored the young men who were drafted, participated in Liberty Bond drives, and held patriotic rallies. In recognition of tireless work giving patriotic speeches at Liberty Bond rallies and receptions honoring draftees, the War Department named attorney William T. Francis an official "war orator," tasked with explaining the government's war aims to the African American community. The Folk-Song Coterie, the musical group led by his wife, Nellie Francis, regularly performed at Liberty Bond rallies and other patriotic events.[23]

The bitter reality, however, was that the state's military forces were just as segregated as the national ones. The Minnesota National Guard had never admitted African Americans, or even created separate African American units as some northern states had done. With an integrated military beyond reach, some African Americans leaders decided that an African American Home Guard battalion would be a step forward.

The idea was first floated by Charles Sumner Smith, editor of the *Twin City Star*, in a speech he gave at a farewell reception for African American draftees in October 1917. About five months later, Clarence Wigington, a St. Paul architect, led a group that petitioned Governor Burnquist to approve the formation of a segregated Home Guard battalion. At the time, Wigington was the senior draftsman in the office of the St. Paul city architect. He may have had a personal connection with the governor, who was president of the St. Paul branch of the NAACP.[24]

Within a few weeks, Wigington had recruited enough St. Paulites to form two companies of about a hundred men each. Two more companies were formed in Minneapolis. The companies elected their own leaders, who were then commissioned by Adjutant General Rhinow. In St. Paul, Wigington became captain of Company A, earning him the lifelong nickname of "Cap." Jose Sherwood, a postal clerk who was a national leader of the Freemasons, was chosen captain of Company B. He was well respected in the community for his strong opposition to the local showing of *The Birth of a Nation*. In Minneapolis, Gale P. Hilyer, a recent graduate of the University of Minnesota Law School, assumed leadership of Company C, and Charles Sumner Smith, a Spanish-American War veteran, became Company D's captain. Smith, who was critical of Burnquist, sarcastically editorialized that the governor approved the battalion just to get the votes of "the cullud people." Nevertheless, he urged men to join and took a leadership role. Subsequently, Jose Sherwood was given command of the entire battalion with the rank of major, and Orrington Hall, a founding member of the local NAACP and a YMCA leader, became the captain of Company B. Dr. Valdo Turner, long associated with the NAACP, led the Medical Corps, and William H. Howard, also a veteran, took command of the battalion band, which was based in Minneapolis. The St. Paul companies also maintained a drum corps.[25]

▪ **Major Jose Sherwood, a respected leader of the NAACP and the Masons in St. Paul, commanded the 16th Battalion of the Minnesota Home Guard.** ***Minnesota War Records Commission, MNHS collections***

The four companies began weekly drills in preparation for the Memorial Day parades. On that day Companies A and B marched with the other Home Guard companies in the St. Paul parade, and Companies C and D marched in the Minneapolis parade. They had not yet received uniforms, but they wore white gloves and carried flags from their fraternal organizations. Charles Sumner Smith's newspaper reported that the Minneapolis companies received compliments and "special applause." He wrote that their appearance "recalled the valor of the Negro troops in all the wars of this nation, and was a strong protest against the many injustices suffered by the Negroes because of sectional lawlessness." The two Minneapolis companies participated in the Flag Day parade, which culminated at the Parade park, where Governor Burnquist and AFL president Samuel Gompers sat in the reviewing stand.[26]

In April, Company B hosted the "first grand Home Guard ball" in St. Paul, kicking off a series of military balls organized by the battalion or one of its four companies. Typically, the battalion band provided the music. Following the Flag Day parade, the Minneapolis companies hosted a reception and dance "attended by many of the most respectable ladies," as well as delegations from the St. Paul companies. To raise funds for the band, Lieutenant William Howard presented his forty-piece band at a formal concert featuring vocalists and comedians at Dania Hall in Minneapolis shortly before the armistice.[27]

Adjutant General Rhinow never ordered the 16th Battalion to participate in the Home Guard's controversial activities such as slacker raids, control of labor unrest, or interference in NPL campaigning. In fact, the battalion's activities were limited to hosting social events and performing ceremonial duties like escorting African American draftees to the train station. Wigington and his colleagues were not able to desegregate Minnesota's military, but they did succeed in cracking open the door that barred African Americans from military service in Minnesota.

The Never Such Primary

The NPL decision to challenge Burnquist in the Republican primary sent a shock wave through the Minnesota political scene. The conservative leadership of the Republican Party, and the many newspaper editors supportive of this wing of the party, were alarmed at the NPL's growing strength. They argued that the NPL was the tool of extreme

Socialists (often described as "Bolsheviki"), and they were convinced that an NPL victory would lead to radical change. The state faced, the *Minneapolis Morning Tribune* proclaimed, the "never such" primary, the "most important political battle ever waged in Minnesota."[28]

Burnquist's campaign had begun with his blistering March 11 open letter rejecting the invitation to speak at the NPL conference. His attack on the NPL thrilled many conservative Republicans, especially businessmen, many of whom wrote letters and sent telegrams to the governor congratulating him for his stand. When writing to the governor, some influential conservative Republicans felt free to speak their minds. For example, Edwin Mead, editor of *Commercial West*, the leading business newspaper of the region, told the governor his newspaper would carry the open letter that was a "splendid service to the people of the Northwest." Slipping into the language of white nationalism, he wrote that the NPL leaders "should all be sent to Russia with the rest of the Bolsheviki and kept out of a white man's country like the United States." Charles Bovey, an executive at Washburn-Crosby Company (later General Mills), expressed the "feeling of pride in you that has arisen in my mind" because of the governor's denunciation of the NPL. When the army begins to suffer casualties in France, he maintained, "I believe that we will hang or shoot anyone who dares to utter a false note." He apparently had lynch mobs in mind, since Minnesota had abolished capital punishment in 1911.[29]

Burnquist officially opened his campaign on May 6, pledging that he would "make no political speeches during the primary" but that he would respond to invitations to make "patriotic addresses." He wrote that "diverting the attention of our people through local politics from the matter of greatest importance is entirely out of place." However, since he claimed that his loyalty, and his opponent's lack of it, was the only issue, "patriotic addresses" were the bread and butter of his campaign.[30]

The MCPS and its county affiliates functioned as the governor's campaign organization. *Minnesota in the War*, its weekly newsletter, published the governor's letter to the NPL under the title "Sharp Rebuke Administered to Breeders of Class Hatred and Discontent During the National Crisis." Two editorials followed: the first heralded Burnquist as "the natural leader of all patriots" and praised him for making the task of winning the war his sole ambition. The second commended the governor, who "wisely pursues" a "straight and undeviating course which will have the sanction and support of the great mass of loyal and patriotic citizenship." Working behind the scenes, John McGee asked his friend Senator Knute Nelson to endorse Burnquist. The question, McGee wrote, was whether the primary would be won by Burnquist or "an anarchist and Bolsheviki like Lindbergh." Nelson responded with an open letter widely printed in the press that urged a vote for Burnquist, who was "a veritable Rock of Gibraltar in maintaining law and order, in sustaining the spirit of loyalty and patriotism among our people, and in faithfully supporting the Federal Government in the prosecution of the war."[31]

Burnquist held his first big campaign rally on March 29 in Worthington, joined by the local company of the Home Guard. The governor told a crowd of twenty-five hundred that immigrants who do not stand for the United States should be deported. In April, he spoke to patriotic rallies at Austin, Two Harbors, and International Falls, among other places. In Austin, he appeared on "Governor's Day," and according to the local newspaper "every heart was throbbing with patriotism." He inspected the local Home Guards and gave a speech in which he again called for deportation of the disloyal, this time adding that their property should also be confiscated. In May, Burnquist continued to travel the state speaking at "patriotic" rallies, usually organized by county affiliates of the MCPS. He spoke at Melrose, sharing the platform with Bishop Joseph F. Busch of St. Cloud, who belonged to the seven-member commission of public safety for Stearns County.[32]

In June, he spoke to large patriotic rallies at Becker, Virginia, Benson, and finally Long Prairie. According to the *Virginia Enterprise*, about twenty thousand people from around the Iron Range came to Virginia on June 9 to watch Burnquist review about a thousand Home Guard troops from two northern Minnesota battalions and deliver a "patriotic address" at a Range Loyalty Day celebration. Marching in the parade were six companies of the 4th Battalion (from Virginia, Hibbing, Chisholm, Grand Rapids, International Falls, and Buhl) and five from the 8th Battalion (from Eveleth, Gilbert, Biwabik, Ely, and Aurora). In his speech, the governor promised to do all he could "to stamp out disloyalists in the state, who by word and deed, stab our fighting boys in the back." He did not mention the coming election, but he was followed to the podium by Lieutenant. J. T. Bergen, pastor of the First Presbyterian Church in Minneapolis and a Home Guard officer. Bergen told the crowd that their country was "being attacked from behind the lines by fearful, treacherous propaganda and if it cannot be stamped out with the ballot, cold steel and the hot bullet may be necessary." The newspaper noted that "it was taken for granted that he referred to the Non-partisan League."[33]

Newspapers generally accepted without comment that Burnquist never addressed the issues that divided the state before the war started, like prohibition, women's suffrage, and taxation of iron ore mining, nor did he comment on the policy proposals of the NPL, like hail insurance for farmers and pensions for workers. His patriotic speeches, however, regularly attacked immigrants; in other words, he continued the "anti-hyphen" campaign of the prewar years. The governor did fulfill his promise to avoid "politics" in the sense that he never mentioned Lindbergh or the NPL.

The active support of the MCPS came with a downside. The governor got an earful about John McGee's notorious testimony in Congress, especially his suggestion that citizens of Swedish descent were not sufficiently loyal. Several Swedish newspaper editors wanted McGee removed from the MCPS, and Burnquist received many angry letters to the same effect. Upon his return to Minneapolis, McGee issued a statement denying any anti-Swedish bias and claiming that "some of my warmest and most intimate friends are of Swedish birth or extraction, and this includes Governor Burnquist." He did admit, however, that he had used Brown County, with a large German population, and Chisago County, which was overwhelmingly Swedish, as examples of places where it would be difficult to get a jury to convict for sedition. He refused to back down from his support for military tribunals, reiterating that the "certainty of conviction of the guilty before such a court with a prompt appearance of the guilty before a firing squad would have had and would still have a most restraining influence on the disloyal, seditious, and traitorous."[34]

Burnquist was not about to fire McGee, but he did try to distance himself. He told the press that Judge McGee was speaking for himself and not for the MCPS. He went on to say that, personally, he thought Minnesota was as loyal as any state in the nation. He defended the loyalty of Minnesotans who were born in Sweden or Germany, claiming that whatever their concerns when war was declared, they had proven by their level of enlistments and Liberty Bonds sales that they would "unquestionably do their part." If that were so, one might ask, why was the leading member of the MCPS calling for firing squads?[35]

* * *

Lindbergh kicked off his campaign on April 25 in the west-central town of Willmar, where he was joined by A. E. Bowen, the former North Dakota Socialist who was part of the NPL's inner circle. Townley probably wanted Bowen to campaign with Lindbergh because he did not think the candidate was a strong stump speaker, a skill for which Bowen was well known. In addition, Townley might have wanted a trusted lieutenant on the platform since Lindbergh steadfastly maintained that he was not an NPL member.[36]

After several appearances in northwest Minnesota, Lindbergh dropped south for a rally at the Rochester armory on May 9. During the next seven weeks, Lindbergh traveled the state, mostly speaking to farmers sympathetic to the NPL. A typical campaign stop was a large, open-air picnic hosted by an NPL farmer in southern or west-central Minnesota. On June 4, for example, Lindbergh, joined by Bowen and Lynn Frazier, the North Dakota governor, spoke at a large picnic near Osakis in Douglas County. Many campaign stops were unmolested, although local authorities were watchful. When Lindbergh and Bowen spoke to twelve hundred at a Sunday picnic in early June on a farm near Madelia, the sheriff and the county attorney of Wantonwan County were present but did not interfere. Lindbergh wrapped up his campaigning at a massive picnic at Wegdahl in Chippewa County on June 14, again with no interference.[37]

Sheriffs, prosecutors, and MCPS county directors in at least nineteen counties banned NPL campaigning. In addition, towns and cities sometimes blocked the Lindbergh campaign even where county officials had not acted. NPL supporters, and Lindbergh himself, were also the victims of vigilante violence. The assaults could be merely symbolic, as when Lindbergh was hung in effigy in two Goodhue County towns. They could also involve kidnapping and assault, as when a group of masked men in Pine County grabbed Nels Hokstad, an NPL farmer, as he was giving a talk at a rural schoolhouse. They took him out in the woods and administered hot tar and feathers to his back. According to the local newspaper, he was "stripped to the waist and

Charles Lindbergh speaking to a Nonpartisan League meeting near the western Minnesota town of Cottonwood. *MNHS collections*

given a liberal coat that denotes infamy." They then brought him into Hinckley, placed him in front of city hall, and rang the fire bell. In Rock County in southwestern Minnesota, someone fired a shotgun at the car carrying Lindbergh when he was campaigning with John Baer, the congressman from North Dakota. Baer recalled that Lindbergh sat up straight and told the driver not to drive too fast, "or they will think we are scared." NPL supporters also were victims of various kinds of vandalism, including painting their houses and barns with yellow paint and ripping campaign posters off their cars. Sometimes NPL supporters reacted violently. In St. Charles, a southern Minnesota town, a fight broke out when several men tore the Lindbergh banners from two automobiles that entered the town. The drivers resisted, and one of the vandals ended up on the ground "unconscious for a time." The visitors were charged with disorderly conduct. In New Prague, an NPL supporter shot at someone who tried to tear posters from his car. He was charged with assault.[38]

Many other campaign stops were blocked by the order of county or city officials, acting on behalf of local business interests, with the ban enforced by police chiefs, sheriffs and their "rural guards," Home Guard units, or groups of militant citizens. In late May, for example, Lindbergh made a swing through northeastern Minnesota, seeking to drum up votes among workers in the lumber and steel industries. Stops were scheduled in Duluth, West Duluth, Two Harbors, Cloquet, and the Iron Range town of Virginia. Halls were booked and paid for in advance, but in each location, the managers of the venues backed out at the last moment, apparently after being contacted by the Duluth chief of police. Lindbergh left the area without speaking to a single audience, blaming the local subsidiaries of the United States Steel Corporation, which, he argued, feared he would "establish the fact that the steel trust should pay taxes in the same proportion to their earnings as the wage-workers and farmers do."[39]

Lindbergh found no support in the local press, most of which was extremely hostile to the NPL. The *Duluth Herald*, for example, editorialized that "Duluth need make no apologies" for locking Lindbergh out of every venue. The paper declared its belief in free speech, but not for Lindbergh because only those "who are wholly and absolutely and devotedly for America" have such rights. Lindbergh could not even count on union support. *The Labor World*, the Duluth newspaper associated with the moderate wing of the labor movement, thought Lindbergh should be allowed to speak, but urged its readers to vote for Fred Wheaton in the Democratic primary.[40]

In what turned out to be an omen of future tragedies, the *Duluth Herald* published a letter from Father Iciek, a well-known Catholic priest, under the title "Notice to Lindbergh." Iciek was gratified that "the doors of large halls were slammed shut in the face of a disloyal candidate." But he went further, warning Lindbergh that "the air of Duluth is too pure for traitors to breathe." If the people of Duluth had not been so law-abiding, he said, "a committee might have been waiting at the depot with a rope and the candidate for high office in the state would certainly hold a high position on our aerial bridge with a red lamp tied to his feet and sign written across his dangling body, 'So shall it be to all traitors'"[41]

On June 10, Lindbergh ran into an ugly situation in Rice County in southern Minnesota, where he had gone to speak at a picnic with Congressman Baer. The sheriff arrived with his deputies and members of the Home Guard and informed the candidate that he could not speak in Rice County. In these situations, the campaign sought an alternative site. An NPL car caravan drove north through Northfield on the way to Waterford, just across the county line. The Home Guard followed the group there and broke up the meeting, which involved several hundred farmers. According to news reports, there was fighting and some injuries. The NPL cars then drove back to Northfield, where townspeople ripped banners off cars, resulting in more fighting.[42]

Lindbergh faced similar problems a few days later in St. Cloud. Herman Mueller, a local NPL legislative candidate, secured permission from the county board to use the Stearns County courthouse for a meeting. One local newspaper, the *Daily Journal Press*, was aghast, reporting that "by a vote of three to two, the county commission invited a riot to hold forth in St. Cloud." The majority, it reported, "seemed to be under the hypnotic spell of Townley and they voted to turn the grounds over to the alleged 'Hun' crowd." The mayor overrode the commissioners by banning the NPL from meeting within the city limits, although he allowed NPL cars to pass through the city to reach the rally that was moved to an outdoor site two miles west of St. Cloud. The mayor called on the Home Guard to patrol the streets, and a deputized contingent attended the rally with the county sheriff.

After all the controversy, about fifteen hundred farmers came to hear a band play patriotic tunes and listen to Lindbergh's and Bowen's speeches.[43]

In letters to Eva, Lindbergh insisted he was unfazed by the bitterness and by the physical danger he sometimes faced. "I do not think I have a single friend who worries less than I do," he told her, adding that "I am absolutely immune from anxiety." His stoicism may have masked a kind of fatalism about the state of Minnesota politics. In three separate letters during these months, he urged Eva to read Mark Twain's *The Mysterious Stranger*, the dark novella that had been published in 1916, six years after the author's death. Throughout the book, the devil indicts the moral weakness and hypocrisy of the human species. In one letter to Eva, Lindbergh typed out a long passage where the devil argues that throughout history a small handful always leads countries into war by shouting down the opposition. Eventually "free speech will be strangled" and "the whole nation—pulpit and all—will take up the war cry, and shout itself hoarse, and mob any honest man who ventures to open his mouth." Obviously thinking about his own experiences, he told her that the book "told life about as it runs." Lindbergh was not as pessimistic as Twain in his final years, but Eva felt the campaign hurt him more than he would admit and undermined his trust in people.[44]

In addition to the bans in many counties, the vigilante violence, and even the mobilizations of the Home Guard, the Lindbergh campaign also had to contend with the ongoing prosecutions brought by the county attorneys of Martin, Jackson, and Goodhue Counties. This trio of aggressive, southern Minnesota prosecutors charged Arthur Townley, Joseph Gilbert, and several other NPL organizers with sedition under the state statute. These charges were used to provide legal justification for banning NPL campaigning in those counties and elsewhere.

In Martin County, Albert Allen charged Townley and Gilbert with sedition based solely on the published resolutions of the NPL. In March, NPL lawyers had entered a demurrer, admitting that the NPL had published the documents but arguing that they did not constitute a crime. The judge agreed to send the case to the Minnesota Supreme Court to resolve the issue prior to trial. This resulted in a significant legal victory for the NPL. On July 5, the Supreme Court reversed the lower court, holding that the pamphlets were not seditious, but nothing more than a political platform, "somewhat flamboyant," intended to recruit citizens to an organization, the purpose of which is to "bring about a more equal distribution of wealth of the world among all classes of mankind." The cocky Martin County attorney had overplayed his hand. Unfortunately for the NPL, the decision came after the primary election had been decided.[45]

In Jackson County, E. H. Nicholas had a better idea, charging Townley and Gilbert with conspiracy to discourage enlistments based on the published resolutions but also on speeches given in the county by Gilbert and by Irving Freitag, an NPL organizer sent to the county by Gilbert. The local grand jury indicted them on May 21, less than a month before the primary. This case did not go to trial until after the armistice, and would end badly for the NPL leaders.

In Goodhue County, Thomas Mohn, the county attorney, persuaded the grand jury to indict three NPL organizers, Joe Gilbert, Louis Martin, and N. S. Randall, with discouraging enlistments in speeches they made in the town of Kenyon in August 1917. Mohn won convictions of Randall and Gilbert before the primary election, allowing Burnquist supporters to argue that a vote for Lindbergh, the NPL's candidate, was a vote for an organization led by convicted traitors.

In a kind of trial run, Mohn first prosecuted a case against Louis Martin not for the Kenyon event but for making an allegedly pro-German speech in the village of Goodhue. At his trial in April, Martin effectively refuted the charges with his own testimony and with the testimony of six defense witnesses who had heard him speak. Mohn made a rookie error by asking Martin to recount what he had said to the Goodhue audience that day. Martin happily responded with his practiced stump speech, complete with a pitch to buy Liberty Bonds. It took the jury about an hour to acquit him.[46]

Mohn had better luck trying Randall, Gilbert, and Martin for their Kenyon speeches. The trial of N. S. Randall began on April 30 and featured a bizarre episode that revealed a great deal about the business community in Red Wing, the county seat. On that evening, a group of masked men kidnapped George Breidel, an NPL organizer, from the St. James Hotel. This was no surprise to Breidel, who had been run out of Kenyon three weeks earlier by a mob. A caravan of about sixteen cars drove him about eight miles into the countryside and left him there. He was told to stay out of Red Wing, and a shot was fired, apparently to intimidate him. He spent the night in a farmer's house.[47]

Would a kidnapping at gun point from Red Wing's most prominent hotel by a group of Red Wing citizens lead to charges? The judge presiding over the Randall trial wanted the grand jury to investigate, but no witnesses could be found willing to identify the assailants or their automobiles. The investigation was dropped in the face of the solidarity of the bankers, merchants, and professionals of Main Street, who maintained their silence. The crime would be remembered, as historian Frederick L. Johnson wrote, "as one of the most brazen and widely witnessed felonies in Red Wing history."[48]

In this atmosphere, Randall's sedition trial began. Thomas Mohn called several Kenyon residents who testified that Randall had made seditious comments. His lawyers had twenty-seven witnesses prepared to refute the charges. The judge decided they could call only twelve. He also ruled that Randall could not repeat the full speech he had made in Kenyon in August. On May 4, the jury returned a guilty verdict after deliberating nine hours. Randall was sentenced to four months and a $250 fine, stayed pending an appeal.[49]

In another incident that exposed the raw political emotions in Red Wing, the court cited Fred Scherf, the NPL leader in Goodhue County, for contempt of court based on the allegation that he had tried to influence a juror in the Randall case. Scherf was unusual in that he was a farmer who also had a house in town. With his brother he ran a hardware and farm implement store in Red Wing. He had served as a county commissioner and as county treasurer. Scherf was Lindbergh's leading supporter in Goodhue County, and in addition, he was running for state legislature with NPL endorsement. He was accused of trying to influence the verdict by offering a juror the position of campaign manager. This implausible charge was dropped a week later. Meanwhile, vandals threw yellow paint at his house, and he was vilified at public meetings as a traitor.[50]

Scherf was running for the state senate seat held by Major Oscar Seebach, a member of another prominent German American family, and one which was deeply divided over the war. McGee had tapped Seebach to organize the Home Guard. After he established the first battalions, he resigned from the MCPS and entered active service in the army. Captain Fred Seebach, his brother, commanded Company A of the Home Guard's 5th Battalion, stationed in Red Wing. The loyalty of the two brothers was beyond question, and they must have been annoyed that John Seebach, their uncle, had been indicted by the Goodhue County grand jury for discouraging enlistments. Their nephew Carl, John's son, was also charged. The case against John Seebach would eventually be transferred to federal court, where he was convicted under the Espionage Act. If the Seebachs got together for Thanksgiving in 1918, one can only imagine the conversations.

On May 9, about a month before the primary, Mohn brought Joseph Gilbert to trial for the alleged seditious speeches in Kenyon. A. G. Hilton, the attorney general and MCPS member, came down from St. Paul to assist. The jury quickly agreed on a guilty verdict, and the judge imposed the maximum twelve-month sentence, which was stayed pending appeal. This conviction would be appealed all the way to the US Supreme Court, which affirmed Gilbert's conviction in a decision that is an important landmark in the development of the free speech law.[51]

The efforts of the trio of county attorneys came to a logical conclusion when Lindbergh himself was arrested in Martin County on June 8, nine days before the voters went to the polls. This was no surprise to Lindbergh, who had warned his daughter Eva in mid-April that he might be charged just "to get votes against me." County Attorney Allen took the position that no NPL candidate could legally speak in Martin County. He had in fact already arrested Meyer Brandvig, the NPL-endorsed candidate for state senate, on charges that he was preaching international socialism and the overthrow of the government on behalf of the NPL. Undaunted, Lindbergh arrived at a picnic in Martin County where about a thousand farmers had come to hear him. Sheriff Carver and his "Rural Guards" arrested Lindbergh as he was about to speak. There was no disturbance, but Carver also arrested Eric Olson, a seventy-two-year-old farmer, for advocating that the rural guard "be thrown over the fence." Local farmers quickly bailed Lindbergh out. The candidate shrugged off the charge, recognizing that the prosecution was a political stunt with no legal validity. Once the primary votes were counted, the charges were dropped.[52]

Criminal prosecutions were not the county attorneys' only contribution to the reelection of Governor Burnquist. Allen and Nicolas hit the campaign trail themselves, embarking on a speaking tour to twenty southern Minnesota cities. Presenting themselves as experts on the NPL, they sometimes appeared together, as at Rochester on May 26, St. Peter on June 1, and Red Wing on June 6, but often individually, appearing in towns from Pipestone on the South Dakota border to Winona on the Wisconsin border. Their rhetoric was unrestrained. "There is no safety, no honor," they told a large Rochester audience, "until Prussianism is crushed and her autocrat captured and caged." They went on to implausibly brand "revolutionary Socialism," which they alleged Townley and Lindbergh represented, as "the child and assistant of militant autocracy." Lindbergh, they argued, was a "Bolshevik" whose book contained enough disloyal statements to land him in Leavenworth Prison. Once the NPL came to power, they charged, all farmland would be seized and owned by the state. Like many Burnquist campaigners, they urged local Democrats to cross over to the Republican primary to save the state from the scourge of socialism.[53]

In the final week of the campaign, the NPL called on its members to come together on a township level to organize a big push. In southern and western Minnesota, many farmers responded by organizing massive car caravans called "booster tours" to demonstrate their strength and invigorate their supporters. By 1918, many farmers had automobiles, and in addition the NPL had purchased a fleet of Model T Fords for its organizers. The caravans, sometimes numbering hundreds of cars bearing NPL banners and Lindbergh campaign signs, drove from town to town, occasionally stopping for a meal or a rally. A band often traveled with the caravan to provide entertainment at the stops. Many townspeople were bitterly hostile to the NPL and the Lindbergh campaign, and the arrival of a caravan in a town often led to trouble.[54]

On June 11, the NPL planned a car caravan through Anoka County, just north of Minneapolis, with the intention of ending in the city of Anoka. In preparation, the local Loyalty League mobilized its Safety Guard of Anoka County, a group of armed automobile owners under the command of sheriff U. S. "Red" Pratt. The mission of the safety guard, among other things, was to "suppress or prevent either private or public meetings which shall have as their purpose the promulgation of any seditious or disloyal sentiments." Large convoys of safety guard cars forced the NPL caravan to avoid some towns on their route, and

■ **In the closing days of the campaign, the NPL organized massive car caravans in southern and western Minnesota. Many farmers owned automobiles, and NPL organizers drove Ford Model T touring cars purchased by the organization.** *MNHS collections*

when the caravan arrived in Anoka, banners were ripped from cars and several fist fights broke out.[55]

On June 12, the NPL organized a motor parade in Goodhue County, with a scheduled stop in Red Wing, the county seat, where NPL speakers hoped to hold a rally in Central Park. Fred Scherf appeared at the city council defending the NPL's right to use the park, but the council voted unanimously to deny the permit, a decision applauded by Jens Grondahl, who editorialized that a group already "pronounced seditious," should not "intrude themselves on a patriotic community." The county MCPS director W. H. Putnam, a local banker, issued a proclamation banning the NPL caravan from entering the city and ordering city and county police to enforce the order. He also mobilized Company A of the Home Guard. As noted by historian Frederick Johnson, the MCPS director had essentially placed Red Wing under martial law without consulting the mayor or the city council. The NPL parade of about 105 cars en route to Red Wing was stopped by the sheriff, who informed them of the ban and urged them not to proceed.

Most of the NPL cars decided to push on, and they succeeded in driving through Red Wing with NPL banners and Lindberg campaign signs displayed. Confronted with the rifles of the Home Guard, however, they did not stop for the scheduled campaign rally.[56]

A week before the primary, farmers from several counties in the Minnesota River valley organized caravans, all of which encountered violence when reaching towns. On June 12, Nicollet County farmers ran into trouble when entering St. Peter, the county seat. There a group of men ripped banners off cars, leading to fights. Later these farmers confronted more violence when they tried to cross the Minnesota River bridge into Mankato. On June 13, an NPL caravan was confronted by angry townspeople at Madison Lake, a town just east of Mankato. A woman from North Dakota who identified herself as an NPL organizer was arrested for pulling a gun on someone who pulled a banner off her car and then got into a fight with her husband. When this caravan reached Mankato, several fights broke out. The chief of police stopped an NPL car caravan at the New Prague city limits on June 16. When they did not immediately turn back, the sheriff was unable to restrain "the large crowd of men and boys" who threw rotten eggs and fruit at the caravan and got into fights with some of the drivers. According to the local newspaper, a few of the NPL women "were especially refractory."[57]

The worst violence might have been on June 14, when a car caravan, which started in Sleepy Eye, in western Brown County, arrived at the small town of Comfrey. The farmers found that the townspeople had barricaded the road. When the farmers tried to get by the barricade, the townspeople threw eggs and stones, and several NPL members were assaulted with clubs. Some townspeople were armed, and shots were fired, although apparently no one was hit. Finally, on June 15, an NPL caravan of about 150 cars entered the village of Elysian, about ten miles east of Mankato, where a rally was planned. There they were met by fifty cars carrying opponents. The Le Sueur County sheriff stopped the rally, on the grounds that it could lead to a riot. In reporting this incident, the *Mankato Daily Free Press* noted that "women in the Nonpartisan party seemed to be the most aggressive."[58]

One of the largest NPL car caravans traveled through Kandiyohi County in west-central Minnesota on June 14. As reported in the *Willmar Tribune*, a newspaper sympathetic to the NPL, the parade started at the tiny town of Svea, about ten miles south of Willmar, the county seat. There were stops for brief rallies at several towns, and by the time it reached Willmar, there were over three hundred cars. Because of threats of violence, the parade leaders decided to drive through town without stopping for speeches. Nevertheless, some townspeople ripped Lindbergh signs off passing cars. By the time the parade reached its last stop in New London, it had grown to seven hundred cars and was over nine miles long.[59]

The Burnquist and Lindbergh campaigns spoke to Minnesotans in essentially different languages. The governor asked voters to choose patriotism over disloyalty. Lindbergh asked voters to choose economic democracy over profiteering. The contest, however, was not decided solely on the merits. The ability of the Lindbergh campaign to communicate its message was severely restricted. The combined efforts of the MCPS, especially its county-level affiliates, the sheriffs of many counties, the Home Guard, the trio of southern Minnesota prosecutors, and vigilantes who acted with impunity made it impossible for the NPL to campaign in some counties and difficult to do so in others. In addition, many voters must have been troubled by the fact that several NPL leaders and, in the end, even Lindbergh himself were being prosecuted for sedition.

Minnesota Politics Reset

Voters got the message that this primary was something special. Nearly 383,000 people came to the polls on June 17, compared to only about 261,000 who voted in the 1916 primary. When the official results were announced, Burnquist had won, with 199,325 votes to Lindbergh's 150,626. In the Democratic primary Fred E. Wheaton beat W. L. Comstock in a close contest that attracted only 32,649 voters. The Democrats were the smaller party, but in the 1916 primary they had polled 93,112 votes. More than 350,000 voted in the Republican primary, far exceeding the 168,308 Republican voters in 1916. Clearly, many Democratic voters had heeded the call to cross over and vote for the governor.[60]

Conservatives celebrated what they characterized as a landslide for Burnquist. Although Townley must have been disappointed, the NPL publicly heralded the results as a victory, arguing that Lindbergh's

Election Results

June 1918 Republican Gubernatorial Primary

Shading indicates the thirty counties in which Charles Lindbergh won a majority of the vote.

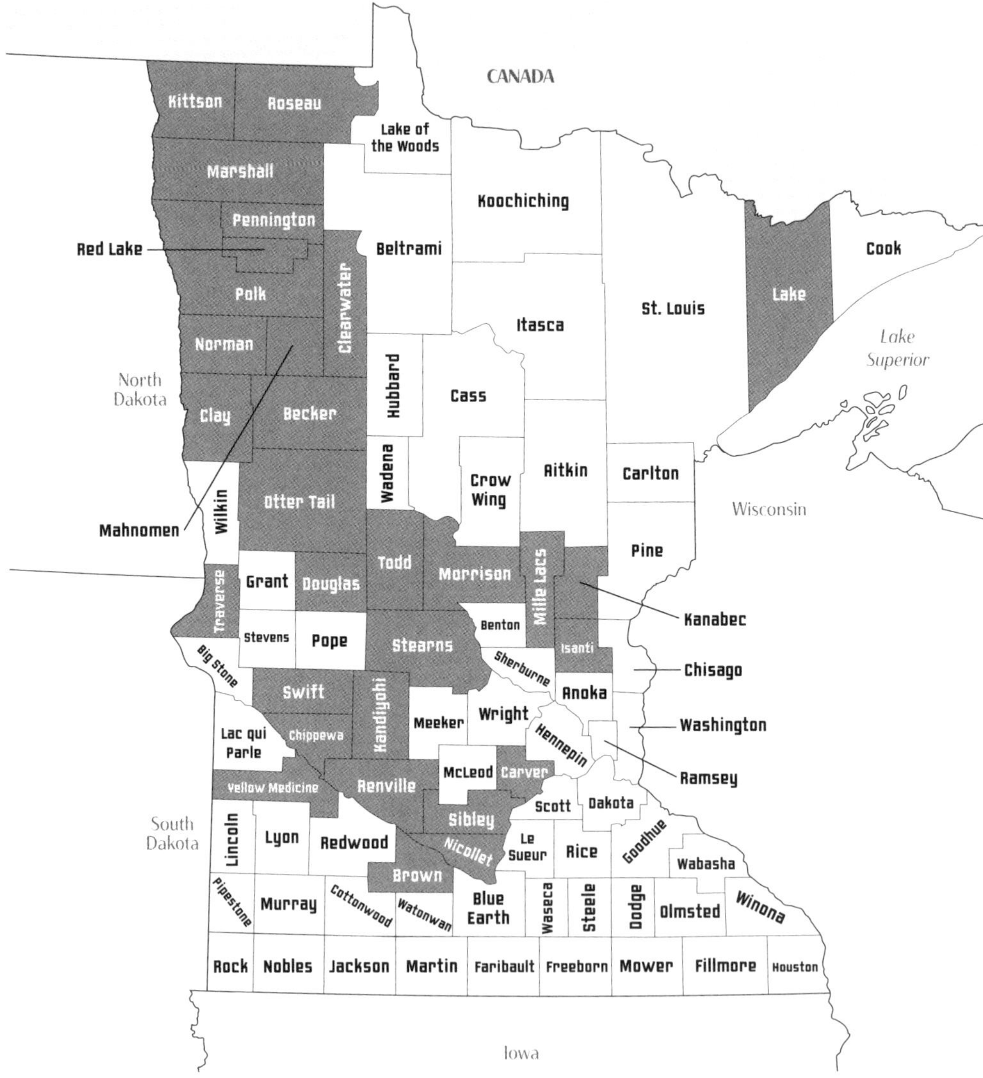

NOTES ■ Two other counties were decided by just a few votes: Burnquist prevailed by one vote in Aitkin County and by five votes in Chisago County. ■ The Canadian border county of Lake of the Woods was created in 1923. Prior to that, its territory was part of Beltrami County.

vote was impressive given the difficulties the campaign faced and the fact that he won 150,000 votes in a state where the NPL had only 50,000 members. The NPL slogan was "We'll stick," and it appeared that its farmer members statewide and organized labor in the Twin Cities did in fact stand firm for Lindbergh. The NPL was also thrilled that a strong majority of its endorsed legislative candidates had done well in the primary and would be on the general election ballot in November.[61]

Lindbergh outpolled Burnquist in thirty of Minnesota's eighty-six counties. These counties included all the wheat-producing Red River Valley counties in the northwest and almost all the counties in the Minnesota River valley, many of which had large German populations. On the other hand, Burnquist prevailed in the two tiers of southern Minnesota counties along the Iowa border, and in almost all the northeastern counties, including St. Louis, home of the Iron Range and Duluth. Despite a strong labor vote for Lindbergh in Minneapolis and St. Paul, Burnquist also prevailed in Hennepin and Ramsey Counties.

A closer look at the results reveals the deep division between townspeople and farmers. Whether a rural county reported a Burnquist or Lindbergh majority, the town votes were overwhelmingly for Burnquist, and the farm votes, collected on a township level, usually showed a Lindbergh majority, often 70 percent and higher. In Clay County in the Red River Valley, for example, Burnquist did very well in Moorhead, the county seat, and several other towns, but lost the county because Lindbergh took almost every rural township. The NPL had a particularly satisfying victory in nearby Douglas County, the home of Senator Knute Nelson, who had personally endorsed Burnquist. Lindbergh won 68 percent of the vote in the county, even though Burnquist prevailed in Alexandria, the county seat. The deep polarization of the county's electorate can be seen in Osakis Township, a few miles east of Alexandria. In the rural parts of the township Lindbergh won 124 votes to 18 for Burnquist. In the village of Osakis, the only urban settlement in the township, Burnquist won 185 votes to Lindbergh's 24. The village boundary marked a stark political divide.[62]

In southern Minnesota, the same pattern prevailed, although Lindbergh did not win every rural township, and when he did, it was by smaller margins. The voting sometimes echoed the violent antagonism of the campaign. In Elysian Township in Le Sueur County, rural voters returned a 119 to 75 vote majority for Lindbergh. In the village of Elysian, which had repelled an NPL car caravan just a week earlier, only 3 of the 96 votes cast went to Lindbergh. Burnquist did very well in Goodhue County, based on a strong showing in Red Wing and other towns. Lindbergh, however, carried many rural townships, and Fred Scherf, the NPL's candidate for the local senate seat, outpolled three other candidates and went on to the general election ballot. Meyer Brandvig, the NPL candidate under indictment for sedition in Martin County, was not successful. In a three-way race for the state senate seat, he came thirteen votes shy of surviving the primary.[63]

Burnquist was victorious in Minneapolis and St. Paul, but Lindbergh did well in wards with significant working-class populations. In St. Paul, Lindbergh won eight of the twelve wards, including the First Ward on the city's east side, where Burnquist had lived before he moved to the governor's mansion. Burnquist had represented this largely Swedish area in the legislature, but the residents who worked for the railroads or Hamm's Brewery turned against him. On the other hand, middle class and wealthy St. Paulites rallied to Burnquist, as indicated by the fact that the governor won 84 percent of the vote in the Seventh Ward, which included Summit Avenue, home to large residences and mansions, and the neighborhoods to the north and south of that opulent street.

The ethnic background of the candidates played little role since each was the son of parents born in Sweden. As it turned out, Lindbergh attracted a majority of the Swedish vote, probably because most Swedish voters were farmers or workers. Burnquist, on the other hand, was closely associated with Twin Cities business leaders, who were almost exclusively old stock Yankees. McGee's suggestion that Swedes were not reliably loyal did little to encourage Swedes to vote for Burnquist, who had appointed McGee and refused to discipline him.[64]

Conservative newspapers heralded the Burnquist victory as a death blow for "Townleyism." In a sense this was true. The Nonpartisan League would not accomplish in Minnesota what it had achieved in North Dakota. Nevertheless, the campaign was a crucial turning point in Minnesota politics. As Carl Chrislock cogently argued, the electoral struggles of 1918 marked the end of the Progressive Era in Minnesota. The bipartisan coalition of moral reformers, farmers, and small-town professionals and businessmen "was shattered beyond repair." The violence that erupted between farmers and Main Street during the campaign provides ample evidence. Moderately Progressive professionals and businessmen, traumatized by the NPL and fearful of socialism, gravitated toward the conservative, "stand-pat," big-business-dominated wing of the Republican Party. The NPL meanwhile had assembled a new coalition of farmers, trade unionists, German Americans, and left-leaning Progressives. It would take a few years for this coalition to develop a stable institutional form. When it did, the Farmer Labor Party would emerge.[65]

NINE

THE LOYALTY REGIME

LATE SUMMER & AUTUMN 1918

> You have proven yourself to be an enemy of America. Let this be your warning. . . . The slacker will not be tolerated in St. Louis County. . . . The knights strike quick and strike well. We do not persecute, but if warning of tar and feathers is not sufficient to your warped and craven soul it is time you take stock of yourself and analyze your soul. America needs you not. . . . This is your final warning, take heed.
>
> Statement of the "Knights of Loyalty" published in the *Duluth Herald* on September 19, 1918, addressed to six immigrants who had renounced their citizenship shortly after one of them had been kidnapped

> If the government wants money from me it will have to tax me. I no longer have any heart in giving help to causes which are controlled by a group of short-sighted, incompetent men.
>
> SARAH COLVIN, Minnesota chair of the National Woman's Party, as quoted in the *St. Paul Pioneer Press*, October 2, 1918, refusing to buy more Liberty Bonds after the US Senate defeated the suffrage amendment

IN JULY, the fifth and last German offensive was sputtering and the massive Allied counteroffensive began. The United States was now a major player, fielding forty-two of the 220 total Allied divisions. American troops held their own in the operation to close the bulge in the front line at St. Mihiel, in the Battle of Meuse-Argonne, and in the Belleau Wood actions. In September, American troops also participated in the Allied intervention in Russia, landing troops in the port of Arkhangelsk in the far north and at Vladivostok in far eastern Siberia. These incursions were initially intended to shore up the eastern front in the wake of Russia's departure from the war, but Allied troops were soon fighting the Bolsheviks in the Russian Civil War.

Besides their enemies, all the armies struggled against the influenza pandemic, the second wave of which roared across the world in the latter half of 1918. Armies proved to be prime breeding grounds for the virus, especially when men lived together in cramped barracks or troopships. The American army shipped to France lost eleven thousand to the pandemic, in addition to many more from combat. The pandemic struck harder at the troops still training in the stateside camps, killing twenty-three thousand.[1]

By mid-October, Germany was all but finished, and its allies Turkey and Austria-Hungary had already capitulated. By November, revolution had broken out in Germany, sparked by a naval mutiny, mass army desertions, and strikes in the cities. General Erich Ludendorf resigned on October 27, Kaiser Wilhelm abdicated on November 9, and the new government led by the Social Democratic Party signed an armistice on November 11.

The Final Months of Training

In mid-August, the 34th Division, including the three Minnesota National Guard infantry units, finally received orders to leave Camp Cody in New Mexico and travel east to board ships bound for France. After almost a year in the desert, the original guard units had been transformed by continual transfers, and it is unclear how many Minnesotans remained. The full division did not reach France until October, too late to join in actual fighting.[2]

Primarily through conscription, the Wilson administration sought to have five million men in the military by 1919. In June 1918, the Selective Service System required the registration of all men who had turned twenty-one since the initial registration of June 1917. In August, the process was repeated for men who had turned twenty-one in the previous two months. When Congress amended the law to extend eligibility for the draft to men as young as eighteen and as old as forty-five, there was a massive new registration on September 12 of men under twenty-one and over thirty. Thirteen million men lined up shoulder to shoulder in post offices and city halls to register, inadvertently spreading the influenza virus.

Minnesotans who entered the army through the Selective Service System went to various camps, but the majority trained at Camp Dodge in Des Moines. Draftees of European and Native American heritage were incorporated into the new 88th Division. Many were later transferred to Camp Lewis, where they joined the 91st Division. The 88th Division left Camp Dodge in August, and was assigned to a quiet sector at the front and saw little action. The 91st Division left Camp Lewis in July and arrived in France in time to participate in combat along the Meuse River.[3]

The many new divisions required thousands of new officers. As a stopgap measure, President Wilson in August created the Student Army Training Corps, which transformed five hundred colleges and universities into training centers for officers and technical specialists. In Minnesota, the university, Dunwoody Industrial Institute, and six private colleges participated. Students were enlisted as privates in the army and studied a combination of academic and military subjects. They lived on campus, often in makeshift barracks, under military discipline. There were about six thousand student-soldiers at the university, 850 at Dunwoody, and smaller numbers at the colleges. By all accounts, the program got off to a rough start, a result of the very short time the institutions had to prepare and the fact that the fall semester coincided with the worst period of the influenza pandemic. There was also the more fundamental problem, articulated by Marion Burton, the university president, that "a true university cannot be a military camp," since the former is about free inquiry and the latter is about strict compliance with orders.[4]

Only two Minnesota units retained their original character. The Minnesota National Guard's 1st Field Artillery, which was sent to Camp Mills, New York, became the 151st Artillery in the 42nd or Rainbow Division. The 151st sailed for France in October 1917, about the same time the 6th Regiment Marines, a unit recruited largely from the University of Minnesota, was making the trip across the ocean. Both units helped stop the German offensive in the Champaigne sector, played a major role at Chateau-Theirry, and were active in pushing the Germans back in the Meuse-Argonne fighting.[5]

African Americans trained in a separate part of Camp Dodge, and some of them joined draftees from six other camps to form the 92nd Division, one of the two African American combat divisions. Although African Americans were barred from the top positions in the division's command structure, many of this division's junior officers were graduates of the African American training camp at Fort Des Moines, a nearby camp. With limited training, the 92nd was sent to France in July, saw combat, and suffered significant casualties.

The 93rd Division, the other African American division, was composed primarily of National Guard units from New York, Illinois, and a few other states that had established African American units. General Pershing loaned the 93rd Division to the French army, and it achieved a legendary record as a fighting unit, in part because the soldiers of the division found more acceptance in the French army than in the American Expeditionary Force.[6]

In 1917, the NAACP had advocated for the Fort Des Moines officer training camp even though it would be segregated, hoping that African American participation in the war effort would lead to positive results after the war. W. E. B. Du Bois, editor of *The Crisis*, the organization's magazine, went further in his July 1918 editorial "Close Ranks," which urged African Americans "to forget our special grievances and close our ranks shoulder to shoulder with our white fellow citizens and the allied nations that are fighting for democracy."[7]

On July 5, 1918, Camp Dodge was the scene of an event that called Du Bois's optimism into question. Over forty thousand soldiers, from both sides of the color line, including about three thousand African Americans, were ordered to assemble at hastily constructed gallows to witness the hanging of three African American soldiers. They had been charged with rape and court-martialed within a week of their arrest. Newspaper reporters described an awful situation, as the condemned men prayed and sang and "the shrieks of Negro soldiers, unwilling and terrified spectators . . . added to the sickening scene."[8]

Rooting Out the Disloyal

The MCPS and its allies held firm control of the home front in the late summer of 1918, although many Minnesotans, including farmers, trade unionists, and German and Scandinavian Americans of all classes, believed that the unelected commission had wielded power far beyond what was appropriate or even constitutional. To counter critics, Ambrose Tighe gave a speech at the State Bar Convention justifying the commission's de facto martial law with a public health analogy. Two months before a real epidemic arrived, he suggested that dissidence about the war created a public danger analogous to a hypothetical epidemic: "If . . . a health board can compel vaccination and prescribe and enforce a penalty for the violation of its orders . . . why, in the event of war, cannot a board or commission, with powers expressed in identical language, promulgate and enforce orders when,

▪ In late 1918 the commissioners posed for this portrait, which shows the Minnesota Commission of Public Safety in its final form. Clockwise around the table are Thomas E. Cashman (who replaced John Lind), Anton C. Weiss, Henry W. Libby (who replaced Charles W. Ames), Governor Joseph Burnquist, Attorney General Clifford L. Hilton (who replaced Lyndon Smith), Ambrose Tighe, John F. McGee, and Charles H. Marsh. ***MNHS collections***

in its judgment, such are needed to preserve the public safety and to protect life and property, and are calculated to most efficiently apply the state's resources to the great job ahead of us, 'the winning of the war'?" His suggestion that war critics were like germs the state could extrajudicially eradicate eerily anticipated the rhetoric of the postwar dictators.[9]

It was the season of loyalty, and a difficult time for war critics like Charles Lindbergh and Thomas Van Lear. In the June primary, Van Lear earned a spot on the November ballot by coming in second behind J. E. Meyers, the Republican candidate. Van Lear's strong suit was his willingness to take on the Twin Cities Rapid Transit Company, seeking the best possible deal for riders. Meyers followed the Burnquist playbook, campaigning as a loyalist who would save Minneapolis from socialism, which he equated with Bolshevism and opposition to the war.[10]

After the bruising June primary, Lindbergh took a break and did some traveling by train. He wrote to his daughter Eva that he preferred day coaches to Pullmans because he wanted to talk to people traveling short distances and learn about local conditions. In August, he was offered an appointment to join the War Industries Board. Lindbergh went to Washington to work out the details with Bernard Baruch, the wealthy financier who led the board. He expected to begin work in two weeks.

When news of his appointment became public in Minnesota, conservatives raised a storm of protest. The *Minneapolis Morning Tribune*, for example, editorialized that it was "past all comprehension" that the Nonpartisan League's candidate for governor "should be chosen for a position of trust" in the federal government. The *Tribune* and other newspapers argued that Lindbergh's *Why Is Your Country at War* book alone disqualified him. There was even talk of boycotting the Fourth Liberty Loan campaign if Lindbergh was appointed. Senator Knute Nelson received many letters and telegrams protesting Lindbergh's appointment, which he bundled and forwarded to Baruch. The Republican State Central Committee, for example, wrote that "the mere mention of his name is an insult to the Loyal citizens of our State." Nelson responded to each protester by saying that Lindbergh had not yet been appointed, which was not true, and that he was not likely to hold the position, which was accurate.[11]

Lindbergh withdrew on September 10, noting in a letter to Baruch that the "the forces of opposition within the state have had their effect." Stoic as ever, he refused to publicly attack those who blocked his appointment, but in a letter to Eva he mentioned the "well understood forces who were willing to subvert their loyalty to selfish personal ends," including heads of Liberty Bond committees, the major newspapers, and "certain U.S. senators." Once again battered, Lindbergh sought respite by joining James Manahan, the NPL lawyer, at his lake cabin north of St. Paul later in the fall. Manahan remembered Lindbergh's "very neat sense of humor," and how he stripped down and swam in the cold lake water. Lindbergh told Manahan that "there isn't any better medicine for the mind and body than just what we have been enjoying."[12]

Why the Wilson administration offered Lindbergh a job is a mystery. Very likely George Creel played a role, although Lindbergh denied it. Creel steadfastly defended the loyalty of the NPL and argued that the league was a dependable ally of the Wilson administration. Surveying the scene from their Washington offices, Creel and Baruch underestimated the depth of hostility toward the NPL in conservative Republican circles in Minnesota. The debacle of Lindbergh's appointment was another example of the chasm separating the Wilson administration from the forces controlling Minnesota during the war.

Theodore Roosevelt had a better understanding of Minnesota. He came to Minneapolis on October 8 to promote the Fourth Liberty Bond Drive, which officially kicked off on September 28, 1918. Speaking to five different audiences, he delivered "the gospel of thoroughgoing Americanism" and, as he did in his earlier visit, denounced both the "Hun without" and the "Hun within our gates." The latter, he made clear, included the IWW, the Socialist Party, and the Nonpartisan League. To stop the "Hun within," he urged crowds to vote for Senator Knute Nelson, Governor Burnquist, Walter Newton (who had beaten anti-war congressman Ernest Lundeen in the Republican primary), and of course J. E. Meyers, who was Van Lear's opponent in the mayor's race.[13]

In the fourth campaign, the voluntary program to finance the war with loans from the population completed its transformation into a coercive system of regressive taxation. In the third campaign, local committees began computing the amount each person was expected to purchase and then pressured individuals to purchase their assigned allotments. In support of the fourth campaign, the MCPS issued Order 44, which gave the public safety director of each county the power to subpoena and question under oath any citizen (usually a farmer) who the chair of the local Liberty Loan committee (usually a banker) determined had not met their allotment. The director could require a farmer to bring financial records to the interrogation.[14]

The farmer was asked about the value of his land, buildings, house, and personal property; his income, expenses, and debts; and whether he owned a motorcar. If he resisted, he might be asked about his attitude toward Germany and whether he wanted the United States to win the war. Often a farmer was willing to buy bonds but disputed the amount of the allotment. In Redwood County, for example, Carl Drusch testified that he could buy $250 in bonds, but not the $600 required. He was told that the local bank was ready to loan whatever funds needed to purchase the full allotment.[15]

These inquisitions were generally effective in encouraging the purchase of the required bonds. Some farmers, however, would not budge. The local directors felt there must be some way to compel compliance, but in fact no law required citizens to buy Liberty Bonds. Henry Libby, the MCPS secretary, responded to frustrated local directors by explaining that "slackers" would be adequately punished by the public scorn of their neighbors.[16]

Order 44, however, stated that the evidence elicited during these investigations could not be made public without MCPS approval (which they never gave). Local directors sometimes threatened to punish "slackers" by publicizing their names in local newspapers. The Liberty Loan committee in Morrison County, for example, produced a handout entitled "Yellow Slacker List for the Fourth Liberty Loan" with names organized by town and township. They asked the MCPS if it would be "libelous" to publish the list in local newspapers. Libby did not answer that question but told them they had better subpoena and question every person on the list before publicizing their names. In fact, newspapers generally declined to publish slacker lists. They may have worried that determination of a slacker was based on the arbitrary and opaque system of determining allotments. Men listed as slackers might simply be too poor to buy bonds, or even to pay the interest on a loan to buy bonds.[17]

Although not legally required to buy bonds, citizens who refused could still find themselves in legal trouble. In several cases, citizens who did not respond to a subpoena, or who refused to answer questions about their finances, found themselves in contempt of court. When a judge threatened them with fines and jail time, they usually agreed to buy some bonds. In Jackson County, for example, three men cited for contempt agreed to subscribe to their full allotment, and additionally two paid a fifty-dollar fine and the third was sentenced to ninety days. On several occasions a frustrated farmer under intense questioning responded with a statement that led to an indictment under the state sedition statute. Albert Allen, the ultrapatriotic Martin County attorney, charged several farmers with sedition for what they said when they refused to buy Liberty Bonds. In neighboring Watonwan County, a farmer was indicted months after the armistice for telling the bond committee that "the U.S. has no business in this war."[18]

The coercive tactics of the Fourth Liberty Bond campaign bore fruit. Minnesota raised about $133 million, approximately 8 percent over its quota. The organizers must have been pleased that even though Minneapolis, St. Paul, and Duluth continued to perform well, the urban share of the total sales had shrunk to 42 percent, suggesting the latest campaign had succeeded in selling more bonds in rural counties than in previous campaigns.[19]

Meanwhile, the American Protective League and the Home Guard continued the "slacker raids" for draft evaders, a process that had begun the past spring in Minneapolis, St. Paul, and Duluth. On July 6, 1918, the four companies of the 1st Battalion aided by the Motor Corps raided sites throughout St. Paul, netting between four and five hundred men. News reports indicated that only six were still being held the next day and that most of them were expected to provide proof of compliance. Two weeks later, the APL and the Home Guard carried out a larger raid in St. Paul, involving both St. Paul Home Guard battalions (the 1st and 15th) and the Motor Corps. APL vigilantes and the Home Guard arrested over fifteen hundred men in hotels, saloons, parks, theaters, the YWCA, and the railroad station. The newspapers reported interesting anecdotes, like the story of Fred Brown, a draftee on his way to a farewell party in his honor. Unfortunately for him, the Home Guard repeatedly stopped and searched the streetcar he was riding. The last time, he refused to show his draft card and was "severely handled" by the guardsmen who arrested him. In another episode, the guard met a Mississippi River excursion boat docking at midnight downtown. All the men were searched and about fifty were arrested, leaving their wives and girlfriends to find their own way home. Until then, the newspapers had reported the raids as an amusing adventure, kind of a lark, but the paper now reported anger and resentment among the detainees.[20]

During the summer, the Home Guard battalions of northern Minnesota held many "slacker raids," especially in Duluth and Iron Range towns. The 3rd Battalion, which had run a spectacular dragnet in downtown Duluth in May, held four smaller raids in Duluth and aided in raids in Proctor and Two Harbors. Later in the summer the battalion also spent two weeks checking passengers arriving at the train station. The 4th Battalion, headquartered in Virginia, conducted raids in Chisholm, Grand Rapids, and Deer River. The five companies of the 8th Battalion held raids in their home towns, which included Eveleth, Gilbert, Biwabik, Ely, and Aurora. Company A of the 21st Battalion bragged that it was the first Home Guard unit in the state to meet trains in search of slackers. For five weeks, it reported, it met every train arriving in Bemidji, its home base.[21]

The slacker raids ended in the fall after the APL overplayed its hand and tested the patience of even the most conservative politicians. In July, the APL participated in a massive three-day operation in Chicago in which more than 150,000 men were questioned. In September, a force of several thousand APL agents, soldiers, and policemen conducted a three-day roundup of young men in New York City that resulted in sixty thousand arrests of men without the proper papers, of which 199 were eventually identified as draft evaders, along with a smaller number of army deserters. This threw the city into chaos and brought business in the nation's commercial capital to a halt. Senator George Chamberlain, chair of the Senate Military Affairs Committee (who had earlier proposed military tribunals), demanded that the draft be enforced by sworn government agents rather than overeager volunteers. Other senators objected to the brazen way in which the raiders disrupted businesses. One senator proposed a national investigation of the APL. This idea died in committee, but the New York raid spelled the beginning of the end for the APL.[22]

The MCPS created the Home Guard in part because the business organizations feared that the federalization of the National Guard would leave them defenseless against labor activism. Indeed, the transit workers might have won union recognition if the MCPS had not brought Home Guard battalions from around the state to St. Paul in December 1917. In July 1918, the commission mobilized the Home Guard against a less formidable opponent, the newsboys who distributed the three daily Minneapolis newspapers. Early in 1918, the *Tribune*, *Journal* and *Daily News* increased the price of a daily paper and raised the cost that newsboys had to pay per one hundred copies. In July, the frustrated newsboys organized a boycott and tried to disrupt circulation. The newspapers argued that the newsboys were committing wholesale vandalism and even personally assaulting customers, and that Mayor Van Lear and his police chief were ignoring, even abetting, their criminal acts. The MCPS threatened to depose Van Lear and mobilized the Minneapolis companies of the Home Guard to aid newspaper circulation. After four days of disruption, the newspapers negotiated a settlement with the newsboys, which gave them a slightly better deal and a grievance procedure.[23]

The rhetoric and activity of the MCPS, the Home Guard, the APL, the Liberty Bond committees, and others inspired some vigilante groups to acts of domestic terrorism. In Rock County, in the far southwest corner of the state, the Loyalty League sought to purge the county of anyone it deemed disloyal. The NPL did poorly in southern Minnesota areas like Rock County, where Lindbergh received only 424 votes of the 1,930 cast in the June primary. Shortly after the primary, Mayor C. O. Meyer announced that the Loyalty League had ordered all Rock County farmers who had voted for the NPL to come to Luverne, the county seat, to publicly record that they had renounced their NPL membership. If they refused to do so, they must leave the county or face deportation and the confiscation of their property. The order, to state the obvious, had no legal basis. According to news reports, most farmers complied.[24]

One farmer who did not comply was John Meints, who had been involved with a short-lived attempt to create an NPL newspaper called the *Rock County Leader*. In June of 1918, the mayor had ordered the newspaper closed, ostensibly to keep it from being sacked by a mob. At about that same time, the Loyalty League forced Meints to leave Rock County, and he apparently resided for a time in nearby Sioux Falls, South Dakota. In late August, John Meints returned to help his son Fred with the harvest. At that point, a posse of about thirty masked men came to his son's farm, kidnapped John Meints, and on the way to the Iowa border applied a coat of hot tar to his back and told him never to return. Still covered with tar, Meints made his way to St. Paul to file a complaint with the Department of Justice and be photographed. Meints sued members of the mob whom he could identify, including several Luverne bankers, a minister, and the clerk of court.[25]

In Duluth, a secretive vigilante group's use of hot tar ended in tragedy. The Knights of Liberty, apparently modeled after the Ku Klux Klan, began terrorizing men deemed insufficiently loyal in the spring of 1918. The newspapers reported that eleven masked men kidnapped Gustaf Landin, a photographer, in March, drove him out of town, whipped him, forced him to kiss an American flag, covered him with tar, and then left him to find his way home. Both the *Duluth Herald* and the *Duluth News Tribune* published the Knights' description of the events and their statement that they had sent warning letters to other men who they believed had made "disloyal utterances."[26]

In the fall, the group appeared in the press again, this time calling itself the Knights of Loyalty. On September 18, three of them, one dressed in a military uniform, took Olli Kiukkonen, a Finnish immigrant, from his boardinghouse in Duluth's west end. It was the last time he was seen alive. Kiukkonen had begun the naturalization process but after war was declared had decided not to seek citizenship, apparently to avoid being drafted.

The *Duluth News Tribune* reported that on the evening of September 18 it received "a mysterious telephone call" from someone who said the Knights had taken and tarred Kiukkonen because he had renounced citizenship to avoid the draft. On that same day, the *Duluth Herald* reported it had received a typed unsigned letter that claimed to contain the questions the Knights put to Kiukkonen about his draft avoidance and his responses. Not satisfied with his answers, they decided to tar and feather him. The *Herald* also received a copy of a letter sent by the Knights to five other men who had announced they were withdrawing their claim to citizenship. The letter warned them of dire consequences if they did not complete the citizenship process immediately. "The knights strike quick and strike well," the letter said, concluding with "this is your final warning, take heed."[27]

On September 30, Kiukkonen's body was found in a wooded area near the Lester River. There was a noose around his neck, and the rope was attached to a tree branch. His feet were touching the ground and his knees were bent. The police reported that there were no signs of a struggle and that he had $450 cash in his pockets, along with some Liberty Stamps. He had tar on him, and it looked like he had tried to remove it. The death certificate prepared by the coroner listed the cause of death as "suicide by hanging." The estimated time of death was sometime between September 18, when Kiukkonen was kidnapped, and September 22. The death certificate lists his age as thirty-seven, and if that is true, he was not required to register for the draft until September 12, 1918, when the age of eligibility was extended from thirty to forty-five. Since the war ended two months later, he never would have been drafted.[28]

What happened to Kiukkonen remains a mystery, but even if he committed suicide, the Knights of Loyalty were ultimately responsible for his death. The federal government agreed. Bruce Bielaski, head of the Bureau of Investigation in Washington, ordered a federal agent in Duluth to investigate. Bielaski was responding not only to the facts of the case but also to President Wilson's response to the lynching in Missouri of Robert Praeger, a young man whose only crime was his German ancestry. The president gave a stern lecture that mob action was a betrayal of democracy, and asked law enforcement to do all it could to end "this disgraceful evil." Governor Burnquist also acted. He had never commented on vigilante violence, even in Rock County, but given the loss of life, he issued a proclamation offering a reward for information leading to the arrest of the Knights of Loyalty vigilantes. His victory in the Republican primary now behind him, he was willing to say unequivocally that "mob violence shall not be tolerated."[29]

The federal agent interviewed Kiukkonen's housemates, the newspaper reporters, the police, and the coroner. He learned that Kiukkonen was a "harmless, easy-going, taciturn person, who easily yields to the advice of others." He uncovered no information about the perpetrators and no arrests were made. This result satisfied the *News Tribune,* which editorialized that "a lesser Judas Iscariot in Duluth, followed the example of his prototype—he went out and hanged himself." Since Kiukkonen had betrayed his adopted country, "his end was fitting." The paper concluded that the kindest thing to do was to forget him. No mention was made of the Knights of Loyalty. This provoked an angry rebuke from *Truth*, the Socialist paper, which rejected the conclusion that Kiukkonen had killed himself and argued that the real Judas was the capitalist who profited from the war while Kiukkonen was laboring in the mines.[30]

The Criminalization of Words

During the war, Alfred Jaques, the US attorney, prosecuted thirty-four cases in Minnesota for saying or writing something in violation of the federal Espionage Act. Most of the action, however, was in the state courts, where prosecutors charged 170 cases using the sedition statute passed by the Minnesota legislature in April 1917.[31]

Nationwide, the federal government prosecuted about two thousand Espionage Act cases, the most famous of which was the trial of Eugene Debs, leader of the Socialist Party, who was convicted for a speech he made in 1918 and sentenced to ten years. Since federal prosecutors had a great deal of discretion, the number of indictments per capita varied greatly across the country. US Attorney Jaques was relatively restrained, at least when compared to neighboring districts. In North Dakota, with half the population of Minnesota, the federal prosecutor brought 103 cases. The two federal districts that made up Wisconsin, which had a population slightly higher than Minnesota, together had ninety-two cases. John McGee found Jaques's moderation infuriating, and went so far as to blast him, in testimony before Congress, for lacking "a fighting stomach." Conservatives were peeved that Jaques did not charge NPL leaders.

The federal sedition cases in Minnesota fall into two categories. Some were against well-known political figures who intended to influence public opinion in speeches or in publications. Shortly after the declaration of war, Jaques indicted Jacob Bentall and Abraham Sugarman, two leaders of the Socialist Party in Minnesota. Other well-known defendants included James A. Peterson, a Progressive Republican who had been the Hennepin County attorney and served one term in the Minnesota House; Albert Steinhauser, the *New Ulm Review* editor; and Jack Carney, the Irish radical who was editor of *Truth*, the Socialist newspaper in Duluth.

The government charged Peterson with two counts of "willfully causing or attempting to cause insubordination, disloyalty, mutiny, or refusal of duty, in the military or naval forces of the United States" by publishing two articles in a local weekly. The jury acquitted him of one count but found him guilty for an article commenting on Wilson's "14 Points" speech in January, in which the president endorsed some of the Allies' plans to seize territory from the German, Austrian, and Turkish empires. Peterson questioned whether seizing territory would lead to peace and democracy. He called on the US Senate to intervene, since American soldiers were in effect fighting and dying to expand the British and French empires. Judge Page Morris imposed a four-year sentence, which was stayed pending appeal.[32]

■ **Alfred Jaques of Duluth served as US attorney for Minnesota during World War I.** ***MNHS collections***

Peterson was a well-known opponent of US involvement in the European war. He had also mounted a spirited primary campaign against Senator Knute Nelson in 1912, and was in fact again challenging Nelson in the 1918 Republican primary. The Minnesota secretary of state ruled that his name would remain on the ballot because he had filed his candidacy before his conviction. As noted earlier, Nelson cruised to victory in 1918, although some observers were dismayed by how many Minnesotans voted for a man who had been convicted of sedition.

Jaques sought the indictment of Steinhauser for reprinting several articles from German newspapers in the *New Ulm Review* in 1918. He had, however, been targeted for prosecution since July 1917 when he was one of the four main speakers at the notorious rally in New Ulm. The MCPS had punished the other three, removing city attorney Albert Pfaender and mayor Louis Fritsch from office, and pressuring Martin Luther Seminary to fire its president, Adolph Ackermann. The US attorney indicted Jack Carney for two pieces he published in *Truth*; the anti-war US Senate campaign platform of Victor Berger, the Wisconsin Socialist; and an editorial protesting the Allied intervention in the Russian civil war.[33]

It is not surprising that the government sought to imprison dissident public figures who had access to large audiences. Most federal indictments, however, were brought against citizens with no political affiliation who voiced criticisms of the government to a few people in a nonpublic setting. The federal grand jury convened in Winona in May 1918, for example, indicted five men under the Espionage Act. Two were farmers who had made a critical comment to a few others; the third was a doctor accused of making a seditious comment in a letter; the fourth was Charles Anding, the Winona County auditor, accused of making an anti-draft statement to a young man in a hardware store; and the fifth was John V. Free, a farmer accused of making an anti-war statement while recruiting for the NPL on a Wabasha County farm. All had German ancestry.

The first three defendants were found guilty and sentenced to sixty or ninety days and a fine. Charles Anding denied any wrongdoing and went to trial in Winona before Judge Morris. The city was treated to a captivating drama as Jaques called the postmaster, the county attorney, the sheriff, and several other notables to testify against Anding. The defense responded by calling the probate judge, two former Winona mayors, the head of the Masons, and an executive of the Laird Norton Lumber Company to testify for Anding. The jury found him guilty, and Judge Morris sentenced him to eighteen months in Leavenworth Prison in Kansas. The sentence was stayed so that Anding could move for a new trial.[34]

John V. Free was the only person affiliated with the NPL charged under the federal Espionage Act in Minnesota. His trial was moved to St. Paul and not held until shortly after the armistice. He testified that he grew up on a Wabasha County farm and that he would not have made anti-war statements because his four brothers were soldiers. Judge Morris instructed the jurors that Free had a "perfect right" to campaign for the NPL and that the jury should consider whether he would be capable of "stabbing his brothers in the back." The jury returned a not guilty verdict in thirty minutes.[35]

The trial of John Seebach was also a public spectacle. Seebach, an official at a Red Wing grain mill, was the uncle of Oscar Seebach, the military officer whom John McGee tapped to organize the Home Guard, and Fred Seebach, the captain of the Red Wing company. The Goodhue County attorney indicted Seebach under the state sedition statute, but dropped the case when Jaques obtained a federal indictment. Witnesses testified that Seebach made various comments to them about the foolishness of the war, all of which he denied. Seebach admitted that he told a woman to ask her brother, a soldier, to aim high when he got to France so as not to hit Seebach's relatives, but he said this was meant as a joke. He was also charged with discouraging the enlistment of his sons and other young men. After deliberating over three hours, the jury returned a verdict of guilty but recommended leniency in sentencing. Judge Wilbur Booth sentenced Seebach to eighteen months in federal prison and a $3,000 fine, but as was customary, stayed the sentence pending appeal.[36]

As in the Winona trial, both sides called a phalanx of witnesses who testified that Seebach did or did not have a good reputation for loyalty. Among the prosecution witnesses was Jens Grondahl, the ultrapatriotic editor of the *Red Wing Daily Republican*. He testified that he knew Seebach was disloyal because the defendant had complained several times about Grondahl's pro-war editorials. When Seebach's attorney asked Grondahl how he could be sure the defendant read his editorials, Grondahl replied that if Seebach was an intelligent man he presumed Seebach read his newspaper. This produced laughter in the courtroom, but things turned serious when the attorney asked Grondahl if he belonged to a secret organization that took the law into its own hands. When Grondahl denied it, the attorney asked if an automobile owned by the newspaper was used in the recent kidnapping of NPL organizer George Breidel during the trial of N. S. Randall. Grondahl replied that his employee, "prompted by curiosity," followed a procession of cars leaving town, not knowing they had kidnapped Breidel.[37]

* * *

The state court prosecutions, in addition to being far more numerous, posed a real threat to the NPL leaders, especially in Martin, Jackson, and Goodhue Counties. These prosecutions were begun in the months before the June 1918 Republican primary to weaken the NPL's ability to attract votes. Albert Allen, the Martin County attorney, charged Townley and Gilbert with sedition based on the published resolutions of the NPL. The Minnesota Supreme Court held that they were not seditious. Thomas Mohn, the Goodhue County attorney, successfully prosecuted Joseph Gilbert, who managed Minnesota NPL activities in May 1918. This case was making its way through the appellate courts. E. H. Nicholas, the Jackson County attorney, charged Townley and Gilbert with conspiracy based on published documents and speeches. This case would not be tried until 1919.

These high-profile cases were exceptions. Most indictments were brought against people with no political affiliation, usually farmers, who expressed personal views to a few people. Generally, defendants were charged with saying that "we had no business in this war" or that it was "a rich man's war" or that Germany would likely prevail, or even that Germany would hopefully win, and that, therefore, the young men should not submit to the draft and neighbors should not buy Liberty Bonds. The Minnesota statute limited punishment to a $500 fine and a year in jail, or both. Those who pled guilty often paid a fine and had jail time suspended, but those who went to trial often served at least some time in the county jail.[38]

The bulk of these cases were charged in a handful of southern Minnesota counties. In Wantonwon County, for example, at least nine were indicted for making allegedly disloyal statements. Occasionally, juries felt that prosecutors had gone too far, as when a Wantonwan County jury acquitted August Ahl of saying "who made this country what it is today: the Germans did." He never mentioned the war. There were seven cases in Rice County, three of which involved the owners and editor of a Socialist newspaper called *Referendum*. They received twelve months, the maximum sentence. Not surprisingly, Albert Allen, the ultrapatriotic Martin County attorney, brought at least a dozen cases, and was still prosecuting disloyalty after the war. On the day of the armistice, he charged Rev. Otto Bruntsch, a Lutheran pastor, with sedition for saying that France and England started the war and the United States was doing their bidding. A jury acquitted the minister after a December 1918 trial.[39]

Today, most, if not all, of the World War I sedition prosecutions would be dismissed on First Amendment grounds. At the time, however, the US Supreme Court held that the right of expression was severely limited during wartime. Even so, the courts might have dismissed many cases based on a close reading of the statute. After all, if a cranky farmer grumbled about the war to a few other farmers, did that really amount to "willfully causing or attempting to cause insubordination, disloyalty, mutiny, or refusal of duty, in the military or naval forces of the United States"? Usually, the federal courts ruled that it did based on the "bad tendency" rule. Disapproval of the war was not a crime, the courts held, but the defendants should have realized that the "natural and probable tendency" of expressing critical thoughts would be to encourage insubordination or other unlawful conduct. On this basis, any negative comment related to the war could sustain a sedition charge and lead to a sentence of up to twenty years.[40]

The Minnesota Supreme Court agreed that the right to free expression was limited in wartime, but did reverse a few convictions based on a common-sense reading of the state sedition statute. For example, two brothers in Wantonwan County were convicted of sedition when a traveling salesman leaning out of his hotel window happened to overhear their private conservation about the war. The court reversed, holding that the legislature intended to punish only those who were actively proselytizing their views. In a Wright County case, a farmer made a negative comment about the war to Red Cross volunteers who had entered his home aggressively seeking a donation. The court reversed the conviction, holding that the defendant had not intended to promote his views, but was reacting to people who had come into his private dwelling. In a third case, the court reversed the conviction of a Redwood County farmer who was heard complaining about the poor food at the army's training camps and the censorship of the soldiers' letters.[41]

After the armistice, the federal government lost its appetite for the Espionage Act. Jaques quietly dropped pending cases, including those against public figures like Albert Steinhauser and John Carney. When James Peterson's case reached the Supreme Court on appeal, the Department of Justice moved to dismiss the case, "confessing error," that is, admitting that the indictment was unjustified. John Seebach lost his appeal, but his prison sentence was commuted by President Wilson in 1920. Socialist leaders Bentall and Sugarman did serve time in Leavenworth Prison, but were released early.[42]

Charles Anding, the Winona County auditor convicted for his hardware store comment, did not serve his sentence. Judge Morris waited until after the armistice and then granted the motion for a new trial, indicating that he understood, belatedly, that the federal courts had been swept up by war fever: "After carefully reading and considering the whole testimony, bearing in mind the condition of public feeling and the consequent atmosphere of the Courts at that time in regard to anyone shown to entertain or even suspected of entertaining, sentiments favorable to Germany or of disloyalty to our Government or to our President, I find myself in such extreme doubt as to the Defendant's guilt . . . that I feel constrained to grant a new trial." The judge may have also guessed that unscrupulous politicians in Winona had conspired to exploit Anding's German ancestry to push him out of his elected office. After the judge's order, Jaques declined to retry the case. Although Anding avoided prison, he was forced to resign as county auditor and mount a legal defense for two years while he and his family were subject to public humiliation.[43]

The Skies Darken: Cyclone, Fire, and Plague

As if a world war and bitter conflicts on the home front were not enough, Minnesotans also experienced three natural disasters in the late summer and fall of 1918. A powerful tornado hit the small town of Tyler in the southwestern corner of the state near the South Dakota border. A massive group of forest fires ripped through northeastern Minnesota near Duluth, wiping out entire towns and killing hundreds. Adjutant General Rhinow responded quickly to both disasters, mobilizing Home Guard, including the Motor Corps, and National Guard units. Meanwhile, the virus of the great influenza pandemic spread rapidly through the nation, facilitated by troop movements, patriotic rallies, and Liberty Bond campaigns.

On the evening of August 21, a cyclone, as it was called at the time, ripped through Tyler, killing thirty-six of the town's approximately eight hundred residents, most of whom were of Danish ancestry. The next morning, Rhinow was on a special train heading for the devastated town. He stopped briefly in Mankato to pick up medical and relief workers organized by the Minnesota National Guard's newly formed 5th Infantry Regiment. In Tyler, he assigned Home Guard troops from nearby towns to cordon off the destroyed area and search for victims. Several companies of the Motor Corps headquartered in Fairmont came with doctors, medicine, and supplies. Major W. R. Stephens, the commander of the corps, drove from Minneapolis to direct their work. The next day, Rhinow's troops began clearing streets of debris and controlling the thousands of visitors who drove to Tyler to see the damage. Three days after the disaster, a military detail acted as pallbearers as the dead were carried in a funeral procession from the makeshift morgue in the opera house to the Danish Lutheran Church.[44]

* * *

Two months later, Minnesotans in the northeast suffered a much bigger disaster, the Cloquet–Moose Lake fires, which consumed 1,500 square miles of timber, killed 453 people, badly burned 85 others, and displaced 11,832 families. Several towns, including Cloquet and Moose Lake, were destroyed, and many others, including Duluth, sustained major damage. Forest fires were common in northern Minnesota, made more frequent and dangerous by the extensive drainage of wetlands, the combustible debris (called "slash") left over from logging, and railroad locomotives spewing sparks. In the fall of 1918, northern Minnesota was above average in temperature and below average in rainfall. Just as the fires were breaking out on October 12, there was a sharp drop in humidity and a rapid rise in wind speed, which eventually reached sixty-five miles per hour. The result was catastrophic. In towns, many people escaped by automobile or railroad, but some isolated farm families tried to save themselves in lakes and ponds or, tragically, in their root cellars, which often became their tombs. The survivors returned to find their homes and all their belongings reduced to ash. More than a century later, these fires still rank as the worst natural disaster in Minnesota history.[45]

Minnesota National Guard and Home Guard units stationed in Duluth were the first on the scene, including companies of the 4th Infantry, one of the newly formed MNG units, the 3rd Battalion of the Home Guards, and the 7th Battalion of the Motor Corps. They fought the fire and helped get some people to safety. They were assisted by other National Guard units, Home Guard companies from as far south as Anoka, and Motor Corps companies from the area and from Minneapolis and St. Paul.[46]

Adjutant General Rhinow set up a command post and a hospital in the few Moose Lake buildings that had survived. His troops searched for survivors, cared for the injured, and helped in the burying of the dead. He declared martial law in the area and deployed his troops to control access to the afflicted areas. Governor Burnquist came to Moose Lake two days after the disaster, and a few days later the MCPS convened a special meeting there to create the Minnesota Forest Fires Relief Commission to coordinate the work of the military, local officials, the Red Cross, and other relief organizations.[47]

This mobilization marked a tiny breakthrough in the Jim Crow segregation of Minnesota's military forces. The governor had approved the creation of the 16th Battalion, an African Americans contingent of the Home Guard, but the MCPS never ordered the unit to do anything beyond ceremonial duties. After establishing himself in Moose Lake, Rhinow ordered two of the 16th Battalion's officers to join his staff. First, Captain Charles Sumner Smith, the editor of the *Twin Cities Appeal*, was assigned to intelligence gathering and communication work. A few days later he was joined by Captain Gale Hilyer, the Minneapolis attorney who had spearheaded the local NAACP's campaign against *The Birth of a Nation*.[48]

* * *

Minnesota's first influenza cases were reported in late September, and once present, the virus spread quickly. By early October, there were already a thousand reported cases in Minneapolis alone. Among the first victims were cadets in the university's Student Army Training Corps, many of whom were hospitalized at Fort Snelling. The city's health commissioner ordered the closure of all schools, churches, movie theaters, dance halls, and similar places. On October 21, the state board of health issued a statewide public meeting ban, and on October 22, the MCPS endorsed the ban and "requested" that people comply. The ban did not include schools, churches, or even movie theaters; these public places were left to the discretion of local authorities. As cases mounted, St. Paul ordered its schools, churches, and theaters closed on November 4. Both cities lifted their bans on November 15, but a second peak in cases in December (the third wave) led Minneapolis to close its schools once again. Minneapolis had fewer deaths per capita than St. Paul, but still had over a thousand confirmed fatalities.[49]

The virus traveled quickly around the state, having an impact in every county. For example, in Martin County, whose population was about twenty thousand, there were 456 cases reported, resulting in nineteen deaths, including a thirty-seven-year-old doctor. Six died in Welcome, a small town of about six hundred. In Winona County, also in southern Minnesota, several manufacturing firms noted that less than a third of their employees were reporting for work in mid-October. Only one death had been documented in Winona, but the manufacturers accused the city leaders of negligence for not ordering a thorough shutdown to contain the virus. Four days later, Winona recorded nine deaths from influenza in a single day, with eleven more in the next two days. Local physicians noted that the East End, home of many recent Polish immigrants, was hardest hit.[50]

By the end of January 1919, the crisis was over. Nationwide, the 1918 influenza killed about 675,000, including about 10,000 Minnesotans, mostly in the last three months of 1918. By comparison, the COVID-19 virus killed almost 1.2 million Americans. Nevertheless, the 1918 influenza still ranks as the nation's most deadly pandemic because the population of the United States in 2019 was about three times what it was in 1918.

The areas ravaged by the forest fires were especially hard hit by influenza, and in response, Rhinow brought fresh Minnesota National Guard troops from Minneapolis to Moose Lake and Cloquet in early November. The MNG medical staff cared for influenza patients at several field hospitals. In mid-December, Hubert Eva, the general manager of the Forest Fire Relief Commission, informed Rhinow that the troops were no longer needed and should be withdrawn. Rhinow replied that citizens wanted the troops to stay. On January 2, 1919, Eva wrote to the governor, stating that he could not find anyone who wanted the guard to stay, and that their continued presence "is more apt to stir up sentiment against the military than for them." Getting no response, Eva renewed his request on January 16, noting that businessmen in Cloquet and Moose Lake wanted the soldiers gone. Within a few days, Rhinow withdrew his troops.[51]

Except for overstaying their welcome, the National Guard and Home Guard responded admirably to the natural disasters that hit Minnesota during 1918. The cyclone victims in Tyler and the fire victims in Moose Lake, Cloquet, and surrounding areas appreciated their help. Adjutant General Rhinow singled out the Motor Corps, who he said were "highly paid executives" volunteering their time, for special praise, noting that they provided crucial mobility that greatly enhanced the relief efforts. The men of the Home Guard, motorized and on foot, could be justifiably proud of their relief work, especially in the devastated fire zone.[52]

Women at War

Alice Ames Winter continued to wear two hats, chairing both the MCPS Women's Committee and the local branch of the National Woman's War Organization. She maintained her ideological balancing act, operating within the loyalist milieu of the MCPS while trying to stay true to the moderate progressivism of the women's clubs from which she and most of her colleagues emerged. She accomplished this in part by recruiting a large advisory group, the war council, composed of representatives of statewide women's organizations, religious denominations, and organizations in which women played a significant role. Here could be found, for example, Clara Ueland, representing the Minnesota Woman Suffrage Association, sitting at the table with Lavinia Gilfallan of the Anti-Suffrage Association. Winter even found a place for Hope McDonald, representing the Woman's Peace Party. The National Woman's Party, however, was conspicuous by its absence.[53]

The Women's Committee developed a statewide structure with women active in every county. Under Winter's leadership, the committee worked on food conservation, patriotic education, Liberty Loan drives, monitoring and protecting women working in industry, child protection, and Americanization. In the second half of 1918, she prioritized the last two programs, which together illustrate the political schizophrenia of the committee.[54]

Winter put increasing emphasis on Americanization because she was alarmed by reports from around the state that many foreign-born Minnesotans, even if citizens, were lacking in loyalty. This was also the view of John McGee and organizations like the America First Association. The early strategy of honoring the cultural traditions of immigrants to encourage assimilation was replaced by a more forceful indoctrination into "100% Americanism," a concept that assumed that the model citizen was an old stock American of English or Scot ancestry. The Americanization campaign was politicized, in the sense that expressing doubts about the war or joining the NPL was deemed to be incompatible with being a true American. The Americanization campaign continued after the war, focusing especially on making English the exclusive language of instruction in schools.[55]

On the other hand, Winter enthusiastically endorsed the Year of the Child program initiated by the US Children's Bureau, a campaign consistent with the Progressive agenda of women's clubs in Minnesota. The goal was to greatly increase child health through baby clinics, school and county nurses, improved playgrounds, and a statewide education program. Winter asked the MCPS for funding, arguing that these programs were "war work" given the fact that draft boards had found so many young men physically unfit for service. Pointing to infant mortality statistics, she noted that it was safer to be a soldier on the western front than an infant in Minnesota.[56]

The project got off to a strong start, with child welfare boards created in most counties. The commission provided some initial funding, but ultimately decided that it was up to the legislature to fully fund the project. Then the influenza pandemic derailed the full development of the ambitious program that Winter envisioned. Nevertheless, Winter's bold plans encouraged the eventual development of government-sponsored child welfare programs in the 1920s.[57]

The Women's Committee also encouraged women to support their local Red Cross chapters. In early 1917, the Red Cross was a young organization that had not yet sunk deep roots into American society. Once war was declared, the organization grew rapidly. By the end of the year, there were eighty-eight chapters across Minnesota, roughly corresponding to the counties, and over eight hundred branches reporting to those chapters. Eventually the membership reached about 476,000, roughly one out of every five Minnesotans. Although statewide and chapter leaders were often men, women did the bulk of the volunteer work, which included knitting sweaters, socks, and mufflers; preparing and packaging hospital supplies; operating canteens at railway stations; helping soldiers' families; and organizing recreation for the men at Fort Snelling. The Red Cross also recruited and trained nurses. Many women were also involved in the extensive fund-raising program that supported this work. In addition, some Minnesota women went to France to work for the Red Cross, some as nurses and others in a wide variety of jobs, including canteen workers, office workers, and drivers.[58]

On the household level, most women also supported the war through food conservation efforts. Women reorganized their household's shopping and cooking routines to follow various conservation programs, including avoiding wheat or meat on the designated days, prioritizing ingredients like cornmeal and potatoes, cutting down on sugar, and expanding vegetable gardening.[59]

* * *

Prior to the war, the movement for women's suffrage appeared to be on the verge of a great breakthrough. The war postponed progress and divided the movement. In 1918, the National Woman Suffrage Association continued its support of the war effort, believing this was the best approach to pave the way for suffrage after the war. Clara Ueland, chair of the MWSA, not only sat on the War Council of the Women's Committee but played an active role in the committee's work. On the other hand, the National Woman's Party, led by Alice Paul, believed that Wilson's war for democracy should start at home. Paul resumed public protests near the White House in August 1918, starting with a public burning of a speech by Wilson. Once again NWP picketers went to jail.

The MCPS Women's Committee sent Senator Knute Nelson its September 1918 resolution urging the Senate to pass the suffrage amendment, while at the same time "pledging all our powers to the winning of democracy for the peoples of the world." The resolution noted that "there can be no true democracy in our own country until women as well as men are enfranchised." Nelson was already on record as supportive of suffrage. All factions of the suffrage movement thought the Senate might finally approve the amendment, especially because President Wilson finally agreed to endorse it. He made a speech in the Senate urging passage, but on October 1, the Senate defeated the amendment by two votes.[60]

All suffrage advocates were frustrated, but Minnesota NWP chair Sarah Colvin crossed a line by publicly boycotting a war program. She and her husband regularly purchased Liberty Bonds, but after the October 1 vote, she told a St. Paul reporter that money she might have used for additional Liberty Bonds would now be used to help defeat

Democrats in the congressional elections of 1918. "I no longer have any heart in giving help to causes," she was quoted as saying, "which are controlled by a group of short-sighted, incompetent men."[61]

This triggered a minor scandal. The local agent of the Department of Justice promised to investigate her. The local Liberty Bond chairman attacked her "for boldly declaring herself out of sympathy with America's war program." The president of MWSA in St. Paul made clear that her organization opposed the militant tactics of the NWP and, as if to compensate for Colvin, had suspended all suffrage work to "give all the help we could to the Liberty Bond campaign."

Writing about the incident years later, Colvin said she voluntarily met with the Department of Justice agent, who said she would not be charged since she had not urged others to boycott Liberty Bonds. She wrote that the incident "increased my contempt for the hybrid patriotism that develops in times of war."[62]

On the other end of the political spectrum was the Daughters of Loyalty, a women's militia from the small town of Woodstock in Pipestone County. At the 1918 Independence Day celebration in Pipestone, the county seat, Captain Bessie Hartigan led about two dozen women who paraded in "feminine uniforms of military cut," carried real rifles, and performed a "splendidly executed" military-style drill. Governor Burnquist came to Pipestone, in the far southwestern corner of the state, spoke at the event, and formally reviewed the unit.[63]

Hartigan, who ran a millinery shop in the same location as her husband's barbershop on Woodstock's main street, created the Daughters of Loyalty in part because three of her brothers and many other relatives were in the military. She may have also been influenced by the fact that the 6th Battalion of the Home Guard, which included a company based in Pipestone, had just been mustered into the Minnesota National Guard. The MCPS had begun the process of creating a new Home Guard battalion in its place, but it did not include a Pipestone County company.[64]

▪ OPPOSITE
Sarah Tarleton Colvin, Minnesota leader of the National Woman's Party, was not pleased when the Senate failed to pass the suffrage amendment while the country was fighting in Europe to make the world safe for democracy. ***MNHS collections***

Hartigan made no effort to have the Daughters of Loyalty recognized as an official unit of the Home Guard, but she did make sure to align her group with the rhetoric of John McGee. Every member, she said, is "a true blue American at heart, as well as body and soul." She was sure of this, because "each member has been subjected to a loyalty test" in which their past and present was thoroughly investigated. Her outfit would "go on the battle line to fight for democracy," although who she was prepared to fight was left unsaid. However, she introduced her squad shortly after the June primary election at which Burnquist easily carried Pipestone County. Some of the agricultural townships voted overwhelmingly for Lindbergh. The town of Woodstock, twelve miles east of Pipestone, voted for Burnquist 46 to 7, but the farmers in the township just north of town favored Lindbergh 42 to 19. Hartigan, like townspeople throughout the state, understood they were surrounded by people they considered traitors.[65]

Winners and Losers

Minnesotans had a wild ride in early November. Election day was November 5, with all statewide offices and the legislature on the ballot, and Democratic control of Congress up for grabs nationwide. Two days later, many newspapers announced the end of the war, and people poured into the streets to celebrate. The *Red Wing Daily Republican,* for example, featured a huge headline shouting "HUNS SURRENDER," accompanied by editor Jens Grondahl's front-page story claiming that "the greatest newspaper scoop in history was put over today" by his newspaper. Grondahl and many other editors had jumped the gun, however. On November 11, the real armistice was declared, sparking renewed, and much more ecstatic, statewide celebrations.[66]

The election was overshadowed by the armistice, but it was important nevertheless. Wilson and the Democrats suffered a disastrous defeat, losing their majorities in both the House and the Senate. In a letter to Wilson, George Creel wrote a remarkable postmortem, noting that the president had successfully won over Progressives and radicals by casting the war as a crusade for democracy. However, "the Department of Justice and the Post Office were allowed to silence or intimidate them," and as a result, "there was no voice left to argue for your sort of peace." The upshot, according to Creel, was that Republicans were the chief beneficiaries of Wilson's war policy.[67]

Knute Nelson, now seventy-five years old, won another term in the Senate. Having beaten James Peterson in the Republican primary, the grand old man of Minnesota politics expected a cakewalk, especially since the Democratic Party did not advance a candidate. However, the Democrats did endorse Willis Calderwood of the prohibitionist National Party, who put up a surprising fight and got 40 percent of the vote. Nelson was embarrassed again in Douglas County, his home, where he managed only 37 percent of the vote.[68]

Following the defeat of Charles Lindbergh in the June primary, the Nonpartisan League leaders and the Minnesota Federation of Labor looked for another way to unseat Governor Burnquist. In August, the two groups endorsed David E. Evans, a Progressive farmer and hardware merchant from southwestern Minnesota, for governor. He appeared on the ballot as the candidate for "Farmer-Labor," although the actual party of that name was not organized until later. Evans campaigned much like Lindbergh, but with the advantage of having unreservedly supported Wilson's war policies from the beginning.[69]

Burnquist continued to campaign on the loyalty issue, arguing that he had saved the state from pro-Germanism and socialism. When the votes were counted, Burnquist prevailed, but with only 45 percent of the votes. Evans and Wheaton, the Democrat, combined for 51 percent of the vote. The many newspapers that supported the governor celebrated, but it was the first indication that Minnesotans were tiring of the loyalty issue. The Republican Party would soon conclude that Burnquist, burdened by his close association with John McGee, was a political liability.[70]

The Nonpartisan League elected seven senators and twenty-five representatives, while their allies in the Twin Cities Labor movement elected five senators and nine representatives. A league activist occasionally won a seat in relatively hostile territory, including Fred Scherf's victory in Goodhue County. As historian Frederick Johnson wrote, "Scherf had been arrested, assaulted, threatened at public meetings, publicly censured by city and village leaders and labeled pro-German, and had his house splashed with yellow paint." Nevertheless, he beat David Neill, a prominent Red Wing businessman and

The people of Minneapolis fill Nicollet Avenue to celebrate the end of the war. *Courtesy of Hennepin County Public Library Special Collections*

president of the local America First Association, because his impressive vote totals in rural townships outweighed Neill's margins in the city of Red Wing. The NPL hoped that this farmer-labor bloc could push through some Progressive legislation. However, when the legislature convened in 1919, the Republican leadership in the house and the senate made sure that those twelve senators and thirty-four representatives were kept isolated and powerless.[71]

For John McGee, Burnquist, and their fellow MCPS commissioners, the best election news was undoubtedly the defeat of Thomas Van Lear, the Socialist who had become the mayor of Minneapolis in 1916. Throughout the war, McGee had criticized the mayor and tried to find ways to depose him. Predictably, his opponent, J. E. Meyers, a conservative businessman, campaigned as a loyal patriot, claiming the election was about "Americanism vs Socialism." The Socialist Party had in fact expelled Van Lear because he had not adopted the party's total opposition to the war and conscription. Nevertheless, Van Lear refused to publicly repudiate the Socialist Party. Meyers won by a small margin, although Van Lear carried eight of the city's thirteen wards, just as he had in 1916.[72]

The Associated Press broadcast news of the actual armistice at about 2:15 AM on November 11. When the editor on duty at the *Winona Republican Herald* read the wire, he called a friend at the Northwestern Railroad's roundhouse, who blew the company's whistle to rouse the town. Soon thousands of Winonans poured into the streets to celebrate. By daylight, people from neighboring towns joined Winona's victory party. At 6:30, the municipal band and the Home Guard led a parade to Levee Park on the Mississippi River to kick off a huge rally. The newspaper took a giddy tone, proclaiming that "everyone must have some sort of a noisemaker or be arrested tonight." The rally evolved into a massive party that lasted until after midnight. Winona's Polish community, which had supported the war from the start, joined in the celebrations and, according to the newspaper at least, "Polish national anthems were for the first time heard on Winona's streets." Every city and town had a similar celebratory story.[73]

The experience of the United States in the Great War was marked by its brevity. In Europe, four years of war and millions of casualties brought down empires and put enormous strains on the victors. The United States was at war for about nineteen months. What would have happened in Minnesota, so deeply divided about the war, if the United States had fought for another year or two, and had begun to suffer losses comparable to France or Germany?

The war was good for conservative business leaders. They created the MCPS to govern the state and fostered several popular organizations to encourage war work and promote "100% Americanism." They had vanquished the IWW, curbed the Socialist Party, defeated the NPL's attempt to unseat the governor, kept Minneapolis an "open shop" town, and, aided by the US attorney, county attorneys, and vigilantes, suppressed dissident voices. With the war over, these leaders would try to consolidate their gains.

The end of the war left many Progressives in a hopeful mood. They had supported the war because Wilson promised it would make the world safe for democracy abroad and foster democratic reform at home. Similarly, the women's movement, especially the NWSA, hoped their support for the war would lead to quick passage of the suffrage amendment. The African American movement, led by the NAACP, hoped their support for the war would lead to the end of Jim Crow and lynching. The time for reckoning had arrived.

PART III

The War about the War

TEN

THE TRAUMATIC PEACE

WINTER 1918–WINTER 1920

> The Commission assumed that it had the right, if in its judgment the public interest so required, to use the strong arm of force to suppress disloyalty, to prevent wastage of men and materials, and to preserve public order.
>
> *Report of the Minnesota Commission of Public Safety* (1919)

> . . . the State Public Safety Commission stood like iron, barred our speakers absolutely, and inaugurated a campaign of terrorism. . . . There is no doubt as to the political nature of the persecution. . . . These leaders made no bones about confessing that the disloyalty issue was the means by which they hoped to crush and destroy the Non-Partisan League as a political organization.
>
> GEORGE CREEL, head of the Committee for Public Information, in "Our 'Aliens'—Were They Loyal or Disloyal," *Everybody's Magazine* (March 1919)

THE GREAT CARNAGE WAS OVER. The warring armies suffered between nine and ten million deaths. At least ten million civilians lost their lives, the result of war crimes, malnutrition, and disease. The cease-fire on the western front, however, did not end the killing. The British refused to lift the blockade against Germany until the final peace treaty was signed, continuing a kind of violence that cut short the lives of thousands of German noncombatants. Within Germany, Socialist revolutionaries tried to overthrow the new parliamentary government and establish something like the Soviet Union. They were defeated by the returning German army and right-wing militias. In the lands of the former Russian empire, the Bolsheviks were fighting a bloody civil war against several armies trying to restore the old regime, increasingly aided by Allied forces, including thirteen thousand American troops, who were not withdrawn until April 1920.

Wilson sailed for Europe on December 3, 1918. He was given a hero's welcome by the people of Paris and a stern lesson in diplomatic reality by the British, French, and Italian leaders. He had hoped for a more just and democratic international order but was forced to acquiesce to his allies' desire to punish Germany and enrich their empires. Representatives of the new German government signed the Treaty of Versailles on June 28, 1919. Wilson took solace in the fact that the treaty created the League of Nations, which he believed would achieve his goals.

Wilson came home to find that most Republicans would not ratify the treaty unless the language defining the League of Nations was amended. Rather than negotiate with Henry Cabot Lodge, he embarked on a nationwide barnstorming tour to win popular support for the treaty as written. When the president and his wife arrived in the Twin Cities on September 9, 1919, they were greeted by enthusiastic crowds. Speaking at both the Minneapolis and St. Paul auditoriums, Wilson defended the League in nationalist terms, arguing that it was in American interests to create a mechanism for stopping expansionist powers, adding that the United States was the only nation that could "lead the world in organizing peace." He recycled his old rhetoric against hyphenated Americans, arguing that those who opposed the treaty were like the German Americans who opposed United States entry into the war.[1]

A few weeks later he fell ill and had to return to Washington, where he suffered a debilitating stroke. He survived but never spoke again in public. Most Republicans, including Knute Nelson and Frank Kellogg, continued to demand amendments to the treaty, which Wilson refused. The Treaty of Versailles was never ratified by the United States.

Winding Down and Coming Home

The country soon discovered that the armistice did not mean the war would pass quickly into history. Many were mourning their lost loved ones, and governments were considering ways to memorialize the dead. Thousands of returning soldiers needed long-term care; many of them were permanently disfigured or totally disabled. Converting from a wartime to a peacetime economy would be a disruptive process.

A sure sign that the war was not completely over was the fifth Liberty Bond campaign in April 1919, advertised as the Victory Bond Campaign. The Treasury Department realized that selling war bonds in peacetime posed a unique challenge. In Minnesota, the first four Liberty Bond campaigns had relied on a combination of advertising, rallies, and parades on the one hand, and a heavy dose of coercion on the other. With the war over, bond campaigners could no longer rely on the MCPS's statewide network of county directors who wielded subpoena power to bully farmers into compliance. However, local Liberty Bond committees continued to use the allotment system, by which small town bankers, for example, computed how much each local farmer should "voluntarily" purchase.

Washington, however, had a powerful new advertising tool, the Victory Loan Flying Circus, a group of aviators flying World War I biplanes, including the Fokker DVII, the famous German fighter. They toured the country putting on air shows that featured aerobatics and sham battles between American "aces" and Germans. In Minnesota, the Flying Circus performed in the Duluth-Superior area on April 20 and in the Twin Cities on April 21. The popular shows were accompanied by parades and rallies encouraging bond sales. In Duluth, a pilot thrilled the crowds by flying underneath the arch of the Aerial Lift Bridge. The Twin Cities show was held at the Fort Snelling parade grounds and was followed by an elaborate banquet at the Minneapolis Club, where Governor Burnquist spoke. The Victory Loan campaign did not raise as much money as the Third and Fourth Liberty Bond campaigns, but Minnesota exceeded its quota, selling bonds worth over $92 million.[2]

When the war ended, the army began discharging the 200,000 men then in training camps to make room for the troops soon to return from abroad. Demobilized soldiers began to trickle back to Minnesota as individuals or in small groups in December 1918. In January whole units began to arrive, and they were greeted by dignitaries, marching bands, and large crowds. The biggest reception marked the arrival of the 151st Field Artillery, a unit of the Minnesota National Guard that

A GRATEFUL PEOPLE PAUSE IN THEIR WELCOME
TO THE VICTORIOUS LIVING TO PAY SILENT
TRIBUTE TO THE ILLUSTRIOUS DEAD

had stayed intact as part of the American Expeditionary Force's 34th Division (the Rainbow Division). After arriving at St. Paul's Union Station on May 8, the 151st marched in a morning parade and passed through a triumphal arch erected at Sixth and Wabasha. An estimated 200,000 cheered the parade. Even larger crowds cheered the 151st in an afternoon parade that proceeded down Nicollet Avenue in downtown Minneapolis. All returning soldiers, marines, and sailors were invited to participate in formations assembled behind the 151st. Wounded soldiers participated in both parades, driven in some cases by members of the Motor Corps.[3]

Those wounded soldiers were probably from Fort Snelling. In September 1918, the army expanded Fort Snelling's base hospital into General Hospital 29, a twelve-hundred-bed facility created to handle the large influx of casualties returning from France. In its first few months, the hospital's doctors and nurses also dealt with hundreds of influenza patients. The hospital was designated a Reconstruction Hospital, meaning that in addition to treating wounds, it helped in the rehabilitation of individual soldiers, including, for example, providing prosthetic limbs. The hospital operated for about one year, during which it served about seventy-five hundred patients.[4]

Over 3,600 Minnesotans did not return from war, either killed in action or struck down by disease or other cause. Another 5,000 were wounded. Of the 104,416 Minnesotans in the army, 1,319 died in combat and 2,024 died from other causes. Over 11,000 Minnesotans served in the navy, and 145 died. Of the 2,845 marines from Minnesota, there were 119 deaths. Overall, the United States had about 324,000 casualties, of which about 114,000 were deaths.[5]

In February 1919, Colonel Theodore Roosevelt, the former president's son, was in Paris, where he presided over a meeting of officers who created the American Legion as an organization to represent the interests of veterans of the Great War, except conscientious objectors and those dishonorably discharged. The city of Minneapolis hosted its founding convention the following November. The Legion declared

▪ OPPOSITE
The 151st Field Artillery, the sole unit of the Minnesota National Guard that stayed intact during the war, parading through the triumphal arch in downtown St. Paul, 1919. ***MNHS collections***

itself to be "absolutely non-political," which meant neutrality in contests between Republicans and Democrats. Its founders, however, envisioned a powerful political organization, intent on "fostering and perpetuating one hundred percent Americanism." Fearing that returning soldiers might be influenced by "Bolsheviks," they were anxious to recruit veterans to a conservative organization. The Legion was anything but neutral when it came to pacifists, the IWW, the Socialist Party, and the Nonpartisan League.[6]

In Minnesota, NPL and trade unionists had some success organizing an alternative to the American Legion called the World War Veterans. When American Legion posts in Minnesota held a state convention in St. Paul a month before the national convention, delegates told the press they had adopted the entire World War Veterans platform except some "ultra-radical" items like honorable discharges for conscientious objectors. A legion official told the press the two organizations should merge.[7]

Leaders of the World War Veterans rejected the idea. Thomas Van Lear told a trade union assembly at the St. Paul Auditorium that no enlisted men were involved in creating the American Legion, that "big business" funded it, and that the Legion would ultimately be used against labor. A few weeks later, World War Veterans published a statement detailing these charges, noting that the Legion had helped break a steelworker strike in Gary, Indiana. They also noted that Colonel Roosevelt often spoke about destroying the NPL and that a Legion post in Aitkin, Minnesota, had passed a resolution banning the NPL from speaking in that county.[8]

By the time the American Legion gathered in Minneapolis for its founding convention, there were 360 local posts in Minnesota, while the World War Veterans was floundering and would soon become dormant. Resolutions were passed calling for universal military training, a key demand of the preparedness movement. They also passed "Americanization" measures, including resolutions in support of deporting aliens who claimed exemptions from military service, banning Japanese immigration, repealing birthright citizenship, and condemning any resumption of German opera productions or performances by German or Austrian performers.[9]

The Time of Troubles

The immediate postwar period was a time of turbulence. The country suffered through the third and final wave of the influenza pandemic in the first few months of 1919. The rapid, unplanned demobilization of nearly four million soldiers inevitably led to unemployment and inflation. Farmers, especially in an agricultural state like Minnesota, found themselves in a recession as demand for their crops diminished. The farm crisis also hurt manufacturers and retailers who supplied the farm market. The return of railroads to private management boosted transportation costs. Prohibition would soon cripple the brewing industry, a thriving part of the Minnesota economy. These disruptions set the stage for "the year of great unrest," as historian Nell Irvin Painter put it, and things were not much calmer in the following year.[10]

The armistice ended the federally mediated truce between employers and the labor movement. Trade unions had grown during the war and were anxious to take advantage of their new strength. Business leaders were intent to maintain the "open shop." As a result, 1919 saw a record number of workplace confrontations, some of which had nationwide significance. In January, a strike of shipyard workers in Seattle escalated into a general strike. The confrontation ended only when federal troops occupied the city. Later in the year, there was a major strike in the steel industry, and the United Mine Workers struck in the coalfields. Meanwhile, the police staged a dramatic strike in Boston.

In addition to the strikes, outbursts of political violence triggered a period of intense public panic about socialism that degenerated into what historians have called the Red Scare. Bombs were sent to various government officials, including federal officials involved in prosecution of radicals. On May Day, labor marches led to violent street confrontations. More bombs exploded in June. In November, American Legion members marching in an Armistice Day parade attacked the IWW office in Centralia, Oregon. The Wobblies fired back, and several Legionnaires were killed. This led to more violence and the lynching of one of the IWW leaders.

Business leaders blamed the strike wave and the bombs on the revolutionary turmoil in Europe, especially the Bolsheviks in Russia. American trade unions, however, were primarily interested in better pay and working conditions, and few unions were led by Socialists. For the Socialist movement in the United States, the Bolshevik Revolution was a mixed blessing. More people were attracted to the idea of socialism, but the movement was weakened as two small parties split from the Socialist Party, eventually uniting to form the American Communist Party, which closely allied itself with Moscow.

Many felt the country was coming apart. In Washington, a Senate committee found that Bolsheviks were about to stage a revolution in the United States. Under pressure to act, Attorney General Mitchell Palmer, assisted by a young J. Edgar Hoover, ordered sweep arrests of people associated with radical organizations. The Palmer Raids, as they came to be called, resulted in thousands of arrests, and the summary deportation of hundreds, including Emma Goldman, perhaps the best-known radical activist in the country.

The backlash against radicalism overlapped with a backlash against immigrants. During the war, the fear that immigrants would sabotage the war effort sparked the demand for 100 percent Americanism. Even though immigrant communities generally participated with enthusiasm in home front mobilization for the war, anti-immigrant feelings deepened after the war, fueled by the new fear that immigrants were bringing revolutionary ideologies across the ocean. As a result, Congress passed a drastic restriction on immigration in the early 1920s.

Business leaders in Minnesota shared in the general fear of revolution. In 1919, leaders of the Minneapolis Civic and Commerce Association formed a new group to fight socialism in the name of Americanism. Typical of the times, the membership letter of the American Committee of Minneapolis was apocalyptic in its tone: "This nation is rapidly drifting into anarchy—more rapidly than the average loyal citizen dreams. The black and dismal pit of national chaos is yawning just ahead. Revolution is in the air. The mob spirit is rampant in the land."[11]

The claim that the United States was on the brink of revolution justified the continuation of wartime repression. Shortly after the armistice, the Socialist Party announced a demonstration in the Gateway district of Minneapolis. Sheriff Otto Langum called it a so-called "red flag" demonstration and banned it. Governor Burnquist ordered the 4th and 6th Regiments of the Minnesota National Guard and the Minneapolis and St. Paul Motor Corps to secure the district. They were joined by sheriff's deputies, Minneapolis Police, Department of

Justice agents, and a large anti-Socialist crowd. When about twenty Socialists tried to parade, they were forced into an early retreat. Led by an elderly man carrying an American flag, they held signs demanding that US troops be withdrawn from Russia and that the United States diplomatically recognize the Soviet government.[12]

In the western Minnesota town of Ortonville, just ahead of a speech from the stage of the opera house, former 5th District congressman Ernest Lundeen was arrested in November 1919 by the sheriff, who was backed by a group of American Legionnaires. His topic was the League of Nations, but he was attacked because as a congressman he had voted against declaring war on Germany. The mob marched him to the train station and locked him in a refrigerator car as the train left the station. Fortunately, the train crew heard his calls and released him. Once home, Lundeen demanded that Burnquist remove the sheriff from office, which the governor refused to do after a hearing.[13]

In Minnesota, the Palmer Raids included the arrest of twenty-four in the Twin Cities and another eight on the Iron Range on January 2, 1920. T. E. Campbell, special agent of the Department of Justice, told the press that "nearly a ton of literature, photographs, stationery, and correspondence" was seized in the homes of those arrested, all of whom were alleged to be aliens who were members of either the Communist Party or the IWW.[14]

Coinciding with the federal raids, the county attorney in Duluth arrested seven men associated with the Finnish Socialist paper *Industrialisti* in January 1920. They were charged with violating the state syndicalism law, which prohibited advocating the violent overthrow of the government. In March, two of the men, and the company that owned the paper, were convicted for publishing an article that criticized the moderation of traditional labor unions and called on workers to seek to overthrow the capitalist class "with all possible and impossible means."[15]

Minnesota also saw its share of strikes in the postwar period, starting a few days after the armistice when telephone operators and linemen walked out of the telephone company. Myrtle Cain, the twenty-four-year-old business agent of the union, led the women who operated the telephone exchanges. In support of their demands, they marched through the Minneapolis and St. Paul downtowns in a carnival-like atmosphere. The strike lasted twelve weeks but ended in a stalemate thanks to the resistance of Albert Burleson, the postmaster general, who had control of telephone and telegraph companies during the war. He banned the strike and would not allow a rate increase to finance the union's wage demands. Nevertheless, the militancy of the "hello girls," as the press called them, invigorated the labor movement.[16]

■ **Woman's Party activist Myrtle Cain led the telephone workers strike in late 1918, and later won a seat in the Minnesota legislature as a Farmer Labor Party candidate.** ***MNHS collections***

In December 1919, about seventy workers struck the Backus-Brooks Company in International Falls. They worked for the railroad that the company operated to serve its lumber mill and paper mill on the Rainy River. In these situations, the Citizens Alliance in Minneapolis advised businesses to follow its strategy, which included hiring strikebreakers and deploying the National Guard. The company complained that sheriff Hugh McIntosh was failing to protect the company and, in fact, had arrested and disarmed several strikebreakers. Governor Burnquist heard their plea and sent the National Guard. Adjutant General Rhinow rushed to International Falls with a National Guard company on December 13. Various companies were rotated through International Falls for the next three months.[17]

The decision to send the National Guard provoked a backlash, and not just from the union. Shortly after the guard arrived, city and county officials signed an angry telegram to Burnquist contending that there was no disorder in town and that residents viewed the presence of the guard as a "deliberate insult." The telegram was written by the mayor and the commander of the American Legion post. Burnquist responded with a telegram lecturing the post commander on his duty to uphold "law and order" and advising the elected officials to resign. The commander responded with a letter assuring the governor that his American Legion post had welcomed their fellow soldiers of the National Guard to their clubrooms, and suggesting that Burnquist might see things more clearly if he had seen fit to serve in the army during the war.[18]

The union never threatened any violence, and the soldiers were never asked to guard the mills. In March, the strike was amicably settled. Even the pro-business *Duluth Herald* commented that only strikebreakers caused any trouble. By assuming a McGee-like stance, Burnquist alienated many people, but he did earn the praise of O. P. Briggs, president of the Citizens Alliance, who thanked him for acting against the "outlaws in northern Minnesota." If this could be done everywhere, Briggs wrote, "all these radical difficulties would disappear."[19]

In the two years after the armistice, two great reform movements achieved their long-sought victories. In 1917, Congress passed the Eighteenth Amendment, making the production and sale of alcohol illegal, and in 1919 the required three-quarters of the states approved it. The country went dry in January 1920. The women's suffrage movement had a more difficult time getting the Nineteenth Amendment through Congress. When the war ended, the House had approved the amendment, but not the Senate. The National Woman Suffrage Association responded with renewed lobbying efforts, while the militant National Woman's Party inaugurated its "watchfire of freedom" protests, featuring a perpetual flame across from the White House. The NWP used the fire to highlight the hypocrisy of Wilson, who had gone to Paris to preserve democracy even though he could not provide the same at home. They fueled it with copies of his speeches. This led to a new round of arrests. Several young women from Minnesota went to jail, including Bertha Berglin Moller, a seasoned NWP organizer who had been arrested several times before; Gertrude Murphy, a teacher; and Rhonda Kellogg, a student at the University of Minnesota.[20]

By this time, Sarah Colvin was in Baltimore working as a nurse at the Fort McHenry hospital, where her husband, an army doctor, had been transferred. As Minnesota's NWP leader, she felt she must join the protest, though she was older than many of the women who went to jail. Without telling her husband, she went to Washington, where she was twice arrested, the second time at the controversial February protest where the NWP burned an effigy of Wilson. After serving a short jail sentence, Colvin joined the NWP "Prison Special" train tour that traveled around the country publicizing the watchfire campaign. In her memoir, she wrote that Dr. Colvin was shocked to learn "that I could possibly consider anything of more importance than his career." After a "very full and frank discussion of the whole situation," she wrote, they put the matter to rest and never discussed it again.[21]

Congress adjourned in March without passing the amendment, forcing Wilson to call a special session of the newly elected Republican-dominated Congress. In June, the Senate finally approved the Nineteenth Amendment, and three-fourths of the states approved it the following summer. Women nationwide were eligible to vote in the 1920 presidential election.

The End of the Public Safety Commission

The nationwide strife was the result, in Nell Irwin Painter's words, of "conflicts between forces of restoration and of resistance to old ways," that is, whether the traditional dominance of business elites over workers and farmers could be restored or weakened. The situation in Minnesota, however, was somewhat different, since the Minnesota Commission of Public Safety had not only maintained the "old ways" but went beyond them, for example, by organizing a businessmen's militia in the guise of the Home Guard. The question in Minnesota was whether business organizations could institutionalize the gains they had made during the war.

With Germany defeated and the legislature set to convene in 1919, business leaders realized the MCPS would have to be abandoned, and the commissioners agreed. At their January 1919 meeting, they noted that the armistice had "made renewal of the war practically impossible." Accordingly, they voted to make their official orders inoperative. At their February meeting, they clarified that this did not apply to the Home Guard and the Motor Corps. They hoped the legislature would make these forces permanent.[22]

In the inaugural message to the 1919 legislature, the governor proposed to incorporate the Home Guard and the Motor Corps into the state's military establishment. He also called for a "red flag" law that would prevent the display of red flags, which, he said, signified the violent overthrow of the government by force, and for the strengthening of the state sedition statute, apparently because the courts had thrown out some prosecutions. To promote "Americanization," he asked for a law making the learning of English "compulsory," since no one had the right to live in this county, he asserted, "unless he is willing to learn its language." Finally, he called for "proper schooling" that would make citizens understand that the common ownership of property would destroy individual initiative.[23]

The legislature did pass "the flag bill," which in its final form outlawed red flags, black flags, or any flags having "an inscription antagonistic to the existing government of the United States, or the state of Minnesota." When the governor's allies introduced a bill to make the Motor Corps permanent, representatives associated with the labor unions and the NPL passionately opposed it, arguing that recent history confirmed that a motorized militia would primarily be used against them. Several thousand union members came to the capitol in early February to demonstrate their disapproval. The bill passed the house but ran aground in the senate, undone by the fact that the Minnesota National Guard opposed it, apparently fearing that the Motor Corps would take money away from the existing guard units.[24]

Although the MCPS was winding down, Progressives introduced a bill to abolish it, wanting to make sure it did not rise from the dead. That bill sailed through the house but was defeated in the senate after a bitter debate. The senate action had no practical effect. The commissioners ended the employment of Ambrose Tighe, its chief counsel, and Charles W. Henke, the publicity director, in 1919, and at its final meeting in January 1920 rescinded all orders. Nevertheless, the senate debate demonstrated that the MCPS was a highly divisive subject.[25]

The 1919 legislature ratified the Eighteenth Amendment to the constitution but had adjourned before the US Senate approved the Nineteenth Amendment. Governor Burnquist called a special session in the summer, during which Minnesota became the fifteenth state to approve the right of women to vote. Against his wishes, the legislature also passed an iron ore tax. He vetoed it, which contributed to his growing unpopularity.

Not So Normal

The MCPS was a great success for the business organizations that created it, except for one unintended consequence. John McGee's heavy-handed leadership encouraged the collaboration of the NPL and the labor movement, something that employers feared. The farmer-labor coalition continued to develop after the war, leading eventually to the Farmer Labor Party. "Third parties" are difficult to establish in the United States, but aided by the weakness of the Democrats, the Farmer Labor Party became the second-largest party in Minnesota.

At a convention in July 1919, the Minnesota State Federation of Labor established the Working People's Nonpartisan League as its political arm. Under the leadership of William Mahoney, president of the St. Paul Trades and Labor Association, and Thomas Van Lear, the former mayor, the new group solidified its alliance with the NPL. The two leagues stuck with the strategy of trying to take over the Republican Party. At coordinated conventions in March 1920, they simultaneously nominated Henrik Shipstead, a dentist from western Minnesota and a state legislator, as their candidate for governor in the Republican primary.

League leaders shortlisted Charles Lindbergh as a possible candidate, but he was not interested in running again for governor. Meanwhile, he pursued other ways of advancing his reform ideas. In March 1919 he unveiled a new monthly farm magazine called *Lindbergh's National Farmer.* Besides articles on practical agriculture, it served as a platform for his views on politics and economics, especially as they affected farmers and workers. He wrote favorably about Wilson's trip to Versailles, but he was greatly disappointed in the treaty, including the League of Nations, because it did not confront economic injustice, the fundamental problem. Lindbergh had much to say, but he was a poor manager of a national publication. The magazine, sixteen pages in large format, lost money from the beginning and ended in March 1920.[26]

Business leaders were busy too, creating the Minnesota Sound Government Association in 1920 to coordinate their statewide fight against the two leagues. They recruited university president Cyrus Northrop as its figurehead leader, and raised several hundred thousand dollars to fund literature, lecturers, and several newspapers, all geared to painting the NPL as Socialist. The association published the newspaper *Minnesota Issues*, which was mailed free to farmers. It ran for about a year starting in February 1920. Business leaders also contributed to the entrepreneurs who organized the short-lived Northwest Warrior Americanization Association that sought to attract veterans to the fight against anarchism and Bolshevism. This group published *Northwest Warrior Magazine* for several years.[27]

Southern Minnesota prosecutors also kept the pressure on the NPL. In 1918, the county attorneys of Martin, Goodhue, and Jackson Counties had charged NPL leaders with sedition to undermine the league's campaign in the June 1918 Republican primary. The Martin County prosecution against Arthur Townley and Joseph Gilbert fell apart when the Minnesota Supreme Court held that the NPL documents upon which the charges were based were not seditious. Goodhue County, however, convicted Gilbert in May, and the Minnesota Supreme Court affirmed his conviction in December. Gilbert appealed to the US Supreme Court, which did not rule until 1920. E. H. Nicholas, the Jackson County attorney, charged Townley and Gilbert with conspiracy based on published documents and speeches. Once again, the defendants were allowed a pretrial appeal to the Minnesota Supreme Court to contest the charges. In May 1919, the court held that the charges were legal.

Although many sedition charges were dropped after the armistice, Nicholas decided to take this case to trial, most likely because the league was at least as much a threat at the polls in 1919 as a year earlier. The trial was a three-week spectacle featuring Fred Tiegen, a disgruntled former NPL employee, as the star prosecution witness. The judge blocked Arthur Le Sueur, the NPL attorney, from presenting evidence of the loyalty of Townley and Gilbert, including testimony of federal officials. The jury found them guilty, and the judge imposed a ninety-day sentence, stayed pending appeal. As in 1918, conservative newspapers once again pointed to the verdict as proof of the treasonous nature of candidates endorsed by the NPL.[28]

Meanwhile, Republican leaders quietly convinced Governor Burnquist not to run for reelection, probably because they wanted a candidate unburdened by the baggage of "McGeeism," the term the labor movement coined to refer to the reign of the MCPS. Afraid that Shipstead would win the primary if there were more than two candidates, the conservative Republicans held an extralegal elimination convention, at which they chose Jacob Preus, the secretary of state. Preus framed the election as a choice between "Americanism and Socialism." Although the NPL/WPNPL platform was, as usual, primarily about economic issues, Preus also claimed that the leagues advocated "free love." Twin Cities newspapers urged Democrats to cross over and vote for Preus to save Minnesota from socialism. Preus beat Shipstead in the June primary by just a few percentage points. The vote total in the Democratic primary was meager.[29]

The NPL/WPNPL leaders were encouraged by the result. Shipstead had carried fifty-four counties, an improvement over the thirty counties won by Lindbergh in 1918. They were able to put the same slate on the general election ballot by petition. In November, Shipstead was overwhelmed by the landslide for conservative Republicans. Warren Harding scored a sweeping victory nationwide and in Minnesota carried every county. The era of "normalcy" had begun, meaning renewed power by conservative Republicans, who promoted friendly relations with business, a kind of return to the age of McKinley.[30]

After the 1920 election, the NPL and the WPNPL abandoned the strategy of capturing the Republican Party and began functioning as an independent party. In 1922, the emerging Farmer Labor Party nominated Shipstead for US Senate and Magnus Johnson for governor. Shipstead defeated incumbent Republican senator Frank Kellogg, and Johnson came close to unseating Governor Preus. The farmer-labor coalition won seventy seats in the Minnesota legislature. Four women were elected to the legislature, one of whom was the Farmer Labor–endorsed Myrtle Cain, the young woman who led the telephone worker strike in 1918.[31]

The Farmer Labor Party was now established, a product of the home front conflicts and the repressive rule of John McGee. In the next decade, it would become Minnesota's dominant party, electing the governor in 1930, 1932, 1934, and 1936.

Thank You for Your Service

After the armistice, W. E. B. Du Bois was eager to get to France. As editor of the NAACP journal *The Crisis*, he had urged African Americans to "close ranks" and support the war effort, hoping that it would lead to reform. He wanted to investigate what African American soldiers had done and how they had been treated. He learned that the 93rd Division, which had fought in the French army, had been treated well and were considered heroes in France. The US Army, however, had treated the 92nd Division poorly, subjecting them to racist abuse, even to the point of officially warning the French that African American soldiers were likely to be sexual predators. In May 1919, Du Bois issued another stirring editorial, "Returning Soldiers," celebrating the African Americans who had fought for democracy in France and proclaiming that returning soldiers would resume the fight for democracy at home. He concluded with "We return. We return from fighting. We return fighting."[32]

Local communities welcomed returning soldiers and, occasionally, people of all backgrounds cheered African American troops, as when the Harlem Hellfighters (the 369th Infantry Brigade of the 93rd Division) marched down New York's Fifth Avenue led by James Reese Europe and his legendary band. The African American community in St. Paul hosted a reception to celebrate the return of Samuel L. Ranson, who had joined the 8th Regiment of the Illinois National Guard, which became the 370th Infantry Regiment of the 93rd Division. Known as the "Black Devils," the regiment had been highly honored by the French, and Ransom had been promoted to first lieutenant. Speeches were given, poems read, and much music performed, all under the direction of William T. Francis, who chaired the event. A few weeks later, Francis presided over another reception, this time for about twenty-five returning soldiers.[33]

It soon became clear, however, that loyally supporting the war effort, even fighting in France, changed nothing. The summer of 1919 was a time of horrible racial violence, which NAACP leader James Weldon Johnson called the Red Summer. The mass demobilization of soldiers complicated already explosive tensions involving jobs, housing, and the use of public space. The new factor was that many African Americans, especially veterans, had heightened expectations for racial equity, and were willing to fight back. The first major outbreak of violence was in Washington, DC, where fighting stopped only after federal troops intervened. Then the stoning of an African American boy swimming off a Lake Michigan beach sparked street battles in Chicago that left thirty-eight dead, twenty-three of whom were African

American. Finally, a seven-day pogrom against African American sharecroppers in a rural Arkansas county left several hundred dead, and many more facing the death penalty for resisting.[34]

Lynching surged across the country during 1919, with seventy-six African Americans murdered, the highest annual total since 1908, including at least eleven who were veterans. On occasion, soldiers still in uniform were targets of violence, especially in the South. President Wilson remained silent. There would be no desegregation of the armed forces, no dismantling of Jim Crow laws, not even an anti-lynching law, until after the next war.

The 1919 Minnesota legislature passed a bill that might have transformed the 16th Battalion of the Home Guards into an African American unit of the Minnesota National Guard. As the war ended, some officers of the 16th Battalion, including Charles Sumner Smith, the editor of the *Twin Cities Star*, convinced Governor Burnquist to support the bill. In *The Appeal*, however, John Quincy Adams argued that the creation of a separate battalion of African Americans was a bad precedent because it reinforced the color line. A group of Nonpartisan League representatives won passage of the bill in the house, and on the last day of the session, the senate also approved it. The governor signed the bill, but the Minnesota National Guard had little interest in the project, and the battalion apparently had difficulty recruiting. By 1921, it was forgotten.[35]

The notion that racist violence was something that happened south of Minnesota was shattered in July 1920 when a circus came to Duluth. The night the circus train was preparing to depart, the sheriff took fifteen of the 150 African American circus workers off the train at random and held them in connection with a rape that most likely did not occur. They were brought to the jail in downtown Duluth, where the next day, a mob of at least five thousand stormed the jail, grabbed three of the jailed circus workers, and hanged them from a streetlight in downtown Duluth. One of the victims, Elmer Jackson, was identified by his parents as an army veteran.[36]

African American migration to an industrial area sometimes raised fears of loss of jobs and provoked a racist backlash. In this case, however, the victims were transient circus workers, and only one of the twenty men charged with participating in the mob worked for U.S. Steel, the dominant industry. Most of those arrested were Protestants of northern European backgrounds, the kind of men who were increasingly attracted to the white nationalist ideology of the Ku Klux Klan. Roy Wilkins, the future president of the NAACP who was at the time a St. Paul teenager, wrote in his autobiography that reading about the lynching left him feeling "sick, scared, and angry all at the same time." He was shaken by the fact that the "mob was in touch with something—an awful hatred I had never seen or felt before."[37]

The acceptance of vigilante violence in Duluth may have also been a contributing factor. The *Duluth Herald* had published Father Iciek's letter threatening to hang Lindbergh from the lift bridge, and it was in Duluth that the Knights of Loyalty kidnapped, tarred, and perhaps lynched Olli Kiukkonen. The Knights were allowed to threaten violence against others in the pages of the Duluth newspapers, and no one was willing to come forward to expose their identities. They might well have been in the mob that murdered the circus workers.[38]

The NAACP in the Twin Cities investigated the lynching and organized the defense of the circus workers still on trial. In St. Paul, William and Nellie Francis spearheaded an NAACP campaign to win passage of an anti-lynching bill in the Minnesota legislature in 1921. Du Bois came to St. Paul and Duluth in March to speak at NAACP events in support of the campaign. The bill passed both houses and Governor Preus signed it. The law made any county in which a lynching occurred liable for damages in a civil suit, and required the governor to remove from office any law enforcement officer who failed to resist a lynching.[39]

Generally, however, the ideology of white supremacy deepened and broadened. "Whiteness," as Du Bois noted, was celebrated and defended in polite society, and the hope for an equitable, multicultural society receded. In Minnesota, the term "white man's country" was commonly used in the press, including in editorials, as when a Rochester paper called for immigration restrictions because "this is a White man's country." In the *Red Wing Daily Republican*, Jens Grondahl quoted with approval a National Security League statement demanding that Germany be subjected to a "white man's vengeance." In serialized fiction in newspapers, the expression "thanks, that's mighty white of you" routinely appeared. This was also the period when the deeds of many homes in the Twin Cities area were written with racial covenants that made it illegal for an owner to sell or rent to an African American.[40]

The armistice marked the beginning of the rapid rise of the Ku Klux Klan, the rebirth of which was related to the experience of the home front. William J. Simmons, who worked with the Atlanta office of the American Protective League, began the revival in Georgia during the war. He combined violent vigilantism, 100 percent Americanism, and Protestant evangelism into a formula that attracted many. The Klan had a banner year in 1919, organizing the same kinds of people—small businessmen, ministers, and professionals—who were involved in the Home Guard, the Loyalty Leagues, the America First Association, and the APL. In the 1920s, millions would belong to the Klan nationally, and thousands in Minnesota.[41]

Every War Is Fought Twice

To win support for the war effort and to attack its political adversaries, the Minnesota Commission of Public Safety devoted considerable resources to propaganda, including its newsletter, its catalog of patriotic publications, speeches by the governor and the commission's many allies, and a steady stream of press releases. The commissioners also took the long view, paying attention to how the conflicts on the home front would be remembered after the war was over. They sought to control the writing of the commission's history.

The first effort was its final report, a bound volume of over three hundred pages published in 1919. Most likely written by Henry Libby, an MCPS commissioner and its secretary, and Charles W. Henke, the publicity director, the report presents the commission as an unusual but necessary reaction to the dire situation that Minnesota confronted in 1917. It argues that strong measures are justified when the "the country's life is at stake," and that Minnesota, which supplied timber, iron ore, and food to the nation, had a high percentage of foreign-born residents who had opposed US entry into the war. "It goes without saying," the report continued, that if the United States had the right "to crush its foreign enemies" it could also "protect itself against those at home whose behavior tends to weaken its war capacity." The MCPS therefore "assumed it had the right . . . to use the strong arm of force to suppress disloyalty." The "test for loyalty," the report stated, was whether a man was "wholeheartedly for the war and subordinates everything else to its successful conclusion." Quietly stifling one's objections while obeying the law was not enough. The commission identified three groups as disloyal—"professional pacifists," "men of pro-German traditions and sympathies," and politicians associated with the Socialist Party and the Nonpartisan League. "With the leaders," the report proudly proclaimed, "it used the mailed fist."[42]

At first glance, the report appears to be a comprehensive survey of the commission's activities. It contains, for example, the full text of each of its fifty-nine orders. Its silences, however, speak volumes. "The commission's top objective," Carl Chrislock wrote, was "defeating trade unionism and the Nonpartisan League." The climax of this battle was the June 1918 Republican primary election in which Charles Lindbergh challenged Governor Burnquist. The MCPS used every weapon available to keep Burnquist in power, even to the extent of mobilizing Home Guard troops to block the Lindbergh campaign. The report, however, never mentions the primary, or Lindbergh for that matter, and in fact has little to say about the NPL, except to reprint the resolution opening an investigation of the NPL for disloyalty. It does not mention that the investigation came to nothing and was quietly dropped.[43]

Before the commission had the time to get its story before the public, George Creel, the director of the Committee of Public Information in Washington, bluntly refuted it. In the March 1919 *Everybody's Magazine*, a popular monthly, Creel defended immigrant groups, including German Americans, holding that they were overwhelmingly loyal to their adopted country, despite being maligned by "Americanizers," a sect whose distinguishing mark was their "passion for minding other people's business." He singled out Minnesota, where "politics played an ugly part" and the MCPS "inaugurated a campaign of terrorism" against the NPL and labor unions. He mentioned tarring and feathering, the stopping of parades by Home Guards, and deportations. The commission, Creel wrote, "made no bones about confessing that the disloyalty issue was the means by which they hoped to crush and destroy the Nonpartisan League as a political organization."[44]

Burnquist angrily rebutted Creel in a speech at a Republican event. He repeated his familiar claims that the Nonpartisan League was a disloyal organization led by Socialists and that the MCPS itself had never prohibited the NPL from holding meetings, although he admitted that "certain county officials" had done so because of the "proven disloyalty" of the NPL. He concluded that Creel's "malicious fabrications" could only be explained by the "probable collusion between him and the radical element within our nation." Burnquist submitted a copy of his speech to *Everybody's Magazine*, but the editors asked him to submit a shorter piece, specifically prepared for the magazine, rebutting Creel. He apparently never did.[45]

In October 1918, the MCPS created the War Records Commission to begin collecting materials in partnership with the Minnesota Historical Society (MNHS). When the commission disbanded, the legislature created a new War Records Commission with Solon Buck, director of the Minnesota Historical Society, as president, and MNHS staff member Franklin Holbrook as secretary. The new WRC was tasked with collecting and preserving material relating to Minnesota's participation in the war, and to create a "comprehensive documentary and narrative history of the part played by the state in the world war, including conditions and events within the state relating to or affected by the war."[46]

An initial plan for a ten-volume series eventually shrunk to a two-volume work entitled *Minnesota in the War with Germany* written by MNHS staffers Franklin Holbrook and Livia Appel, and a one-volume history of the 151st Artillery Brigade written by one of its officers. The former was a comprehensive survey of the home front in which the commission was presented as a benign institution whose actions were governed by what was reasonable under the circumstances. The authors note that the commission "on numerous occasions forbade gatherings" of the NPL, but imply that this directive was a prudent necessity.[47]

Official histories are valuable in that they bring together a great deal of basic information, usually quite reliable, organized and presented by skilled researchers and writers. Critical readers can take institutional bias into account when evaluating them. The larger danger is that an official history may simply omit significant parts of the story. Taking a cue from the commission's report, Holbrook and Appel, for example, found no room in their weighty two-volume work to mention the tumultuous Republican primary in 1918.

In addition to these statewide histories, the War Records Commission encouraged counties to publish books memorializing local contributions to the war. About thirty were produced, usually assembled by a local newspaper and financed by advertising. They bear a strong resemblance to high school yearbooks. They list every county resident who served in the military, with special attention to those who were killed, and members of the Home Guard, Public Safety Commission, draft board, Red Cross, and other organizations, illustrated with individual pictures of each soldier and group photos of the various organizations. Some books also have substantial narrative sections.[48]

In Red Wing, Jens Grondahl took responsibility for publishing *Goodhue County in the World War*, a 190-page book of which the last fifty-five pages were advertising. It contains overviews of the activities of the county's Public Safety Commission, Home Guard, Motor Corps, draft board, and War Advertising Committee, among others. Grondahl also mentioned the local American Protective League, noting that it had six agents working in Red Wing alone. He claimed that the APL apprehended "German spies" working in the United States, which is doubtful, since not a single spy or saboteur was convicted in the federal courts during the war. Strangely, he makes no mention of how W. H. Putnam, the county public safety commission director, took control of the city and mobilized the Home Guard to prevent the NPL from holding a rally in Red Wing during the June 1918 Republican primary campaign.[49]

William Watts Folwell was the first writer to tell the story of Minnesota's home front outside the confines of an official history. Folwell was the first president of the University of Minnesota, and in retirement he wrote his groundbreaking, and still valuable, four-volume *A History of Minnesota*. He provided a detailed assessment of the Minnesota Commission of Public Safety, which he characterized as a "dictatorship," and noted that "if a large hostile army had already landed at Duluth and was about to march on the capital . . . a more liberal dictatorship could hardly have been conceded to the commission." He left the impression, however, that its repressive ways were justified.[50]

In a separate section, he recounted the history of the Nonpartisan League in Minnesota and the subsequent development of the Farmer Labor Party. He briefly mentioned the league's nomination of Charles Lindbergh to challenge Burnquist in the 1918 Republican primary, but said nothing about the campaign itself, including the fact that the league was barred from campaigning in many counties, faced violence throughout the state, and even had its candidate arrested. As far as one could tell from Folwell's history, the MCPS played no role in the election. In a telling error, Folwell reported that Lindbergh received 50,000 votes, when in fact he received 150,000 votes, 43 percent of the total. Given Folwell's background, it may have been that he found it difficult to take the NPL seriously as a political organization.[51]

The story that the commissioners wanted Minnesotans to remember about the home front was not questioned by historians until after the next world war, when a new generation began to explore the Minnesota scene between 1914 and 1920. The experience of World War II and the McCarthy era encouraged a reappraisal of the repressive policies in World War I. After the Vietnam War, and the massive protests against US policy, yet another generation of historians was motivated to explore World War I tensions in Minnesota. Today, when a polarized population confronts issues of democracy, immigration, unionization, and military intervention abroad, the conflicts of Minnesota's home front during the Great War takes on renewed significance.[52]

EPILOGUE

LIVES AFTER WARTIME

THERE WAS NO ESCAPING THE GREAT WAR. European society was shattered by the massive death and enormous destruction of the interminable war. The United States was also transformed by the national mobilization for war, even though the experience was relatively brief and the casualties small by comparison. When a major catastrophe like World War I grips a society, individual lives are necessarily altered. Some go to war and never come back, leaving behind families and friends who grieve them. The soldiers, nurses, and aid workers who return come back changed by the powerful experience they have shared. Those who stay home, and live through the tensions and conflicts of the home front, are also changed.

* * *

The war was hard on Charles Lindbergh, although he stoically denied it. He had been a successful lawyer, speculating in real estate, investing in local banks, and hobnobbing with the young lumber barons who were his clients in Little Falls. The voters of the Sixth District sent him to Congress five times by big margins. Then came the war. In the 1918 Republican primary for governor, most newspapers called him a traitor, a Socialist, even a Bolshevik. He was hung in effigy, arrested for sedition, shot at. As an ally of the NPL and the trade unions, he was generally persona non grata in the social circles of the middle class or wealthy. He could not return to the quiet life of a small-town lawyer in Little Falls. He rented an office in Minneapolis, dabbled in real estate

■ Charles Lindbergh sat for this portrait in 1919. *MNHS collections*

■ The young Lindbergh's Jenny after a mishap in a farmer's field during his father's 1924 campaign. *MNHS collections*

development, and looked for ways to help build a reform movement based on populist principles.[1]

There were various false starts. The farm journal he started in spring 1919 lasted only a year. In 1920, he made an ineffective attempt to win back his congressional seat, and perhaps reclaim the stability of his life before the war. He played a major role behind the scenes in building the Farmer Labor Party, serving, for example, with William Mahoney and Harry Teigen on the twelve-member state committee of the developing organization. He wrote a book, *The Economic Pinch*, published in April 1923, a new appeal for structural reform based on an analysis of the postwar economy. He worried that so many Progressives had abandoned reform. To get back on track, he argued, "we must substitute reason for tradition if we are to unshackle ourselves from the arbitrary domination of property privilege over human right."[2]

Knute Nelson died on April 28, 1923, leading to a special election with party primaries in June. Lindbergh entered the Farmer Labor primary, and the campaign gave Lindbergh the chance to spend time with his son who was by this time a barnstormer who owned and maintained his own airplane. Charles Jr. had studied mechanical engineering for two years at the University of Wisconsin and then attended flight school in Nebraska. He flew his two-seat open cockpit biplane to Minnesota in the spring of 1923 to carry his father between campaign stops. It was a brief experiment. As the young pilot and the candidate were taking off from a farmer's field near Glencoe, one wheel dipped into a ditch, causing the plane to crash. Neither were hurt, but the plane was too damaged to fly. Lindbergh once again did poorly at the polls, coming in third behind Magnus Johnson and Louis Fritsche. Johnson went on to beat Jacob Preus in the general election, and for a time, the neophyte Farmer Labor Party held both Senate seats.[3]

Despite the poor showing in 1923, friends convinced Lindbergh to enter the Farmer Labor Party primary for governor in March 1924. A month later, he was diagnosed with a brain tumor. He was sixty-five years old. When doctors at the Mayo Clinic confirmed it was inoperable, he was transported to a hospital in Crookston to be near the home of his daughter Eva and her husband. He died there May 24, and as he requested, Eva brought his body to Minneapolis for a funeral at the First Unitarian Church. He was cremated, and later his son flew over the farmstead at Melrose where he had grown up and spread his ashes.[4]

Lindbergh was the premier populist politician in Minnesota, contributing to the Progressive wing of the Republican party, to the Nonpartisan League, and finally to the Farmer Labor Party in Minnesota. On a national level, his main contribution was articulating a radical critique of the financial system and making the case for structural reform on democratic principles. He had many enemies, especially because of his anti-war views, but it was hard to take issue with either his honesty or his courage.[5]

In 1931, the Lindbergh family donated his house and farm near Little Falls to the State of Minnesota, which developed it as a state park. In 1940, the sculptor Paul Fjelde created a bronze bust of Lindbergh that occupied a prominent place in the central corridor of the Minnesota Historical Building. In 1969, the Minnesota Historical Society took over management of the Little Falls house, a National Historic Landmark, presenting it as the boyhood home of Charles Jr., famous for his transatlantic flight in 1927.[6]

* * *

After a two-year stretch of being the most powerful man in Minnesota, John McGee found law practice less than satisfying. In 1921 when Congress debated a bill to expand the federal judiciary, McGee set his sights on becoming a federal judge. If it passed, Minnesota would gain a judgeship.[7]

Presidents nominate federal judges who must be approved by the Senate. The custom is for the president to consult with the senators from the district, and if they are from the same party, follow their recommendations. Fortunately for McGee, his friend Knute Nelson was still a senator, and he agreed to sponsor McGee's candidacy. As chair of the Senate Judiciary Committee, he was well placed to usher McGee through the process. Nelson knew McGee would be a controversial candidate. He hoped the other senator, Frank Kellogg, would endorse McGee before his candidacy became public. Kellogg would not commit.[8]

McGee told Nelson that the three sitting federal judges in the Minnesota District would support his nomination, as well as some of his former colleagues among state court judges. He also told Nelson that "the most powerful men in this community" had agreed to write letters for him, including A. C. Loring, president of Pillsbury Company, and

John Crosby, president of Washburn-Crosby Company (later General Mills). He also mentioned that the president of the Soo Line Railroad, three bank presidents, the president of the *Minneapolis Tribune*, and the owner of the *Minneapolis Journal* had written strong letters. He had the support of Governor Preus and former governor Burnquist, who recommended McGee "as emphatically as possible." He cited his service on the MCPS and mentioned "his fearless stand always for what he believed to be right and his love of his country, together with a broad mindedness which will lead to the right kind of decision on the bench." It was, however, McGee's role on the MCPS that worried Nelson. Former US senator Moses Clapp hinted at this when he told Nelson that McGee did not have "the temperament" required for a federal judge.[9]

Congress did not pass the judicial bill until 1922. By then, McGee's campaign was common knowledge and "McGeeism" had become a major stumbling block. Nelson received a letter from the Minnesota State Federation of Labor "most emphatically" opposing the nomination of McGee because of his "intolerant" attitude while on the MCPS. His "expression against certain classes of our citizens," the letter concluded, "was not such as should come from a man who is to sit upon the Federal bench." The Minneapolis Trade and Labor Assembly's letter was even blunter. McGee had proven himself to be "bigoted, prejudiced, and entirely unfitted by temperament for the judiciary," citing his incendiary testimony before the congressional committee in Washington when he lamented the lack of "firing squads." His appointment, the letter concluded, would be "a slap at the intelligence of the citizenry."[10]

Edward J. Lee, a Minneapolis attorney, told Nelson that McGee was not as popular as the senator appeared to think, especially in the Scandinavian community and among lawyers, at least in the Twin Cities. Nelson responded that Lee's letter was the first he had received opposing McGee, aside from "two or three heads of labor organizations, who are evidently of Bolshevik leanings." Lee pointed to the Hennepin County Bar Association poll in which McGee got only 48 of the 299 votes cast. McGee told Nelson that "Bolshevik elements" among young attorneys had called for the vote and that only about a quarter of the attorneys participated.[11]

McGee shrugged off the political criticism, but was obsessed by a rumor that Kellogg thought he was too old. McGee was sixty-one, and he set out to prove that he had the vigor to serve productively for many years. Borrowing from eugenic theories popular at the time, McGee wrote a long statement to demonstrate, as he told Nelson, "that I both inherited and transmitted energy and vitality to a remarkable degree." His paternal grandparents, he noted, had lived to 102 and 100 respectively. His mother lived into her late eighties and his father was still alive at eighty-seven. He also put great emphasis on the "rugged health" he bequeathed to his children, especially his eldest son, Hugh, even to the point of mentioning that he "measured twenty-eight inches around the waist, forty inches around the bust, had a six-inch chest expansion, stood five feet ten and a half in height, and weighed one hundred and sixty-two pounds." McGee related how his son was shot through the chest in the Philippine War but that "on the thirty-first day after he was wounded, he was not only back in the saddle, but as in action under fire."[12]

He was peeved that Kellogg, who was four years his senior, would question his age, since it is "generally conceded that I can do as much work as half a dozen ordinary men." He concluded his personal statement with a claim that in retrospect appears as a tragic irony: "I have no doubt that my physical and mental conditions are such that I am good for from twenty to twenty-five years on the Bench."

Kellogg lost the election in November 1922 but was still a senator when McGee's nomination was considered in the March 1923 lame duck session. He decided to support McGee, countering the Progressive Republican senators led by Robert La Follette and William Borah, who bitterly opposed the nomination. Back in Minnesota, state senators endorsed by the NPL and labor unions introduced a resolution opposing McGee, whose attitude was characterized as "notoriously un-American." The resolution cited McGee's testimony before Congress where he argued that "civil courts should be suspended and martial law put into effect to control citizens." Before the Minnesota Senate could vote on the resolution, the US Senate confirmed McGee with forty-six senators in favor, eleven opposed, and thirty-nine registered as not voting, including Knute Nelson himself, who was ill.[13]

Nelson and Kellogg congratulated McGee, but told him in strict confidence that the main objection to his nomination was his alleged "non-judicial temperament," and the feeling that he was "arbitrary, dictatorial, and prejudiced." These charges, they said, came from "many sources in Minnesota" and almost defeated his nomination. Nelson warned McGee "to be as judicious and patient" as possible. Kellogg separately telegraphed McGee warning him not to criticize those who had opposed him in the Senate. Neither senator mentioned McGee's age.[14]

In response, McGee wrote to Nelson that he owed him a debt of gratitude that he could never repay. He also noted that Kellogg's warning was unnecessary because he had the sense not to stir up further antagonism. He recalled that when he had been a judge earlier in his career, he had been very careful to say as little from the bench as possible and to decline invitations to make public speeches. He understood that "a good many people think that I will make lots of copy for the newspapers, . . . but they will be woefully disappointed."[15]

The new federal judge was soon making news, however. He earned a reputation for being hard on bootleggers, processing a remarkable number of cases and imposing harsh sentences. The newspapers covered Judge McGee's "sentencing days," when defendants who had pled guilty or were convicted at trial were sentenced, starting with fourteen sentenced in Winona in May 1923. The next month he sentenced sixty people in St. Paul, twelve of whom received jail time. He singled out defendants who were not citizens, stating in court that he would contact the US attorney to see if these defendants could be deported. In December, he sentenced 114 people in one day in Minneapolis, sixty of whom were given jail sentences and two of whom were sent to Leavenworth Prison for three years, "the severest sentence ever pronounced in federal court in Minnesota," for an alcohol-related charge. On the final day of the term, McGee sentenced 108 men and six women, "at the rate of one per minute" according to the news report. Over that two-month term in Minneapolis, McGee sentenced a record-breaking 450 defendants, almost all for liquor violations, imposing prison terms that collectively added up to 130 years. He dispatched the civil trials on his docket in the same heavy-handed way. In 1924, he dismissed several lawsuits brought against the railroads by several local attorneys. He called the lawyers "ambulance chasers," and referred their names to the board of law examiners for disciplinary action.[16]

Judge McGee had to follow a rigorous schedule to move all these cases through his court. He heard cases for about forty-five hours per week by running his court until 6:00 PM daily and holding court on Saturdays. He spent Sundays writing opinions and orders. He reportedly told friends that he worked "nine days a week" but that "I've always worked like this and work has never hurt me."[17]

On February 15, 1925, he traveled from his south Minneapolis home to the federal courthouse in the Gateway district, his normal Sunday routine. He was expected home for lunch, and when he had not returned by 2:00, his daughter Dorothy drove to the courthouse. She gained admittance with the help of a janitor and found McGee's body in the vault of his office. He was dead from a bullet wound in the head. A pistol he had recently purchased was on the floor.[18]

Because McGee had received some threatening letters, the police briefly considered foul play. However, they quickly confirmed the authenticity of the signed, handwritten note left on his desk. McGee wrote that "the state of mental depression I am in is difficult for anyone to understand—everything looks dark, and the bottom seems to have fallen out." He wondered if it was "worthwhile to lead the strenuous life I have led particularly since 1917 in April," referring to the month he was appointed to the MCPS. He described mental exhaustion going back to March 1924, when he "practically collapsed" at the end of the court term. By January 1925, however, he realized he was much worse, especially when he tried unsuccessfully for a month to write an important legal opinion. "My mind would not work—would not, I might say, focus." He was unable to sleep and was losing weight. His doctor, he reported, told him he was exhausted from overwork and the cure was "rest and then more rest." McGee then stated his dilemma: "I thought how foolish to say rest with my desk drawers full of undecided cases." He felt betrayed by the wealthy men to whose service he had dedicated his life. His work for the MCPS, he wrote, "burned my nerves and weakened me." He wondered if "a more selfish life on the whole is not better." The people who benefited from his work, he thought, "forget the sacrifices made for them" when the emergency is over.[19]

Two doctors told the press that McGee, who was sixty-four years old, was in a state of mental exhaustion and imbalance. Dr. M. J. Lynch saw him two days before his death and was shocked by his condition. McGee was rambling and incoherent. The doctor confirmed he was not suffering from a physical ailment, and then urged him to take a long rest. The judge only mumbled, "It's no use." Dr. W. A. Jones stated that he had also warned the judge that he was suffering from overwork and that he must take a rest of several months. In fact, the doctor said, he had seen the judge the day before his death and told him once again that he must rest. It appeared that after consulting with his doctors, McGee decided to take his life.[20]

After a brief service for family and intimate friends at the McGee home, an overflow crowd attended the funeral mass at St. Stephen's Catholic Church, the family's parish church. Among the honorary pallbearers were Governor Theodore Christenson, and two former governors, Jacob Preus and Joseph Burnquist. The federal bench and the justices of the Minnesota Supreme Court were well represented. All federal and state courts were closed in recognition of the event. McGee was buried at St. Mary's Cemetery in south Minneapolis.

Acquaintances and allies of John McGee were shocked by his death and tried in various ways to explain and justify his act in the newspapers. They perhaps recognized that his suicide made his funeral and burial in the Catholic Church somewhat awkward. Before McGee's note became public, US attorney Lafayette French claimed the threatening letters he had received had "undermined his brain" because he was so fearful for his wife and children. His suicide note, however, made no mention of his family. The newspapers suggested instead that Judge McGee had "lost his mind by hard work." Editorials praised his record as a public servant on the MCPS and on the federal bench, and celebrated his resolution not to "surrender" in the face of his workload. In the words of the *Minneapolis Tribune*, McGee "died a martyr to his own ardent zeal for and devotion to his duties as a public servant."[21]

* * *

During the war, Joseph Burnquist exhausted his political capital supporting John McGee's loyalty regime. Even though he was the incumbent governor and the darling of the business elite, Republican leaders in 1920 persuaded him to step aside for a candidate less associated with McGeeism. Burnquist made a feeble attempt to resurrect his political career when Knute Nelson's death led to a special election in 1923. He came in sixth in the Republican primary with about 5 percent of the vote. He was, however, still in his early forties and could afford to wait for memories to fade. In 1938, the year the Republicans finally won the governorship back from the Farmer Labor Party, he was elected attorney general, a position he held for the next sixteen years, finally retiring at age seventy-five.

In the years between the two chapters of his political career, he practiced law and developed an interesting hobby—writing history. In 1924 he published a massive four-volume work entitled *Minnesota and Its People.* This work was similar in style to many of the county histories being published at this time, with two volumes for chapters on specific topics such as railroads or banking, and two volumes for biographies of notable figures. A reader who picks up this work to learn about the war period from an insider's perspective would be disappointed. Burnquist recounts the MCPS official view of itself and lists the original commissioners, but does not mention that he fired Charles Ames and that John Lind quit because of John McGee. He recounts his reelection in November 1918, but makes no mention of the violent June primary. The Nonpartisan League and Lindbergh are absent from his history. Overall, this work seems to be another attempt to control how the home front would be remembered by omitting critical pieces of the story.[22]

* * *

Alice Ames Winter's reputation as a leader was enhanced by her efficient management of the Women's Committee of the MCPS. Things went well for her during the war, except that her heightened profile might have led to the Winter home being burglarized while Thomas Winter was in France with the Red Cross and Alice Winter was visiting friends. Thieves pried open and looted three built-in jewel safes. Her record of accomplishments was recognized nationally and locally. In 1921, she was elected president of the General Federation of Women's Clubs and President Warren Harding chose her to be one of four women advisers to the disarmament conference held in Washington. When the women's clubs in Minneapolis built a "demonstration house" in 1925 to provide a "daily visualization of efficient home management," they named it the Alice Ames Winter House in her honor. She continued to write, publishing several books, including a lyrical, impressionistic history of women.[23]

In 1928, the Winters sold their Minneapolis home and moved to Pasadena, California. That same year, the Motion Picture Producers and Distributors of America hired Alice Ames Winter to be the national liaison between the movie industry and the women's club movement. Two years later the studios adopted the Motion Picture Code, a system of self-regulation created to protect Hollywood from the growing criticism of movies on moral grounds. Ames focused on encouraging women to support the morally uplifting films she urged the studios to produce. She held this job until 1942, and two years later died in Pasadena.[24]

* * *

Thomas Van Lear, who was elected mayor of Minneapolis in 1916 and narrowly lost the office in 1918, ran one more time for mayor in 1921. He was again defeated by a small margin, this time by the war hero George Leach, the former commander of the 151st Field Artillery. The *Minneapolis Tribune* and the *Minneapolis Journal* did all they could to aid Leach, while Van Lear had the support of the *Minnesota Daily Star*, the Farmer Labor newspaper he helped organize. In 1922, the paper had better luck supporting the candidacy of Henrik Shipstead, who won the US Senate seat, but it continued to have trouble attracting advertising. Van Lear became president of the paper's parent company in 1923, but the following year the paper went bankrupt.[25]

In 1931, Van Lear and his wife traveled to Miami, the first leg of a trip in which he planned to visit places in Florida and Cuba where he was stationed while serving in the army during the Spanish-American War. He died in a hospital in Miami from complications after an operation for appendicitis. He was sixty-two years old. He was buried in Minneapolis with full military honors, and his honorary pallbearers included both Farmer Labor allies, like Governor Floyd B. Olson, and opponents, like former mayors J. E. Meyers and George E. Leach.[26]

Both of Van Lear's sons initially claimed exemption from the draft based on their Socialist beliefs, but in the end, both served in the military during World War I and were honorably discharged. Ralph Van Lear served time in the brig but eventually came to an understanding with his superiors at Fort Dodge. By the end of the war, he was a sergeant major in the Headquarters Battalion of the 163rd Depot Brigade, the unit charged with managing the camp. He ran unsuccessful campaigns for Congress and Minneapolis mayor in the 1930s. His older brother, Howard, who had finished law school before being drafted, was also promoted to sergeant. He managed his father's 1921 mayoral campaign. He went to work for Floyd B. Olson, at that time the Hennepin County attorney, and had a long career as a criminal prosecutor.

* * *

Some of the well-known victims of the loyalty campaign persevered and were rewarded after the war. The MCPS had removed Dr. Louis Fritsche, New Ulm mayor, and Albert Pfaender, the city attorney, from office for their participation in the notorious July 1917 anti-draft meeting. Both men also had to fight off attempts to bar them from practicing their professions. In 1920, Louis Fritsche ran for mayor against the man whom Burnquist had appointed to replace him. Openly identifying with the Working People's Nonpartisan League, he swept to victory with 64 percent of the vote, a result understood locally as a "vindication at the hands of fellow citizens." He appointed Albert Pfaender to his former job as city attorney. Several months later, Pfaender ran for judge in a district that included Brown County, where New Ulm was the county seat, and three other counties. He was not elected, but easily carried Brown County.[27]

* * *

In 1938, the University of Minnesota board of regents passed a resolution rescinding the firing of William Schaper and awarding him emeritus status and $5,000 compensation for his loss of salary during the 1917–18 academic year. The resolution stated that the board "recognizes with regret . . . that periods of national crisis are characterized by widespread loss of social perspective and a strain upon the values that prevail when conditions are more normal."[28]

John McGee wrote Fred Snyder, the board chair and local director of the Minnesota Commission of Public Safety, demanding that Schaper be investigated based on a statement of an anonymous informant. President Marion Burton called Schaper before the board without notice, and he was grilled by regent Pierce Butler, the St. Paul lawyer who had built a career representing James J. Hill's railroad interests. At the end of meeting, Schaper was fired.

This reversal was the result of six years of Farmer Labor rule in Minnesota. Pierce Butler and other conservatives had been replaced by people like labor leader George Lawson and, most remarkably, Albert Pfaender, the New Ulm attorney who was himself a victim of the MCPS. Guy Stanton Ford, the acting president of the university at the time, remembered Pfaender's impassioned comment in support of Schaper. Ford noted the "blood rises from his neck to his face" as he was about to speak.[29]

■ **William Schaper in an image from a campaign poster from his unsuccessful bid to win the Farmer Labor nomination for governor in 1924.** ***MNHS collections***

Fred Snyder was still the board chair and had not changed in the intervening two decades. He refused to support the resolution that he correctly understood to be a profound criticism of the 1917 regents. He included in the minutes his statement that he thought that during the war the board was duty bound to fire a teacher who was not "loyal." He saw no reason to reopen the case unless Schaper would come forward with new evidence of his loyalty. This perspective was echoed years later by Burnquist, then the attorney general, who contended that the board should be praised rather than criticized for firing Schaper. Burnquist, who as governor sat on the board of regents in 1917, wrote that Schaper's dismissal did not violate academic freedom, since no faculty member had the freedom to be disloyal in time of war.[30]

Ford supported the resolution but believed Schaper was partly at fault because of his "prickly" personality. In the end, however, Schaper acted with greater grace than his adversaries. Eight years after Minnesota fired him, the University of Oklahoma hired him, and in a few years, he was again a department chair. When he died in 1955, Schaper left bequests of $10,000 to both the University of Oklahoma and, remarkably, to the University of Minnesota.[31]

* * *

Maria Sanford never slowed down, following a rigorous schedule of travel and lecturing right up until the end. She died in Washington, DC, in April 1920, the day after she had addressed the national convention of the Daughters of the American Revolution. The title of her last talk was "Apostrophe to the Flag," a lyrical paean to patriotism: "Stalwart, strong hearted men have willingly laid down their lives at the command, to guard the outposts of freedom. . . . Thousands upon thousands of our bravest and our best followed thee across the seas for the glorious privilege of defending the weak and helpless or of reinforcing the hard-pressed lives of brave men who would not yield."[32]

Sanford was part of a cohort of Progressives in the academic community who were wary of militarism during the period of neutrality, but adopted a quite different tone after the break with Germany. Cyrus Northrop, former president of the university, and James Wallace, the Macalester College political scientist, who had been president and vice president respectively of the Minnesota Peace Society, and George Vincent, university president in 1917, became advocates of uncompromising war against Germany and critics of the "cowards" who were not wholly committed to the war effort. Sanford avoided the demonization of the enemy, and she criticized the tendency to suspect all Minnesotans of German ancestry of disloyalty. Her patriotic speeches generally echoed President Wilson by presenting the war as a historic battle between democracy (the United States and the Allies) and autocracy (Germany). She lived long enough to witness the Allied victory, but not long enough to observe that the military defeat of Germany did not advance the democratic project either at home or abroad.[33]

* * *

Jens Grondahl, the editor of the *Red Wing Daily Republican*, must have been flummoxed by the rapid rehabilitation of men like Pfaender and Fritsche. In his "Mark of Cain" editorial, he had confidently predicted that pro-Germans like them were "branding their children and their children's children with the Mark of Cain." They would be called to account, he stated, "as sure as there is a God in heaven." When the war was over, however, most people, whatever their views of the conflict, were not called to account, much less their descendants. Even before the armistice, Fred Scherf, the NPL leader in Red Wing, won a seat in the Minnesota legislature, even though Grondahl endorsed his rival. Worse yet, Scherf started a newspaper, *The Organized Farmer*, to express the views of the emerging Farmer Labor movement and compete with Grondahl's *Daily Republican*. Even John Seebach, another Red Wing citizen whom Grondahl worked hard to convict, never served time.[34]

Grondahl also railed against German culture, arguing that everything made in Germany bore the mark of Cain. He was happy to see Wagner and Beethoven discarded, as they sometimes were. After some patrons protested an all-Wagner program, the Minneapolis Symphony opened its new season in October 1918 with no German composers on its schedule. The Germans soon returned. When the Paris Orchestra visited Minneapolis in December, shortly after the armistice, the Minneapolis Symphony Orchestra treated their guests to a concert that opened with a rousing Le Marseillaise and continued with a Beethoven symphony. By March, even Wagner was back in their repertoire. The *Minneapolis Morning Tribune* wondered why we would want to "stultify ourselves and cast doubt upon our good sense" by banning Beethoven, Bach, Goethe, and Schiller. Banning German works, the editors thought, was misguided Americanism.[35]

* * *

Not all efforts to reverse the worst abuses of the war years went so smoothly. John Meints, the Rock County farmer who was "deported" to South Dakota and then tarred and feathered when he returned, sued thirty-two prominent citizens of Luverne, the county seat, who he alleged had formed the mob that attacked him. The suit was tried in federal court at Mankato in November 1919. Meints was represented by Arthur Le Sueur and William Lemke, two NPL attorneys. The defendants were represented by Pierce Butler, who likely took the case, quite unlike his normal work of defending railroads, because of ideological affinity with his clients. Butler constantly reminded the jury that many in Rock County thought Meints was "disloyal," and he also found alibi witnesses for the three men who Meints testified had applied the hot tar to his back. The judge would not allow Le Sueur and Lemke to present evidence about the political situation in Luverne. The jury quickly returned a verdict for the defendants.

When they returned home to Luverne, they were welcomed with a band and celebrated as heroes. The Commercial Club raised money to cover their legal expenses. In 1921, however, the Eighth Circuit Court of Appeals reversed the judgment for the defendants

■ **President Warren G. Harding nominated Pierce Butler for the Supreme Court not long after Butler defended the vigilantes who tarred and feathered John Meints. Progressives in the Senate tried but failed to block his nomination.** ***MNHS collections***

and sent the case back for a new trial. The following spring, Meints dropped the case when the defendants agreed to pay him $6,000 in damages. Later that year, President Herbert Hoover nominated Pierce Butler to become an associate justice of the US Supreme Court. Over the objections of Progressive senators like Robert La Follette, his nomination was confirmed.[36]

* * *

Three years after the armistice, NPL leaders Arthur Townley and Joseph Gilbert were serving time for their alleged sedition during the war. The US Supreme Court affirmed Gilbert's Goodhue County conviction in December 1920. It was one of the landmark free-speech cases of the period, and although the majority affirmed the conviction, Justice Louis Brandeis dissented, paving the way for the eventual strengthening of First Amendment protections of political dissent. Gilbert, his appeals exhausted, reported to Red Wing in February 1921 to begin serving his twelve-month sentence in the Goodhue County jail. Against Gilbert's wishes, his attorney James Manahan prepared an application to the pardon board, and, remarkably, Ambrose Tighe appeared before the board in April to support Gilbert's release. Tighe testified that Gilbert was not a bad man, "and surely not disloyal." Nevertheless, the board refused to issue a pardon. Several Progressive newspapers then mounted a petition drive. In July about three thousand petitions were delivered to the board, but pardon was again denied.[37]

In 1921, the Minnesota Supreme Court affirmed the Jackson County convictions of Townley and Gilbert. As several hundred supporters stood in solidarity, Townley reported to the county jail in Jackson on November 2, 1921, to serve his ninety-day sentence. Gilbert, meanwhile, was still in the Goodhue County jail. When he completed his twelve months there, he reported to Jackson County, shortly after Townley had left, to serve his ninety days.[38]

In 1922, Townley resigned from the leadership of the NPL. He tried in several other ways to organize farmers, but nothing led to success. The league, as Robert Morlan wrote, was his "one great work." After the NPL faltered, Joseph Gilbert was active in the midwestern cooperative movement, and eventually became the editor of the *Midwest Cooperator*, the journal of Midland Cooperatives.[39]

* * *

James Manahan's war years were exciting. As one of the Nonpartisan League's main attorneys, he was indicted, nearly lynched, and generally castigated as a pro-German traitor. Postwar life was calmer but, in his view, disappointing. He continued his lifelong work of building and representing organizations fighting for equity for farmers, but he was increasingly depressed. His daughter thought it might help if he wrote a memoir, and after his death in 1932, she published it. Much of it is lively and engrossing, as when he described his defense of Gilbert in Lakeville and how he managed to escape. When he reached the 1920s, his postwar gloom was evident. He felt that farmers were less inclined to "organize as a class for self-protection," and that the labor movement "lost its zeal for political affiliation with agriculture." Strangely, he never mentioned the Farmer Labor Party. He ended his book with the election of Herbert Hoover, which, he feared, was "a death blow to the Independent American farmer."[40]

* * *

Sarah Colvin, the leader of the Minnesota branch of the National Woman's Party, had worked hard to secure passage of the Nineteenth Amendment. She had been arrested twice at the White House in the months following the armistice. However, she and her compatriots saw this victory as only a beginning. The fundamental issue, Colvin thought, was economic inequality. Accordingly, she cast her very first vote for Eugene Debs in the 1920 presidential election, and later became active in the Farmer Labor Party. She sought reforms that would strengthen the economic status of working women, like improved pay and status for nurses.

While Colvin was in Washington getting arrested, Myrtle Cain, also a Woman's Party activist, was busy leading the telephone workers strike in the Twin Cities, another approach to strengthening women economically. After the strike, she led the local Women Trade Union League and worked for the American Federation of Labor as an organizer. In 1922, she ran for a seat in the legislature as a Farmer Laborite and was one of four women elected to the house of representatives (none were elected to the senate).[41]

She served only one term in the legislature, but it was a productive one. In the face of aggressive and successful Ku Klux Klan organizing in Minnesota, she succeeded in passing an anti-Klan bill that made it a misdemeanor to wear masks or other disguises in public places. She also sponsored a bill to grant "equal rights, privileges, and immunities to both sexes." This bill failed, in part because of the opposition of established women's groups like the Federation of Women's Clubs, who feared it would undermine protective legislation for women. Cain, backed by Sarah Colvin and the Woman's Party, asked for equal opportunity unhampered by legal disabilities and opposed special protections for women that she considered paternalism.[42]

Cain watched the Minnesota Senate pass the Equal Rights Amendment in 1973, toward the end of a long career working for progressive causes. She died in 1980, still living in the same northeast Minneapolis house from which she ran her 1922 campaign for legislature.[43]

* * *

Clarence Wigington led the campaign to create the 16th Battalion, the African American unit of the Home Guard, and commanded one of its companies, earning the nickname "Cap," which stuck with him for the rest of his life. In 1918, Wigington was working in the office of the St. Paul city architect, and he held this position for the next two decades, designing many public buildings, especially schools and park buildings. He also had private design commissions, among them the first clubhouse for the Sterling Club, a fraternal organization for African Americans men in St. Paul. He was also famous in St. Paul for his designs of the massive ice palaces built for the Winter Carnival.

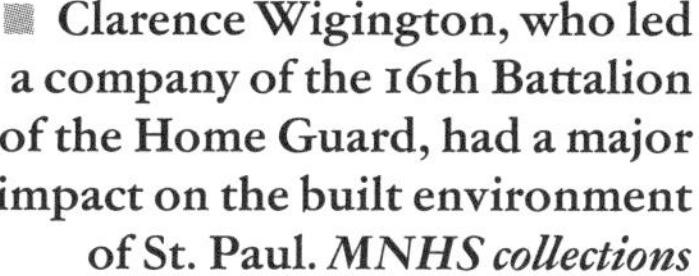

■ Clarence Wigington, who led a company of the 16th Battalion of the Home Guard, had a major impact on the built environment of St. Paul. *MNHS collections*

He continued to work as an architect into the early 1960s, having an enormous impact on the built environment of his city. Many of his buildings are still in use, and three have been added to the National Register of Historic Places.[44]

Jose Sherwood, who commanded the 16th Battalion, had played a major role in the NAACP's campaign against *The Birth of a Nation* in St. Paul before the war. On the eve of World War II, he was still fighting for racial justice. In what must have been a painful déjà vu, the state of Minnesota excluded African Americans from the Home Defense Force, a militia created in anticipation of the federalization of the Minnesota National Guard. Sherwood helped organize the Minnesota Negro Defense Committee, a coalition of organizations, which met with Governor Harold E. Stassen in June 1941 to demand that he desegregate the Home Defense Force. It was a long and lively meeting, but changed nothing. At one point, the governor said that if he admitted African Americans, the officers might quit. Lee Turpin, a young businessman in St. Paul, then sued the state in federal court after he was denied induction into the Home Defense because of race. To settle the suit, Stassen offered to create two African American companies of the Home Defense Force. Turpin, backed by the Negro Defense Committee, refused to accept segregated units, and the judge dismissed the suit. The Minnesota National Guard would not be integrated until 1949, by executive order of Governor Luther Youngdahl.[45]

* * *

Ambrose Tighe might be called the father of the Minnesota Commission of Public Safety. He was in the room when it was conceived, and he wrote the statute that brought it into being. When the commissioners assembled, they hired him as chief counsel. The commissioners were volunteers, but Tighe was paid, and reasonably well, although certainly less than his normal earnings as a very successful St. Paul attorney.[46]

Tighe defended the commission before the Supreme Court, advised the commissioners that they had extensive powers (for example, to remove elected officials for disloyalty), acted as prosecuting attorney (as in the hearing of the New Ulm officials), and spoke for the commission (as when he threatened the board of Martin Luther

College). He used his prestige to win acceptance in the legal community of an institution that pushed the boundaries of constitutional law, as when he delivered a spirited defense of the MCPS in a speech to the state bar convention in 1918.[47]

Privately, however, he had misgivings about his creation. When John Lind quit the commission because of his conflict with McGee, Tighe wrote a poignant letter to Lind, explaining that "a great deal of the joy of life is gone because of your absence." He went on to say that "the ruthlessness of the commission's procedure shows . . . how dangerous it is to vet even good men with arbitrary power." Very likely he appreciated the fact that Lind had been the only check on McGee's authoritarian instincts. It was also surprising that he was willing to appear before the pardon board on behalf of Joseph Gilbert.[48]

After the war, Tighe returned to his thriving private practice. He was local counsel for corporations such as the Eastman Kodak Company and Fairbanks, Morse and Company, an armament manufacturer. He represented several municipalities, including St. Paul. He was elected to various positions in the Minnesota State Bar Association, serving as president in 1920–21. He served on the board of St. Paul College of Law, which he helped found, and taught the course on corporate law.[49]

He was doing very well economically. He owned a large home in the Cathedral Hill neighborhood of St. Paul, where he lived with his wife, four children, and three servants. Shortly after the war, they moved to a bigger home, one of the Summit Avenue mansions designed by architect Cass Gilbert before he moved to New York in 1898.

Below the surface, however, something was terribly wrong. In the fall of 1928, readers of the *St. Paul Pioneer Press* were surprised to learn that he had died at his home. He was sixty-nine and appeared to be in good health. The newspaper did not report that the coroner had concluded that he had died from a self-inflicted gunshot to the head. The family held a private funeral, and would only say that he had been suffering from acute insomnia that had "induced a condition of nervous depression."[50]

Perhaps it was a coincidence, but Ambrose Tighe killed himself on November 11, the tenth anniversary of the armistice ending World War I.

OBSERVATIONS AFTER A CENTURY

Centennials are one way we remember the past, and true to form, there were many attempts to remind Minnesotans about how the state experienced World War I during 2017 and 2018. Local historical societies mounted exhibits and hosted lectures that generally focused on the young men who fought, and sometimes died, in France and the volunteers back home who worked for the Red Cross or helped with Liberty Bond campaigns. The story presented in most of these commemorations was simple and clear: except for a few "slackers," Minnesotans cheerfully rallied together to support a great and noble cause in a spirit of self-sacrifice and patriotism.[1]

Although it was sometimes mentioned that anti-German prejudice went too far, the bitter and often violent conflicts of the period were mostly forgotten. This is unfortunate. Although Minnesota's home front experience was the product of a particular confluence of events and personalities, a study of those events can help us navigate the present, not by presenting simple lessons but by alerting us to dangers and opportunities. While working on this book, I was struck by several aspects of the Minnesota home front that seemed particularly instructive.

First, I was surprised by how deeply polarized Minnesotans were in those years, reflected in the animosity between employers and workers, and most especially in the angry, sometimes violent, conflicts between business owners, both city and small-town, and farmers. Fear and resentment toward immigrants added fuel to these tensions, but the primary driver of conflict was class rather than ethnic divisions. The Minnesota Commission of Public Safety argued that victory over Germany was endangered by the disloyalty of immigrant communities, but its loyalty campaign was focused on weakening groups like the NPL and the trade unions, which threatened the power of the business interests.

A close study of this period should alert us that American politicians have often played the anti-immigrant card when seeking power. The basic move is to characterize immigrants as outsiders with alien languages and inscrutable customs, and link them to an external enemy, in this case, the German Kaiser, but at other times, perhaps Mexican drug lords or Muslim terrorists. Informed by this history, we should be on guard when politicians proclaim that the country faces disaster unless millions of immigrants are deported. The story of Minnesota's home front should also remind us that anti-immigrant campaigns often function to distract attention from conflicts about economic justice unrelated to ethnicity.

Second, I was struck by the fragility of the state's democratic institutions when faced with the stressful conditions of the war years. The creation of the MCPS was a kind of "coup" by Twin Cities businessmen that represented a suspension of representative government for the duration of the war. Under the leadership of John McGee, the commission used its power to create a kind of dictatorship and something approaching martial law. He justified his calls for firing squads and internment camps by arguing that the war in Europe was an existential crisis for Minnesota.

During the war, conservative leaders exhibited a disturbing impatience with those democratic processes that might lead to outcomes not to their liking. When Congress legislated an eight-hour day for interstate railroads, for example, the state's leading business journal editorialized that it might now be necessary to move to an autocratic form of government to regain control of the industrial situation. Forces associated with the MCPS even resorted to the use of military force to suppress the electoral campaign of the opposition.[2]

Democracy depends not only on governmental structures but also on civil society, the institutions between government and the population that ideally model democratic norms and act as a check on state power. Unfortunately, civil society often failed to defend democracy during the war. Minnesota, for example, was fortunate to have a thriving print media in this period, but most newspapers decided it was their patriotic duty to adopt uncritically the political views of the MCPS and, worse yet, sometimes even encourage and justify mob violence. One would expect lawyers to defend the rule of law, but nevertheless an audience at the Minnesota State Bar Convention in 1917 rose to their feet cheering a county attorney's call for summary executions of the disloyal. The University of Minnesota regents did not go that far, but they were willing to abandon any pretense of due process and abruptly fire a professor whom John McGee had accused based on an anonymous report.[3]

Studying the Minnesota home front should leave no one complacent about the democratic values of their fellow citizens. This history suggests that democratic institutions must be defended even in the best of times. It also shows that times of crisis pose the biggest danger, when individuals and groups seeking power are prone to argue that the nation faces a threat so extreme that only an autocratic government can save the day.

Third, I was fascinated by the fierce style of the pro-war forces in the state, observed for example in the frenzied rallies and parades, the threatening rhetoric of speeches, and the official and vigilante violence against opponents, phenomena occasionally summed up as "war hysteria." The causes of this phenomenon are complex, but the history of this period points to nationalism, which George Orwell defined as "the habit of identifying oneself with a single nation or other unit, placing it beyond good or evil, and recognizing no other duty than that of advancing its interests." An aggressive nationalism first appeared in Minnesota during the Spanish-American War, and flamed up again during the Great War, for example, in the loyalty regime of John McGee, who demanded that everyone be "100% American" and proudly proclaimed "my country right or wrong." Another source of the belligerent stance of the pro-war forces was militarism, a belief that military force is the best way to deal with international conflict and, further, as Theodore Roosevelt constantly argued, that the vigorous use of armed force would lead to the moral regeneration of the United States, which, he maintained, had grown soft and effeminate. Some Progressives concurred, at least to the point of believing, along with President Wilson, that militarism opened a path to democratic reform at home and abroad.[4]

Studying this period reinforces Orwell's warning not to confuse nationalism with patriotism, which he defined as a devotion to one's way of life with no wish to force it on others. Nationalism, he noted, tends to be aggressive and imperialistic, while patriotism is defensive and respectful of others. This history should also make us wary of those who trumpet the virtues of militarism. A military capable of effective national defense is necessary, but reviewing the events that unfolded in the United States and Europe after the armistice should make one skeptical of claims that wars lead to moral regeneration or democratic reform.

Fourth, I was intrigued by the fact that the war years led to a remarkable shift in Minnesota politics, when farmers aligned with the Nonpartisan League found common cause with the trade unionists, brought together by a shared adversary, the MCPS. The Twin Cities trade unions took up the NPL program, and the NPL farmers supported trade union demands. This coalition laid the groundwork for a new party that dominated Minnesota politics in the 1930s. Studying this development suggests that significant political change is possible, especially when people look outside their own narrow identities and support the demands and aspirations of others.

Readers will likely find other aspects of the home front story that catch their attention and provoke serious thought about what can be learned from this history. Studying our past can be challenging, especially since it can undermine comfortable myths about our ancestors and the place we call home. But it can be intellectually rewarding, and perhaps provide some help, even some hope, as we face today's conflicts.

ACKNOWLEDGMENTS

I CONDUCTED MUCH OF MY RESEARCH for this book at the Minnesota Historical Society's Gale Family Library at the Minnesota History Center in St. Paul. I spent hundreds of hours there, ably cared for by helpful and congenial staff. My work was supported by two of the library's yearlong Legacy Research Fellowships, the first in 2015, managed by Katie Jean Davey, and the second in 2022, managed by Anne Thayer.

Staff from several other Minnesota archives also provided much-appreciated help, including Walt Bennick and Andy Bloedorn of the Winona County Historical Society, Katelyn Morken of the University of Minnesota Archives and Special Collections, Ted Hathaway and Bailey Diers of Special Collections at the Minneapolis Central branch of the Hennepin County Public Library, and archivists from the Kathryn A. Martin Library at the University of Minnesota Duluth.

At the Minnesota Historical Society Press, Shannon Pennefeather expertly and graciously guided me through the process of turning a manuscript into a book. I was also fortunate to benefit from the input of Ann Regan during the final months of her illustrious forty-six-year career at the press. Lizzie Ehrenhalt edited three MNopedia entries I wrote on Minnesota's World War I home front and in the process helped clarify my ideas. Thanks to all.

Over the years several local historians have helped me understand the issues surveyed in this book. While I was a graduate student at the University of Minnesota, Theofanis Stavrou, Kim Munholland, and

Kinley Brauer impressed upon me the crucial significance of World War I. In recent years, John Sayer, Peter Rachleff, William Millikan, Paul Nelson, and Jeff Goldthorpe provided ideas, sources, and encouragement.

Most of all, my wife and frequent coauthor Marsha Neff assisted me in many ways, offering excellent advice and perspective, occasionally editing text, and sharing many experiences related to this book, from cultural performances on World War I themes to a visit to the Verdun battlefield in France. Over the years, she has also taken on the burden of organizing aspects of our lives not related to this project. I cannot imagine completing this book without her.

I am fortunate to be a member of a group of men who have shared friendship and generally looked out for each other for over forty years. They include Phil Bush, Tom Homme, Roger Luckmann, Bob Lyman, Jerry Peterson, Harry Pontiff, John Sayer, John Sims, John Stuart, and Mark Wernick. I appreciate their support and encouragement.

Finally, I have greatly benefited from the work of historians who have written books and articles touching on Minnesota's World War I home front. I want to especially acknowledge the books written by Carl Chrislock, Daniel Hoisington, Richard Hudelson, Frederick L. Johnson, Michael J. Lansing, Bruce L. Larson, William Millikan, Robert L. Morlan, Carl Ross, and Mary Lethert Wingerd. They are exemplary members of a cohort of historians who have explored Minnesota history. So much of our state's past remains unexamined. I hope many others will join them.

NOTES

See bibliography for full citation details.

ABBREVIATIONS

MCPS	Minnesota Commission of Public Safety
MNHS	Minnesota Historical Society

Notes to Introduction

1. Vasily Grossman, *Stalingrad*, trans. Robert Chandler and Elizabeth Chandler (New York: New York Review of Books, 2019), originally published in the Soviet Union in a censored form as *For a Just Cause* in 1952; Vasily Grossman, *Life and Fate*, trans. Robert Chandler (New York: New York Review of Books, 2006), never published in the Soviet Union and first published in Western Europe in 1980. Grossman died in 1962.

2. Stephane Audoin-Rouzeau and Annette Becker, *14–18: Understanding the Great War* (New York: Hill and Wang, 2002), 210.

3. Kennedy, *Over Here*, 41.

4. Lindbergh's home in Little Falls, Minnesota, for example, is a National Historic Landmark interpreted as the boyhood home of his son, although the future aviator mostly grew up elsewhere. For clarity's sake, I refer to the elder Lindbergh as "Sr.," although father and son had slightly different names. Charles August Lindbergh and his wife Evangeline Lodge Land named their only son Charles Augustus Lindbergh, adding one syllable to the father's name: Berg, *Lindbergh*, 26.

5. Viet Thanh Nguyen, *Nothing Ever Dies: Vietnam and the Memory of War* (Cambridge, MA: Harvard University Press, 2016), 4; *Report of the Minnesota Commission of Public Safety* (St. Paul, 1919), 30, 32.

6. Folwell, *A History of Minnesota*, 3:556; Blegen, *Minnesota: A History of*

the State, 473; see also Hilton, "Minnesota Commission," 1–2. Writing about growing up in Minnesota, the journalist and historian Harrison Salisbury wrote that during the war Minnesota "was transformed into a pre-fascist fief." He characterized the MCPS as a "dictatorship" that had "totalitarian" powers: Harrison E. Salisbury, *A Journey for Our Times: A Memoir* (New York: Harper and Row, 1983), 13. Chrislock *Watchdog of Loyalty*, x.

7. One leading historian of World War I has suggested that it became the "forgotten war" because "Americans never developed a unifying collective memory about its meaning or the political lessens it offered": Keene, "Finding a Place for World War I in American History," 449.

8. Pifer, *The Great War Comes to Wisconsin*; Glad, *The History of Wisconsin, Volume 5*.

Notes to Chapter One: Let Us Be Neutral

1. "Woodrow Wilson: Statement on Neutrality," in Berg, ed., *World War I and America*, 30–32; Josephine Schain, "Minneapolis Enlists in World Peace Army: Big Audience in Auditorium Joins Nation-Wide Neutrality Movement," *Minneapolis Morning Tribune*, September 22, 1914, 1.

2. "Fred Beal Snyder," *Progressive Men of Minnesota* (Minneapolis: Minneapolis Journal, 1897), 141; "F. B. Snyder, U. Regent for 39 Years, Dies," *Winona Republican Herald*, February 14, 1951, 1.

3. *Red Wing Republican*, August 5, 1914, 1.

4. Johnson, *Patriot Hearts*, 5–8, 28–29.

5. Buhl, "The Crisis of the German-American Press in World War I," part 1, p1–12.

6. Hoisington, *A German Town*, 66–68, 119; "Kaiser's Gift is Accepted," *New Ulm Review*, June 18, 1907, 1.

7. Hoisington, *A German Town*, 122–23.

8. Kelley, "Irish-Americans and World War I," 3–29; Chrislock, *Progressive Era in Minnesota*, 99.

9. "Praying for Peace," *The Labor World*, August 29, 1914, 4; "Let Monarchs Fight Say Workers," *Labor Review*, August 28, 1914, 3; *Labor Review*, September 4, 1914, 8; Holbrook and Appel, *Minnesota in the War with Germany*, 1:9–10.

10. Nord, "Minneapolis and the Pragmatic Socialism of Thomas Van Lear," 3.

11. Frederick G. Vogel, *World War I Songs: A History and Dictionary of Popular American Patriotic Tunes* (Jefferson, NC: McFarland and Co., 1995), 15–16, 20–21; Christina Gier, *Singing, Soldiering and Sheet Music in America During the First World War* (Lanham, MD: Lexington Books, 2017), 15; Mark W. Van Wienan, *Partisans and Poets: The Political Work of American Poetry in the Great War* (Cambridge: Cambridge University Press, 1997), 54–59; "A Song Aimed to Check Warfare," *Duluth Herald*, February 16, 1915, 7.

12. In general, I have adopted the interpretation of Progressivism of Lears, *Rebirth of a Nation*, 195–200, 306–21.

13. Chrislock, *Progressive Era in Minnesota*, 9; William Lass, *Minnesota: A History*, 2nd ed. (New York: W. W. Norton, 1998), 207–17.

14. Chrislock, *Progressive Era in Minnesota*, 51–52, 58; Manahan, *Trials of a Lawyer*, 184. The seat was at large because the legislature did not develop a redistricting plan before the election. Manahan had earlier been a William Jennings Bryan–inspired Democrat.

15. Kazin, *War Against War*, 15.

16. See for example Gabriel Kolko, who argued in *The Triumph of Conservatism: A Re-Interpretation of American History, 1900–1916* (New York: The Free Press, 1963, 2) that the Progressive Era was essentially conservative, in the sense that the solutions chosen by national political leaders to the economic problems of the age were almost always those "advocated by the representatives of concerned business and financial interests." Lears, *Rebirth of a Nation*, 200.

17. Lovoll, "*Gaa Paa*: A Scandinavian Voice of Dissent," 87–99; Chrislock, *Progressive Era in Minnesota*, 115.

18. Berg, *Lindbergh*, 10–15; Larson, *Lindbergh of Minnesota*, 4–9. His parents were not typical immigrants. They left Sweden in a hurry because August Lindbergh was in legal trouble, and he and Louisa were both married, but not to each other. The couple took the name of Lindbergh en route, and began calling the baby Charles August Lindbergh.

19. Berg, *Lindbergh*, 16–17; Larson, *Lindbergh of Minnesota*, 12–20. The University of Minnesota did not establish a law school until 1888.

20. Clara K. Fuller, *History of Morrison and Todd Counties, Minnesota: Their People, Industries, and Institutions* (Indianapolis, IN: Bowen and Co., 1915), 181–94, 204; "Remarkable Growth of Little Falls," *Northwest Illustrated Monthly Magazine* 10, no. 11 (November 1892): 24; Harold Fisher, *"The Land Called Morrison": A History of Morrison County*, 2nd ed. (St. Cloud, MN: Volkmuth, 1976), 131–32; Ralph W. Hidy, Frank Ernest Hill, and Allan Nevins, *Timber and Men: The Weyerhaeuser Story* (New York: Macmillan Co., 1963), 50–77.

21. Berg, *Lindbergh*, 17–31; Larson, *Lindbergh of Minnesota*, 28–31.

22. Berg, *Lindbergh*, 32–33; Larson, *Lindbergh of Minnesota*, 38–56. He had been elected Morrison County attorney in 1891, but elections for this office did not involve party designations. He did not seek reelection when the two-year term ended.

23. Berg, *Lindbergh*, 33–34; Larson, *Lindbergh of Minnesota*, 57.

24. Larson, *Lindbergh of Minnesota*, 90–96.

25. Larson, *Lindbergh of Minnesota*, 96–98, 106–32.

26. Larson, *Lindbergh of Minnesota*, 133–49.

27. Larson, *Lindbergh of Minnesota*, 99; Ida M. Tarbell, "The Hunt for a Money Trust," *American Magazine* (May 1913): 11.

28. Larson, *Lindbergh of Minnesota*, 150–69.

29. Stephenson, *John Lind of Minnesota*, 208–63.

30. Larson, *Lindbergh of Minnesota*, 170.

31. Frank M. Surface and Raymond L. Bland, *American Food in the World War and Reconstruction Period: Operations of the Organizations under the Directions of Herbert Hoover, 1914 to 1924* (Redwood City, CA: Stanford University Press, 1931), 3–5; Edgar, *The Medal of Gold*, 305–7.

32. See, for example, "Correspondent Lauds Conduct of Kaiser's Men," an Associated Press story debunking the German atrocity stories which the *Minneapolis Morning Tribune* published on page 4 of the September 17, 1914, edition. "Our German Cables Cut at the Azores," *New York Times*, August 6, 1914, 6.

33. Doenecke, *Nothing Less Than War*, 47–48.

34. Doenecke, *Nothing Less Than War*, 43–44, 54.

35. Kazin, *War Against War*, 26–27; Chrislock, *Progressive Era in Minnesota*, 102; Doenecke, *Nothing Less Than War*, 57.

36. Holbrook and Appel, *Minnesota in the War with Germany*, 1:11; Annual Report (1915), Minnesota Peace Society records, 1913–1922, Minnesota Historical Society, St. Paul; "Woman Asks America to Act in Peace Cause," *Minneapolis Morning Tribune*, November 28, 1914, 7; Kazin, *War Against War*, 39–40. Schwimmer was also the leader of the campaign for women's suffrage in her native Hungary.

37. Kazin, *War Against War*, 18; "Invited to Hague Meeting," *Minneapolis Morning Tribune*, March 28, 1915.

38. Kazin, *War Against War*, 47; Kennedy, *Over Here*, 31.

39. Congressional Record, 63rd Congress, 2nd Session, p15708; Larson, *Lindbergh of Minnesota*, 179–81.

40. Larson, *Lindbergh of Minnesota*, 182.

Notes to Chapter Two: Neutrality under Siege

1. Morris, *Colonel Roosevelt*, 429.

2. Doenecke, *Nothing Less Than War*, 158–66.

3. Doenecke, *Nothing Less Than War*, 176–77, 183–87.

4. Morris, *Colonel Roosevelt*, 397, 420, 469.

5. Holbrook and Appel, *Minnesota in the War with Germany*, 1:30–31.

6. Kennedy, *Over Here*, 31.

7. Chrislock, *Progressive Era in Minnesota*, 94; Chrislock, *Watchdog of Loyalty*, 22–23; Holbrook and Appel, *Minnesota in the War with Germany*, 1:26–27.

8. Albro Martin, *James J. Hill and the Opening of the Northwest* (St. Paul: Minnesota Historical Society Press, 1991), 604–8; James J. Hill, *Preparedness for Peace* (St. Paul, MN: First National Bank of St. Paul, 1916). On Morgan's role in organizing the loan, see David Stevenson, *Cataclysm: The First World War as Political Tragedy* (New York: Basic Books, 2004), 184–85.

9. Doenecke, *Nothing Less Than War*, 194.

10. "Col. Roosevelt Scores the Pacifists," *Duluth Herald*, July 20, 1915, 10; Morris, *Colonel Roosevelt*, 442, 450.

11. Morris, *Colonel Roosevelt*, 433–36.

12. Holbrook and Appel, *Minnesota in the War with Germany*, 1:28; Chrislock, *Watchdog of Loyalty*, 103.

13. Cooper, *Pivotal Decades*, 237–38; Doenecke, *Nothing Less Than War*, 101–3.

14. Stephenson, *John Lind of Minnesota*, 343.

15. Kazin, *War Against War*, 84; "Slaughter for Private Profit Must Be Ended: Three Thousand People Pack Auditorium to Hear Anti-Preparedness Speakers," *Labor Review*, April 14, 1916, 1, 3.

16. Buhl, "The Crisis of the German-American Press in World War I," part 1, p8; Hoisington, *A German Town*, 122–24; Chrislock, *Progressive Era in Minnesota*, 97.

17. Kelley, "Irish-Americans and World War I," 3–29; "Munitions Check Is Lawler Plan for New Platform," *Minneapolis Morning Tribune*, June 14, 1926, 1; "Senator Lewis, With Flow of Wit, Defends All Wilson Policies," *Minneapolis Morning Tribune*, September 19, 1916, 1, 4.

18. Kazin, *War Against War*, 102. After April 1917, Bishop John Ireland strongly supported the war, seeing it as an opportunity for Irish immigrants to prove they were genuine Americans: Marvin R. O'Connell, *Pilgrims to the Northland: The Archdiocese of St. Paul, 1840–1962* (Notre Dame, IN: University of Notre Dame Press, 2009), 385.

19. "Local Clubs Endorse Peace Resolution," *Minneapolis Morning Tribune*, November 14, 1915, 13; Kazin, *War Against War*, 45, 66–67.

20. "Women Members of Peace Party Will Attend the Production, 'War Brides,'" *Minneapolis Morning Tribune*, October 8, 1915, 9; "Maria Sanford Adds to Peace Message 'War Brides' Brings," *Minneapolis Morning Tribune*, October 12, 1915. William Watts Folwell called Sanford "Minnesota's apostle of culture and patriotism," in his *History of Minnesota*, rev. ed., 4:465.

21. "Spend Money to Relieve Unemployment, Not to Slaughter Workers in War Said Last State Federation Convention," *Labor Review*, May 21, 1915, 3; "Who Pays?" *The Labor World*, October 13, 1915, 4.

22. "Don't Let Them Send You to Hell," *Labor Review*, March 16, 1917, 1; "What Labor Thinks of Training Camps," *Labor Review*, August 27, 1915, 1.

23. Chrislock, *Progressive Era in Minnesota*, 93.

24. Chrislock, *Progressive Era in Minnesota*, 91–92, 103–4.

25. Larson, *Lindbergh of Minnesota*, 186–87.

26. Larson, *Lindbergh of Minnesota*, 188–89.

27. "Minnesota's Shame," *Duluth Herald*, March 8, 1916, 8.

28. "Views of Lusitania Sinking Varied Here," *Minneapolis Morning Tribune*, May 8, 1915, 1.

29. Millikan, *A Union Against Unions*, 74; John G. Rice, "The Old-Stock Americans," in *They Chose Minnesota: A Survey of the State's Ethnic Groups*, ed. June Drenning Holmquist (St. Paul: Minnesota Historical Society Press, 1981), 55–72.

30. Chrislock, *Progressive Era in Minnesota*, 113–14; Millikan, *A Union Against Unions*, 13–15.

31. Wingerd, *Claiming the City*, 66, 97–113.

32. Haynes, "Revolt of the 'Timber Beasts,'" 163–74.

33. Millikan, *A Union Against Unions*, 90–95; "Team Owners Quit Conference; Refuse to Recognize Union," *Minneapolis Morning Tribune*, June 11, 1916, 10; "200 Business Men Discuss Teamsters' Strike at Meeting," *Minneapolis Morning Tribune*, June 28, 1916, 9; "Resolution of C & C Demands the Police Safeguard Laborers," *Minneapolis Morning Tribune*, July 1, 1916, 8.

34. Rachleff, "Turning Points in the Labor Movement," 195–222; Robert M. Eleff, "The 1916 Minnesota Miners' Strike Against US Steel," *Minnesota History* 51, no. 2 (Summer 1988): 63.

35. Chrislock, *Progressive Era in Minnesota*, 120–21. Some union locals passed a resolution condemning Burnquist for "taking the part of the rich and carefree against the poor and suffering": Resolution to the Governor of the State of Minnesota passed by Teamsters' Union Local No 338, Fort Worth, Texas, September 17, 1916, J. A. A. Burnquist Papers, alpha box 1 (148.G.17.4F), MNHS.

36. "Clearing the Air for Some Straight Thinking" [editorial], *Commercial West*, September 9, 1916, 7.

37. Haines and Haines, *The Lindberghs*, 225–34.

38. Ross, "White Supremacy on Parade," 170–80.

39. Ross, "White Supremacy on Parade," 170–71, 177–78; "Nightriders to Ride in Broad Daylight," *Minneapolis Morning Tribune*, January 26, 1917, 9; "'White Hopes' to Be Auto Show Feature," *Minneapolis Morning Tribune*, January 28, 1917, 4; "Ku Klux Will Invade St. Paul in 500 Autos to Give Parade Today," *Minneapolis Morning Tribune*, February 2, 1917, 2. Ross links the screening of *The Birth of a Nation* with the auto show event.

40. "Crush Disloyalty, Cries the President," *New York Times*, June 15, 1916, 1, 3. At the time, almost one out of every three Americans was foreign born or had at least one foreign-born parent, and almost all of these were workers or farmers.

41. "Americanization Day Is Nation's Sanest Fourth" and "Taking Out the Hyphen," *Minneapolis Morning Tribune*, July 5, 1915, 1, 8.

42. "Roosevelt Urges Unity in America as Great Issue," *New York Times*, May 20, 1916, 1, 4.

43. Morris, *Colonel Roosevelt*, 446, 459.

44. Biographical details come from *Progressive Men of Minnesota* (Minneapolis: Minneapolis Journal, 1897), 500–501, and John McGee's fifteen-page typed manuscript entitled "A Statement of Facts by John F. McGee," in which he summarized his personal biography during his campaign to be appointed

a federal judge in 1922. It can be found in Knute Nelson Papers, box 69, MNHS.

45. David Riehle, "Labor Found a Friend: W. W. Erwin for the Defense," *Ramsey County History* 42, no. 4 (Winter 2008): 18–26; "Oswald on Trial," *Devils Lake Inter-Ocean*, May 1, 1886, 1; "Manslaughter: This Is the Verdict in the Oswald Case," *Devils Lake Inter-Ocean*, May 8, 1886, 1.

46. "Colonel McGee Is Popular with First," *Minneapolis Morning Tribune*, March 7, 1917, 12; "A Statement of Facts by John F. McGee," Knute Nelson Papers, box 69, MNHS.

47. *Brass v. North Dakota*, 153 U.S. 391 (1894); *Ex parte Young*, 209 U.S. 123 (1908).

48. The conservative movement that emerged from the crucible of World War I was unified around the ideas of preserving the "white" Protestant character of the United States against ethnic and racial pluralism and defending private enterprise against socialism. It would be decades before the conservative movement was reconciled to Catholicism.

49. John McGee to Knute Nelson, September 11, 1916, Knute Nelson Papers, box 23B, MNHS.

50. John McGee to Hon. Moses E. Clapp, February 14, 1916, J. A. O. Preus and Family Papers, box 13, MNHS.

51. "Are We Cowards or Effeminate? Minister Asks," *Minneapolis Morning Tribune*, February 14, 1916, 1; "Ireland Flays Pacifists: 'War Holy at Time,'" *Minneapolis Morning Tribune*, February 13, 1916, 10.

52. McGee to George R. Smith, March 1, 1916. McGee sent a copy to Nelson, noting that he had no doubt Nelson "occupied the same position": McGee to Nelson, March 1, 1916, Knute Nelson Papers, box 23A, MNHS. "Scuttlers" refers to sailors who sink their own ships. McGee referred to the Gore-McLemore resolutions as "the scuttle bill."

53. Chrislock, *Progressive Era in Minnesota*, 104.

54. Theodore Roosevelt, "Speech at Cooper Union," in Berg, ed., *World War I and America*, 261–70. In this speech a few days before the election, Roosevelt said that if the country reelected Wilson, it would have deliberately shown itself to be "a sordid, soft, and spineless nation."

55. Chrislock, *Progressive Era in Minnesota*, 125.

56. "Governor Hammond Dies Suddenly in Louisiana," *Duluth Herald*, December 30, 1915, 1.

57. Chrislock, *Progressive Era in Minnesota*, 120; Charles A. Lindbergh Sr. to Hon. J. A. Burnquist, February 21, 1917, J. A. A. Burnquist Papers, box 5, MNHS.

58. Chrislock, *Progressive Era in Minnesota*, 126–27; Larson, *Lindbergh of Minnesota*, 190–93.

59. Larson, *Lindbergh of Minnesota*, 192–97. Larson reprints La Follette's letter to Manahan lamenting Lindbergh's decision. Berg, *Lindbergh*, 46. In November of that year, Lindbergh lost his eldest daughter, Lillian, to

tuberculosis. His relationship with his younger daughter, Eva, became even more important, and they exchanged hundreds of letters: Larson, *Lindbergh of Minnesota*, 132, 172–73, 210.

60. Chrislock, *Progressive Era in Minnesota*, 125–29.

61. McGee to Nelson, November 15, 1916, Knute Nelson Papers, box 24, MNHS.

Notes to Chapter Three: The War Comes Home

1. Doenecke, *Nothing Less Than War*, 223–27.

2. Doenecke, *Nothing Less Than War*, 230–46.

3. Nord, "Minneapolis and the Pragmatic Socialism of Thomas Van Lear," 4–7; "Citizens' Non-Partisan Committee Urges Votes Against Socialism"; "Mr. Gould Explains His Reasons for Withdrawing from Contest"; "Mr. Gould Tells of Events That Led to Withdrawal"; and "Mr. Gould's Stand Praised"—all in *Minneapolis Morning Tribune*, November 3, 1912, 1, 2.

4. Nord, "Minneapolis and the Pragmatic Socialism of Thomas Van Lear," 9; Nathanson, "Thomas Van Lear: City Hall's Working-Class Champion," 215–17.

5. Haynes, "Revolt of the 'Timber Beasts,'" 163–74; Rachleff, "Turning Points in the Labor Movement," 195–222. On the earlier iron miners' strike, see Kaunonen, *Flames of Discontent*.

6. Lansing, *Insurgent Democracy*; Morlan, *Political Prairie Fire*.

7. Lansing, *Insurgent Democracy*, 35–41.

8. Lansing, *Insurgent Democracy*, 43–44, 56–57.

9. Kazin, *War Against War*, 148–49.

10. Larson, *Lindbergh of Minnesota*, 201.

11. "Van Lear Is Indefinite on Backing President" and "On Standing by the President," *Minneapolis Morning Tribune*, February 6, 1917, 9–10.

12. Everts, *Stockwell of Minneapolis*, 199–200; "Van Lear Gives Views of Peace at Mass Meeting," *Minneapolis Morning Tribune*, February 11, 1917, 1, 11.

13. Holbrook and Appel, *Minnesota in the War with Germany*, 1:43–46.

14. "Minneapolis to Assert Loyalty to U.S. and President Tomorrow," *Minneapolis Morning Tribune*, February 10, 1917, 1; "Telegram to Notify President that Minneapolis is Loyal," *Minneapolis Morning Tribune*, February 12, 1917, 1.

15. "Minneapolis Flashes Word of Loyalty to Wilson from Three Monster Mass Meetings," *Minneapolis Morning Tribune*, February 12, 1917, 1.

16. Kennedy, *Over Here*, 39–42, 50–51; Chrislock, *Progressive Era in Minnesota*, 135–36. On the support for the war among intellectuals, see Lasch, *The New Radicalism in America*, and especially the chapter "*The New Republic* and the War," 181–224.

17. "Minneapolis Flashes Word of Loyalty to Wilson from Three Monster Mass Meetings," *Minneapolis Morning Tribune*, February 12, 1917, 1.

18. Holbrook and Appel, *Minnesota in the War with Germany*, 1:42;

Chrislock, *Watchdog of Loyalty*, 42. After the former president's death, Farnham toured the country delivering a hagiographic lecture on his hero. A published version of his lecture, *Theodore Roosevelt, 1858–1919: A Memorial*, is in the collection of the Minnesota Historical Society.

19. "Ambrose Tighe, B.A. 1879," Obituary Record of Graduates, *Bulletin of Yale University*, November 1, 1929, 77–78; Henry A. Castle, *History of St. Paul and Vicinity* (Chicago: Lewis Publishing Co., 1912), 483.

20. "Record Naval Bill Passed by House," *New York Times*, February 14, 1917, 8. As his time in Congress was expiring, Lindbergh took one final shot at the Money Trust. In February he presented on the floor of the House articles of impeachment against five members of the Federal Reserve Board for collaborating with J. P. Morgan and Company and other major bankers to subvert the constitution. The House took no action: Larson, *Lindbergh of Minnesota*, 208–9.

21. Larson, *Lindbergh of Minnesota*, 203.

22. Haines and Haines, *The Lindberghs*, 256–57.

23. Chrislock, *Watchdog of Loyalty*, 44–45; "Flame of Patriotism Sweeps Senate," *Minneapolis Morning Tribune*, February 9, 1917, 2.

24. "President Scored, Germany Defended in Neutrality Meet," *Minneapolis Journal*, March 30, 1917, 1.

25. "Big Patriotic Mass Meeting," *St. Paul Daily News*, April 1, 1917, 1, 2; "Prison or Death Defied by Peace Meeting Speaker," *Minneapolis Journal*, April 1, 1917, 1, 2; Chrislock, *Watchdog of Loyalty*, 47, 130–31. The speech by Willis was printed and a copy is held by the Minnesota Historical Society: John W. Willis, *Peace or War? A Speech Delivered by John W. Willis, A. M. Ph.D. at a Public Meeting Held in the City of St. Paul, Minnesota, March 31, 1917*. Other speakers at the rally included Sylvanus Stockwell and Jack Carney, an Irish Socialist who edited *Truth*, the party's Duluth newspaper. On Anna Maley, see Nathanson, "Thomas Van Lear: City Hall's Working Class Champion," 228.

26. Hoisington, *A German Town*, 129; "Patriotism Rings at Peace Meeting," *New Ulm Review*, April 4, 1917, 1, 2; "Peace Delegates Tell of Journey," *New Ulm Review*, April 11, 1917, 1, 2.

27. Chrislock, *Watchdog of Loyalty*, 47–48; "Defense Speeches Inflame Citizens with Patriotism at Commerce Club Luncheon," *Minneapolis Morning Tribune*, August 7, 1917, 1.

28. "Poles Here Pledge Loyalty, Fortunes, Lives to Nation," *Minneapolis Journal*, March 30, 1917, 1, 2. On the Polish American attitude toward the war, see Frank Renkiewicz, "The Poles," in *They Chose Minnesota: A Survey of the State's Ethnic Groups*, ed. June Drenning Holmquist (St. Paul: Minnesota Historical Society Press, 1981), 373.

29. Kazin, *War Against War*, 176; Doenecke, *Nothing Less Than War*, 284.

30. "'U' Professors Urge Congress to Declare War," *Minneapolis Morning Tribune*, April 1, 1917, 1; "Resigns Leadership in Peace Society," *Minneapolis Morning Tribune*, March 6, 1917, 3; Skidmore, "On Courage and Cowards," 14–15.

31. Skidmore, "On Courage and Cowards," 14–20; "Macalester Faculty Members Wire Wilson, Urge Aggressive Warfare Against the Teutons," *Minneapolis Morning Tribune*, March 22, 1917, 1.

32. "Woodrow Wilson: Address to Congress on War with Germany," in Berg, ed., *World War I and America*, 313–22.

33. Chrislock, *Progressive Era*, 125, 135; Doenecke, *Nothing Less Than War*, 295.

34. McGee to Nelson, April 5, 1917, Knute Nelson Papers, box 25, MNHS. Lundeen, however, was elected to the US Senate as a Farmer Labor Party candidate in 1936: Chrislock, *Progressive Era in Minnesota*, 196.

35. Chrislock, *Watchdog of Loyalty*, 61; Holbrook and Appel, *Minnesota in the War with Germany*, 1:75.

36. Ambrose Tighe to Charles W. Farnham, March 29, 1917, with draft of commission bill, and letter from Charles W. Farnham to Ambrose Tighe, March 29, 1917—both in the files of the Patriotic League of Minnesota, 103.K.8.12F, MNHS; Chrislock, *Watchdog of Loyalty*, 52; Millikan, *A Union Against Unions*, 103.

37. Julius A. Schmahl, Secretary of State, *Legislative Manual of the State of Minnesota Compiled for the Minnesota Legislature in 1919*, 407.

38. George Ackerson, "State Preparing to Do Bit When U.S. Enters War," *Minneapolis Morning Tribune*, April 4, 1917, 1; "What the States Can Do" [editorial], *Minneapolis Journal*, April 4, 1917, 16; "Aliens May Not Have to Register," *St. Paul Daily News*, April 4, 1917, 1. On Charles Ames, see Wingerd, *Claiming the City*, 148. Wingerd suggests that Ames, whose firm had a national focus, was close to the MCCA even though he was based in St. Paul. Cushman Davis, Frank Kellogg, and Cordenio Severance founded their firm in 1887, and among their many corporate clients were the Minnesota subsidiaries of U.S. Steel. Davis had been governor of Minnesota, and in 1887 was elected to the US Senate. When he died, Kellogg and Severance made Robert Olds a partner, retaining the firm's original name. Olds defended meat-packers like Swift and Armour against lawsuits, like the case of a large cockroach found in a tin of meat. He was known for resolving these cases without negative publicity. The partners defended corporate clients against Progressive regulation, but were also hired by President Theodore Roosevelt to prosecute antitrust cases against Standard Oil and other corporate giants. Kellogg's success as a "trust-buster" aided his campaign for US Senate in 1916. Later he would be secretary of state. Davis, Kellogg, and Severance eventually became Briggs and Morgan: Dave Kenney, *Briggs and Morgan, P.A.: The First 125 Years* (Minneapolis and St. Paul: Briggs and Morgan, 2008), 16–20, 29–30.

39. "Bitter Words Used in House Debate on Registering Aliens," *Minneapolis Journal*, April 5, 1917, 1, 2; George Akerson, "War Measures Due for Final Action in Legislature Monday," *Minneapolis Morning Tribune*, April 6, 1917, 1; Chrislock, *Watchdog of Loyalty*, 53; Johnson, *Patriot Hearts*, 5, 13.

40. "Governor Orders War Police Here, Urges Safety Bill," *Minneapolis Journal*, April 7, 1917, 1, 2; Chrislock, *Watchdog of Loyalty*, 56–57.

41. Chrislock, *Watchdog of Loyalty*, 58.

42. Chrislock, *Watchdog of Loyalty*, 51–52, 59–60.

43. McGee to Nelson, April 11, 1917, Knute Nelson Papers, box 26, MNHS. The amendment McGee proposed became Section 10 of the act: *Session Laws of Minnesota for 1917*, 377.

Notes to Chapter Four: Forging the Weapons

1. Ferguson, *The Pity of War*, 329.

2. Chambers, *To Raise an Army*, 186.

3. Chambers, *To Raise an Army*, 167.

4. Holbrook and Appel, *Minnesota in the War with Germany*, 1:125–27. Representative Van Dyke's comments are in the *Congressional Record* for the 65th Congress, Session 1, Vol. 55, House of Representatives, April 26, 1916, 1241–42.

5. Holbrook and Appel, *Minnesota in the War with Germany*, 1:127–30.

6. Chambers, *To Raise an Army*, 188–89. The Selective Service Act required draft boards to exempt federal and state legislative, executive, and judicial officers and clergy, seminarians, and divinity students. The act gave the administration the authority to also exempt county and local officials, which was later extended to include firefighters and police. Aliens who had not declared their intention to become citizens were exempt because they could theoretically be drafted by their home countries. At first, boards were unwilling to exempt men who claimed, or whose employers claimed, they were indispensable to the economy. This stance would change when labor shortages in agriculture and industry became a problem.

7. Capozzola, *Uncle Sam Wants You*, 58.

8. Kennedy, *Over Here*, 99–101; Cooper, *Pivotal Decades*, 292–94. In addition to the fact that the well-off were well positioned to oppose a tax on their wealth, McAdoo wanted to divert as much money as possible away from current consumption to dampen the growth of the price inflation likely to occur in a wartime economy when wages could outpace the availability of consumer goods.

9. Holbrook and Appel, *Minnesota in the War with Germany*, 2:190–201.

10. Kennedy, *Over Here*, 117–23; Edgar, *The Medal of Gold*, 289–301.

11. Chrislock, *Watchdog of Loyalty*, 56; Hilton, "Minnesota Commission," 1–44.

12. *Session Laws of Minnesota for 1917*, Chapter 261 (S.F. No 1006). O. A. Hilton, who studied and wrote about both world wars, considered the MCPS's dictatorial powers "the most sweeping powers probably every accorded any state agency to that time" ("Minnesota Commission," 1). Paul L. Murphy, scholar of American constitutional history, called the MCPS "the most powerful state council in the nation" in *World War I and the Origin of Civil Liberties in the United States* (113). In an exhaustive history of the World War I home front,

William J. Breen surveyed state councils nationally and found that the Minnesota legislature had given the MCPS "draconian" powers that made it among the most powerful in the nation: see *Uncle Sam at Home*, 72.

13. Chrislock, *Watchdog of Loyalty*, 55, 325.

14. Chrislock, *Watchdog of Loyalty*, 68–83; Millikan, *A Union Against Unions*, 102–3. McGee had told Knute Nelson that he had the support of influential men in "banking, grain, and milling circles." Ambrose Tighe tried unsuccessfully to persuade the governor to appoint his colleague Charles Farnham: Ambrose Tighe to Charles Farnham, March 29, 1917, in the files of the St. Paul Patriotic League, 103.K.8.12F, MNHS.

15. "Public Safety Commission," *Minneapolis Morning Tribune*, April 18, 1917, 8.

16. Chrislock, *Watchdog of Loyalty*, 94–95.

17. "Minneapolis Citizens, 8000 Strong, Renewing Days of '75," *Minneapolis Morning Tribune*, April 20, 1917, 1, 2.

18. Jens Grondahl, "America, My Country," *Red Wing Daily Republican*, April 6, 1917, 1; George F. Authier, "Minnesota Poet Honored by Having Poem Read into Records by Congressman," *Minneapolis Morning Tribune*, April 8, 1917, 8; Johnson, *Patriot Hearts*, 5–7. The sheet music contained a testimonial from the leaders of the National Editorial Association, noting that when they heard the song played at their national convention, they felt a new national anthem had been born, because it expressed the "true spirit of America." The sheet music is available online at the Library of Congress website: https://lccn.loc.gov/2007499064.

19. "Vincent Calls Americans to Country's Aid" and "Red Wing Citizens Stand Solidly by the President," *Red Wing Daily Republican*, April 20, 1917, 1, 7.

20. Minutes, April 23, 2017, Minnesota Commission of Public Safety, MNHS.

21. *Mobilizing Minnesota*, 13; Millikan, *A Union Against Unions*, 104; Wingerd, *Claiming the City*, 166; Johnson, *Patriot Hearts*, 16, 39, 74–75. The commission published *Mobilizing Minnesota* in September 1917 to publicize its early activities. This booklet also provided a statewide directory of commission personnel.

22. Chrislock, *Watchdog of Loyalty*, 98–99, 104–6; *Mobilizing Minnesota*, 6–9.

23. Chrislock, *Watchdog of Loyalty*, 159–60; *Mobilizing Minnesota*, 15; Zieger, *America's Great War*, 78–80.

24. The text of the speeches given by McGee and Ames are in *Mobilizing Minnesota*, 55–57.

25. David Kennedy noted the parallels between the American experience and George Orwell's *1984*, in particular "the overbearing concern for 'correct' opinion, for expression, for language itself, and the creation of an enormous propaganda apparatus to nurture the desired state of mind and excoriate all dissenters": Kennedy, *Over Here*, 62.

26. *Mobilizing Minnesota*, 57. McGee made this comment in a letter to

congressman George R. Smith on March 1, 1916. McGee sent a copy of this letter to Senator Knute Nelson, noting that he had no doubt Nelson "occupied the same position": McGee to Nelson, March 1, 1916, Knute Nelson Papers, box 23A, MNHS.

27. 40 Stat. 217 (Public Law 65-24); Scheiber, *The Wilson Administration and Civil Liberties*, 6–12; Murphy, *World War I and the Origin of Civil Liberties in the United States*, 76–80. Although Section 3 had nothing to do with spying or foreign agents, prosecutions under that section are commonly referred to as espionage cases because of the name of the act.

The Sedition Act of 1918 amended Section 3 to make explicit what had been implicit in the earlier act. It imposed the same penalties for, among other things, "uttering, printing, writing, or publishing any disloyal, profane, scurrilous, or abusive language intended to cause contempt, scorn, contumely or disrepute as regards the form of government of the United States, its Constitution, its flag, or the uniform of the Army and Navy": 40 Stat. 553 (Public Law 65-150).

28. Woodrow Wilson, "Flag Day Address in Washington, D.C. June 1917," in Berg, ed., *World War I and America*, 366–72.

29. William H. Riker, *Soldiers of the States: The Role of the National Guard in American Democracy* (Washington, DC: Public Affairs Press, 1957).

30. Order No. 3, *Report of the Minnesota Commission of Public Safety* (1919), 74–75. See also minutes, May 29, 1917, Minnesota Commission of Public Safety, MNHS, and Chrislock, *Watchdog of Loyalty*, 99–100. To keep the Home Guard from being merely a security service for property owners, Lind won approval of a resolution that units should not be called on to perform "any duty that can be as well performed by civilian officers or private watchmen": *Report of the Minnesota Commission of Public Safety* (1919), 165.

At the time, the adjutant general was Fred B. Wood, who was under investigation for not adequately accounting for federal funds supplied to equip the MNG. On May 7, the commission appointed Captain Walter F. Rhinow, an instructor in the military department at the university, as the "military secretary of the governor," and by the end of the summer the governor appointed Rhinow the adjutant general. In this role, Rhinow oversaw the MNG, the Home Guard, and the local operation of the Selective Service System: Holbrook and Appel, *Minnesota in the War with Germany*, 1:77–78.

31. Minutes, May 7, 1917, Minnesota Commission of Public Safety, MNHS; Johnson, *Patriot Hearts*, 5, 13.

32. "Business Men Rally to Flag by Enlisting in Civilians' Auxiliary," *Minneapolis Morning Tribune*, April 11, 1917, 9; "New Steps for Preparedness," *Duluth Herald*, March 31, 1917, 29; "Citizens in New Company," *Duluth Herald*, April 6, 1917, 4; "Forced to Divide Training Corp," *Duluth Herald*, April 24, 1917, 9: Watne, "Intolerance and Conformity," 89–90; Holbrook, *St. Paul and Ramsey County in the War of 1917–1918*, 73–75. Holbrook, the official historian of Ramsey County's war effort, wrote that a "special appeal was made to business men, on the ground that with first-hand knowledge of the rudiments, at least, of

military practice, business men as such could the more effectively co-operate with the government in meeting the requirements of fighting forces."

33. Holbrook and Appel, *Minnesota in the War with Germany*, 2:29–30; Rhinow, *Report of the Adjutant General*, 253–61. In early 1918, the Minneapolis Civilian Auxiliary was absorbed into the Home Guard as the 13th Battalion, and the St. Paul Civilian Auxiliary became the Home Guard's 15th Battalion.

34. Order No. 4, *Report of the Minnesota Commission of Public Safety* (1919), 75–76; see also Chrislock, *Watchdog of Loyalty*, 100.

35. Chrislock, *Watchdog of Loyalty*, 117–23.

36. Chrislock, *Watchdog of Loyalty*, 126.

37. Chrislock, *Watchdog of Loyalty*, 227–29.

38. Chrislock, *Watchdog of Loyalty*, 107–9. The Bobbs-Merrill Company published Winter's novels *The Prize to the Hardy* in 1905 and *Jewel Weed* in 1906.

39. Chrislock, *Watchdog of Loyalty*, 231–48.

40. Kennedy, *Over Here*, 117–20, 123. Alice Ames Winter issued a detailed bulletin to her membership outlining the program of the Women's Committee, reprinted in *Mobilizing Minnesota*, 60–64. Chrislock, *Watchdog of Loyalty*, 233.

41. *Mobilizing Minnesota*, 62.

42. According to Holbrook and Appel, *Minnesota in the War with Germany* (1:374), 104,416 were in the army, 11,236 in the navy, and 2,845 in the marines.

43. Holbrook and Appel, *Minnesota in the War with Germany*, 1:73–95.

44. Holbrook and Appel, *Minnesota in the War with Germany*, 1:96–122, 370–71.

45. Holbrook and Appel, *Minnesota in the War with Germany*, 1:133, 141.

46. Chrislock, *Watchdog of Loyalty*, 87–88, 116; "Mayor's Draft Exemption List Scratched Hard," *Minneapolis Morning Tribune*, May 31, 1917, 1.

47. *Mobilizing Minnesota*, 28; Chrislock, *Watchdog of Loyalty*, 121; Holbrook and Appel, *Minnesota in the War with Germany*, 1:135, 137, 143; Nathanson, "Thomas Van Lear: City Hall's Working Class Champion," 227; Order No. 6, *Report of the Minnesota Commission of Public Safety* (1919), 76.

48. Chrislock, *Watchdog of Loyalty*, 121–22; "Grand Jury Indicts 113 Alleged Slackers in Duluth," *Duluth Herald*, July 13, 1917, 25; "Slackers to Pay Penalty for Defying Draft Law," *Duluth Herald*, July 22, 1917, 9; "Thirty Men Are Released," *Duluth Herald*, July 27, 1917, 18; "Trials About Completed," *Duluth Herald*, August 1, 1917, 17.

49. Chambers, *To Raise an Army*, 219–20; Douglas, "The Germans Would Court-Martial Me, Too," 287–301. The Supreme Court decision bears the name of one of the St. Paul defendants: *Arver et al. v. United States*, 245 U.S. 366 (1918).

50. Mjagkij, *Loyalty in Time of Trial*. The National Guard of Tennessee, Massachusetts, Maryland, Ohio, Illinois, Connecticut, New York, and the District of Columbia had segregated units.

51. Schaffer, *America in the Great War*, 77.

52. "Lawyer W. T. Francis Appointed Representative of the Public Safety Commission," *The Appeal*, July 21, 1917; "Governor Appoints Francis," *Twin City Star*, July 21, 1917, 1; "Fund to Aid Americanism," *The Appeal*, April 14, 1917, 2; untitled editorial in *Twin Cities Star*, April 21, 1917, 4; see also Nelson, "William T. Francis, at Home and Abroad," 3–13.

53. Mjagkij, *Loyalty in Time of Trial*, 78.

54. "An Insult to Patriots" and "With 'Marked Cards,'" *The Appeal*, June 9, 1917, 2; "Negroes Specially Identified by Government Registration," *Twin Cities Star*, June 9, 1917, 4.

55. "Samuel L. Ranson was Banqueted by his Friends at Union Hall Wednesday Night," *The Appeal*, July 21, 1917, 3.

56. Williams, *The Wounded World*, 46–49, 77–78.

57. Chambers, *To Raise an Army*, 231.

58. William Convery, "Little Wolf, William (1899–1953), MNopedia, accessed March 31, 2024.

59. Quoted in Britten, *American Indians in World War I*, 57.

60. Nelson Baker, Secretary of War and Chairman of the Council of National Defense, to Hon. J. J. A. Burnquist, Chairman, Public Safety Commission, May 26, 1917, MCPS main files, John McGee file, MNHS. On the letter someone has handwritten, "original sent to Judge McGee June 7, 1917." Meyer, *We Are What We Drink*, 172. German Americans generally, not to mention the many German Americans who owned breweries, opposed liquor regulation, and especially prohibition: Chrislock, *Progressive Era in Minnesota*, 34.

61. Chrislock, *Progressive Era in Minnesota*, 20, 31, 87; Meyer, *We Are What We Drink*, 166–67.

62. Chrislock, *Watchdog of Loyalty*, 97–98; Meyer, *We Are What We Drink*, 173; Orders No. 1, 8, *Report of the Minnesota Commission of Public Safety* (1919), 72–73, 78–79. McGee claimed to have never used intoxicating liquor, in "a Statement of Facts by John F. McGee," which he wrote on May 16, 1922, as part of his campaign to marshal support for his quest to become a federal judge. It can be found in Knute Nelson Papers, box 69, MNHS. As lieutenant governor, Burnquist had played a major role in maneuvering the county option law through the Minnesota senate, where it faced a closer battle than in the house: Chrislock, *Progressive Era in Minnesota*, 120.

63. "Unjust to Minneapolis" [editorial], *Minneapolis Labor Review*, May 4, 1917, 2.

64. Orders No. 2, 6, *Report of the Minnesota Commission of Public Safety* (1919), 73–74, 77.

65. Chrislock, *Watchdog of Loyalty*, 110; Meyer, *We Are What We Drink*, 173; Order No. 7, *Report of the Minnesota Commission of Public Safety* (1919), 77–78.

66. "Autocrats of Minnesota Rule with Iron Hand," *Minneapolis Labor Review*, June 15, 1917, 1, 2; "Are Members of the Minnesota Safety Board Kings?," *Minneapolis Labor Review*, June 22, 1917, 1.

67. Chrislock, *Watchdog of Loyalty*, 111; Meyer, *We Are What We Drink*, 173.

68. *Cook v. Burnquist et al.*, 242 Federal Reporter 321 (D. Minnesota, July 16, 1917). The full text of the decision is reprinted in *Report of the Minnesota Commission of Public Safety* (1919), 57–62.

Notes to Chapter Five: Opening Salvos

1. Holbrook and Appel, *Minnesota in the War with Germany*, 2:32–34; Rhinow, *Report of the Adjutant General*. In June 1918, Washington agreed to the reorganization of the Minnesota National Guard into three new units, the 4th, 5th, and 6th Infantry Regiments. The 4th Infantry was expanded by adding eight companies from the two Minneapolis Home Guard battalions, the 2nd and the 13th. The latter was the Minneapolis Civilian Auxiliary, which was briefly the 13th Battalion of the Home Guard: "New Infantry Units Reviewed First Time," *Minneapolis Morning Tribune*, August 14, 1917, 4; "Col. Harrison Reviews Fourth and Home Guard," *Minneapolis Morning Tribune*, August 28, 1917, 9.

2. Minutes, July 24, 1917, Minnesota Commission of Public Safety, MNHS; "Aides to Home Guard to be Organized," *Minneapolis Morning Tribune*, July 26, 1917, 5.

3. Chrislock, *Watchdog of Loyalty*, 157–58; *Mobilizing Minnesota*, 12.

4. Buhl, "The Crisis of the German-American Press in World War I," part 2, p4–5.

5. Knight, *Jane Addams*, 218; Jane Addams, *Peace and Bread in Time of War* (New York: Macmillan, 1922), 140.

6. Kennedy, *Over Here*, 50–51; Lasch, *The New Radicalism in America*, 181–205; "Maria Sanford Wins Plaudits," *Glencoe Enterprise*, August 2, 1917, 1, 4.

7. Kennedy, *Over Here*, 51–53; Lasch, *The New Radicalism in America*, 205–13; Randolph Bourne, "War and the Intellectuals," in Berg, ed., *World War I and America*, 373–84.

8. Kennedy, *Over Here*, 27; Kazin, *War Against War*, 212–13.

9. Kennedy, *Over Here*, 27–29.

10. "For the Freedom of the World" [editorial], *The Labor World*, April 7, 1917, 4; "Labor Hears the Call" [editorial], *The Labor World*, June 9, 1917, 4.

11. Chrislock, *Watchdog of Loyalty*, 184–86; Nord, "Hothouse Socialism," 144–45; "Resolutions Acted on by the Convention in Faribault," *The Labor World*, July 26, 1917, 2.

12. Egge, *Woman Suffrage and Citizenship in the Midwest*, 172–73.

13. Zahniser, "The Fifteenth Star," 154–61; Colvin, *A Rebel in Thought*.

14. Zahniser, "The Fifteenth Star," 158–59. Fuller favorably reviewed Lindbergh's *Why Is Your County at War* in "Lindbergh's Book," *Little Falls Transcript*, August 23, 1917.

15. "Minnesota Women Repudiate Work of Washington Group," *Daily Post and Bulletin*, July 8, 1917, 5. In addition to this Rochester paper, Ueland's statement appeared in several other newspapers.

16. Haines and Haines, *The Lindberghs*, 158–59.

17. Larson, *Lindbergh of Minnesota*, 205; Chrislock, *Watchdog of Loyalty*, 296.

18. Charles A. Lindbergh, *Why Is Your Country at War and What Happens to You After the War and Related Subjects* (Washington, DC, 1917), 16, 42; Larson, *Lindbergh of Minnesota*, 211–13, 233–34. Walter Quigley later prepared a reprint of the original book under the title *Your Country at War and What Happens to You After a War* (Philadelphia: Dorrance and Co., Inc., 1934). Citations are to the reprint edition. In the introduction, Quigley claimed the federal government had ordered the destruction of the original plates of the book after only several hundred had been printed. Larson could not confirm that federal agents had destroyed the original plates. There is no doubt, however, that very few copies of the original edition were ever printed or distributed.

19. Lindbergh, *Your Country at War*, 208–13.

20. Lindbergh, *Your Country at War*, 214–15.

21. Lindbergh, *Your Country at War*, 17.

22. Nord, "Hothouse Socialism," 144; Nathanson, "Thomas Van Lear: City Hall's Working-Class Champion," 228. Van Lear's position reflected the stand taken by his union, the International Association of Machinists. Although a stronghold of socialism before the war, the union quickly pledged its allegiance to Wilson.

23. "Reds Bolt Convention of State Federation," *The Labor World*, July 21, 1917, 2.

24. Nathanson, "Thomas Van Lear: City Hall's Working Class Champion," 228; "Mayor's Son Changes Exemption Blank to Suit His Own Case," *Minneapolis Morning Tribune*, August 1, 1917, 9. Their June 5, 1917, draft registration cards are available on Ancestry.com.

25. Mjagkij, *Loyalty in Time of Trial*, 71.

26. Untitled editorial, *Twin Cities Star*, April 7, 1917, 4; "Col. Young to Be Retired," *Twin Cities Star*, June 30, 1917, 2; Mjagkij, *Loyalty in Time of Trial*, 62–64; Lewis, *W. E. B. Du Bois: Biography of a Race*, 531–34.

27. Kennedy, *Over Here*, 282; Carlos F. Hurd, "*Post-Dispatch* Man, an Eye-Witness, Describes Massacre of Negroes," in Berg, ed., *World War I and America*, 385–93. This is an excerpted reprint of Hurd's article in the *St. Louis Dispatch* for July 3, 1917.

28. *The Appeal*, August 4, 1917, 2; Schaffer, *America in the Great War*, 77; James Weldon Johnson, "An Army with Banners," 629–30, in *James Weldon Johnson: Writings*, ed. William L. Andrews (New York: Library of America, 2004). This piece was originally an editorial in the *New York Age*, August 3, 1917.

29. Mjagkij, *Loyalty in Time of Trial*, 66–69; Williams, *Torchbearers of Democracy*, 32–39.

30. Mjagkij, *Loyalty in Time of Trial*, 70–71.

31. L. A. Fritsche, ed., *History of Brown County, Minnesota: Its People, Industries and Institutions*, vol. 2 (Indianapolis, IN: B. F. Bowen and Co., 1916).

32. Hoisington, *A German Town*, 127.

33. Fritsche, *History of Brown County*, 2:144–48, 368–69.

34. "New Ulm Loses Last Military Unit," *Sleepy Eye Herald-Dispatch*, July 13, 1917, 1.

35. "War Protest Meeting in New Ulm Tonight; Mayor on Program," *Minneapolis Morning Tribune*, July 25, 1917, 9; "Mass Meeting Is Planned Tonight," *New Ulm Review*, July 25, 1917, 1.

36. "New Ulm Anti-War Meeting Protests Selective Draft," *Minneapolis Morning Tribune*, July 26, 1917, 1, 2; "Big Crowd Hears Draft Discussion," *New Ulm Review*, August 1, 1917, 1; "Don't Want Draft Men Forced to Go to Europe," *Brown County Journal*, July 28, 1917, 1, 2.

37. The quoted words are from the *Minneapolis Morning Tribune* account. The *New Ulm Review* and the *Brown County Journal* quote Pfaender as saying substantially the same thing.

38. Chambers, *To Raise an Army*, 160–61, 219–20. In January 1918, the Supreme Court upheld the constitutionality of the draft in *Arver v. United States*, 245 U.S. 366.

39. The *New Ulm Review*, of which Steinhauser was the editor, reported his comment about *The Masses* but not his endorsement of the Nonpartisan League. The *Minneapolis Morning Tribune* article reported that he praised the Nonpartisan League. The *Brown County Journal* mentioned that he quoted from the *Nonpartisan Leader*. On July 17, 1917, the editors of *The Masses* received a letter from the post office informing them that their August issue was "unmailable" under the terms of the Espionage Act of June 15, 1917: see John Sayer, "'Art and Politics, Dissent and Repression': *The Masses Magazine* Versus the Government, 1917–1918," *American Journal of Legal History* 32, no. 1 (January 1988): 42–78.

40. The quote comes from the *New Ulm Review*. It is not included in the *Brown County Journal* article. The *Minneapolis Morning Tribune* article makes no mention of Ackermann. Only the *Brown County Journal* mentioned that Ackermann criticized the congressman. It also speculated that Albert Pfaender was weighing the possibility of running for that seat. M. J. Wagner, a Martin Luther College professor, also spoke and strongly criticized the draft as undemocratic. He is mentioned in the *Brown County Journal* and *New Ulm Review* accounts. Although Ackermann lost his job, it does not appear that Wagner, who was also a practicing Lutheran minister, was punished.

41. "Gibbon Meeting Deplores Draft," *New Ulm Review*, August 8, 1917, 1; "Patriotic Glencoe Rejoice Meeting Was Quiet," *Minneapolis Morning Tribune*, August 9, 1917, 4.

42. "Treason Must Be Stopped," *Red Wing Daily Republican*, August 11, 1917, 2; "Tyranny in America" [editorial], *Minneapolis Morning Tribune*, August 25, 1918, 10; "The New Ulm Traitors," *Princeton Union*, August 16, 1917, 4.

43. "Loyalty Meeting Is Great Success," *New Ulm Review*, September 5, 1917, 1; "Loyalty Talk Is Attraction Here," *New Ulm Review*, September 12, 1917, 1.

44. "Stars and Stripes League Asks Every Minnesotan to Declare Loyalty

to Nation," *Minneapolis Journal*, August 12, 1917, 2; "Burnquist at Parade Gives Internal Foes Stern Warning," *Minneapolis Journal*, August 17, 1917, 1.

45. Chrislock, *Watchdog of Loyalty*, 186; "Labor's Loyal Legion to Fight Acts of Treason," *Minneapolis Morning Tribune*, August 12, 1917, 1; "Labor's Loyal Legion Now Fully Formed," *Minneapolis Morning Tribune*, August 15, 1917, 1.

46. "No Peace if Kaiserism Lasts, Say Gerard and Darrow: Great Outpouring of Patriots Puts Labor and City Right," *Minneapolis Morning Tribune*, August 25, 1917, 1, 2. On Gerhard, see Doenecke, *Nothing Less Than War*, 10.

47. "Internment for Antidraft Fighters Urged at Windom," *Minneapolis Journal*, August 16, 1917, 5; "Twelve Counties Urged to Attend Loyalty Meeting," *Minneapolis Journal*, August 10, 1917, 1.

48. Chrislock, *Watchdog of Loyalty*, 138–39. At first the commission focused on Fritsche, Vogel, and county treasurer Henry J. Berg. Later they added Pfaender and dropped Berg when it became clear to them that he had done nothing they found objectionable.

49. Chrislock, *Watchdog of Loyalty*, 137–40; Hoisington, *A German Town*, 134–36.

50. "Movement to Disbar Albert Pfaender on in Bar Association," *Minneapolis Morning Tribune*, August 9, 1917, 1; "Pfaender, New Ulm Lawyer, Defends His Talks as Moderate," *Minneapolis Morning Tribune*, August 11, 1917, 13.

51. "Van Lear Escapes Threatened Removal Request by Lawyers of the State on Technicality," *Minneapolis Morning Tribune*, August 10, 1917, 1.

52. "Two More Jailed in Big Drive for War Obstructors," *Minneapolis Morning Tribune*, August 10, 1917, 1.

53. "Peoples' Council to Open Office Here," *Minneapolis Morning Tribune*, August 8, 1917, 8.

54. Chrislock, *Watchdog of Loyalty*, 147–51.

55. Peterson and Fite, *Opponents of War*, 52–60; "The I. W. W.," *New York Times*, August 4, 1917; "A Federal Job," *Minneapolis Morning Tribune*, August 2, 1917, 10.

56. Chrislock, *Watchdog of Loyalty*, 125–26. Eventually 150 municipalities adopted the ordinance. "Eighteen I. W. W. Members, Including Elizabeth Gurley Flynn, in Court," *Duluth Herald*, June 25, 1917, 5; "Joan D'Arc of I. W. W. Leaves," *Duluth Herald*, June 29, 1917, 25.

57. Chrislock, *Watchdog of Loyalty*, 143–44.

58. Chrislock, *Watchdog of Loyalty*, 142; Lee, "Hometown Hysteria," 74; "Crookston Mill No. 1 Swept by Fire: Loss over $200,000; 450 Out of Work," *Bemidji Daily Pioneer*, July 23, 1917, 1; Kaunonen, *Flames of Discontent*, 207–8.

59. *Bemidji Daily Pioneer*, July 26, 1917, 1.

60. Lee, "Hometown Hysteria," 53. Like other northern units of the Home Guard, Bemidji's Company A, which was originally in the 10th Battalion, was transferred several times as new battalions were organized, first to the 11th Battalion, then to the 14th Battalion, and finally to the 21st Battalion. Captain Thomas W. Swinson, the original commander of Company A, was later promoted to major and given command of the 21st Battalion: Adjutant General

Files, Home Guard, 21st Battalion Report, and Morris Kaplan and Family Papers, MNHS.

"First Conviction under I.W.W. Law; Beltrami Shows State Her Stand," *Bemidji Daily Pioneer*, September 28, 1917, 1; "I.W.W. Official Awaits Trip to 'State Pen,'" *Bemidji Daily Pioneer*, December 10, 1917, 1.

61. "Soldiers Demolish I.W.W. Headquarters—Room Wrecked; 100 Soldiers in Raid; Investigation Ordered," *Duluth News Tribune*, August 19, 1917, 1; Hudelson and Ross, *By the Ore Docks*, 84.

62. "What Is a 'Mob'?," *Duluth News Tribune*, August 22, 1917; Holbrook and Appel, *Minnesota in the War with Germany*, 1:91.

63. "41 I.W.W.'s Driven from County by Police and 'Minute Men' Today," *Moorhead Daily News*, September 21, 1917, 1; "36 I.W.W.'s in 'Bull Pen,'" *Moorhead Daily News*, September 22, 1917, 4. Hopeman set up a rapid strike force within the Home Guard which he called the "minute men." See also Watne, "Intolerance and Conformity." Watne notes that the *Fargo Courier-News*, a newspaper sympathetic to the Nonpartisan League, interviewed the workers and found them willing to work but not at the rates being offered. They came back after being expelled because some farmers were offering reasonable rates for harvesting potatoes. This reporting was exceptional. Most local newspapers printed unsourced rumors of IWW mayhem.

64. "U.S. Hits with Concerted Blows at I.W.W. Menace," *Minneapolis Morning Tribune*, September 6, 1917, 1, 12; Chrislock, *Watchdog of Loyalty*, 145–46.

65. Chrislock, *Ethnicity Challenged*, 89; Fred Snyder to Senator Knute Nelson, August 18, 1917, Knute Nelson Papers, box 26, MNHS; "Three Thousand Gather to Hear Nonpartisan League Speakers," *Glencoe Enterprise*, June 28, 1917, 1, 4.

Notes to Chapter Six: Brandishing the Weapon of Loyalty

1. Holbrook and Appel, *Minnesota in the War with Germany*, 1:307–9; Smith, *Confluence*, 185–86. The MCPS created the dry zone with Order 2, *Report of the Minnesota Commission of Public Safety* (1919), 73–74.

2. Holbrook and Appel, *Minnesota in the War with Germany*, 1:309–24.

3. Holbrook and Appel, *Minnesota in the War with Germany*, 1:260–62.

4. Holbrook and Appel, *Minnesota in the War with Germany*, 1:147–49.

5. Chambers, *To Raise an Army*, 225–26; Barbeau and Henri, *The Unknown Soldiers*, 35–37.

6. "Minnesota Negroes Entrain for Camp Dodge," *Twin City Star*, November 3, 1917, 1, 5; "Our Camouflage Friends—At the 'Chicken Dinner,'" *Twin City Star*, November 3, 1917, 4. In the *Adjutant General of the Minnesota National Guard's Biennial Report for 1917–1919* (17), General Rhinow wrote that "the send off the colored men received was worthy of their often-repeated assertion that they were 'good fighting men.' This boast was later made good on the battle fields of France."

7. That "a kind of officially blessed vigilantism" was allowed to exist was symptomatic of the state of US society during World War I. Kennedy, *Over Here*, 81–83; Chrislock, *Watchdog of Loyalty*, 273; Operative No. 71, *Summary and Report of War Service, Minneapolis Division, American Protective League* (Minneapolis: n.d.), 1–3. For a general history of the APL, see Jensen, *The Price of Vigilance*.

8. Operative No. 71, *Summary and Report of War Service*, 2.

9. Order No. 4, *Report of the Minnesota Commission of Public Safety* (1919), 75–76. There are letters from Charles Davis to McGee requesting peace officer commissions for APL agents dated February 6, February 16, March 21, and April 25, 1918, in MCPS main files, Peace Officer file, 103.L.8.7B, MNHS. Thanks to Andrew McGuire for sharing his research on the MCPS peace officers.

10. "Taking of Testimony Ends Abruptly with Pfaender Statement," *Minneapolis Morning Tribune*, October 3, 1917, 9.

11. "Taking of Testimony Ends Abruptly with Pfaender Statement," *Minneapolis Morning Tribune*, October 3, 1917, 9.

12. Chrislock, *Watchdog of Loyalty*, 155.

13. Hoisington, *A German Town*, 134.

14. Chrislock, *Watchdog of Loyalty*, 155–56.

15. The Schaper incident is described in Matsen, "Professor William S. Schaper," and Gruber, *Mars and Minerva*, 174–87. John McGee to Fred Snyder, July 12, 1917, with unsigned enclosure "Concerning German Department at State University," Office of the President, box 24, file William A. Schaper, University of Minnesota Archives. John Lind later told Shaper that there had been no letter from the commission to the university, but Lind's relationship with the commission, and especially with McGee, was tenuous at that point, and he may not have been aware of all commission actions: Chrislock, *Watchdog of Loyalty*, 348n43.

16. "More U Faculty Men Questioned by Board on Patriotism Stand," *Minneapolis Morning Tribune*, September 15, 1917, 18; Gray, *The University of Minnesota*, 245–48.

17. Schaper's contributions to local government reform were frequently covered by the Minneapolis papers: see for example, "Charter Differences Are Nicely Overcome," *Minneapolis Morning Tribune*, July 3, 1913, 12, and "Women Hear Address on Charter Situation," *Minneapolis Morning Tribune*, February 8, 1917, 5.

18. There is no transcript of the meeting. This quotation comes from Schaper's statement of what transpired in "Schaper Issues Explanation of Opinion on War," *Minneapolis Morning Tribune*, September 18, 1917, 8.

19. M. L. Burton to Prof. W. A. Schaper, September 13, 1917, Office of the President, box 24, file William A. Schaper, University of Minnesota Archives.

20. "I.W.W. Teacher Dismissed by School Board," *Minneapolis Morning Tribune*, September 17, 1917, 1; Chrislock, *Watchdog of Loyalty*, 147.

21. Chrislock, *Watchdog of Loyalty*, 159–60; Holbrook and Appel, *Minnesota in the War with Germany*, 2:69–72.

22. Holbrook and Appel, *Minnesota in the War with Germany*, 2:68–69.

23. Chrislock, *Watchdog of Loyalty*, 163; Holbrook and Appel, *Minnesota in the War with Germany*, 2:70.

24. Holbrook and Appel, *Minnesota in the War with Germany*, 2:70–72; Chrislock, *Watchdog of Loyalty*, 161. In a December 20, 1917, letter Henke told Alice Ames Winter that in the previous six weeks, he had sent out 47,500 copies of her flyer, and that they were now posted in every railroad station, school, and post office and many restaurants and business offices: MCPS, Publicity Department files, MNHS.

25. *Minnesota in the War*, September 15, 1917, 1; Holbrook and Appel, *Minnesota in the War with Germany*, 2:65–66. Isobel Field was a member of the Vigilantes, a group of writers and publishers who committed themselves to publishing patriotic materials during World War I.

26. "Wall Street and the War: A Concise Argument against 'Rich Man's War' Propaganda" (St. Paul, MN: Publicity Department of the Commission of Public Safety, n.d.). The contents of this pamphlet provided the lead article in *Minnesota in the War* 1, no. 14 (December 8, 1917): 1, 3. Both in MNHS collections.

27. "Every Loyalist Must Be on Guard," *Minnesota in the War* 1, no. 13 (December 1, 1917): 1.

28. See generally Philip Knightley, *The First Casualty: The War Correspondent as Hero and Myth-Maker from the Crimea to Kosovo* (Baltimore, MD: Johns Hopkins University Press, 2000), and Read, *Atrocity Propaganda*. "Hilles' Tales of German Cruelty Stuns Audience," *Minneapolis Morning Tribune*, October 18, 1917, 2. The story describes the talk by Rev. Newell Dwight Hilles, a "noted Brooklyn pastor," speaking at the Minneapolis Auditorium to a crowd of three thousand on behalf of the Second Liberty Bond campaign committee.

29. Hilton, "Minnesota Commission," 7–8.

30. "What German Americans Owe to Themselves: A Message to Americans of German Stock," issued by the MCPS Publicity Department; Otto H. Kahn, "The Poison of Prussianism, an Address Given at the Auditorium, Milwaukee, Wisconsin, January 13, 1918," issued by the MCPS Publicity Department; Rudolph Heinrichs, "A Family Letter: From a German American to His Brother," issued by the MCPS Publicity Department, 1918; J. W. Olsen, "Our Adopted Country: Some Special Duties of the Foreign-Born American," issued by the MCPS Publicity Department; see also Herman Hagedorn, "Where Do You Stand? An Appeal to Americans of German Origin," issued by the MCPS Publicity Department with special permission of *McClure's* magazine. The department also produced one pamphlet aimed at all immigrants: "Our Adopted Country: Some Special Duties of the Foreign-Born American," by J. W. Olsen, the former superintendent of public instruction. All held in MNHS collections.

31. "Blood on their Hands" [editorial], *Red Wing Daily Republican*, August 23, 1917, 2; "Sixty Years Young" [editorial], *Red Wing Daily Republican*, September 3, 1917, 4; "Away with the Traitors" [editorial], *Red Wing Daily Republican*, September 21, 1917, 4.

32. Advertisement, *Red Wing Daily Republican*, September 7, 1917, 2; Jens K. Grondahl, "We Go to 'Get' the Kaiser," *Red Wing Daily Republican*, August 27, 1917, 1; Holbrook and Appel, *Minnesota in the War with Germany*, 1:7.

33. Buhl, "The Crisis of the German-American Press in World War I," parts 1 and 2; Chrislock, *Watchdog of Loyalty*, 160.

34. Gieske and Keillor, *Norwegian Yankee*, 309; Chrislock, *Watchdog of Loyalty*, 160–61.

35. Knute Nelson to John McGee, June 7, 1917, MCPS main files, box 103, MNHS; Knute Nelson to A. S. Burleson, Postmaster General, August 11, 1917, Knute Nelson Papers, box 26, MNHS; Gieske and Keillor, *Norwegian Yankee*, 309–10; Chrislock, *Watchdog of Loyalty*, 131. Alexandria had three newspapers, the *Echo*, the *Post News* (Republican), and the *Citizen* (Democratic).

36. Gieske and Keillor, *Norwegian Yankee*, 310–12.

37. Chrislock, *Watchdog of Loyalty*, 206–7; *Report of the Minnesota Commission of Public Safety* (1919), 16–17.

38. Chrislock, *Watchdog of Loyalty*, 207; "7,000 Pounds of Carp to Go on Sale Here," *Minneapolis Morning Tribune*, January 8, 1918, 2; *Report of the Minnesota Commission of Public Safety* (1919), 16–17.

39. Chrislock, *Watchdog of Loyalty*, 208; Order No. 13, *Report of the Minnesota Commission of Public Safety* (1919), 87.

40. Chrislock, *Watchdog of Loyalty*, 209–11; Order No. 18, *Report of the Minnesota Commission of Public Safety* (1919), 91–94.

41. Chrislock, *Watchdog of Loyalty*, 211; Holbrook and Appel, *Minnesota in the War with Germany*, 2:167–68; *Report of the Minnesota Commission of Public Safety* (1919), 148–49.

42. Holbrook and Appel, *Minnesota in the War with Germany*, 2:170–75.

43. Holbrook and Appel, *Minnesota in the War with Germany*, 2:176–80.

44. Holbrook and Appel, *Minnesota in the War with Germany*, 2:184–89.

45. Chrislock, *Watchdog of Loyalty*, 215, 217–18; Orders No. 10, 17, *Report of the Minnesota Commission of Public Safety* (1919), 79–80, 90–91. Order 10 also required that all alcohol purchased be consumed on the premises.

46. "Two Mayors and Sheriff Ousted," *Minneapolis Morning Tribune*, October 9, 1917, 13; Chrislock, *Watchdog of Loyalty*, 219–20; Orders No. 11, 12, 19, 20, 24, *Report of the Minnesota Commission of Public Safety* (1919), 80–82, 94–95, 99–100.

47. Chrislock, *Watchdog of Loyalty*, 222–24.

48. Chrislock, *Watchdog of Loyalty*, 224–25.

49. Holbrook and Appel, *Minnesota in the War with Germany*, 2:202–3; *Minnesota in the War*, January 26, 1918, 5.

50. Lansing, *Insurgent Democracy*, 103–5.

51. Lansing, *Insurgent Democracy*, 99–101; National Nonpartisan League, *Origin, Purpose and Method of Operation and War Program and Statement of Principles* (1917), Nonpartisan League Papers, M182, roll 1, frame 181–82, MNHS.

52. Morlan, *Political Prairie Fire*, 110.

53. Chrislock, *Watchdog of Loyalty*, 169; Lansing, *Insurgent Democracy*, 103;

"Patriotism Plus Protest Urged on Nonpartisans," *Minneapolis Morning Tribune*, September 19, 1917, 1; "Blaze of Disloyalty Ends Conference of Nonpartisan League," *Minneapolis Morning Tribune*, September 21, 1917, 1, 2.

54. Larson, *Lindbergh of Minnesota*, 216–18. A typescript of his speech, entitled "Profits of Finance in the High Cost of Living," is in the Arthur Le Sueur Papers, MNHS.

55. Chrislock, *Watchdog of Loyalty*, 170; "Red Wing Honors Departed Heroes," *Red Wing Daily Republican*, May 30, 1917, 1. Grondahl's paper reported that Manahan "stirred the audience to great patriotic fervor in a splendid address."

56. Chrislock, *Watchdog of Loyalty*, 170–71; Lansing, *Insurgent Democracy*, 103.

57. Chrislock, *Watchdog of Loyalty*, 171; Lansing, *Insurgent Democracy*, 104.

58. "Blaze of Disloyalty Ends Conference of Nonpartisan League," *Minneapolis Morning Tribune*, September 21, 1917, 1, 2.

59. This paragraph and the next based on George E. Akerson, "'Huns Within Our Gates' Put to Rout by Roosevelt," *Minneapolis Morning Tribune*, September 29, 1917, 1, 2 (with four related articles on page 2); "St. Paul Proves Its Loyalty as Roosevelt Scores 'Huns,'" *St. Paul Pioneer Press*, September 29, 1917, 1, 2 (with a series of related articles on both pages); and "Roosevelt Flays La Follette Talk," *St. Paul Pioneer Press*, September 28, 1917. Both the *Minneapolis Morning Tribune* and the *St. Paul Pioneer Press* reprinted Roosevelt's full address.

60. "St. Paul Proves Its Loyalty as Roosevelt Scores 'Huns,'" *St. Paul Pioneer Press*, September 29, 1917, 1. Although this may sound like an editorial, it was news reporting of the event.

61. Morlan, *Political Prairie Fire*, 127–28. The *Nonpartisan Leader* published a four-part exposé of the affair in 1919 when Clarence Johnson, who was the editor of the ill-fated faux newspaper, sued a group of St. Paul businessmen for failing to pay him as promised for the anti-league work. His lawsuit opened the project to public view and exposed the names of the businessmen behind it: see "How the Fake League Was Started," *Nonpartisan Leader*, June 9, 1919, 4–5, 13. The series continues for the next three issues of the newspaper.

62. Chrislock, *Watchdog of Loyalty*, 171–74.

63. Chrislock, *Watchdog of Loyalty*, 177–78; MCPS resolution, September 25, 1917, *Report of the Minnesota Commission of Public Safety* (1919), 163.

64. Chrislock, *Watchdog of Loyalty*, 175. The MCPS resolution of October 2, 1917, appointing Ames to oversee the NPL investigation, is reprinted in the *Report of the Minnesota Commission of Public Safety* (1919), 164.

65. Chrislock, *Watchdog of Loyalty*, 177–79; Louis Keane, secretary, Otter Tail County Public Safety Commission, to Arthur Townley, October 3, 1917, reprinted in *Nonpartisan Leader*, October 18, 1917, 4; Henry G. Dahl, chairman, Otter Tail County Public Safety Commission, to H. W. Libby, October 3, 1917, in MCPS main files, 103.L.8.4F, MNHS.

66. L. Benshoof, director, Becker County Safety Commission, to H. W. Libby, October 4, 1977, and the reply to Benshoof on October 5, 1917, in MCPS main files, 103.L.8.4F, MNHS. The city of Detroit changed its name to Detroit Lakes in 1927. The attorney general stated his opinion in his October 11, 1917, letter to Hon. J. A. A. Burnquist. Libby reprinted the letter and addressed it to "county directors, sheriffs, county attorneys and all peace officers in Minnesota": MCPS main files, Lyndon Smith file, MNHS.

67. "Nonpartisan League Barred from Holding Meetings in Three Towns in Minnesota," *Minneapolis Morning Tribune*, October 3, 1917, 1; "More About Those Big Meetings," *Nonpartisan Leader*, October 25, 1917, 7, 22.

68. This account is based on the affidavits of N. S. Randall and Perry Aronson in *Memorial to Congress of the United States Concerning the Conditions in Minnesota, 1918* (40–48), a 120-page booklet published by the National Nonpartisan League. See also the affidavit of H. A. Paddock (48–56), a detective who visited Pine County after the incident on behalf of the NPL. He found people willing to brag about how they had almost lynched the two NPL members, and that the Home Guard was "in on the fun too."

69. "Shock troops" quote from Chrislock, *Watchdog of Loyalty*, 175; Sheriff James Mitchell to Hon. Lyndon Smith, October 11, 1917, MCPS main files, 103.L.12.4F, MNHS. On the Kandiyohi sheriff, see E. B. Fussell, "Ain't Farmers Legal?," *Nonpartisan Leader*, October 18, 1917, 5.

70. "Minnesota Loyalty Meeting Called to Combat Traitors," *Duluth News Tribune*, October 8, 1917, 1, 12. The meeting was intended to be private, but one journalist wrote a full report. See also Chrislock, *Watchdog of Loyalty*, 176–77; Morlan, *Political Prairie Fire*, 146–47.

71. "County Loyalty Meeting Opened at Armory; Five Hundred Delegates," *Winona Republican Herald*, November 10, 1917, 7. After the Twin Cities transit strike, Lawson's outlook would change significantly. In 1918, Edward Lees would defend a Winona man charged under the federal Espionage Act.

72. "U.S. Looks to Great Northwest in Crisis—Minnesota Again Attests Loyalty in Monster Rally" and "Minnesota Loyalty Attested [editorial]," *Minneapolis Morning Tribune*, November 17, 1917, 1, 2, 20; "Minnesota Proclaims to Entire World It Is 100 Percent Loyal," *Minneapolis Sunday Tribune*, November 18, 1917, 1.

73. "Loyalty of Towns Throughout State Pledged at Meetings," *Minneapolis Morning Tribune*, December 20, 1917, 8; Frank N. Murphy, "Twin City Loyalty Meetings Add New Chapter to State's Already Glorious History," *Minneapolis Morning Tribune*, November 23, 1917, 9. Murphy was the president of the America First Association.

Notes to Chapter Seven: Urban and Rural Skirmishes

1. Holbrook and Appel, *Minnesota in the War with Germany*, 1:317–31, 345–46.

2. *Arver v. United States*, 245 U.S. 366 (1918). The case took its name from one of the Minnesota Socialists who was appealing his conviction. Douglas, "The Germans Would Court-Martial Me, Too," 286–301. In World War I, it was possible to be prosecuted in federal court for failure to register, and then be forcibly registered and drafted out of order and without regard to possible exemptions, and then also court-martialed for continued noncooperation within the military. During the Vietnam War, the Supreme Court ended this duplication in yet another case arising in Minnesota: *Gutknecht v. U.S.*, 396 U.S. 295 (1970).

3. "Ralph O. Van Lear to Face Further and More Serious Charges," *Minneapolis Morning Tribune*, October 14, 1917, 4; "Van Lear Released from Guard House," *Minneapolis Morning Tribune*, November 1, 1917, 15; application for headstone marker, September 5, 1952, available on Ancestry.com.

4. *Report of the Attorney General of the United States*, for the fiscal years ending June 30, 1917, 1918, 1919, 1920.

5. Holbrook and Appel, *Minnesota in the War with Germany*, 1:270–83, 285–88; Hardy, "The Americanization of Bjorn Winger," 78–85. This article includes the full text of this poem and others.

6. Chrislock, *Watchdog of Loyalty*, 187–88. The story of employers' efforts to block unionization in Minneapolis is well told in Millikan, *A Union Against Unions*.

7. Millikan, *A Union Against Unions*, 125.

8. Wingerd, *Claiming the City*, 187; Millikan, *A Union Against Unions*, 126–27; Holbrook, *St. Paul and Ramsey County in the War of 1917–1918*, 235–42.

9. Wingerd, *Claiming the City*, 184–85, 195.

10. Wingerd, *Claiming the City*, 188–89; Millikan, *A Union Against Unions*, 128–31; Order No. 16, *Report of the Minnesota Commission of Public Safety* (1919), 90.

11. Millikan, *A Union Against Unions*, 131; MCCA telegram to President Wilson et al., MCPS main files, Twin Cities Street Car Strike file, MNHS; Burnquist telegram to Acting Secretary of Labor Louis Post, December 1, 1917, *Report of the Minnesota Commission of Public Safety* (1919), 40.

12. "Unions Score Governor and Safety Board," *St. Paul Pioneer Press*, December 2, 1917, 1, 2.

13. "Five Thousand Riot in St. Paul Streets; Cut Trolley Wires," *Minneapolis Morning Tribune*, December 3, 1917, 1, 2. Although this newspaper was extremely hostile to the NPL and the strikers, its reporter acknowledged that the Rice Park speakers urged people to refrain "from disturbances." The quote from Manahan's speech comes from his biography, *Trials of a Lawyer*, 229–32.

14. "Governor Ousts Sheriff Wagener for Riot Laxity," *St. Paul Daily News*, December 3, 1917, 1, 10.

15. This list of Home Guard units brought to St. Paul is based on Rhinow,

Report of the Adjutant General, and "State Guard Mobilizes to Keep Order," *St. Paul Daily News*, December 5, 1917, 1.

16. Millikan, *A Union Against Unions*, 132; Chrislock, *Watchdog of Loyalty*, 196; Burnquist telegram to Baker, *Report of the Minnesota Commission of Public Safety* (1919), 40–41.

17. "Fifteen Thousand Unionists Demand Arbitration in Street Car Dispute," *Minnesota Union Advocate*, December 7, 1917, 1.

18. Millikan, *A Union Against Unions*, 133–34.

19. Millikan, *A Union Against Unions*, 134.

20. Report from the President's Mediation Commission to Newton D. Baker, February 14, 1918, with a cover letter from Newton Baker to the Minnesota Commission of Public Safety, February 15, 1917, MCPS main files, Twin Cities Street Car Strike file, MNHS.

21. Chrislock, *Watchdog of Loyalty*, 252–53; Millikan, *A Union Against Unions*, 135–36.

22. Order No. 30, *Report of the Minnesota Commission of Public Safety* (1919), 108–9.

23. Chrislock, *Watchdog of Loyalty*, 256–58; Millikan, *A Union Against Unions*, 137–38.

24. Chrislock, *Watchdog of Loyalty*, 258–59; Millikan, *A Union Against Unions*, 139.

25. Transcript of telegram from John F. McGee to Harry A. Garfield, March 11, 1918, MCPS main files, Twin Cities Street Car Strike file, MNHS.

26. "Labor Unions Prepare for Walkout; Saloons to Close; 2,000 Guards"; "U.S. Asks 'Button' Order Suspension"; and "Burnquist Warns Ames 'Hands Off'"—all *St. Paul Daily News*, December 4, 1917, 1.

27. Chrislock, *Watchdog of Loyalty*, 196–97; telegram from Ames to Burnquist, December 7, 1917, 3:28 AM, J. A. A. Burnquist Papers, box 11, MNHS.

28. "Libby Scored by Union Machinists," *Minnesota Union Advocate*, December 7, 1917, 5; "H. W. Libby Is Ousted from Union Ranks," *Winona Republican-Herald*, December 19, 1917, 7.

29. Chrislock, *Watchdog of Loyalty*, 196–97; Millikan, *A Union Against Unions*, 133; Wingerd, *Claiming the City*, 201–2. The quotation comes from a letter Burnquist wrote to Ames in January 1921, responding to Ames's letter asking Burnquist about his dismissal, which he said "was like a slap in the face by a friend": Charles W. Ames to Hon. J. A. A. Burnquist, January 11, 1921, and Governor Burnquist to Charles W. Ames, January 12, 1921. Ames could not let the matter rest and wrote a second letter on February 1, 1921, contending that his actions in Washington had been misunderstood. Burnquist responded one more time, on February 8, 1921, reiterating his position. All in J. A. A. Burnquist Papers, box 21, MNHS.

30. Stephenson, *John Lind of Minnesota*, 334–36; Chrislock, *Watchdog of Loyalty*, 201–2.

31. Stephenson, *John Lind of Minnesota*, 335–36; Chrislock, *Watchdog of Loyalty*, 203–4.

32. Chrislock, *Watchdog of Loyalty*, 204.

33. Wingerd, *Claiming the City*, 150, 169, 220, 239; Chrislock, *Watchdog of Loyalty*, 208, 210; Nord, "Hothouse Socialism," 148–49. The transformation of the labor moderates can also be seen in the editorial stance of the *Union Labor Bulletin*, a pro-war, anti–La Follette labor monthly published in Minneapolis. Watching the strike unfold, they argued that "union men are fighting for their future existence in the face of autocratic resistance on the part of the public safety commission, headed by Gov. Burnquist": *Union Labor Bulletin* 6, no. 12 (December 1917): 17.

34. Manahan, *Trials of a Lawyer*, 229–32. Manahan includes a lengthy quote from Judge Frederick M. Dickson's dismissal order.

35. "Victory of Right Brings Rejoicing: Unionists and Farm Men Celebrate Triumph of Sense Over Fanaticism," *Minnesota Union Advocate*, February 8, 1918, 1, 8.

36. The telegram to Senator Nelson was signed by Captain Ten Broek and dated December 5, 1917: Knute Nelson Papers, box 26, MNHS. I can find no mention of a Captain Ten Broek in the records of the Minnesota National Guard or the Home Guard. He might have been a regular army officer stationed at Fort Snelling. "Judge McGee Under Fire," *St. Paul Daily News*, December 6, 1917, 1, 5; see also Chrislock, *Watchdog of Loyalty*, 197.

37. Oscar Seebach to Hon. J. A. A. Burnquist, December 6, 1917, J. A. A. Burnquist Papers, box 11, MNHS.

38. "Governor Replies to Non-Partisan Resolutions," *Minnesota in the War* 1, no. 25 (February 23, 1918): 1, 3. Since the MCPS was created by business organizations to advance their own interests, there was little chance the governor would appoint commissioners sympathetic to unions or the farmers. In Wisconsin, on the other hand, the legislature mandated that there be "one representative of labor" and "one representative of farmers" on the Wisconsin State Council of Defense, the analogous body: Wisconsin Session Laws 1917, Chapter 82, Section 1; see Pifer, *The Great War Comes to Wisconsin*.

39. "Defiant Agitators Driven Out," *Akeley Herald-Tribune*, January 18, 1919, 1. Affidavits from two NPL organizers are in *Memorial to the Congress of the United States Concerning Conditions in Minnesota* (St. Paul, MN: National Nonpartisan League, 1918), 19–26.

40. "Non-Partizan's Attempt Foiled," *Freeborn County Standard*, March 4, 1918, 1. The Home Guard members were likely from the 7th Battalion's Company D, which was headquartered in Albert Lea but had platoons in smaller towns. Affidavits from the NPL organizer involved are in *Memorial to the Congress of the United States Concerning Conditions in Minnesota* (St. Paul, MN: National Nonpartisan League, 1918), 17–18.

41. Johnson, *Patriot Hearts*, 50–51; "Held Caucus and Drove Out Breidal," *Kenyon News*, March 7, 1918, 1.

42. Morlan, *Political Prairie Fire*, 159, 162.

43. Director of Publicity to the Editor, January 19, 1918, Arthur Le Sueur Papers, P1004, box 2, MNHS. The NPL reprinted this letter in the *Nonpartisan Leader*, February 18, 1918, 9.

44. Morlan, *Political Prairie Fire*, 163.

45. Morlan, *Political Prairie Fire*, 159–61; Douhit, *Nobody Owns Us*, 117–25.

46. Manahan, *Trials of a Lawyer*, 232–38; Douhit, *Nobody Owns Us*, 123–25; Morlan, *Political Prairie Fire*, 159–61.

47. *Session Laws of Minnesota for 1917*, Chapter 463, p764–65. The war resolutions were contained in a pamphlet entitled *The Nonpartisan League: Its Origin, Purposes and Methods of Organization*. The Minnesota statutes severely limited free expression since any criticism of the government could be construed to discourage enlistment. However, the Minnesota statute only restricted public speech if there was an audience of at least five. There was no such limitation in the federal act, and some federal prosecutions in Minnesota involved purely private comments to one other person. The federal statute was also much more punitive, allowing for sentences up to twenty years.

48. Morlan, *Political Prairie Fire*, 167–71.

49. "Strong Arm of Law to Stop Sedition," *Red Wing Daily Republican*, March 14, 1918, 1, 4.

50. Jens Grondahl, "To Make Old Goodhue 100 Percent American," *Red Wing Daily Republican*, March 15, 1918, 4; "The Mark of Cain," *Red Wing Daily Republican*, March 14, 1918, 4.

51. Kennedy, *Over Here*, 68, 81; Schaffer, *America in the Great War*, 20–25.

52. Order No. 25, *Report of the Minnesota Commission of Public Safety* (1919), 108–9. Earlier, the MCPS had issued Order 23, requiring the registration of all property owned by aliens.

53. Chrislock, *Watchdog of Loyalty*, 281.

54. Chrislock, *Watchdog of Loyalty*, 283. The Iowa governor ordered not only that English be the only medium of instruction in all schools but also that "all conversations in public places, on trains, or over the telephone should be in the English language." He even ordered religious worship not in English to be conducted only in private homes: Governor William Harding, *A Proclamation to the People of Iowa*, May 23, 1918.

55. Luebke, *Bonds of Loyalty*, 246–49.

56. Sherman, *Music and Maestros*, 37–54, 66–67; Millikan, *A Union Against Unions*, 82–83.

57. Caryl Storrs, "Program Notes," *Minneapolis Morning Tribune*, March 14, 1918, 16; "Symphony Orchestra Season Closes with Easter Concert," *Minneapolis Sunday Tribune*, March 31, 1918, section 13, p7; Gladys M. Hamblin, "Minneapolis Symphony Orchestra," *Minneapolis Morning Tribune*, April 1, 1918, 4.

58. "Accused Member of Symphony Reinstated," *Minneapolis Morning Tribune*, October 20, 1918, 3; Sherman, *Music and Maestros*, 139.

59. "Remember the Lusitania," *Red Wing Daily Republican*, August 14, 1918, 2. Later in the editorial, Grondahl explained that the abandonment of everything German did not mean discarding Martin Luther, because if "Luther was alive today he would be fighting on the side of democracy with all his tremendous vigor." The auditorium board did not remove the three German names, and they can be viewed in the Sheldon's lobby today, joined by Chopin,

Shakespeare, Michelangelo, Raphael, Rembrandt, and Longfellow, along with the architects Sir Christopher Wren and Richard Hunt and the painter and sculptor Rosa Bonheur.

60. "Decorators Blotting Out German Mottoes," *Minneapolis Morning Tribune*, April 18, 1918, 14. Governor Theodore Christianson ordered the mottoes restored in 1930, although with some of the drinking mottoes altered to please the temperance lobby. All the mottoes were covered up again in later remodels, but fully restored in the 1990s: Denis Gardner, *Our Minnesota State Capitol: From Groundbreaking to Restoration* (St. Paul: Minnesota Historical Society Press, 2017), 35.

61. The Little Falls bank, which currently houses a law firm, is on the corner of Broadway and Southeast First Street. The remains of the word "German" can be seen on the Broadway facade. On the St. Paul building, see Larry Millett, *Lost Twin Cities* (St. Paul: Minnesota Historical Society Press, 1992), 216–17.

62. "Loyal Germans Form Patriotic League in State," *St. Paul Pioneer Press*, April 3, 1918, 1. Emil Leicht of Winona, who was working to keep his newspaper, the *Westlicher Herold*, afloat, was elected treasurer. See also Nathanson, *World War I Minnesota*, 74.

63. Robert A. Rice to whom it may concern, July 18, 1918, Hiram D. Frankel Papers, MNHS. Frankel was the adjutant of the 15th Battalion. Rice retained Auerbach as his middle name. In Rhinow, *Report of the Adjutant General*, the Company H commander is listed as Captain R. A. Rice (265).

Notes to Chapter Eight: The Decisive Battle

1. Holbrook and Appel, *Minnesota in the War with Germany*, 1:155, 322.

2. "Governor, Rhinow to Protest Breaking of Units at Camp Cody," *Minneapolis Morning Tribune*, May 28, 1918, 1; Holbrook and Appel, *Minnesota in the War with Germany*, 1:280–81.

3. Crosby, *America's Forgotten Pandemic*, 9–25; Barry, *The Great Influenza*, 170.

4. Larson, *Lindbergh of Minnesota*, 221; letters from Charles A. Lindbergh to Eva Christie, 1918 (undated), and February 1, 1918, Lindbergh Family Papers, MNHS. The NPL endorsed Victor Power, the mayor of Hibbing, as its candidate for auditor, but he declined.

5. Platform and Declaration of Principles adopted by the delegates of the State Convention of the Minnesota Branch of the National Nonpartisan League, St. Paul, Minnesota, March 19, 1918, National Nonpartisan League Papers, M128A, roll 1, MNHS.

6. Lindbergh, *Your Country at War*, 6; Charles Lindbergh to Eva Christie, February 1, 1918, Lindbergh Family Papers, MNHS.

7. "A Non-Partisan Leaguer," *New York Times*, May 29, 1918, 12; "Congressman Calls League Seditious," *New York Times*, June 9, 1918, 7; Rep. C. B.

Miller, *The Poison Book of Lindbergh, Officially Endorsed by the Townley League Organ* (St. Paul, 1918).

8. Arthur Le Sueur to Hon. J. A. A. Burnquist, March 6, 1918, Arthur Le Sueur Papers, box 2, MNHS. See, for example, "Governor Excoriates Nonpartisans," *Minneapolis Morning Tribune*, March 12, 1918, 1, 4.

9. Chrislock, *Progressive Era in Minnesota*, 164. In *Watchdog of Loyalty*, Chrislock more judiciously called it a "miscalculation" (294). Arthur Le Sueur to Hon. J. A. A. Burnquist, March 12, 1918, Arthur Le Sueur Papers, box 2, MNHS.

10. Larson, *Lindbergh of Minnesota*, 222; Lindbergh's acceptance speech, March 21, 1918, Arthur Le Sueur Papers, box 2, MNHS.

11. Abraham Lincoln, for example, suspended the writ of habeas corpus, but only in the context of a bitter civil war that threatened the future of the United States as a political entity. Article II, Section 9 of the US Constitution states that the "privilege of Writ of Habeas Corpus shall not be suspended, unless when in Cases of Rebellion or Invasion the public Safety may require it."

12. "McGee Urges Firing Squads for Seditionists," *Minneapolis Tribune*, April 20, 1918, 1; "Minnesota Fight against Disloyal Impresses Solons," *St. Paul Pioneer Press*, April 20, 1918, 1; "Firing Squads for Traitors, Demands Judge J. F. McGee," *Minneapolis Journal*, April 20, 1918, 2.

13. "M'Gee [*sic*] Denies He Cast Reflection on Loyalty of Swedish Citizens," *Minneapolis Journal*, May 5, 1918, 1, 2; "McGee Denies He Attacked the Swedish Race," *St. Paul Pioneer Press*, May 5, 1918, 1, 4.

14. Chrislock, *Watchdog of Loyalty*, 218, 285–87; Orders No. 33, 37, *Report of the Minnesota Commission of Public Safety* (1919), 115, 117–18.

15. Chrislock, *Watchdog of Loyalty*, 158; Rhinow, *Report of the Adjutant General*, 271. Privately owned motorcars were a relatively new phenomenon, although they were common in prosperous middle-class urban households by 1918. Many farmers also owned a motorcar. Only after World War I did car ownership became widespread.

16. Chrislock, *Watchdog of Loyalty*, 218; Rhinow, *Report of the Adjutant General*, 41–42, 286.

17. Capozzola, *Uncle Sam Wants You*, 41–53; Jensen, *The Price of Vigilance*, 188–218.

18. "21 Are Seized as Evaders in Lodging House Raids Here," *Minneapolis Journal*, March 26, 1918, 3; Operative 71, *Summary and Report of War Service, Minneapolis Division, American Protective Service* (Minneapolis, n.d.), 5–6; Jensen, *The Price of Vigilance*, 191; "Slacker Raid Catches 200 Who Are Held," *Minneapolis Morning Tribune*, April 7, 1918, 1, 2; "Raid by Home Guard Fails to Reveal Any Slackers Captured," *Minneapolis Morning Tribune*, April 8, 1918, 7.

19. "Deserts and Enemy Aliens Caught by Home Guards' Net in City Wide Loyalty Coup," *Duluth News Tribune*, May 12, 1918, 1, 12; "Raid on Slackers Success; Forty-Four Still in Custody," *Duluth Herald*, May 13, 1918, 2; *History of the Third Battalion Minnesota Home Guard* (n.d.), 15–17. The last source gives the number of arrests at two thousand.

20. Holbrook and Appel, *Minnesota in the War with Germany*, 2:203–6.

21. Holbrook and Appel, *Minnesota in the War with Germany*, 2:207.

22. "War Board Will Hear Loan Cases Tonight," *Fairmont Daily Sentinel*, April 27, 1918, 1; "War Board 'Sells' $5,100 Bonds; More Cases to be Heard," *Fairmont Daily Sentinel*, April 29, 1918, 1, 8. On August 27, 1918, the MCPS issued Order 44, appointing local directors as their agents for the purpose of investigating Liberty Bond purchases. Clearly the MCPS thought local directors could not issue subpoenas prior to this order. To protect the privacy of those under suspicion, Order 44 held that the investigations not be publicized. In Martin County, however, the local newspaper reported the questions asked and the answers given in detail. The finances and the attitudes of the farmers brought before the local commission were front-page news.

23. "Attorney Francis Appointed War Orator," *The Appeal*, July 13, 1918; Nelson, "William T. Francis, at Home and Abroad," 3–13.

24. DeCarlo, "Loyalty Within Racism," 211; "Farewell Reception to Drafted Men by Local Elks," *Twin City Star*, October 20, 1917, 5; Taylor and Larson, *Cap Wigington*, 53–56; "Clarence W. Wigington," *The Appeal*, May 18, 1918, 2.

25. DeCarlo, "Loyalty Within Racism," 212–13.

26. "Negro Home Guards Receive an Ovation on Memorial Day," *Twin City Star*, June 1, 1918, 5; "Battalion Parade and Ball a Big Success," *Twin City Star*, June 22, 1918, 7.

27. "First Grand Home Guard Ball" [advertisement], *St. Paul Appeal*, April 20, 1918, 3; "Battalion Parade and Ball a Big Success," *Twin City Star*, June 22, 1918, 7; "First Musical Concert and Grand Ball of the 16th Battalion Home Guard Band" [advertisement], *Twin Cities Star*, September 28, 1918, 4.

28. George E. Ackerson, "Forces of Loyalty Mass for Drive on Townleyism at 'Never Such. Primary,'" *Minneapolis Morning Tribune*, June 8, 1918, 14.

29. Letters in J. A. A. Burnquist Papers, box 13, MNHS.

30. "Burnquist Files for Renomination: Makes Loyalty Watchword," *Minneapolis Morning Tribune*, May 7, 1918, 8.

31. *Minnesota in the War* 1, no. 28 (March 16, 1918): 1, 5; *Minnesota in the War* 1, no. 33 (April 20, 1918): 2; *Minnesota in the War* 1, no. 35 (May 4, 1918): 2; John McGee to Sen. Knute Nelson, May 23, 1918, Knute Nelson Papers, box 29, MNHS; "Nelson Endorses Gov. Burnquist in Note to Northrop," *Mower County Transcript-Republican*, June 12, 1918, 7.

32. "Governor's Day: Company C of the Seventh Battalion Minnesota Home Guard Passing Review before Governor, Who Afterwards Address[es] the Big Crowd," *Mower County Transcript Republican*, April 10, 1918, 1; "Bishop Says Townley Men Won't Hoodwink Stearns County Folk," *Minneapolis Morning Tribune*, May 5, 1918, 2.

33. "20,000 People Witness First Review of Guard Battalions Here by Governor Burnquist," *Virginia Enterprise*, June 10, 1918, 1, 5.

34. "McGee Denies He Attacked the Swedish Race," *St. Paul Pioneer Press*, May 5, 1918, sec 2, p1, 4; "Swedish Loyalty Not Questioned, Asserts McGee,"

Minneapolis Sunday Tribune, May 5, 1918, 1. On the angry letters, see, for example, Gunnar B. Bjornson, "He Should Resign," *Minneota Mascot*, May 10, 1918, 4, or A. G. Johnson to Burnquist, J. A. A. Burnquist Papers, box 14, MNHS. Johnson was the publisher of *Svenska Folkets Tidning* of Minneapolis.

35. "Minnesota as Loyal as Any State in the Union: Gov. Burnquist Takes Issue with Judge McGee—State is Loyal," *Sleepy Eye Herald-Dispatch*, May 3, 1918, 1.

36. "Lindbergh Rally Drew Big Crowd," *Willmar Tribune*, May 1, 1918, 8; see also the full-page advertisement for the rally, *Willmar Tribune*, April 24, 1918, 5.

37. "C.A. Lindbergh Airs His View," *St. James Plaindealer*, June 15, 1918, 1. Although the newspaper was hostile to Lindbergh, it thought county officials should let him speak.

38. "Give Him Tar: Nels Hokstad, Non-Partisan Organizer, Given Coat of Infamy," *Hinckley Enterprise*, May 10, 1918, 1; Larson, *Lindbergh of Minnesota*, 237. This anecdote is based on Larson's interview of Congressman Baer in 1965. "Non-Partisan League Is Bound Over: John Walters Will Be Tried in Winona in September," *Winona Republican-Herald*, July 3, 1918, 2. This case was sent to the Winona County grand jury in September. If they indicted Walters, the case never came to trial, possibly because county attorneys were less willing to prosecute such cases after the armistice. "Murder Case Will Feature District Term," *Winona Republican Herald*, September 10, 1918, 2.

39. "Won't Rent to Lindbergh," *Duluth Herald*, May 27, 1918, 4; "Lindbergh Leaves City," *Duluth Herald*, May 28, 1918, 5; "Lindbergh Fails," *Duluth Herald*, June 1, 1918, 16; "Halls Closed to Lindbergh," *Minnesota Leader*, June 8, 1918, 2. Lindbergh's statement about being barred from campaigning was reprinted in the *Minnesota Leader* on June 8, 1918.

40. "Dealing with Mr. Lindbergh," *Duluth Herald*, May 30, 1918, 10; "Duluth Press Misrepresents Him, Charges Lindbergh," *The Labor World*, June 1, 1918, 5; "Wheaton for Governor," *The Labor World*, June 15, 1918, 4.

41. "The Open Court: Notice to Lindbergh," *Duluth Herald*, May 29, 1918, 9.

42. "No League Meeting Held," *Faribault Journal*, June 12, 1918, 1; "Sheriff Livingston Stops Nopartisan-Lindbergh [*sic*] Meeting," *Northfield Independent*, June 13, 1918, 1.

43. "County Dads by Close Vote Invite a Riot" and "Mayor Freeman Puts Lid on Non-Loyalty Meeting," *Daily Journal-Press*, June 14, 1918, 1; "Quiet Gathering of Nonpartisans Held Near Here," *St. Cloud Times*, June 17, 1918, 5.

44. Charles A. Lindbergh to Eva Christie, 1918 (undated), February 18, April 28, and July (undated), 1918, Lindbergh Family Papers, MNHS; Larson, *Lindbergh of Minnesota*, 241–42. *The Mysterious Stranger* should perhaps not be attributed to Twain, since his literary executor assembled the text from three fragments which Twain never finished or published. Twain's late life pessimism, however, is well documented: Robert Douglas, "The Pessimism of Mark Twain," *Mark Twain Quarterly* 9, no. 1 (Winter 1951): 1–4.

45. *State v. A. C. Townley and Another*, 140 Minn. 413, 168 N. W. 591 (July 5, 1918).

46. "'Not Guilty' Is Jury's Verdict in Martin Trial," *Red Wing Daily Republican*, April 5, 1918, 1.

47. "Breidel Returns After Being Spirited Out of City by Force," *Red Wing Daily Eagle*, May 1, 1918, 1.

48. Johnson, *Patriot Hearts*, 78; "Investigation into Kidnapping Stopped," *Red Wing Daily Eagle*, June 18, 1918, 1.

49. The sentence was never served. The Minnesota Supreme Court reversed the conviction because Randall's right to mount a defense was restricted by the court. The vindication, however, came in 1919, after the war had ended: *State of Minnesota v. N. S. Randall*, 142 Minn. 203, 173 N. W. 425 (July 3, 1919).

50. Johnson, *Patriot Hearts*, 61–62.

51. Shortly after the primary election, Mohn brought Louis Martin, the third defendant, to trial for his role in the August 1918 speeches in Kenyon. Although Mohn had bungled his first prosecution of Martin, this time he managed to convict him. However, this conviction was overturned by the Minnesota Supreme Court, although not until 1919.

52. Charles A. Lindbergh to Eva Christie, May 18, 1918, Lindbergh Family Papers, MNHS; "Non-Party Candidate for Senate Arrested in Waverly Township," *Fairmont Daily Sentinel*, May 6, 1918, 1; "Rural Guardsmen, 141 Strong, Fill Armory at Drill," *Fairmont Daily Sentinel*, May 7, 1918, 1; Larson, *Lindbergh of Minnesota*, 237–41.

53. "Martin and Jackson Counties Gain Fame," *Fairmont Daily Sentinel*, June 17, 1918, 1; "Speakers Assail Townley and Lindbergh in Talks; Bolshevism Trying to Bring Ruin to This Nation," *Rochester Daily Post and Record*, May 29, 1918, 5; "Nonpartisans' Aim to Seize all Land, E. H. Nicholas Says," *Minneapolis Sunday Tribune*, June 2, 1918, 16; "Declare League to be Disloyal," *Red Wing Daily Republican*, June 6, 1918, 1, 5; "Nonparty is Scored by E.H. Nicholas," *Red Wing Daily Eagle*, June 7, 1918, 1, 4; "Kaiser's Hand Seen in War Program of Townley's League," *Minneapolis Journal*, June 11, 1918, 9.

54. "Primaries Arouse Keen Excitement," *New Ulm Review*, June 12, 1918, 1.

55. "Keep Them Out," *Anoka Union*, June 12, 1918, 1; "Friends of the Hun," *Anoka Herald*, June 18, 1918, 1; Chase Roe, *With the Colors from Anoka County* (1919), 42–43, 72–73.

56. Johnson, *Patriot Hearts*, 87–92; "Non-Partisan Parades Forbidden in City," *Red Wing Daily Eagle*, June 11, 1918, 1, 4.

57. "Mankato Backs Up Acts of Hoodlums," *New Ulm Review*, June 19, 1918, 1; "Threats to Shoot Charge Is Lodged," *Mankato Daily Free Press*, June 14, 1918, 1; "Nonparty Tour Stopped Short," *New Prague Times*, June 20, 1918, 1.

58. "Bullets Were Fired; Blood Was Spilled," *Mankato Daily Free Press*, June 15, 1918, 1; "Comfrey Goes Mad—Froths at Mouth," *New Ulm Review*, June 19, 1918, 1.

59. "Farmers Parade Was a Long One," *Willmar Tribune*, June 19, 1918, 1.

60. All vote totals from the *Legislative Manual of the State of Minnesota, 1919*.

61. "Farmer-Labor Candidates Named in State-Wide Primaries June 17," *Minnesota Leader*, July 6, 1918, 3.

62. Relations between the NPL and the small-town middle class had grown antagonistic even before the NPL won the 1916 elections in North Dakota. Merchants, bankers, insurance salesmen, and newspaper editors, for example, felt threatened by the NPL program, which included a state bank and government-sponsored crop insurance, and NPL tactics, such as publishing its own newspapers: Lansing, *Insurgent Democracy*, 96–97; see also Catherine McNichol Stock, *Main Street in Crisis: The Great Depression and the Old Middle Class on the Northern Great Plains* (Chapel Hill: University of North Carolina Press, 1992), 71–74.

63. "Great Victory for Loyalty," *St. James Plaindealer*, June 20, 1918, 1. In the state senate race, Albert Wood got 753 votes, George Sutherland 737, and Meyer Brandvig 724. Just four months later, Brandvig died of heart disease: "Death of Mr. Brandvig," *St. James Plaindealer*, October 20, 1918, 1. The editor wrote that although he disagreed with Brandvig about the NPL, he considered him "a high-minded man and patriotic to a marked degree."

64. Blanck, "Swedish Americans and the 1918 Gubernatorial Campaign in Minnesota," 322–28.

65. Chrislock, *Progressive Era in Minnesota*, 181.

Notes to Chapter Nine: The Loyalty Regime

1. Crosby, *America's Forgotten Pandemic*, 46–47, 150–51.

2. Holbrook and Appel, *Minnesota in the War with Germany*, 1:305–6.

3. Kennedy, *Over Here*, 166–67; Holbrook and Appel, *Minnesota in the War with Germany*, 1:154–55, 331, 356–58, 367–69.

4. Holbrook and Appel, *Minnesota in the War with Germany*, 1:235–59. The participating colleges were Hamline University, Macalester College, and the College of St. Thomas in St. Paul; St. Olaf and Carleton Colleges in Northfield; and Gustavus Adolphus in St. Peter. See also Gray, *The University of Minnesota*, 249–52.

5. Holbrook and Appel, *Minnesota in the War with Germany*, 1:353–55, 363–69.

6. Mjagkij, *Loyalty in Time of Trial*, 103–5, 112–13; Williams, *Torchbearers of Democracy*, 119–28.

7. Lewis, *W. E. B. Du Bois: Biography of a Race*, 555–57; Mjagkij, *Loyalty in Time of Trial*, 135–36; Williams, *The Wounded World*, 71–78.

8. Bill Douglas, "Wartime Illusions and Disillusionment: Camp Dodge and Racial Stereotyping, 1917–1918," *Annals of Iowa* 57 (Spring 1998): 111–34. The newspaper quotation is from the *Des Moines Register*, July 5, 1918.

9. Tighe later published the speech: Ambrose Tighe, "The Legal Theory

of the Minnesota 'Safety Commission' Act," *Minnesota Law Review* 3, no. 1 (December 1918): 1–19. The quotation is at 12–13.

10. "J. E. Meyers Leads Mayoralty Ticket by More than 1,000 Votes," *Minneapolis Morning Tribune*, June 18, 1918, 3; Nathanson, "Thomas Van Lear: City Hall's Working-Class Champion," 231–32.

11. Charles Lindbergh to Eva, August 13, 1918, Charles A. Lindbergh Family Papers, box 16, MNHS; "Capital Stunned Over Mystery of Lindbergh Berth," *Minneapolis Morning Tribune*, September 8, 1918, 1, 9; "Northwest Is Aroused over Nonpartisan Appointment," *Bemidji Daily Pioneer*, September 10, 1918, 1; "Past All Comprehension," *Minneapolis Morning Tribune*, September 9, 1918, 6; "Will Not Stand for Lindbergh: Liberty Loan Committeemen Protest Against His Appointment," *Duluth Herald*, September 10, 1918, 12; Sidney J. Huntley, publicity bureau, Republican State Central Committee, to Hon. Knute Nelson, September 10, 1918, Knute Nelson Papers, box 30, MNHS.

12. Charles Lindbergh to Hon. B. M. Baruch, September 10, 1918, and Charles Lindbergh to Eva, September 13, 1918—both in Charles A. Lindbergh Family Papers, box 16, MNHS; Haines and Haines, *The Lindberghs*, 296.

13. "Roosevelt Lashes Foe-Apologist in Five Talks," *Minneapolis Morning Tribune*, October 8, 1918, 1, 4.

14. Order No. 44, *Report of the Minnesota Commission of Public Safety* (1919), 125–26. The Home Guard from Virginia took over the job of questioning alleged bond "slackers": "Slackers Taken by Home Guards," *Tower Weekly News*, October 11, 1918, 1.

15. Typed transcript of Redwood County attorney questioning Carl Drusch on October 23, 1918, MCPS main files, file 249, MNHS. This file includes six other transcripts of Order 44 interrogations that local public safety directors sent to the MCPS. They usually end with the interrogator urging the witness to borrow money to buy the required bonds.

16. Charles Pitkin, Pennington County MCPS director, to MCPS, October 31, 1918, and Henry Libby, Secretary, to Charles E. Houston, Traverse County, December 20, 1918—both MCPS main files, F249, MNHS. In this letter Libby makes the case that "public sentiment which no doubt will be aimed against these people can be made a sufficient punishment."

17. R. B. Millard, Chair of Morrison County Liberty Loan Organization, to MCPS, December 11, 1918, with attachment, "Yellow Slacker List of the Fourth Liberty Loan for Morrison County, Minn," MCPS main files, F249, MNHS; "Insistent Demand May Force Early Publication of Names," *Winona Republican-Herald*, October 11, 1918, 2; "Will Publish Blue Carders," *Long Prairie Leader*, December 12, 1918, 1. I could find no evidence in these cases that the newspaper published any names.

18. *Minnesota in the War*, November 2, 1918.

19. Holbrook and Appel, *Minnesota in the War with Germany*, 2:207.

20. "Home Guards Arrest 500 in Slacker Raid," *St. Paul Dispatch*, July 6, 1918, 1; "Only Six Held as Result of Raids Against Slackers," *St. Paul Pioneer Press*, July 6, 1918, 1; "Many Draftees Without Cards Are Detained," *St. Paul Pioneer Press*, July 21, 1918, 1.

21. *History of the Third Battalion Minnesota Home Guard* (n. d.), 17; information from the "Unit Reports" file, Minnesota National Guard, Home Guard Records, MNHS, and in Rhinow, *Report of the Adjutant General.*

22. Jensen, *The Price of Vigilance*, 195–96; Capozzola, *Uncle Sam Wants You*, 50.

23. "Readers of the Minneapolis Tribune," *Minneapolis Morning Tribune*, July 4, 1918, 1; "Newsboys Ask Square Deal from Tribune," *Minneapolis Labor Review*, January 11, 1918, 1, 3; "City Wide Disorder Blinked at by Police, Watched by Military," *Minneapolis Morning Tribune*, July 8, 1918, 1, 7; "Newspaper Price Scale Established," *Minneapolis Morning Tribune*, July 8, 1918, 1; "Daily Papers, Burnquist, Langum Fight Newsies," *Minneapolis Labor Review*, July 5, 1918, 1; "Home Guard Called to Suppress Newsies," *Minnesota Leader*, July 13, 1918, 1, 2; "Glorious Victory Won by Newsboys and Fairminded People from Daily Combine," *Minneapolis Labor Review*, July 12, 1928, 1.

24. "Must Renounce the N.P. League or Leave," *Mankato Free Press*, June 28, 1917, 4; "Lindbergh's Backers Desert Nonpartisans," *Minneapolis Morning Tribune*, June 25, 1918, 7.

25. "Newspaper Office Closed by Mayor," *Rock County Herald*, June 21, 1918, 1; "J. Meints Deported; Held to be Disloyal," *Rock County Herald*, June 28, 1918, 1, 2; "Meints Returns; Is Again Deported," *Rock County Herald*, August 23, 1918, 1, 2; "Meints Files Two Damage Suits," *Rock County Herald*, September 27, 1918, 1, 2; "Mobbists Face $200,000 Damage Suit," *Minnesota Leader*, September 28, 1918, 1, 3.

26. "Duluth Man Is Beaten, Tarred for Disloyalty," *Duluth News Tribune*, March 25, 1918, 1; "Gustav Landin Tarred and Feathered for Disloyalty," *Duluth Herald*, March 25, 1918, 6.

27. "Tar Coat Given Alien; Renounced U.S. Rights," *Duluth News Tribune*, September 19, 1918, 1; "Knights of Liberty Tar and Feather Slacker," *Duluth Herald*, September 19, 1918, 4.

28. "Victim of Tar Party in Duluth Suicide, Belief," *Duluth News Tribune*, October 1, 1918, 1; State of Minnesota Certificate of Death, Olli Kiukkonen, #32567, October 1, 1918.

29. Peterson and Fite, *Opponents of War*, 205–7.

30. The notes of John T. Kenney, the lead federal investigator, are in Investigative Records Relating to German Aliens ("Old German Files"), 1915–1919, RG 65, Entry 31, Identifier 833644, "Victims of Knights of Loyalty," roll 729, National Archives; "$500 for Arrest of Tar and Feather Party," *International Falls Press*, October 10, 1918, 1; Chrislock, *Watchdog of Loyalty*, 290–91.

"A Twentieth Century Judas," *Duluth News Tribune*, October 7, 1918, 6; "Is Olli Kiukkonen the Judas?," *Truth*, October 11, 1918, 1. The *News Tribune* also said that in the country Kiukkonen left he would have been forced to serve under the "flag of rapine and murder," words usually used to describe Germany. Kiukkonen came from Finland, which was part of the Russian empire, a US ally until 1917, and after that independent.

31. The total of thirty-four federal cases is based on the *Annual Report of the Attorney General of the United States* for the years 1918, 1919, and 1920. The

number of state cases collated from the data in the *Biennial Report of the Attorney General of Minnesota for the Two Years Ending December 31, 1918* and the *Biennial Report of the Attorney General of Minnesota for the Two Years Ending December 31, 1920*.

32. "James A. Peterson Found Guilty on First Count of Espionage Indictment," *Minneapolis Journal*, April 14, 1918, 1, 10. Also indicted was Paul Dehnel, who edited the newspaper in which Peterson's articles appeared. His trial ended in a hung jury, at which point the government, having discovered that he was a German citizen, interred him as an enemy alien: "President Wilson Signed the Document to Incarcerate Editor," *Mankato Free Press*, October 25, 1918, 6.

33. "New Ulm News Story Puts Editor in Jail," *Minneapolis Morning Tribune*, August 30, 1918, 1; Richard Hudelson, "Jack Carney and the *Truth* in Duluth," *Soathar* 19 (1994): 129–39.

34. This prosecution, and what led to it, is closely examined in Gaut, "Hardware Store Sedition," 178–89.

35. "John V. Free, Non-Partisan, Is Acquitted," *Winona Republican-Herald*, December 14, 1918, 6; "Federal Court Clears League Organizer," *Minnesota Leader*, December 21, 1918, 2.

36. Johnson, *Patriot Hearts*, 13, 52–54, 98–99.

37. The details are from the *Red Wing Daily Republican*'s front-page coverage of the trial on June 25–29 and July 2. The early coverage of the trial came from United Press reports. Starting on June 27, Grondahl added his own stories detailing testimony at the trial, especially his own.

38. *Session Laws of Minnesota for 1917*, Chapter 463.

39. "Disloyalty Cases Tried," *St. James Plaindealer*, May 18, 1918, 1; "Grand Jury Return Many Indictments," *Faribault Journal*, November 21, 1917, 1; "Editor Ed. Bosky Gets Year's Term," *Faribault Journal*, December 5, 1917, 1; "Bruntsch Case Goes to Jury," *Martin County Sentinel*, December 24, 1918, 1.

40. Stone, *Perilous Times*, 170–73.

41. *State v. Bernard Rempel* and *State v. Peter W. Rempel*, 143 Minn. 50 (1919); *State v. William Ludemann*, 143 Minn 126 (1919); *State v. Fred Deike*, 143 Minn. 23 (1919). The court noted that "the legislature never intended by this law to deprive the citizens of the right to talk about, discuss, speculate upon, or to even criticize matters pertaining to the war."

42. "Peterson Case to Be Dropped," *Rochester Daily Post and Record*, October 20, 1920, 6; "Seebach Escapes Prison; Need Only Pay His Fine," *Minneapolis Morning Tribune*, February 18, 1920, 10. The Circuit Court of Appeals opinion affirming his conviction is at *Seebach v. United States*, 262 F. 885 (8th Circuit, 1919).

43. Gaut, "Hardware Store Sedition," 185–87. The judge's statement can be found in Memorandum to the Order Granting a New Trial in *United States v. Charles W. Anding*, April 26, 1919, RG 21, Identifier 582973, National Archives, Kansas City.

44. Rhinow, *Report of the Adjutant General*, 287–91. The 5th Infantry

Regiment was one of the new National Guard units created to replace the federalized MNG units. It consisted mostly of the former 6th Battalion of the Home Guard headquartered in Mankato. The Home Guard soldiers from Worthington and Pipestone were likely members of the new 6th Battalion, which was in the process of being organized. The Danish Lutheran Church is one of the four buildings in the Danebod Historic Complex, which was added to the National Register of Historic Places in 1975.

45. Carroll and Raiter, *The Fires of Autumn*, 4–13; Brown, *Minnesota, 1918*; Luukkonen, "Brave Men in Their Motor Machines," 3–8.

46. Carroll and Raiter, *The Fires of Autumn*, 103–9; *Report of the Adjutant General, 1918*, 303–96.

47. *Report of the Adjutant General, 1918*, 296–97. Some residents blamed the railroads for starting the fires. Since the railroads were nationalized during the war, this meant suing the federal government. Congress finally passed legislation with a final settlement of claims in 1935: Carroll and Raiter, *The Fires of Autumn*, 129–74.

48. *Report of the Adjutant General, 1918*, 306; "Negro Assistant to Adjutant General," *Twin Cities Star*, October 26, 1918, 5.

49. *Eighth Biennial Report (New Series) of the State Board of Health and Vital Statistics of Minnesota, 1918–1919* (Minneapolis: 1920); Susan Dowd, "The Spanish Influenza in St. Paul in 1918, the Year the City Found the 'Wolf' at Its Door," *Ramsey County History* 40, no. 1 (Spring 2005): 19–24; Influenza Encyclopedia: The American Influenza Epidemic of 1918–1919, "Minneapolis, Minnesota," minutes, October 22, 1918, https://www.influenzaarchive.org.

50. Brown, *Minnesota, 1918*, 117–23; "Winona Manufacturers Voice Loud Protest at Manner in Which the Influenza Situation Is Handled Here," *Winona Republican Herald*, October 14, 1918, 5; "Influenza Takes Nine in Last 24 Hours," *Winona Republican Herald*, October 18, 1918, 2; "Six More Victims of Influenza," *Winona Republican Herald*, October 21, 1918, 5.

51. "Military Takes Charge at Cloquet," *The Pine Knot*, November 1, 1918, 1; Hubert V. Eva to Rhinow, December 13, 1918; Rhinow to Eva, December 21, 1918; Eva to Burnquist, January 2, 1919; Eva to Burnquist, January 16, 1919; Governor's Executive Clerk to Eva, January 20, 1919—all Governor J. A. A. Burnquist Records, Forest Fire file, box 84, MNHS. Eva appended letters from the Cloquet mayor and the commission's Moose Lake manager, both asking for troop removal, to his January 2 letter.

52. *Report of the Adjutant General, 1918*, 295.

53. *Report of the Minnesota Commission of Public Safety* (1919), 312–16.

54. The last issue of *Minnesota in the War* (vol. 2, no. 18, February 15, 1919) was designated a "Special Edition for the Women's Committee" and reported on its organizational structure and various aspects of its work, along with a directory of its leadership, including the war council, and the "chairmen" of the district and county committees.

55. Chrislock, *Watchdog of Loyalty*, 242–45.

56. Chrislock, *Watchdog of Loyalty*, 239–42.

57. Minutes, June 27, 1918, Minnesota Commission of Public Safety, MNHS.

58. Holbrook and Appel, *Minnesota in the War with Germany*, 2:89–115; Nancy O'Brien Wagner, "Red Cross Women in France During World War I," *Minnesota History* 63, no. 1 (Spring 2012): 24–35; Gaul, *The Women of Southwest Minnesota and the Great War*, 20–35.

59. Eighmey, "Food Will Win the War," 272–86.

60. Aimee Fisher, Secretary to Minnesota Women's Committee, to Senator Knute Nelson, September 11, 1918, Knute Nelson Papers, box 30, MNHS.

61. "Woman Stirs Ire," *St. Paul Dispatch*, October 2, 1918, 1, 2.

62. "St. Paul Suffragists Oppose Bond Strike," *Minneapolis Sunday Tribune*, October 6, 1918, section 14, p8; "Discuss Suffrage," *St. Paul Pioneer Press*, October 8, 1918, 7; Colvin, *A Rebel in Thought*, 132–34. Colvin incorrectly recalls the context of her statement, attributing it to Wilson's refusal to speak out on suffrage. Wilson did make a pro-suffrage speech shortly before the vote, but failed to sway even one Democratic senator.

63. Gaul, *The Women of Southwest Minnesota and the Great War*, 59–67; "Home Guardswomen Drill at Woodstock," *St. Paul Pioneer Press*, July 6, 1918; "July 4th Celebration in Pipestone Nets About $8,000 for Red Cross Society," *Pipestone Leader*, July 11, 1918, 1; "Guards of Loyalty Are True Americans," *Pipestone County Star*, July 12, 1918, 1; *In the World War, Pipestone County, Minnesota* (Pipestone, 1919). This unpaginated volume contains a brief description of the Daughters of Loyalty and three photographs. The name of the group varies in news reports.

64. *Report of the Adjutant General, 1918*, 259–60. Gaul speculates that Hartigan got the idea from an article about a women's militia in New York City which was published in the *Pipestone County Leader* on August 30, 1917. In any case, Hartigan's unit was likely the only women's militia in Minnesota during the war.

65. Vote totals from the *Legislative Manual of the State of Minnesota, 1919*.

66. When accurate news of the armistice arrived on November 11, Grondahl's headline was "WORLD AT PEACE: Germany Bows to Allies," and the celebrations were restarted in Red Wing.

67. George Creel, Chairman, Committee on Public Information, to President Wilson, November 8, 1918, WWP22584, World War I Letters, Woodrow Wilson Presidential Library & Museum, Staunton, VA, https://presidentwilson.org/items/show/16421.

68. Burnquist did even worse in Douglas County, gaining only 32 percent of the vote. Statewide Nelson received 206,684 votes to Calderwood's 137,296: *Legislative Manual of the State of Minnesota, 1919*.

69. Chrislock, *Progressive Era in Minnesota*, 172, 179–82.

70. Burnquist received 166,611 votes, Evans 111,966, and Wheaton 76,838. The Socialist candidate got 7,795, and the candidate of the National Party 6,649. Wheaton's vote total was more than twice the total vote in the

Democratic primary in June, when many Democrats voted in the Republican primary to block Lindbergh: *Legislative Manual of the State of Minnesota, 1919*.

71. Johnson, *Patriot Hearts*, 47, 106, 107; *Legislative Manual of the State of Minnesota, 1919*, 678; Morlan, *Political Prairie Fire*, 211; Lansing, *Insurgent Democracy*, 143; "Legislative Victory Is Far-Reaching," *Nonpartisan Leader*, November 25, 1918, 4.

72. Nathanson, "Thomas Van Lear: City Hall's Working Class Champion," 232; Nord, "Hothouse Socialism," 133–66.

73. "Ten Thousand Winonans Celebrate News of Peace," *Winona Republican-Herald*, November 11, 1918, 3; "Monday's Peace Celebrations Will Remain Historic Event in City's History for All Winonans," *Winona Republican-Herald*, November 12, 1918, 5. There is no mention of the ongoing pandemic in these articles.

Notes to Chapter Ten: The Traumatic Peace

1. "Wilson Stirs 15,000 Minnesotans with Americanism Plea," *Minneapolis Morning Tribune*, September 19, 1919, 1, 2, 7.

2. There were three Flying Circus groups, one on the East Coast, one in the Midwest, and one in the Far West: Roesler, "Flying for Dollars," 190–202; "'Flying Circus' Thrills Thousands; Pilot's Quick Work Prevents Crash," *Minneapolis Morning Tribune*, April 22, 1919, 1, 6; Holbrook and Appel, *Minnesota in the War with Germany*, 2:198, 207.

3. Holbrook and Appel, *Minnesota in the War with Germany*, 2:241–42; "300,000 Roar Hoarse 'Well Done' to Boys," *Minneapolis Morning Tribune*, May 8, 1919, 1, 17.

4. Smith, *Confluence*, 188–95.

5. Holbrook and Appel, *Minnesota in the War with Germany*, 1:374; Ferguson, *The Pity of War*, 295.

6. Kennedy, *Over Here*, 217–18; Lansing, *Insurgent Democracy*, 205–7; Capozzola, *Uncle Sam Wants You*, 211.

7. "Soldier Legion to Organize in St. Paul Today," *Minneapolis Morning Tribune*, September 2, 1919, 1.

8. "Van Lear Flays Legionnaires in St. Paul Speech," *Minneapolis Morning Tribune*, October 1, 1919, 1, 4; "World War Veterans Give Organization Purposes," *Minneapolis Morning Tribune*, October 16, 1919, 12. World War Veteran leader George Mallon said that conscientious objectors should be treated like other veterans if they had "soldiered" after entering the military, by which he likely meant that they wore uniforms and followed orders.

9. "Legion Endorses Universal War Training," *Minneapolis Morning Tribune*, November 12, 1919, 1, 2; "Legionaries Decry Members' Murder; Move for Action Against Radicals," *Minneapolis Journal*, November 12, 1919, 1, 2. The convention took no position on bonus payments to compensate veterans for the difference between their military pay and the wages earned by workers on

the home front. Later, the Legion took up this demand, and Congress decided to issue certificates for compensation based on length of service redeemable in 1945. During the Depression, many veterans sought immediate payment, which led to the "Bonus Army" demonstration in Washington in 1932.

10. Painter, *Standing at Armageddon*, 379; Wingerd, *Claiming the City*, 233–34.

11. American Committee membership appeal letter, signed by James F. Gould, February 16, 1920, World War I Homefront Ephemera file, D525, MNHS; Millikan, *A Union Against Unions*, 143–44.

12. "State Guards Called to Check Red Flag Meeting," *Minneapolis Morning Tribune*, November 24, 1918, 1; "Crowd Halts Tiny Parade of Socialists," *Minneapolis Morning Tribune*, November 25, 1918, 1. An editorial stated that generally the sheriff should ban a meeting only after it becomes unlawful, but that banning this one in advance was lawful because the Socialists were likely to provoke their opponents to violence (16).

13. "Anti-Leager Gets Cold Storage Ride," *New York Times*, November 18, 1919, 1; "Lundeen Ousted from Ortonville by Legion Men," *Minneapolis Morning Tribune*, November 18, 1919, 1, 8; "Lundeen Makes Complaint to Governor," *Daily People's Press*, November 19, 1919, 1; "Lundeen Visited Ortonville Unasked," *Sleepy Eye Herald Dispatch*, December 26, 1919, 1; Ernest Lundeen to Governor Burnquist, January 17, 1920, J. A. A. Burnquist Papers, MNHS. The World War Veterans also sent a January 14, 1920, letter to Burnquist protesting Lundeen's treatment.

14. "24 Communist Suspects Held in Twin Cities," *Minneapolis Morning Tribune*, January 3, 1920, 1; "Trials of Men Taken in Raids to Begin Today," *Minneapolis Morning Tribune*, January 5, 1920, 1, 2.

15. "Industrialisti Heads Guilty of Syndicalism Is the Verdict of the Jury," *Duluth Herald*, March 27, 1920, 1, 4. In 1921, the Minnesota Supreme Court upheld the conviction against the company and the managing editor: "Conviction Against Duluth Publisher Affirmed in St. Paul," *Duluth Herald*, December 2, 1921, 2. See also Douglas J. Ollila Jr., "Defects in the Melting Pot: Finnish-American Response to the Loyalty Issue 1917–1920," *Turun historiallinen arkisto*, no. 31 (1976): 397–413.

16. Faue, *Community of Suffering and Struggle*, 47–50; "Phone Employees Threaten Strike for Wage Increase," *Minneapolis Morning Tribune*, November 15, 1918, 1; "Hello Girls Toot Horns to Inform Phoneless Twin Cities of Strike," *St. Paul Pioneer Press*, November 16, 1918, 1.

17. "State Guard Is Called to Border City in Sudden Order," *Bemidji Daily Pioneer*, December 13, 1919, 1; "Burnquist Orders Withdrawal of International Falls Troops," *Minneapolis Morning Tribune*, March 7, 1920, 3. The company contended that McIntosh asked for the troops. See E. W. Backus to Governor Burnquist, December 22, 1919, J. A. A. Burnquist Papers, box 20, MNHS. City and county officials denied it. Sheriff McIntosh disappeared in late January, and Burnquist appointed John Wall as interim sheriff. Several weeks before the strike ended, Wall informed the governor that the troops were no

long needed: "Sheriff M'Intosh of Koochiching County Missing Two Weeks," *Bemidji Daily Pioneer*, February 7, 1920, 1.

18. Telegram to Governor Burnquist from M. E. Withrow, Post Commander, American Legion Wm. Robideau Post, and Pat Lynch, Mayor, International Falls, and others, December 13, 1919 (other signers included the county auditor, register of deeds, treasurer, clerk of court, probate judge, city clerk, municipal judge, an alderman, a legislator, and a former mayor); Burnquist telegram to Withrow and Lynch, December 17, 1919; Withrow letter to Burnquist, December 18, 1919—all in J. A. A. Burnquist Papers, box 20, MNHS.

19. "International Falls Strike Ends: Demands of Men Are Granted," *Duluth Herald*, March 27, 1920, 1; O. P. Briggs to Burnquist, December 22, 1919, J. A. A. Burnquist Papers, box 20, MNHS.

20. J. D. Zahniser and Amelia R. Fry, *Alice Paul: Claiming Power* (New York: Oxford University Press, 2014), 306–14; Doris Stevens, *Jailed for Freedom: American Women Win the Vote*, ed. Carol O'Hare (Troutdale, OR: New Sage Press, 1995), 161–65, 205–11; Barbara Stuhler, "Organizing for the Vote: Leaders of the Minnesota Woman Suffrage Movement," *Minnesota History* 57, no. 4 (Fall 1995): 290–303; Zahniser, "The Fifteenth Star," 154–62.

21. Colvin, *A Rebel in Thought*, 134–42.

22. Orders No. 58, 59, *Report of the Minnesota Commission of Public Safety* (1919), 141–42. The commission also retained the order creating the peace officers, but they were quietly forgotten after the commission ceased to exist.

23. Inaugural Message of Governor J. A. A. Burnquist to the Legislature of the State of Minnesota, 1919.

24. Buell, *The Minnesota Legislature of 1919*, 75–87; "Union Labor Starts Bitter Fight on Motor Corp Bill," *The Labor World*, February 8, 1919, 1; "Workers Are Barred from House Gallery," *Minneapolis Labor Review*, February 14, 1919, 1.

25. Buell, *The Minnesota Legislature of 1919*, 76–79; Chrislock, *Watchdog of Loyalty*, 323.

26. Larson, *Lindbergh of Minnesota*, 255–56.

27. Morlan, *Political Prairie Fire*, 281; Millikan, *A Union Against Unions*, 155–56; "Start Drive on Radicals," *Duluth Herald*, November 12, 1920, 17.

28. Morlan, *Political Prairie Fire*, 256–61; Folwell, *A History of Minnesota*, 3:572–75.

29. Chrislock, *Progressive Era in Minnesota*, 185–96.

30. Socialist candidate Eugene Debs, campaigning from a cell in a federal penitentiary, received over 900,000 votes. Although several cabinet members urged President Wilson to free Debs from his Espionage Act sentence, Wilson steadfastly refused. President Harding finally released Debs on Christmas Day 1921: Hochschild, *American Midnight*, 337–38, 342; Peterson and Fite, *Opponents of War*, 270–79.

31. Chrislock, *Progressive Era in Minnesota*, 182–201. The NPL abandoned its traditional strategy because the legislature changed the primary law in 1921

by requiring conventions to identify endorsed primary candidates for each party and by making it impossible for a losing primary candidate to compete in the general election by petition: Lansing, *Insurgent Democracy*, 202.

32. Williams, *The Wounded World*, 163–65.

33. Williams, *The Wounded World*, 151–53; "Ranson Reception," *The Appeal*, March 8, 1919, 3; "Citizen's Reception," *The Appeal*, April 26, 1919, 3.

34. Lewis, *W. E. B. Du Bois: The Fight for Equality*, 1–11.

35. "Plan Negro Guard Units," *Twin City Star*, December 14, 1918, 2; "A Bad Precedent," *The Appeal*, February 1, 1919, 3; Buell, *The Minnesota Legislature of 1919*, 80–81; DeCarlo, "Loyalty Within Racism," 217–18.

36. Bessler, *Legacy of Violence*, 183–224; Fedo, *The Lynchings in Duluth*. Clifton E. Jackson and his wife told their local newspaper that their son had served overseas in the US Army: "Topeka Youth May Be Victim of Duluth Mob," *Topeka Plaindealer*, June 11, 1920, 1.

37. Roy Wilkins with Tom Mathews, *Standing Fast: The Autobiography of Roy Wilkins* (New York: Viking Penguin, 1982; reprt., New York: Da Capo Press, 1994), 44.

38. Hudelson and Ross, *By the Ore Docks*, 121–28.

39. Bessler, *Legacy of Violence*, 216–20; "Minnesota's Anti-Lynching Law," *The Appeal*, April, 23, 1921, 2; Nelson, "William T. Francis, at Home and Abroad," 5; William D. Green, *Nellie Francis: Fighting for Racial Justice and Women's Equality in Minnesota* (Minneapolis: University of Minnesota Press, 2020).

40. Lewis, *W. E. B. Du Bois: The Fight for Equality*, 96–97; "A Threatened Invasion," *Rochester Daily Post and Record*, November 27, 1920, 8; "Citizens, Be on Your Guard," *Red Wing Daily Republican*, September 28, 1918, 2; Frank Blighton, "Swami Ram's Reincarnation," *Freeborn County Standard*, February 9, 1920, 3; Kirsten Delegard, "Racial Housing Covenants in the Twin Cities," MNopedia, accessed April 19, 2024.

41. Pegram, *One Hundred Percent American*, 7; Capozzola, *Uncle Sam Wants You*, 212–13; Elizabeth Dorsey Hatle and Nancy M. Vaillancourt, "One Flag, One School, One Language: Minnesota's Ku Klux Klan in the 1920s," *Minnesota History* 61, no. 8 (Winter 2009–10): 360–71.

42. *Report of the Minnesota Commission of Public Safety* (1919), 11, 30, 32.

43. Chrislock, *Watchdog of Loyalty*, x–xi; *Report of the Minnesota Commission of Public Safety* (1919), 163–64.

44. George Creel, "Our 'Aliens'—Were They Loyal or Disloyal?," *Everybody's Magazine* 40, no. 3 (March 1919): 36–38, 70–73. Creel repeated his criticism of the MCPS in *How We Advertised America* (New York: Harper and Brothers, 1920), 179–80, where he concluded that "North Dakota, where the League elected every state officer, had a war record of which any state might be proud."

45. "Address of Welcome by Governor J. A. A. Burnquist at the Republican Rally Held in Honor of Will H. Hays, Chairman, Republican National Committee, March 7, 1919," J. A. A. Burnquist Papers, box 1, MNHS; Virginia

Roderick, Managing Editor, *Everybody's Magazine*, to Governor Burnquist, May 22, 1919, J. A. A. Burnquist Papers, box 18, MNHS.

46. *Session Laws of Minnesota for 1919*, Chapter 284, p293–94.

47. Holbrook and Appel, *Minnesota in the War with Germany*, 2:48.

48. Books were produced in at least the following counties: Anoka, Becker, Blue Earth, Chippewa, Chisago, Clay, Cottonwood, Dakota, Dodge, Faribault, Fillmore, Freeborn, Goodhue, Isanti, Jackson, Kandiyohi, Martin, Mower, Nobles, Norman, Otter Tail, Pipestone, Polk, Ramsey, Renville, Rock, Waseca, Washington, Watonwan, Wilkin, Winona. The most extensive of these books is Holbrook, *St. Paul and Ramsey County in the War of 1917–1918*. Most are in the collections of the Minnesota Historical Society.

49. *Goodhue County in the World War: Comprising a Short History of the World War, the Service Records and Photos of Goodhue County Boys and the County's Numerous War Activities* (Red Wing, MN: Red Wing Printing Co., 1919), 160–77.

50. Folwell, *A History of Minnesota*, 3:556, 569. Folwell uses the term "liberal" not in its current political sense, but in the older sense of ample or full. When this volume was published, Folwell was ninety-three.

51. Folwell, *A History of Minnesota*, 3:547. Theodore C. Blegen repeated the same error in his *Minnesota: A History of the State*, 476.

52. Following World War II, for example: Hilton, "Minnesota Commission," 1–44; Morlan, *Political Prairie Fire*; and Peterson and Fite, *Opponents of War*. Following the Vietnam War, for example, Chrislock, *The Progressive Era* (1971) and *Watchdog of Loyalty* (1991); Larson, *Lindbergh of Minnesota* (1973); Millikan, *A Union Against Unions* (2001); and Wingerd, *Claiming the City* (2001).

Notes to Epilogue: Lives After Wartime

1. Richard L. Neuberger noted how deeply the war changed the course of Lindbergh's life, especially the 1918 primary campaign, which "for bitterness and violence . . . was without parallel": "The Hero Had a Father." Neuberger, a journalist at the time, later was the US senator from Oregon.

2. Charles A. Lindbergh, *The Economic Pinch* (Philadelphia: Dorrance and Co., 1923), 245; Larson, *Lindbergh of Minnesota*, 268–70, 288.

3. In May 1923, the young Lindbergh bought an army surplus Curtiss JN-4D, commonly known as a "Jenny." The army used these planes primarily for training during the war, and after the armistice, sold several thousand planes to civilians: Berg, *Lindbergh*, 69–72.

4. "Charles Lindbergh, Governor Aspirant, Dies at Crookston," *Minneapolis Journal*, May 24, 1925, 1; "Lindbergh to Be Cremated, Ashes Strewn on Farm," *Minneapolis Journal*, May 25, 1924, 4.

5. Larson, *Lindbergh of Minnesota*, 282–88.

6. Nute, "The Lindbergh Bust," 294–95. The bust was placed in storage in 1978. The Minnesota Historical Building was the home of the Minnesota Historical Society until 1992. It is now the Minnesota Judicial Center.

7. Chrislock, *Watchdog of Loyalty*, 327–31.

8. Chrislock, *Watchdog of Loyalty*, 327; Knute Nelson to John McGee, June 23, 1921, Knute Nelson Papers, box 59, MNHS.

9. John McGee to Knute Nelson, June 29, 1921; Joseph Burnquist to Knute Nelson, June 29, 1921; Moses Clapp to Knute Nelson, June 24, 1921—all in Knute Nelson Papers, box 59, MNHS.

10. W. A. Lawson, secretary-treasurer of the Minnesota State Federation of Labor, to Knute Nelson, April 14, 1922, and Dan Stevens, Secretary-Treasurer, to Nelson, April 14, 1922—both in Knute Nelson Papers, box 68, MNHS.

11. Edward Lee to Knute Nelson, April 15, 1922; Knute Nelson to Edward Lee, April 19, 1922; Edward Lee to Knute Nelson, May 17, 1922; McGee to Nelson, May 17, 1922—all in Knute Nelson Papers, box 68, MNHS.

12. McGee to Nelson, May 17, 1922, Knute Nelson Papers, box 68, MNHS. Attached to the letter was a fifteen-page typed manuscript entitled "A Statement of Facts by John F. McGee," in which he summarized his personal biography and made a case for his appointment in 1922: Knute Nelson Papers, box 69, MNHS.

13. "Attack on McGee Begun in Senate," *St. Paul Daily News*, March 2, 1923, 3; "Senate Confirms M'Gee [*sic*] as Judge," *St. Paul Daily News*, March 3, 1923, 3; Chrislock, *Watchdog of Loyalty*, 331.

14. Nelson to McGee, March 3, 1923, Knute Nelson Papers, box 74, MNHS.

15. McGee to Nelson, March 5, 1923, Knute Nelson Papers, box 74, MNHS.

16. "What They Got from Judge McGee," *Winona Republican Herald*, May 19, 1923; "McGee Fines 60 Bootleggers in St. Paul Court," *Winona Republican Herald*, June 20, 1923; "Judge McGee Sends 60 Persons to Jail; Fines 53 Others," *Winona Republican Herald*, December 1, 1923; "McGee Punishes 450 Dry Law Violators in Two-Month Term," *Winona Republican Herald*, December 3, 1923; "St. Paul Police Guard Judges from 'Leggers," *Winona Republican Herald*, December 19, 1923. At the time, the federal judges held terms of court in Minneapolis, St. Paul, Duluth, Winona, Mankato, and Fergus Falls.

17. "'Ambulance Chasers' Hit by Judge McGee in Dismissing Suits," *Winona Republican Herald*, March 12, 1924, 3; "Judge McGee, Warned to Give Up Work or Collapse, Ends His Life," *Minneapolis Journal*, February 16, 1925, 1, 8.

18. "Judge J. F. M'Gee [*sic*] Is Found Dead in Office Vault," *St. Paul Pioneer Press*, February 6, 1925, 1, 2.

19. The note is reproduced in full at "Rites Tomorrow for Judge McGee: Farewell Note Left by Judge McGee Is Made Public by Coroner," *St. Paul Daily News*, February 17, 1925, 4, and "Judge McGee Died a Victim of Overwork," *Minneapolis Tribune*, February 17, 1925, 1.

20. "US Courts to Close for Judge McGee; Funeral Tomorrow," *Minneapolis Journal*, February 17, 1925, 1; "Judge McGee Had Lost His Mind by Hard Work," *Minneapolis Tribune*, February 17, 1925, 1.

21. "John Franklin McGee" [editorial], *Minneapolis Tribune*, February 16, 1925, 8; "Judge McGee Had Lost His Mind by Hard Work," *Minneapolis Tribune*, February 17, 1925, 1. McGee left behind his wife, four daughters, and two sons. His wife, Libby, stayed in their home and lived until 1946. Three of his daughters were living there at the time of his death. One had married and lived nearby. His son Hugh, the West Point graduate, was a banker living in New York. His younger son, Jerome, lived in St. Louis.

22. Joseph A. A. Burnquist, *Minnesota and Its People*, 4 vols. (Chicago: S. J. Clarke Publishing Co., 1924). The two biographical volumes do not contain entries on John McGee, John Lind, or Charles Lindbergh.

23. "T. G. Winter Jewel Safes Looted: Loss Unknown," *Minneapolis Morning Tribune*, June 28, 1918, 1; "Club Women Play a Part in International Politics," *St. Paul Pioneer Press*, December 25, 1921, 8; "Alice A. Winter Model Home Will Be Dedicated Friday," *Minneapolis Sunday Tribune*, May 10, 1925, 10; "A Model Home with a Big Purpose," *Minneapolis Morning Tribune*, May 24, 1924, 18. Winter's history of women is *The Heritage of Women* (New York: Minton, Balch and Co., 1927).

24. "Mrs. Winter Retires from Movie Field," *New York Times*, November 17, 1942, 22.

25. The new owners revamped it as the *Minneapolis Daily Star*, with no political affiliation. Many years later it was merged with the *Minneapolis Tribune*, and today it is the *Minnesota Star Tribune*.

26. "Death Claims Van Lear on First Vacation," *Minneapolis Star*, March 5, 1931, 1, 2; "Van Lear Will Be Buried with Military Pomp," *Minneapolis Star*, March 9, 1931, 1, 2.

27. "Fritsche Elected by 2 to 1: Receives Vindication at Hands of Fellow Citizens," *New Ulm Review*, April 7, 1920, 1; "Albert Pfaender Is City Attorney," *New Ulm Review*, April 21, 1920; "Official General Election Returns of Brown County—1920," *New Ulm Review*, November 10, 1920, 2.

28. Text of resolution passed by the Board of Regents of the University of Minnesota, January 28, 1938, includes Fred Snyder letter of dissent, Office of the President, box 24, University of Minnesota Archives.

29. Guy Stanton Ford to James L. Lee, November 5, 1957, William A. Schaper Case papers, University of Minnesota Archives. On Ford's attitude, see Gruber, *Mars and Minerva*, 181–82.

30. J. A. A. Burnquist to Dr. William Anderson, July 11, 1958, William A. Schaper Case papers, University of Minnesota Archives.

31. Matsen, "Professor William S. Schaper," 137.

32. Geraldine Bryan Schofield and Susan Margot Smith, "Maria Louise Sanford: Minnesota Heroine," in *Women of Minnesota: Selected Biographical Essays*, ed. Barbara Stuhler and Gretchen Kreuter (St. Paul: Minnesota Historical Society Press, 1998), 77–93; Helen Whitney, *Maria Sanford* (Minneapolis: University of Minnesota, 1922).

33. "'German Born Not All Spies,' Miss Sanford," *Minneapolis Morning Tribune*, August 27, 1918, 9; "Held Union Services: Patriotic Programs Carried

Out at Congregational and Episcopal Churches," *Little Falls Herald*, December 5, 1918, 2.

34. Jens Grondahl, "The Mark of Cain," *Red Wing Daily Republican*, March 14, 1918, 4; Johnson, *Patriot Hearts*, 106–7, 110.

35. "Oldest Symphony Orchestra Hears One of the Youngest," *Minneapolis Morning Tribune*, December 19, 1918, 1, 11; "Popular Concert Today to Be Conducted by Arthur Bodansky," *Minneapolis Morning Tribune*, March 2, 1919, 20; "Americanism and German Works," *Minneapolis Morning Tribune*, October 22, 1919, 20.

36. "Meints Files Two Big Damage Suits," *Rock County Herald*, September 27, 1918, 1; "Mobbists Face $200,000 Damage Suits," *Minnesota Leader*, September 28, 1918, 1, 3; "Under Cross Exam," *Mankato Free Press*, November 7, 1919, 3; "All Luverne Greets 32 Citizens Freed in Tar-Feather Case," *Minneapolis Morning Tribune*, November 16, 1919, 13; *Meints v. Huntington et al.*, 276 Federal Reporter 245 (1922); "Rock County Man Settles $100,000 War Time Suit Out of Court for $6,000," *Minneapolis Morning Tribune*, April 23, 1922, 10; "Luverne Tarring Party Pay Six Thousand Dollars Damages to John Meints," *The Organized Farmer*, May 11, 1922, 1.

37. *Gilbert v. Minnesota*, 254 U.S. 325 (1920); Murphy, *World War I and the Origin of Civil Liberties in the United States*, 268–69; Douhit, *Nobody Owns Us*, 181–83. "League Worker Denied Pardon," *Minneapolis Morning Tribune*, April 27, 1921, 1; "Pardon for Gilbert," *Truth*, June 10, 1921, 4; "110 Prisoners to Seek Pardon of State Board," *Minneapolis Morning Tribune*, July 8, 1921, 11. The pardon board consisted of Governor J. A. O. Preus, Chief Justice Calvin Brown, and Attorney General C. L. Hilton (a member of the MCPS).

38. Morlan, *Political Prairie Fire*, 336–38.

39. Morlan, *Political Prairie Fire*, 348; Nick Stewart-Bloch, "From Cooperative Commonwealth to Yardstick Capitalism: Midland's Evolving Vision of Cooperation in Mid-Century Minnesota," *Minnesota History* 66, no. 1 (Spring 2018): 7–19.

40. Manahan, *Trials of a Lawyer*, 239, 248; Doug A. Hedin, "Episodes in the Life of James Manahan. Chapter One: The Making of *Trials of a Lawyer*," Minnesota Legal History Project, http://minnesotalegalhistoryproject.org/index.cfm, accessed April 25, 2024. Manahan's memoir was reviewed by George M. Stephenson in *Minnesota History* 15, no. 3 (September 1939): 337–39.

41. Barbara Stuhler and Gretchen Kreuter, *Women of Minnesota: Selected Biographical Essays* (St. Paul: Minnesota Historical Society Press, 1998), 262–63. The election of four women did not signal a trend. In 1971, for example, there was only one woman in the legislature, after which the numbers began to climb.

42. C. J. Buell, *The Minnesota Legislature of 1923* (St. Paul, 1923), 8–9, 30–35; Chrislock, *Progressive Era in Minnesota*, 201.

43. Elizabeth Loetscher, "Cain, Myrtle Agnes (1894–1980)," MNopedia, accessed October 15, 2024.

44. Taylor and Larson, *Cap Wigington*. The buildings on the National

Register are the Highland Park Water Tower, the administration building at Holman Field, and the Harriet Park Pavilion, now called the Clarence W. Wigington Pavilion.

45. "Governor Confers with Group to Discuss Defense; Urged to Ban Discrimination," *St. Paul Recorder*, June 13, 1941, 1, 4; "Turpin Case Is Closed, Defense Committee Reports," *Minneapolis Spokesman*, April 30, 1943, 1.

46. Tighe was paid $6,521.44 by the commission for roughly two years of work. This would be the equivalent of $134,882 today. Report of Examination of the Books and Affairs of the Minnesota Commission of Public Safety, January 2, 1919, MPSC main files, MNHS.

47. The speech was reprinted as Ambrose Tighe, "The Legal Theory of the Minnesota 'Safety Commission' Act," *Minnesota Law Review* 3, no. 1 (December 1918): 1–19.

48. Stephenson, *John Lind of Minnesota*, 334–36; Chrislock, *Watchdog of Loyalty*, 201–2.

49. Ambrose Tighe, B.A. 1879, Obituary Record of Graduates of Yale University, *Bulletin of Yale University*, November 1, 1929, 77–78.

50. "Ambrose Tighe, Leading Attorney, Dies at His Home," *St. Paul Pioneer Press*, November 12, 1928; "Ambrose Tighe, Lawyer and Civic Leader, Is Found Dead at Home After Long Illness," *St. Paul Daily Star*, November 12, 1928, 1; Coroner's Certificate of Death, #8088, Ambrose Tighe, November 13, 1928. Despite its headline, the *Daily Star* article noted that Tighe had killed himself.

Notes to Observations After a Century

1. There were exceptions that provided insightful exploration of the conflicts of the period, including Johnson, *Patriot Hearts*, Nathanson, *World War I Minnesota*, and the Brown County Historical Society's exhibit "Loyalty and Dissent: Brown County in World War I," written by Daniel Hoisington, at the society's museum in New Ulm, Minnesota.

2. "Clearing the Air for Some Straight Thinking" [editorial], *Commercial West*, September 9, 1916, 7.

3. "Van Lear Escapes Threatened Removal Request by Lawyers of the State on Technicality," *Minneapolis Morning Tribune*, August 10, 1917, 2.

4. George Orwell, "Notes on Nationalism," in *Collected Essays, Journalism, and Letters of George Orwell, Vol. 3: As I Please, 1943–1945* (New York: Harcourt, Brace and World, 1968), 362. Orwell also observed that nationalism assumed that "human beings can be classified like insects and that whole blocks of millions or tens of millions of people can be confidently labelled 'good' or 'bad.'" Mickelson, "Nationalism in Minnesota During the Spanish-American War," 11–12.

SELECTED BIBLIOGRAPHY

Abrams, Ray H. *Preachers Present Arms: The Role of the American Churches and Clergy in World Wars I and II, with Some Observation on the War in Vietnam.* 2nd rev. ed. Scottsdale, PA: Herald Press, 1969.

Barbeau, Arthur E., and Florette Henri. *The Unknown Soldiers: Black American Troops in World War I.* Philadelphia: Temple University Press, 1974.

Barry, John M. *The Great Influenza: The Epic Story of the Deadliest Plague in History*. New York: Penguin, 2004.

Berg, A. Scott. *Lindbergh*. New York: Putnam, 1998.

Berg, A. Scott, ed. *World War I and America: Told by the Americans Who Lived It*. New York: Library of America, 2017.

Bergman, Klas. *Scandinavians in the State House: How Nordic Immigrants Shaped Minnesota Politics*. St. Paul: Minnesota Historical Society Press, 2017.

Bessler, John D. *Legacy of Violence: Lynch Mobs and Executions in Minnesota*. Minneapolis: University of Minnesota Press, 2003.

Blanck, Dag. "Swedish Americans and the 1918 Gubernatorial Campaign in Minnesota." In *Swedes in the Twin Cities: Immigrant Life and Minnesota's Urban Frontier.* Edited by Philip J. Anderson and Dag Blanck, 322–28. St. Paul: Minnesota Historical Society Press, 2001.

Blegen, Theodore C. *Minnesota: A History of the State.* Minneapolis: University of Minnesota Press, 1963, 1975.

Breen, William J. *Uncle Sam at Home: Civilian Mobilization, Wartime Federalism, and the Council of National Defense, 1917–1919*. Westport, CT: Greenwood Press, 1984.

Britten, Thomas A. *American Indians in World War I: At War and at Home*. Albuquerque: University of New Mexico Press, 1997.

Brown, Curt. *Minnesota, 1918: When Flu, Fire, and War Ravaged the State*. St. Paul: Minnesota Historical Society Press, 2018.

Buell, C. J. *The Minnesota Legislature of 1919*. St. Paul, MN: C. J. Buell, 1919.

Buhl, Paul. "The Crisis of the German-American Press in World War I: A Study of the Winona *Westlicher Herold*." *Chronicles* (Winona County Historical Society) 7, no. 2 (Summer 1988): 1–12, and 7, no. 3 (Fall 1988): 1–10.

Capozzola, Christopher. *Uncle Sam Wants You: World War I and the Making of the Modern American Citizen*. New York: Oxford University Press, 2010.

Carroll, Francis M., and Franklin R. Raiter. *The Fires of Autumn: The Cloquet-Moose Lake Disaster of 1918*. St. Paul: Minnesota Historical Society Press, 1990.

Chafee, Zachariah. *Free Speech in the United States*. Cambridge, MA: Harvard University Press, 1941.

Chambers, John Whiteclay. *To Raise an Army: The Draft Comes to Modern America*. New York: The Free Press, 1987.

Chrislock, Carl H. *Ethnicity Challenged: The Upper Midwest Norwegian-American Experience in World War I*. Northfield, MN: Norwegian-American Historical Association, 1981.

———. *The Progressive Era in Minnesota, 1899–1918*. St. Paul: Minnesota Historical Society Press, 1971.

———. *Watchdog of Loyalty: The Minnesota Commission of Public Safety during World War I*. St. Paul: Minnesota Historical Society Press, 1991.

Colvin, Sarah Tarleton. *A Rebel in Thought*. New York: Island Press, 1944.

Cooper, John Milton Jr. *Pivotal Decades: The United States, 1900–1920*. New York: W. W. Norton and Co., 1990.

Crosby, Alfred W. *America's Forgotten Pandemic: The Influenza of 1918*. 2nd ed. New York: Cambridge University Press, 2003.

DeCarlo, Peter J. "Loyalty Within Racism: The Segregated Sixteenth Battalion of the Minnesota Home Guard during World War I." *Minnesota History* 65, no. 6 (Summer 2017): 208–19.

Doenecke, Justus D. *Nothing Less Than War: A New History of America's Entry into World War I*. Lexington: University of Kentucky Press, 2011.

Douglas, William R. "'The Germans Would Court-Martial Me, Too': St. Paul's World War I Socialist Draft Resisters." *Minnesota History* 55, no. 7 (Fall 1997): 286–301.

Douhit, Davis. *Nobody Owns Us: The Story of Joe Gilbert, Midwestern Rebel*. Chicago: The Cooperative League of the USA, 1948.

Edgar, William C. *The Medal of Gold: A Story of Industrial Achievement*. Minneapolis: Bellman, 1925.

Egge, Sara. *Woman Suffrage and Citizenship in the Midwest, 1870–1920*. Iowa City: University of Iowa Press, 2018.

Eighmey, Rae Katherine. "'Food Will Win the War': Minnesota Conservation Efforts, 1917–1918." *Minnesota History* 59, no. 7 (Fall 2005): 272–86.

———. *Food Will Win the War: Minnesota Crops, Cooks, and Conservation during World War I*. St. Paul: Minnesota Historical Society Press, 2010.

Everts, William P. Jr. *Stockwell of Minneapolis: A Pioneer of Social and Political Conscience*. St. Cloud, MN: North Star Press, 1996.

Faue, Elizabeth. *Community of Suffering and Struggle: Women, Men, and the Labor*

Movement in Minneapolis, 1915–1945. Chapel Hill: University of North Carolina Press, 1991.

Fedo, Michael. *The Lynchings in Duluth*. 2nd ed. St. Paul: Minnesota Historical Society Press, 2016.

Ferguson, Niall. *The Pity of War: Explaining World War I*. New York: Basic Books, 1999.

Fleming, Thomas J. *The Illusion of Victory: America in World War I*. New York: Basic Books, 2003.

Folwell, William W. *A History of Minnesota*. 4 vols. St. Paul: Minnesota Historical Society Press, 1926; rev. ed., 1969.

Gambrino, Thomas E. "The Editorial Reaction of Alvah Eastman to the Events and Issues of World War I in the *St. Cloud Journal-Press*." MA thesis, St. Cloud State University, 1977.

Gaul, Anita Talsma. *The Women of Southwest Minnesota and the Great War*. Marshall, MN: Society for the Study of Local and Regional History, Southwest State University, 2018.

Gaut, Greg. "Hardware Store Sedition: The Case of Charles W. Anding." *Minnesota History* 67, no. 4 (Winter 2020–21): 178–89.

Gieske, Millard L., and Steven J. Keillor. *Norwegian Yankee: Knute Nelson and the Failure of American Politics, 1860–1923*. Northfield, MN: Norwegian-American Historical Society, 1995.

Glad, Paul W. *The History of Wisconsin: Vol. 5, War, a New Era, and Depression, 1914–1940*. Madison: State Historical Society of Wisconsin, 1990.

Gray, James. *The University of Minnesota, 1851–1951*. Minneapolis: University of Minnesota Press, 1951.

Gruber, Carol S. *Mars and Minerva: World War I and the Use of the Higher Learning in America*. Baton Rouge: Louisiana State University Press, 1975.

Haines, Lynn, and Dora B. Haines. *The Lindberghs*. New York: Vanguard Press, 1931.

Hardy, Rob. "The Americanization of Bjorn Winger: A Norwegian American, World War I Poet from Minnesota." *Minnesota History* 69, no. 2 (Summer 2024): 78–85.

Haynes, John E. "Revolt of the 'Timber Beasts': IWW Lumber Strike in Minnesota." *Minnesota History* 42, no. 5 (Spring 1971): 163–74.

Hilton, O. A. "The Minnesota Commission of Public Safety in World War I, 1917–1919." *Bulletin of the Oklahoma Agricultural and Mechanical College* 48, no. 14 (May 15, 1951): 1–44.

Hochschild, Adam. *American Midnight: The Great War, a Violent Peace, and Democracy's Forgotten Crisis*. New York: Harper Collins, 2022.

Hoisington, Daniel. *A German Town: A History of New Ulm, Minnesota*. New Ulm, MN: City of New Ulm, 2004.

Holbrook, Franklin F. *St. Paul and Ramsey County in the War of 1917–1918*. St. Paul, MN: Ramsey County War Records Commission, 1929.

Holbrook, Franklin F., and Livia Appel. *Minnesota in the War with Germany*. 2 vols. St. Paul: Minnesota Historical Society, 1928–32.

Hudelson, Richard, and Carl Ross. *By the Ore Docks: A Working People's History of Duluth*. Minneapolis: University of Minnesota Press, 2006.

Jensen, Joan M. *The Price of Vigilance*. Chicago: Rand McNally, 1968.

Jenson, Carol E. *Agrarian Pioneer in Civil Liberties: The Non-Partisan League in Minnesota during World War I*. PhD diss., University of Minnesota, 1968. Reprint, New York: Garland, 1986.

———. "Loyalty as a Political Weapon: The 1918 Campaign in Minnesota." *Minnesota History* 43, no. 2 (Summer 1972): 42–57.

Johnson, Frederick L. *Patriot Hearts: World War I Passion and Prejudice in a Minnesota County*. Red Wing, MN: Goodhue County Historical Society, 2017.

Johnson, Jack K. "'Our United Effort': Hamline University's World War I Ambulance Company." *Minnesota History* 64, no. 8 (Winter 2015–16): 320–29.

Jordan, Philip D. *The People's Health: A History of Public Health in Minnesota to 1948*. St. Paul: Minnesota Historical Society, 1953.

Kaunonen, Gary. *Flames of Discontent: The 1916 Minnesota Iron Ore Strike*. Minneapolis: University of Minnesota Press, 2017.

Kazin, Michael. *War Against War: The American Fight for Peace, 1914–1918*. New York: Simon and Schuster, 2011.

Keene, Jennifer D. "Finding a Place for the First World War in American History." In *Writing the Great War: The Historiography of World War I from 1918 to the Present*. Edited by Christoph Cornelissen and Arndt Weinrich, 449–87. New York: Berghahn Books, 2021.

———. *The United States and the First World War*. London: Longman, 2000.

Keillor, Steven J. *The Basis of Belief: A Century of Drama and Debate at the University of Minnesota*. Lakeville, MN: Pogo Press, 2008.

———. *Shaping Minnesota's Identity: 150 Years of State History*. Lakeville, MN: Pogo Press, 2008.

Kelley, Daniel John. "Irish-Americans and World War I: An Analysis of the Response of the Minneapolis *Irish Standard*." *Hennepin County History* 45, no. 2 (Summer 1986): 3–29.

Kennedy, David M. *Over Here: The First World War and American Society*. 25th anniversary ed. Oxford: Oxford University Press, 2004.

Knight, Louise W. *Jane Addams: Spirit in Action*. New York: W. W. Norton and Co., 2010.

Kohn, Stephen M. *American Political Prisoners: Prosecutions under the Espionage and Sedition Acts*. Westport, CT: Praeger, 1994.

Lamb, Charles R. "The Nonpartisan League and Its Expansion into Minnesota." *North Dakota Quarterly* 49, no. 3 (Summer 1981): 108–43.

Lansing, Michael J. *Insurgent Democracy: The Nonpartisan League in North American Politics*. Chicago: University of Chicago Press, 2015.

Larson, Bruce L. *Lindbergh of Minnesota: A Political Biography*. New York: Harcourt Brace Jovanovich, Inc., 1973.

Lasch, Christopher. *The New Radicalism in America, 1889–1963: The Intellectual as a Social Type*. New York: Alfred A. Knopf, 1965.

Lears, T. J. Jackson. *Rebirth of a Nation: The Making of Modern America, 1877–1920*. New York: HarperCollins, 2009.

Lee, Art. "Hometown Hysteria: Bemidji at the Start of World War I." *Minnesota History* 49, no. 2 (Summer 1984): 65–75.

Lewis, David Levering. *W. E. B. Du Bois: Biography of a Race, 1868–1919*. New York: Henry Holt, 1993.

——. *W. E. B. Du Bois: The Fight for Equality and the American Century, 1919–1963*. New York: Henry Holt, 2000.

Lovoll, Odd S. "*Gaa Paa*: A Scandinavian Voice of Dissent." *Minnesota History* 52, no. 3 (Fall 1990): 87–99.

Luebke, Frederick C. *Bonds of Loyalty: German-Americans and World War I*. DeKalb: Northern Illinois University Press, 1974.

Luukkonen, Arnold. "Brave Men in Their Motor Machines—and the 1918 Forest Fire." *Ramsey County History* 9, no. 2 (Fall 1972): 3–8.

Manahan, James. *Trials of a Lawyer*. Minneapolis: Farnham Printing, 1933.

Matsen, William E. "Professor William S. Schaper, War Hysteria and the Price of Academic Freedom." *Minnesota History* 51, no. 4 (Winter 1988): 130–37.

Mayer, Arno J. *Political Origins of the New Diplomacy, 1917–1918*. New Haven: Yale University Press, 1959. Reprint, New York: Vintage Books, 1970.

McCausland, Thomas W. *Rally of Resolve: The Home Front in Lyon County, Minnesota*. Marshall, MN: Southwest State University, 1990.

Meyer, G. J. *The World Remade: America in World War I*. New York: Bantam, 2016.

Meyer, Sabine N. *We Are What We Drink: The Temperance Battle in Minnesota*. Urbana: University of Illinois Press, 2015.

Mickelson, Peter. "Nationalism in Minnesota During the Spanish-American War." *Minnesota History* 41, no. 1 (Spring 1968): 1–12.

Millikan, William. "Defenders of Business: The Minneapolis Civic and Commerce Association versus Labor during World War I." *Minnesota History* 50, no. 1 (Spring 1986): 2–17.

——. *A Union Against Unions: The Minneapolis Citizens Alliance and Its Fight Against Organized Labor, 1903–1947*. St. Paul: Minnesota Historical Society Press, 2001.

Mjagkij, Nina. *Loyalty in Time of Trial: The African American Experience during World War I*. Lanham, MD: Rowman and Littlefield Publishers, 2011.

Mobilizing Minnesota: Powers and Duties of the Minnesota Commission of Public Safety. St. Paul: Minnesota Commission of Public Safety, 1917.

Morlan, Robert L. "The Nonpartisan League and the Minnesota Campaign of 1918." *Minnesota History* 34, no. 6 (Summer 1955): 221–32.

——. *Political Prairie Fire: The Nonpartisan League, 1915–1922*. Minneapolis: University of Minnesota Press, 1955. Reprint with new introduction by Larry Remele. St. Paul: Minnesota Historical Society Press, 1985.

Morris, Edmund. *Colonel Roosevelt*. New York: Random House, 2010.

Murphy, Paul. *World War I and the Origin of Civil Liberties in the United States*. New York: W. W. Norton and Co., 1979.

Murray, Robert K. *Red Scare: A Study in National Hysteria, 1919–1920.* Minneapolis: University of Minnesota Press, 1955.

Nathanson, Iric. "Thomas Van Lear: City Hall's Working-Class Champion." *Minnesota History* 64, no. 6 (Summer 2015): 224–33.

———. *World War I Minnesota.* Charleston, SC: The History Press, 2016.

Nelson, James Carl. *Five Lieutenants: The Heartbreaking Story of Five Harvard Men Who Led America to Victory in World War I.* New York: St. Martin's Press, 2012.

Nelson, Paul D. "William T. Francis, at Home and Abroad." *Ramsey County History* 51, no. 4 (Winter 2017): 3–13.

Neuberger, Richard L. "The Hero Had a Father: Charles A. Lindbergh, Sr., an Even Greater Hero Than His Son, Was a Martyr to Mob Stupidity." *Esquire* 7, no. 3 (March 1937).

Nord, David Paul. "Hothouse Socialism: Minneapolis 1910–1925." In *Socialism in the Heartland: The Midwestern Experience, 1900–1925.* Edited by Donald T. Critchlow, 133–66. Notre Dame, IN: University of Notre Dame Press, 1986.

———. "Minneapolis and the Pragmatic Socialism of Thomas Van Lear." *Minnesota History* 45, no. 1 (Spring 1976): 2–10.

Nute, Grace Lee. "The Lindbergh Bust." *Minnesota History* 21, no. 3 (September 1940): 294–95.

Painter, Nell Irvin. *Standing at Armageddon: A Grassroots History of the Progressive Era.* New York: W. W. Norton and Co., 2008.

Pegram, Thomas R. *One Hundred Percent American: The Rebirth and Decline of the Ku Klux Klan in the 1920s.* Chicago: Ivan R. Dee, 2011.

Peterson, H. C., and Gilbert Fite. *Opponents of War, 1917–1918.* Seattle: University of Washington Press, 1957.

Pifer, Richard L. *The Great War Comes to Wisconsin: Sacrifice, Patriotism, and Free Speech in a Time of Crisis.* Madison: Wisconsin Historical Society Press, 2017.

Pratt, William C. *After Populism: The Agrarian Left on the Northern Plains, 1900–1960.* Pierre: South Dakota Historical Society Press, 2022.

Rachleff, Peter. "Turning Points in the Labor Movement: Three Key Conflicts." In *Minnesota in a Century of Change: The State and Its People since 1900.* Edited by Clifford E. Clark Jr., 195–222. St. Paul: Minnesota Historical Society Press, 1989.

Raff, Willis H. "Coercion and Freedom in a War Situation: A Critical Analysis of Minnesota Culture during World War One." PhD diss., University of Minnesota, 1957.

Read, James Morgan. *Atrocity Propaganda, 1914–1919.* New Haven, CT: Yale University Press, 1941.

Remele, Larry. "The Tragedy of Idealism: The National Nonpartisan League and American Foreign Policy, 1917–1919." *North Dakota Quarterly* 42 (Autumn 1974): 78–95.

Rhinow, W. F. *Report of the Adjutant General of the State of Minnesota Covering the*

Thirtieth Biennial Period Ending December 31, 1918. Minneapolis, MN: Syndicate Printing, 1918.

Rippley, La Vern J. "Conflict in the Classroom: Anti-Germanism in Minnesota's Schools, 1917-1919." *Minnesota History* 47, no. 5 (Spring 1981): 170–83.

Roesler, Alan L. "Flying for Dollars: The Victory Loan Flying Circus in the Twin Ports, April 20, 1919." *Minnesota History* 67, no. 4 (Winter 2020–21): 190–202.

Ross, Drew M., "White Supremacy on Parade: The Fight to Stop *The Birth of a Nation* in the Twin Cities." *Minnesota History* 68, no. 5 (Spring 2023): 170–80.

Schaffer, Ronald. *America in the Great War: The Rise of the War Welfare State*. New York: Oxford University Press, 1991.

Scheiber, Harry N. *The Wilson Administration and Civil Liberties, 1917–1921*. Ithaca, NY: Cornell University Press, 1960.

Schoone-Jongen, Robert. *Patriotic Pressures WW I: The Dutch Experience in Southwest Minnesota during World War I*. Marshall, MN: Society for the Study of Local and Regional History, Southwest State University, 1992.

Sherman, John K. *Music and Maestros: The Story of the Minneapolis Symphony Orchestra*. Minneapolis: University of Minnesota Press, 1952.

Skidmore, Emily. "On Courage and Cowards: The Controversy Surrounding Macalester College's Neutrality and Peace Association, 1917." *Ramsey County History* 43, no. 2 (Summer 2008): 14–20.

Smith, Hampton. *Confluence: A History of Fort Snelling*. St. Paul: Minnesota Historical Society Press, 2021.

Starr, Karen. "Fighting for a Future: Farm Women of the Nonpartisan League." *Minnesota History* 48, no. 6 (Summer 1983): 255–62.

Stentiford, Barry M. *The American Home Guard: The State Militia in the Twentieth Century*. Texas A & M University Military History Series 78. College Station: Texas A & M University Press, 2002.

Stephenson, George M. *John Lind of Minnesota*. Minneapolis: University of Minnesota Press, 1935.

Stone, Geoffrey R. *Perilous Times: Free Speech in Wartime from the Sedition Act of 1798 to the War on Terrorism*. New York: W. W. Norton and Co., 2004.

Stuhler, Barbara. "Charles A. Lindbergh: Radical Isolationist." In *Ten Men of Minnesota and American Foreign Policy, 1898–1968*. St. Paul: Minnesota Historical Society, 1973.

———. *Gentle Warriors: Clara Ueland and the Minnesota Struggle for Woman Suffrage*. St. Paul: Minnesota Historical Society Press, 1995.

Taylor, David Vassar, and Paul Larson. *Cap Wigington: An Architectural Legacy in Ice and Stone*. St. Paul: Minnesota Historical Society Press, 2001.

Thomas, Louisa. *Conscience: Two Soldiers, Two Pacifists, One Family—A Test of Will and Faith in World War I*. New York: Penguin, 2012.

Unger, Nancy C. *Fighting Bob La Follette: The Righteous Reformer*. Chapel Hill: University of North Carolina Press, 2000.

Vaughn, Stephen. *Holding Fast the Inner Lines: Democracy, Nationalism, and the*

Committee on Public Information. Chapel Hill: University of North Carolina Press, 1980.

Walker, Charles R. *American City: A Rank and File History of Minneapolis*. New York: Farrar and Rinehart, Inc., 1937. Reprint, Minneapolis: University of Minnesota Press, 2005.

Ward, Charles S. "The Minnesota Commission of Public Safety in World War One: Its Formation and Activities." MA thesis, University of Minnesota, 1965.

Watne, Joel Andrew. "Intolerance and Conformity: The Fargo-Moorhead Area in the First World War." MA thesis, Morehead State College, 1967.

Weinstein, James. "Anti-War Sentiment and the Socialist Party, 1917–1918." *Political Science Quarterly* 74, no. 2 (1959): 215–39.

Wilkins, Robert P. "Referendum on War?: The General Election of 1916 in North Dakota." *North Dakota History* 36, no. 4 (Fall 1969): 296–336.

Williams, Chad L. *Torchbearers of Democracy: African American Soldiers in the World War I Era*. Chapel Hill: University of North Carolina Press, 2010.

———. *The Wounded World: W. E. B. Du Bois and the First World War*. New York: Farrar, Straus and Giroux, 2023.

Wingerd, Mary Lethert. *Claiming the City: Politics, Faith, and the Power of Place in St. Paul*. Ithaca, NY: Cornell University Press, 2001.

Wolkerstorfer, John Christine. "Nativism in Minnesota in World War I: A Comparative Study of Brown, Ramsey and Stearns Counties, 1914–1918." PhD diss., University Minnesota, 1973.

———. "Persecution in St. Paul: The Germans in World War I." *Ramsey County History* 13, no. 1 (Fall/Winter 1976): 3–13.

Zahniser, J. D. "The Fifteenth Star: Alice Paul and the National Woman's Party in Minnesota." *Minnesota History* 67, no. 3 (Fall 2020): 154–61.

Zieger, Robert H. *America's Great War: World War I and the American Experience*. Lanham, MD: Rowman and Littlefield, 2000.

INDEX

Page numbers in *italics* refer to images.

The War at Home was designed and set in type by Judy Gilats in St. Paul, Minnesota. The text typeface is Garamond ATF Micro and display faces are Haboro Contrast and Liquorstore Regular.